A Guide to Research in Music Education

Fourth Edition

by
Roger P. Phelps
Lawrence Ferrara
Thomas W. Goolsby

The Scarecrow Press, Inc.
Metuchen, N.J., & London
1993

The first edition of *A Guide to Research in Music Education* by
Roger P. Phelps was published by Wm. C. Brown Company in
1969. Second and third editions of this title by the same author
were published by The Scarecrow Press in 1980 and 1986,
respectively.

British Library Cataloguing-in-Publication data available

Library of Congress Cataloging-in-Publication Data

Phelps, Roger P.
    A guide to research in music education / by Roger P. Phelps.
Lawrence Ferrara, Thomas W. Goolsby.—4th ed.
      p.   cm.
    Includes bibliographical references and index.
    ISBN 0-8108-2536-8 (acid-free paper)
    1. Music——Instruction and study——Research. I. Ferrara,
Lawrence. II. Goolsby, Thomas, 1953—   . III. Title.
MT1.P5   1993
780'.7——dc20   92-29643

Manufactured in the United States of America

Printed on acid-free paper

This book is lovingly dedicated to our wives,

Mildred Phelps

Kathi Ferrara

Brenda Goolsby

Contents

PART TWO: WRITING THE RESEARCH
PROPOSAL AND THE RESEARCH DOCUMENT

PART THREE: THE RESEARCH
METHODOLOGIES—CONCEPTS AND
TECHNIQUES

Figures

Preface to the Fourth Edition

It has been twenty years since the first edition of *A Guide to Research in Music Education* appeared in print. This new edition is evidence of its general acceptance by music-education researchers over the years. Both the second and third editions expanded upon the first to keep up with the ever-changing field of research in music education. With the addition of two coauthors this fourth edition points to some new dimensions for music-education research. The original objectives of the previous editions are still valid: namely, to present a concise, practical, and logical approach to the fundamental principles and methods of research that music educators can readily understand and apply.

I am pleased that Lawrence Ferrara, of New York University, with his extensive training and publications in philosophy and aesthetics, has written chapters 3, 4, and 5. Presented in these chapters are some new ideas for music educators to consider as they are confronted with music-education research topics which impinge on philosophy and aesthetics. Thomas Goolsby, formerly of East Carolina University, now of the University of Washington, whose background includes intensive training and experience in descriptive and experimental research, presents some of the most recent concepts and techniques in these methods for researching descriptive and experimental problems. He is responsible for chapters 2, 6, 7, and 8. The responsibility for the largely rewritten chapters 1, 9, and 10 has been my pleasant task.

The fourth edition, like the third, is organized into four logical parts: Part One: Research Problem Identification; Part Two: Writing the Research Proposal and the Research Document; Part Three: Research Methodologies—Concepts and Techniques; and Part Four: Music Education Research—A Glimpse into the Future. Included are some of the recent relevant studies appropriate to the context of each chapter.

This treatise can be especially useful when the concepts and methods it discusses are translated into the formulation of an acceptable research design, its adequate implementation, and the appropriate dissemination of the research results. This is the central theme of the book and the principal reason for its being written.

Sincere appreciation and thanks are due to the following people, who have read portions of the manuscript and offered many constructive suggestions: Dr. Thomas Colwell, Dr. Mildred Phelps, Dr. Fred Rees, Philip Blumberg, Ken Bodiford, Dolores Ciavola, Karen Olsen, Cheryl Range, Robert Tomaro, and Limor Tomer. Valuable assistance also has been given to the writers by library staff members of New York University, East Carolina University, Meredith College, and North Carolina State University.

Roger P. Phelps
Cary, North Carolina

Professor Emeritus
New York University

Acknowledgments

We express our thanks to the authors and publishers listed below for permission to reprint the citations identified in the Notes.

Charles D. Hopkins and R. L. Antes, *Educational Research: A Structure for Inquiry*, 3rd ed.; Itasca, Ill.: F. E. Peacock, 1990, p. 21. Reprinted by permission of Charles D. Hopkins and R. L. Antes.

James H. McMillan and Sally Schumacher, *Research in Education: A Conceptual Approach*, 2nd ed.; Glenview, Ill.: Scott, Foresman and Co., pp. 8, 435. Copyright © 1989. Reprinted by permission of Scott, Foresman and Company.

Edward J. Vockell, *Educational Research*, New York: Macmillan, 1983, p. 287. Reprinted with permission of Macmillan Publishing Company from *Educational Research* by Edward Vockell. Copyright © 1983 by Edward Vockell.

John W. Best and James V. Kahn, *Research in Education*, 6th ed.; Englewood Cliffs, N.J.: Prentice-Hall, 1989, p. 17. Copyright © 1989. Reprinted by permission of Prentice-Hall, Inc., Englewood Cliffs, N.J.

Paul D. Leedy, *Practical Research Planning and Design*, 4th ed.; New York: Macmillan, 1989, pp. 5, 46, 125, 133, 152, 173. Reprinted with permission of Macmillan Publishing Company from *Practical Research Planning and Design* by Paul Leedy. Copyright © 1989 by Paul D. Leedy.

Edward L. Rainbow and Hildegard C. Froehlich, *Research in Music Education: An Introduction to Systematic Inquiry*, New

Shafer, editor, copyright © 1980, 3rd ed. The Dorsey Press, Homewood, Ill.

William W. Cutler III, "Oral History—Its Nature and Uses for Educational History," *History of Education Quarterly*, Summer 1971, 11,2:184. Reprinted by permission of William W. Cutler III.

PART ONE

RESEARCH PROBLEM IDENTIFICATION

In this section you will learn about procedures for selecting a research problem, the scientific method and reflective thinking, sources of information, and procedures for narrowing a research idea into a workable problem.

1. Selecting a Research Problem

What an intriguing and gratifying experience research can be! This is true not only for the research tyro, but also for one who is an experienced researcher. After your research is completed you can know the satisfaction of presenting new knowledge or of finding answers to some of your vexatious problems. Knowledge obtained may be from either personal, firsthand experience, or secondary, which may or may not be reliable, according to Van Dalen.[1] The significance of selecting the right problem or topic is also stressed by Ary, Jacobs, and Razavieh.[2]

You may be wondering in what direction you should go with your research. Are you interested in doing some kind of aesthetic inquiry in music, or is your preference more in researching classroom problems using some type of descriptive techniques? Topics utilizing philosophical, historical, qualitative, or experimental/quasi-experimental procedures should not be overlooked either if you have some idea to pursue in one of those categories. As you study this chapter you should be better able to focus not only on a possible research topic but also on a tentative idea of the method which might be best to use in pursuing that topic. The specifics for applying the method chosen, however, must wait until a later chapter.

Definitions of Research

As used throughout this book, the term "research" will refer to the identification and isolation of a problem into a workable plan; the implementation of that plan to collect the data needed; and the synthesis, interpretation, and presentation of the collected information into some format which readily can be made available to others. This chapter will deal essentially with the first part of the term "research" as just defined—the identification and isolation of a problem. Later chapters will present procedures and techniques for obtaining data and for reporting on the data obtained.

There are many meanings of the term "research." Some are general; others are more specific. In an ambivalent sense, if someone tells you to "research" that question, do you know the context in which that term is meant? Very likely in a nonacademic situation it means nothing more than trying to "cope" with a situation, and does not mean the careful investigative process so important to good research.

Following are some of the more specialized and formal definitions of research. Shulman states that in the field of teaching the term "research" relates to collecting a growing body of knowledge. This is done by many kinds of scholars and professionals: those who are practitioners in a given field, the theoreticians for that field, and other researchers.[3] The quest for all knowledge involves posing questions for which answers are sought. Hopkins and Antes write that research is *"structured inquiry that (1) utilizes acceptable scientific methodology to solve problems and (2) creates new generally applicable knowledge."*[4] All educational research, according to Wiersma, is directed toward either extending knowledge or solving a problem or both.[5] McMillan and Schumacher define research this way: *"research* is a systematic process of collecting and logically analyzing information (data) for some purpose."[6] Vockell considers research to be a hierarchy of four different levels, which he identifies as data collection, internal validity, external validity, and theoretical research.[7] Sowell and Casey aver that research is applying principles of the scientific method to investigate problems.[8] Best and Kahn relate research to the scientific method, stating that research involves systematic procedures to analyze and report on the findings.[9] Leedy says: "Research is a procedure by which we attempt to find systematically, and with the support of demonstrable fact, the answer to a question or the resolution of a problem."[10] Englehart's definition is one that comes fairly close to the practice of music educators. His definition is that research is the identification of generalizations that enable educators to determine what is necessary for the education of children and adults.[11] Madsen and Madsen give a broad definition of research, stating that it is how one thinks rationally and objectively about something that can be examined scientifically.[12] Rainbow and Froehlich label a research problem as the research purpose. Continuing, they state, "Whatever the label, the research purpose/problem is the objective of a specific investigation toward which one initially directs all research efforts."[13] The definition of music-education research that is operational throughout this book is that *research is a carefully organized procedure that can result in the discovery of new knowledge, the substantiation of previously held concepts, the rejection of false tenets that have been widely acclaimed, and the formal presentation of data collected.*

Research Concepts

The researcher in music education can expect to encounter certain terms or concepts that relate to procedures of research. Those that refer only to specific types of research will be discussed in appropriate chapters in this book. Others, which are common to all types of research, follow. An understanding of these terms is important to the logical organization of a study.

When matriculated, especially at the doctoral level, graduate students often are required to make a distinction in their programs of studies between an emphasis that will enable them to pursue a project of *pure* research and one that may be called *applied*, referred to as *action* research in this chapter. The former, sometimes known as "basic" or "fundamental" research, is based on the accurate reporting of results, usually with little attempt to incorporate practical applications of the findings in the study. Those who read the report are expected to make whatever use of the data seems appropriate to their own situation. *Pure* research, often concerned with the development of a theory or model based on previous theories or models, is desirable in almost all fields of endeavor, but frequently is not the type that will produce answers to questions facing music educators in the classroom. A history of eighteenth-century English secular choral music most likely would be regarded as "pure" research, provided the study was concluded according to the concepts of "basic" research. *Applied* (sometimes called "action" research) is conducted and reported in such a way that the investigator includes practical suggestions for applying the data of a study to a teaching situation. An anthology of eighteenth-century English secular choral music would be classified as "applied" research because an anthology, by implication, may consist of compositions that have been collected and edited for a specific group, with rehearsal suggestions also incorporated in the study. The anthology quite properly could contain a history section, but this factor alone is not important enough to change the character of the study, since the basic intent in this type of research is to present practical suggestions for using the results.

As an example of a recent study of "action" research, Clarke composed choral settings to selected psalms based on Jamaican folk melodies, rhythms, and harmonies. He reviewed three centuries of Jamaican history and culture to determine the influence of African and European immigration to that Caribbean island. The nine psalm settings were arranged for three voice parts with piano, guitar, and percussion accompaniment. The settings are appropriate, according to Clarke, for Jamaican students in secondary schools, churches, or music festivals.[14]

Of the six kinds of research discussed in this book, experimental/quasi-experimental, historical, philosophical, qualitative, and aesthetic usually fall under the heading of "pure" research, whereas descriptive and some aesthetic and qualitative studies might fall in the "applied" category. It should be noted at the outset that any attempt to assign arbitrarily any kind of research to one category or the other is risky at best. The purpose and the data included in a research study ought to determine how the study is classified. Pigeonholing can be very hazardous, but researchers who, during the process of planning, consider their research with either a *pure* or an *applied* emphasis in mind will find their projects much easier to organize.

Qualitative and *quantitative* are terms frequently referred to in research jargon, and may have different meanings from those usually associated with those terms. As used in this book, they refer to procedures for looking at information. In the former, research results are largely subjective, that is, not easily translated into scores, whereas in the latter, objective data based on the scores of some type of measurement are given. If you were to count the number of bassoon players in all the public schools of any given state you could obtain *qualitative* data, in other words, "kinds" of information, rather than evaluation of these data. However, the mere counting of the bassoonists would not tell you how proficient these bassoonists were. You would need to obtain some type of objective evaluation to determine their proficiency on the bassoon—this would result in *quantitative* data. Thus, you could combine *qualitative* and *quantitative* data, a most desirable research procedure when it is possible to do so. Travers, in addressing this point, says that qualitative generalizations eventually may lead to pronouncements that are substantiated quantitatively.[15] Leedy puts the difference between qualitative and quantitative data this way: "We think of the data of historical and descriptive studies as *qualitative data*, and the data of analytical survey studies as *quantitative data*."[16] While it is possible for a research project to be so organized that it would contain only qualitative data, it would be virtually impossible for a study to contain quantitative but no qualitative data, because even in a study where data are the result of some type of measurement, narrative is necessary to explain the theoretical rationale for the study, and a rationale statement is a type of information.

In examining research studies in music education, sometimes one can find those that contain qualitative data only, with quantitative data omitted, when there is every indication that they should have been included. Such studies are ineffective and weak because the investigator has not proceeded thoroughly and carefully to the next significant step of quantifying information. For example, a qualitative study might be undertaken to learn which school systems in a given state have instrumental music programs. These data, readily obtainable by a questionnaire or other means, could be useful to school administrators who do not have an instrumental program, thereby enabling them to report to their Boards of Education that such a program is needed if children in the community are to receive the same cultural advantages as youngsters in neighboring school systems. To music teachers, by contrast, these data would be relatively useless because they give no indication of the actual content of the instrumental programs surveyed. They merely signify the presence or absence of instrumental music in the school systems investigated. Music supervisors more likely would be interested in determining how their curricular offerings compare with those of other schools and the quality of these programs. In other words, after hearing the groups, they might point out to their superiors that the level of performance in a certain school that has two orchestras, two bands, two choruses, and two jazz ensembles in the senior high school is such that this pattern should be emulated.

Since music is largely concerned with skills, still unanswered is the question of performing competency of the groups under consideration. This problem also is quantitative, and answers would be dependent on the use of a specialized type of measurement in conjunction with a questionnaire. Such an investigation would be proper under certain conditions. The investigator would need to establish criteria for comparison in order to ascertain how well the groups performed. Researchers who organize their projects so as to obtain quantitative data are in a better position initially to produce a significant research study than are those who merely scratch the surface by seeking only qualitative information. It should be made clear, however, that both quantitative and qualitative studies may produce valid information although different techniques are used for each.

It has been gratifying to note that the quality of research in music education has improved markedly in the last two decades. Much of this improvement is due to greater sophistication in the field of research. This may be attributed to better use of reflective thinking in the organization and development of a problem and in the implementation of the research through better and more objective research techniques.

Categories of Music-Education Research

Most research studies in music education fall under one of the following categories: aesthetic, descriptive, historical, philosophical, qualitative, and experimental/quasi-experimental (sometimes called behavioral). Procedures for obtaining and treating data in each of these methodologies are to be found in later chapters in this book. Sometimes music students will engage in research across different fields, for instance, combining music education and psychology or therapy.

A purview of any standard textbook in educational research will likely reveal a discussion of the descriptive (with its many components), experimental/quasi-experimental, and historical methodologies; unfortunately, aesthetic and philosophical methodologies usually are missing. Texts on musicology and other music topics normally include procedures for conducting historical research but say little, if anything, about the other possibilities included in this book.

Philosophical inquiry is mentioned in some older research sources, such as Smith and Whitney, but many educational researchers in the past have either denied its existence as a separate type of research or suggested that its use was so extremely limited as to be hardly worth serious consideration. Others consider philosophical inquiry to be no different from the process of the scientific method and reflective thinking, to which it is closely related, to be sure. Rainbow and Froehlich are among the more recent writers who devote an entire chapter to philosophical inquiry. Also, the American Educational Research Association (AERA) has begun to recognize that philosophical inquiry is a valid method for obtaining information. Their recent publication *Complementary Methods for Research in Education*, edited by Richard M. Jaeger, contains a chapter by Michael Scriven entitled "Philosophical Inquiry Methods in Education."[17] In music education, philosophical inquiry normally refers to a comparison of ideas, and can be a very fruitful technique to use for investigation.

Aesthetic inquiry (or research) is a designation that usually relates to discovery of the beautiful in the arts, or to the comparison of art objects. Specifically, in music, it may relate to learning about a composer or the composer's music, or to any other investigation that focuses on music. This type of study has received considerable emphasis by researchers in performance-oriented programs (those offered for the D.M.A. or the Ph.D., for instance). When concerned with the study and analysis of certain compositions of a composer, including the latter's role in the mainstream of history, it may be regarded quite properly as quasi-musicological in scope. Many possibilities exist in the aesthetic type of research for a music educator who has a good aesthetic, theoretical, and musicological background. The frequently impersonal nature of behavioral research, which has become prominent in music-education research, now is beginning to lose some ground to the more personal approaches which are possible through applications of aesthetic inquiry techniques.

Qualitative research, found in some of the newer textbooks or more recent editions of textbooks—such as those by Borg and Gall, McMillan and Schumacher, Tuckman, and Van Maanen—may be combined with descriptive research, or listed as a separate entity, especially when it has a strong social-science base. The qualitative method deals with topics which are ethnographic or sociological or involve some type of fieldwork. In 1982 Bogdan and Biklen brought out *Qualitative Research for Education: An Introduction to Theory and Methods*, in which they include both phenomenological and what is labeled "ethnomethodological" approaches. Ethnomethodology refers to the kind of methods researchers use to obtain their data.[18] A series from Sage Publications entitled *Qualitative Research Methods* was in the process of development, with some of the seven volumes already off the press, at the time of this writing. The editor for that series is John Van Maanen. Recent extension of the qualitative method to include a strong philosophical or aesthetic emphasis may be noted in the chapter on qualitative research in this book (chapter 5). Applications of the qualitative method philosophically and aesthetically may be found in the two volumes entitled *Qualitative Evaluation in the Arts*, published by New York University.[19]

Since the techniques, philosophical bases, procedures, and characteristics of each of the six kinds of research referred to earlier will be presented in detail in subsequent chapters in this book, they will be mentioned here only in passing. Any study, of course, may incorporate some aspects of the other research types, but the main emphasis in that study will be upon one or a combination of the six types just listed. The organization of a study largely determines the format under which the research will be conducted. A historical study will emphasize the design for a historical study, in which authenticity and credibility of data become crucial. A descriptive report contains information on some current observations, whereas experimental (behavioral) and quasi-experimental studies will concentrate on techniques which involve statistical comparison of variables. Understandably, labels associated with a given research study should not become a fetish, because the essential factor is *the way the study is organized and implemented, and the information reported*. Categorization, on the other hand, is helpful in determining procedures that will be or have been followed in a research study. The research might be labeled aesthetic-descriptive, aesthetic-historical, aesthetic-qualitative, aesthetic-quasi-experimental, or any other combination. In the aesthetic-descriptive approach, a music or other aesthetic topic would be studied using descriptive techniques, and in the aesthetic-quasi-experimental approach, an aesthetic topic would be studied using quasi-experimental techniques. Most research studies are not developed exclusively with one methodology at the expense of the others. By analogy, no person is completely an introvert or an extrovert; personality traits label you as being inclined in one direction or the other. To cite another example, a musical tone that you have identified as *A* may have a frequency of 220 hertz (Hz). When the sound is analyzed by an oscilloscope it may be found also to possess minor amounts of energy present for E (966 Hz) or C# (1,100 Hz), yet you perceive only the note *A* because it is the dominant sound. Likewise, a study could include both historical and philosophical concepts, yet be regarded as basically an experimental study. Background information on the experiment proposed or theories upon which it is predicated could be philosophically based. Regardless of the kind of organization, the research must meet certain rigid criteria if it is to be solid. Results of any of these types of research are largely dependent on the attitude of the researcher, not the organization, because even the best-organized research plan could be meaningless if it is not implemented carefully by an investigator who uses good research techniques.

Expansion of Degree Programs

In years past teachers of music for the public schools were trained not only in the more formal normal schools and teachers' colleges but also in teachers' institutes, singing schools, and military music schools. From two- to three-year programs in normal schools offering no degree to advanced graduate schools which award some type of doctorate, change has been phenomenal and rapid in the twentieth century. About sixty years ago many state departments of education began to mandate at least a baccalaureate degree as a prerequisite for a teaching certificate. Since then, the increasing demand on the part of state departments of education for a minimum of a master's degree as the requisite for permanent certification has resulted in a monumental growth in graduate programs in music and other fields of education all over the nation, and even abroad. A few master's programs mandate extra course work in place of the usual thesis or some other creative project. Other master's degree programs are organized to allow the student to carry extra course work in lieu of a written project. Still others require some type of creative endeavor (composition, arrangement, thesis, recital, or field project) as partial fulfillment of degree requirements. The option of either extra course work or a project has some advantages. The authors' experiences in advising students at both the master's and doctoral levels, however, suggest that graduate schools should consider the feasibility of making some type of culminating written requirement involving research mandatory for all master's degree recipients. Not only can these students expand their knowledge and receive intellectual stimulation, but they will have had some practical research experience should they eventually pursue a doctorate, which many are doing now.

There is a great proliferation of degree designations in master's degree programs: namely, Master of Music, Master of Arts, Master of Science, and Master of Music Education, among others. Sometimes a graduate student in music may believe that the Master of Music is superior to the Master of Arts. One cannot always tell by the degree designation the actual quality of a master's program. The reputation of the institution, the faculty involved in the program, and the success of graduates are the important criteria to consider, as well as the accrediting associations to which the institutions belong.

Sometimes a graduate student will use a pilot study (to be discussed in chapter 8) to determine the feasibility of pursuing that topic in greater depth at the master's or doctoral level. Howes's study, "Some Effects of Sequential Music Tasks on the Cognitive and Social Skills of Learning Disabled Adults," is an example of this type of pilot study. Howes's subjects (Ss) were nine learning-disabled adults enrolled in an intensive job training program. Various musical tasks were given to the Ss, using Orff-Schulwerk instruments. Both the social and musical skills of the Ss showed marked improvement.[20]

The demand for academic standing above the baccalaureate degree began in the 1920s. Until the advent of World War II the master's degree generally was considered to be the terminal degree for music teachers, even on the college or university level. Apparently it was assumed that musicians were "doers" rather than "thinkers"; thus, advanced-level work beyond the master's degree was believed to be unnecessary because "thinkers" usually were researchers and "doers" often were not. In the past fifty years, moreover, the pressure for advanced degrees on college and university music teachers by administrators has caused a rethinking of graduate music education, with the result that many beginning postbaccalaureate students now anticipate that a master's degree is only the transitional step to the doctorate. An aspirant for a teaching position at the college or university level can hardly hope to rise above the level of assistant professor without an earned doctorate, except in a few isolated situations.

Jones and McFee, writing in the *Handbook of Research on Teaching*, 3rd edition, point out that dissertations in music education largely have been quantitative in scope, based on research methods from general education and psychology.[21] Studies on curriculum in music education, say Jones and McFee, essentially have been directed toward developing performance skills. In comparing art and music education, the same authors indicate little agreement on goals and objectives of instruction by art and music educators. On the positive side, the nod was given to music educators as being in more agreement than art educators in regard to kinds of methodologies needed to provide answers to research questions.[22]

It seems almost incongruous to think of graduate education without some type of research being involved. John Brademas, writing for the Graduate Subcommittee of the National Commission on Student Financial Assistance, pointed out that the highest quality of research is not possible without original research. Furthermore, no matter where the research is done, it is dependent on education at the graduate level.[23]

If you have examined college or university vacancy lists recently, you are fully aware that among the application requirements the phrase "doctorate required or preferred" stares at you boldly. The by-product of the coercion by college and university administrators for an earned terminal degree has been a demand for doctorates with emphases different from those of the traditional Ph.D. and Ed.D. This has been true in specialized fields such as music and the other arts, where the Ph.D., the typical research doctorate, often is not equated with the kind of scholarship possessed by musicians. One of the newer degrees is the Doctor of Arts (D.A.). Dressel reports that the D.A. was originally conceived as a degree for practitioners rather than one for the research-oriented specialist.[24] Thus it would appear that this would be the logical degree for the musician to pursue; however, a more specific degree was desired, so several universities developed curricula leading to the Doctor of Musical Arts (D.M.A.) and the Doctor of Music (Mus.Doc.), to mention a few new designations. The Mus.Doc. actually has been around for a long time, but as an honorary degree conferred upon outstanding composers, conductors, and performers, and not as an earned degree comparable to the D.M.A. or other degree designations.

With few exceptions, all doctorates require some type of terminal project in written form, be it a dissertation, composition, project, or whatever format the creativity takes. The Doctor of Arts is a more flexible, interdisciplinary, and individually oriented program of studies enabling a student to relate music to the other arts more effectively than can the traditional Ph.D. or Ed.D. Sometimes there is confusion between the designations D.A. and D.M.A. You should check carefully to make sure the institution you propose to enter (or presently attend) offers the degree which best fits your needs, be it the D.A., D.M.A., Ph.D., Ed.D., or any other degree designation, for that matter.

The flexible nature of the D.A., for instance, could permit a music educator to develop a study incorporating music as taught one hundred years ago in a living history project. The researcher could employ methods and techniques used to teach music reading to elementary school children. The life of some lesser-known but important music teacher of this period, such as Hosea E. Holt (1836-1898) or Sterrie A. Weaver (1853-1904), would need to be reviewed and then this information incorporated into an actual teaching situation, which could be videotaped, with the researcher in period costume and in a classroom setting of the period. The researcher would actually teach a series of music reading lessons as they would have been presented, using appropriate materials from one hundred years ago. Research would be necessary to bring this project off because much background study would be necessary to make the presentation as authentic as possible.

Often it is believed that a Ph.D. is superior to the Ed.D. This is not necessarily true. The main distinction between the two degrees should be the type of project to be completed. The Ph.D. normally is concerned with the development of a theory or model philosophically, some type of qualitative or descriptive observation, or a report on some historical or aesthetic activity. The action research for the Ed.D. often takes place in the form of a practical project that one can take directly into the classroom. Here are some hypothetical examples of the difference between the Ph.D. and the Ed.D. Suppose you were to complete a study on the development of a model to teach music to multiply handicapped children. This study would be in the realm of the Ph.D. because the model should be theoretically based and would most necessarily be process oriented. On the other hand, a series of lessons for multiply handicapped children in music would be in the category of action research, appropriate for the Ed.D. In this instance your reader could take directly to the classroom what you had outlined and developed in your study. This would assume that you first test it to determine its applicability to the appropriate population. Two of the newer degrees, D.M.A. and Mus.Doc., emphasize musical analysis, musical performance, or other skills, but essentially stay clear of the "action" research concept. Regardless of the degree, the results of the research are what is important. Some institutions do not offer certain degree designations because they are not authorized to do so by an overseeing agency such as a board of trustees. As already stated, this is not to say that one degree is superior to another. The standards expected for any of these degrees should be consistent; the methodology and kind of results sought should be the difference. The egregious canard that the Ed.D., D.M.A., D.A., and Mus.Doc. are inferior to the Ph.D. should be expunged from the literature and from the minds of those who hold such ideas once and for all. Holders of the Ph.D., on the other hand, should not look snobbishly down their noses at any of the newer degrees if the research product is of high quality. Research is not a game of trying to see who is more intellectual than someone else!

Some universities permit a variant of the Ed.D., referred to as the "Alternative Ed.D.," which stresses the development of a product, a series of position papers, or the completion of a textbook, to cite three examples. This type of project is more flexible in format than that for the traditional Ph.D., D.M.A., Mus.Doc., or Ed.D., and the final document may be similar to the projects for the D.A., referred to in previous paragraphs. A hypothetical example of an Alternative Ed.D. topic would be "Three Position Papers on the Teaching of Music Methods to Elementary Education Majors in a College or University."

While doing some research recently, the senior author of this text came across an interesting incident of memorabilia, the Doctor of Pedagogy degree. This designation was used at the end of the last century and the early part of this century. Such a degree in music education was awarded to one John J. Dawson by New York University in 1895, only five years after the School of Pedagogy was established, the first one to award degrees in education. (That dissertation will be discussed in greater depth in chapter 9, "Historical Research: Concepts and Techniques.") What makes this even more unusual is that before a Department of Music Education was formally established at New York University by Hollis Dann (1861–1939) in 1925, two graduate students with musical backgrounds (Dawson being the first) had already written dissertations with a music education emphasis.[25] Since no earlier account has been found to date, this makes Dawson the *first recipient of an earned doctorate in music education.* The title of his dissertation is "The Education Value of Vocal Music."[26]

You will recall that with few exceptions all earned doctorates at present are based upon the acceptance of some type of "creative" project. Therefore, students in music education as well as other disciplines find themselves faced with the reality of engaging in research. Many times selection of an acceptable topic becomes an unnecessarily long and tedious process, one that could be shortened considerably if reflective thinking were used to help locate and develop a topic which is meaningful and interesting to you. The necessity for you to do your own thinking is emphasized by Koefod,

who also observed that an excellent research report is the hallmark
of this kind of investigator.[27]

Common Ways of Obtaining Research Topic Information

There are three common ways that information on a research
topic is obtained: namely, through (1) trial and error, (2) serendipity,
and (3) implementation of a carefully organized plan of research.
If you are a teacher you may have found solutions to some of your
dilemmas by trying out one strategy, then another, until you eventually came up with an approach which seemed satisfactory, at least
on an interim basis. This trial-and-error approach does not fall
under the formal designation of "research."

Serendipitous discoveries have accounted for some of the greatest advances in the scientific world; however, very few solutions to
problems faced by music educators have been the result of serendipity. (The term "music educators" is used throughout this book
in a very broad sense to mean those who teach music of any kind
at any level.) The word "serendipity" is derived from the account
of The Three Princes of Serendip, as told by the eighteenth-century
British novelist Horace Walpole (1717-1797). As they sailed the
Indian Ocean, these princes of Serendip, known more recently as
Ceylon and now as Sri Lanka, were continually finding things they
did not expect. One example of serendipity in the scientific world
will suffice. Often cited is the discovery in 1928, quite by accident,
by Alexander Fleming (1881-1955), of that marvelous antibiotic
penicillin. From his research on influenza he observed by chance
that spores from the *Penicillium notatum* had wiped out a culture
of staphylococcus bacteria, which led him to see the powers of the
mold from which penicillin is made.[28]

A recent serendipitous discovery, related to a connoisseur of the
arts, was the accidental finding by James Gilreath and Douglas L.
Wilson of Thomas Jefferson's (1743-1826) classification catalog of
his personal library. Jefferson's catalog had been assembled by
Nicholas P. Trist, his private secretary, and prepared for publication
in 1815 by George Watterson, Librarian of Congress. Gilreath,
history specialist at the Library of Congress, and Wilson, Knox
College professor, discovered that Jefferson's personal catalog had
been mistakenly bound in the front of the Watterson catalog.
Jefferson placed his books into three categories of knowledge:
history, philosophy, and fine arts. His fine arts collection included

books on architecture, painting, sculpture, and music. Watterson's arrangement, disapproved by Jefferson, involved an alphabetical arrangement of all entries.[29] (You will recall that many of the holdings of the Library of Congress were destroyed when the British burned Washington during the War of 1812. Jefferson subsequently sold much of his personal library to the Library of Congress.)

To approach serendipity from a hypothetical viewpoint, Sir Arthur Sullivan (1842-1900) wrote a vocal composition entitled *The Lost Chord*. The "discovery" of this "lost chord" would have been the result of serendipity had the traditional system of harmony developed by Jean-Philippe Rameau (1683-1764) not been so well established already that a "new" chord was an impossibility. Any significant research findings, except those resulting from serendipity, are usually based on careful and deliberate planning, followed by precise execution of the plan, and then unbiased critique of the results. Frequently this cycle is repeated several times before significant results are achieved. Since problems are ever-present, humanity will continue to be challenged to draw upon its ingenuity for solutions in the future as it has in the past. The continuum is endless, because as answers to questions emerge through various research procedures, new and additional challenges arise as we move up the ladder of progress. Only when our hunger to improve our lot in life is satisfied will we cease our quest for knowledge.

Emphasis in this book will be on the third of the ways commonly used to obtain research topic information: namely, the development and implementation of a carefully organized plan of research. Emphasized throughout the book, this procedure will be discussed by the authors in greater depth in subsequent chapters.

The selection of a topic is the first consideration in this approach. Here is an example. If you are a Union Civil War buff and are thinking about a topic combining music and Civil War events, you might want to examine the role of Union cavalry commander Colonel Benjamin H. Grierson, a former music teacher from Illinois. Colonel Grierson's successful raids of sixteen days in Tennessee, Mississippi, and Louisiana in 1863 diverted the attention of the Confederacy from General Grant's siege of Vicksburg, Mississippi. You might ask: "What was his role as a music teacher?" "Where did he teach?" "What did he teach?" "Did he enlist in the Union Army or was he drafted?" "What musical activities did he engage in during his time in the Union Army?" Grierson, a composer and arranger, also played several instruments. On patrols he is said to have entertained himself and those of his troops within earshot by strumming on a jaw harp as they rode along.[30]

Taking a Confederate point of view of this fratricidal conflict, Ferguson recently investigated the musical and military contribution of bands in the Confederate States of America. About 2,400 bandsmen served in 155 bands for the Confederacy. During combat they usually served as hospital corpsmen and surgeons' assistants. Bands from Louisiana, North Carolina, and Tennessee, about which little had been written previously, were included in Ferguson's study.[31]

The human race is instinctively committed to change, for without it, survival for any length of time is impossible. The "greenhouse effect," pollution, and other life-threatening events are a serious cause for concern. Research by dedicated people will be needed to curtail, or at least arrest, these disturbing trends in our world. The human race does not appear ready yet to go the way of the prehistoric brontosaurus and the fabled dodo bird. Their disappearance from the face of the earth has been attributed to an inability to adjust to environmental changes. The process of metamorphosis has extended to the tools and devices we use not only for our survival but also for our enjoyment. Even a cursory glance at a music history textbook will reveal names of instruments that are no longer in use: the ancient Greek cithara, the medieval shawm, the ophicleide of the last century, and others. Or, witness the changes in instruments used or instrumentation called for in contemporary concert band and wind ensemble arrangements. The soprano saxophone, the Eb mellophone, the Eb cornet, the Db piccolo and flute, and the Eb alto clarinet are often missing from today's band and wind ensembles. Why are they not in vogue today? That is a question which research may or may not be able to answer. Nevertheless, the current disuse of these instruments in ensembles is no reason for failure to learn about them. Any person who is well read in music—as in any discipline—is expected to know about significant developments (and even those less significant) and events pertinent to his or her chosen field. How do you best acquire this knowledge? The answer is through research into many sources.

The term "research" can be an awesome and frightening one at times. Students have entered some of the authors' research classes with fear and trepidation because the world outside of academia often pictures a researcher as one who is isolated from society, one who spends time turning knobs, mixing chemicals, moving rats from one cage to another, or holed up in front of a computer. Is the music educator expected to go into seclusion to search for the solution to a problem? The answer is unquestionably no. Fortunately, research need not be something to dread; it even can be fun!

Change is ever-present not only in society but also in education and brings with it new problems to be solved. The quest for solutions to problems, you will recall, may be labeled "research" in the proper sense of the word. Educators may seek answers to some classroom problem through applying the results of formal research. Some solutions to problems obviously will result from less formally organized procedures because, as Kelley avers, research actually is a process of evolution.[32] In the realm of music, the clumsy, five-key, eighteenth-century clarinet of Johann C. Denner (1655–1707) would be repugnant to the contemporary clarinetist, who performs on an instrument containing up to twenty keys and seven rings. Is it possible that the cithara, shawm, or ophicleide likewise could have been modified and improved to keep pace with changing aesthetic and music concepts? This conjecture hardly seems appropriate; the record is clear. Obsolescence and usefulness are both the result of change, but for different reasons, many of which will never be known. It should be noted, however, that research may hasten either one or the other. From a practical standpoint, research is concerned with utility—or should be—although from a historical perspective, obsolescence could provide appropriate topics for study.

Selection of a Topic

It is a "given" that a master's thesis or a doctoral dissertation is expected to make a contribution to knowledge. Before selecting a topic, some consideration needs to be given to the *purpose* of the research. Other than the obvious reason—to obtain a degree—you need to ask yourself: "Why am I conducting this research?" "Will it help me do better what I already am doing?" "Will this research improve my perspective on education?" Or, "Will the research supplement my résumé and enable me to obtain a better position?" You may give a positive answer (or a negative one) to all four, or to only some of these questions. Since the topic selection procedure is so important, you need to go about selecting a topic for your research which is oriented toward the goal of providing knowledge in your field relating to that topic.

As a starter, here are some specific questions which relate to your *purpose* for the research as well as to provide additional knowledge to the field: "What am I interested in?" "Are there problems in my classroom that might be resolved by research?" "Am I sure that I have the background to successfully complete the research I plan to do?" "Is the topic I propose to pursue one that is supported by my adviser or department?" "Has this proposed research been done before?" "How can I be sure I can obtain all the answers I need to successfully complete my study?" Obviously there are no complete answers for all these questions, but they can stimulate your mind and help you to focus your problem properly.

Davis and Parker identify several sources of possible topics. Those that are relevant for music students are: (1) current problems in the classroom, (2) suggestions for further research listed in theses and dissertations, (3) suggestions from authorities in the field, and (4) procedures or methods generally accepted as being valid, but without substantiation.[33] Sometimes problems encountered by the teacher in the classroom do not lend themselves to formal research procedures. As mentioned earlier, answers are sometimes found by the "trial and error" method. This is usually true when an answer to a classroom problem cannot wait for the usual development of a research proposal and its implementation. The question of why students use drugs is not one that can be answered quickly. It is too complex and involves the assistance of professionals in many fields working together with the teacher.

Most theses and dissertations include a final chapter which lists suggestions for further research. These can be a most promising source of possible topics. Then there are several sources which list the titles of completed studies. Among the most valuable for music students are *Doctoral Abstracts International, Master's Abstracts,* and *Doctoral Dissertations in Musicology International.* For dissertations not yet completed, *Directory of International Music Education Dissertations in Progress,* issued by the Council for Research in Music Education, is the best source. From the list of completed studies, however, one must actually review the abstract—notice the first two sources listed—or better yet, the study, to find potential topics. The titles are an indication, but not a complete idea, of what remains to be done in the field.

Research suggestions often are presented by authorities in the field as they lecture at conferences, in the classroom, and by personal conferences with them. It must be assumed that they are the leaders in the field and thus they can offer valid suggestions for topics which need to be researched.

Teaching techniques and approaches often are handed down from one generation of teachers to another. Some of them are "time tested"; but this does not necessarily mean they have been validated through some careful research process. While not numerous, these topics can be fruitful sources. Tuckman reports that the selection of a research problem or topic is one of the most difficult in the entire research process, and one to which little guidance can be given. Yet, he does offer the encouragement that a problem may be expressed as the relationship which exists between two or more variables.[34]

One of the most respected and concise accounts of topic selection takes into account the relationship which should exist between the student and his or her adviser. The suggestions by Chambers, paraphrased from the *Phi Delta Kappan*, indicate that potential researchers should: (1) avoid asking their advisers for "assigned" topics, but rather seek those that are in accord with their own interests and initiative; (2) select subjects that are in harmony with their interest and background instead of those that are suited to the "predilections" of their advisers; (3) manifest erudition by not expecting their advisers to serve as "intellectual nursemaids"; (4) define their problems clearly; (5) become familiar with literature in their field so as to find out what has or has not been done; (6) determine what methods, techniques, or instruments will be needed; and (7) find out whether field trips or visits to museums, libraries, private archives, and other repositories of information are necessary. After continuing with suggestions for student-adviser conferences and for writing up the study, Chambers concludes by stating, "Research is not necessarily as complex, difficult, mysterious, or esoteric as a pedantic attitude can make it seem. In common with all things that are really great, it is essentially simple in concept. It has been comprehensively and simply defined in eight words as 'the orderly treatment of data to answer questions.' "[35]

Referring to Chambers's first point, topics that are "assigned" by advisers have validity for investigators *only if they are interested in the subject and can involve themselves wholeheartedly in it.* By analogy, there are too many exercises in music theory that result in a mediocre or mechanical sound because the persons writing them have not been given the freedom to express themselves in a manner that is meaningful and significant to them. This, obviously, is not to imply that all principles and rules should be abrogated. They are certainly needed as guidelines, but students need to be encouraged to express themselves in a manner that is in accord with their own initiative and creativity. All too prevalent are research projects in a "series," usually at the master's level, which are "assigned" by advisers to certain of their students. A group of studies of this type might center on a general title, such as a survey of elementary private method instruction books for specific instruments, with students examining and comparing materials for each instrument of the band and orchestra. Such projects, if well organized and implemented, can be very beneficial to students in instrumental-techniques classes who are unfamiliar with those publications. It is in this spirit, no doubt, that advisers make such assignments. Koefod takes a less optimistic viewpoint when he states that students beg for this type of assignment frequently because they have been led to believe that this is the way to find a research topic.[36] Whether the "assignments" are voluntary or involuntary, the results will usually be of little value unless you are interested and completely immersed in the subject, which is Chambers's second point. The process of reflective thinking, to be discussed later in this chapter, will be more effective when the choice of a topic is the result of your initiative, since the decision undoubtedly will be one of the most important you will make in your educational career, and thus should be predicated on something in which you are intensely interested.

Chambers's third point, referring to advisers who serve as "intellectual nursemaids," is both amusing and tragic. The implication is that students will merely put the "flesh" on "skeletons" constructed by their advisers. Advisers can no more do your reflective thinking for you than they can take your examinations. Advisers should direct attention to questionable patterns of thinking and organization of materials. Their suggestions should be practical, relevant, and within the framework of the research proposal. Advisers' remarks are suggestions, not mandates, with full responsibility for accepting or rejecting them resting with you, upon whom also the onus eventually falls for defending your research.

Fortunately, many students give considerable thought to potential topics prior to enrollment in a graduate program. Others depend on expediency, mandate, suggestions from an adviser, or some other extrinsic factor in choosing a research topic. Such ambivalence can hardly result in anything more than inferior productivity. You should choose a topic for investigation in which you have an intense interest, one to which you may lay claim as "your own." It is inconceivable that you would want to become involved in a research topic in which you are neither totally engrossed nor in general agreement philosophically. School administrators recognize that personnel perform tasks more efficiently in areas in which they are competent and interested. In the interest of educational efficiency, good administrative practice dictates that such predilections be honored wherever possible through appropriate assignments. Why should involvement in research operate under a different procedure? As if in reply, Kelley notes that the conduct of worthwhile research is not easy, and he also deplores those who dismiss its importance too lightly.[37] Because the selection of an appropriate topic is very significant, it will be treated more comprehensively in the next chapter.

While most graduate students pursue research in music education for pragmatic reasons, a gratifying trend is evident in the ever-increasing number of postdoctoral titles. Governments, philanthropic agencies, colleges and universities, and foundations have supported many of these postdoctoral projects. Regrettably, much of the money allocated for research by the various agencies has dried up, especially for the arts. One positive example of recent funding for the arts is the National Arts Education Research Center, which was established at New York University in October of 1987 by the National Endowment for the Arts and the U.S. Department of Education. At the time of this writing the focus of this ongoing research was to investigate practical teaching strategies and to identify quality curricula. Teachers have been selected nationwide and their research has been developed to produce theoretical bases and substantive means for the improvement of arts education. These teachers met in summer institutes in 1988 and 1989 at New York University. The center's staff is interdisciplinary and includes members in art, music, psychology, elementary and early childhood education, educational technology, sociology, and statistics.[38]

Many of the projects which have not received subsidization because of the paucity of funds likely would have been funded if monies were available. The proposed research procedures that were reviewed by these authors seem to have been solid and the research potentially could be important. Certainly, experience received in developing and pursuing a graduate project ought to make it easier to prepare an acceptable proposal for funding from agencies and organizations that still support research in the arts. On the other hand, it would be inaccurate to infer that all research plans rejected for funding are exemplary in organization. Many proposals are deficient and most likely would not be subsidized even if funding were endless.

Chambers's fourth point relates to defining a problem clearly. It has been gratifying for us to note that the quality of research in music education has risen over the past several years. This is not to state that research in the field is still without fault. Like that of education in general, some studies in music education have been open to question. Some of this criticism is justified. Sometimes a research study consists of a superficial treatment of some insipid topic that the busy music educator does not really find pertinent. Actually, there are innumerable significant problems in music education that need to be solved. Might it not be more useful to concentrate on those that are of immediate concern and practical value for the profession? When realistic solutions have been found to those, then some attention may be given to other topics that are of less import to music educators. Realistically, it must be admitted that some of the most critical areas do not lend themselves to easy and quick solutions. The time schedule of a researcher and financial subsidization are frequently both limiting factors. Since times change, as indicated earlier, some solutions may be neither found nor needed for certain perplexities. One might ask, why engage in research if it will not be beneficial or if the results will be inconclusive? Significant research rarely results when answers to problems are obtained in haste. In addition, such findings may even be erroneous or impractical, note Borg and Gall.[39]

A literature review is the fifth concern of Chambers. Even a cursory review of the studies published for the past several years in journals such as the *Journal of Research in Music Education* or the *Bulletin of the Council for Research in Music Education* will reveal that the vast number of them are those which involve behavioral approaches to music education problems. The preponderance of behavioral studies is substantiated by Jones and McFee.[40] Yarbrough came to the same conclusion in her content analysis of articles published in the *Journal of Research in Music Education* for a thirty-year period (1953–1983). Yarbrough found that descriptive and experimental (including behavioral) studies, in that order, composed over 73 percent of the articles published. Historical and philosophical studies made up about 21 percent. The remaining 6 percent consisted of articles categorized by Yarbrough as "other."[41]

Methods and techniques constitute Chambers's sixth point. The experimental approach has been used largely because it is believed that the most valid data can be obtained only by using the behavioral approach to problem solving. This is almost like saying, "Now I have a working knowledge of the behavioral approach so I must find a topic which will fit this methodology." Or, could it be that this is an attempt to overcome the inferiority complex which many musicians have had for so long because their colleagues in the behavioral and pure sciences have dismissed their efforts in music-education research as inferior at best? One axiom that any fledgling researcher should keep in mind is this: *Selection of the topic should come first; the methodology to best deal with that problem should come next.*

Should an experimental or quasi-experimental approach be used where quantification of data will be by statistical concepts, or should a more qualitative approach be used employing aesthetic, philosophical, or historical techniques? These latter approaches would involve visits to repositories of information, Chambers's last point. Now it is true that the behavioral or experimental approach usually does result in data which are very objective, but they sometimes can also be rather artificial and arbitrary. Many answers can best be obtained with experimental procedures; however, some questions can better be answered by using other methodologies, as the senior author pointed out in an article in a state music educators' journal.[42] The careful structuring of research projects in music education, regardless of methodology used, should be accompanied by a subsequent meticulous implementation of the research plan to bring about valid and objective results that, when interpreted and disseminated, will be meaningful and practical to members of the profession.

The Scientific Method

In order for research to be judged as solid, it must consist of three steps: logical organization, objective implementation, and precise interpretation. Logical organization involves the thought process which will enable you to develop an effective research proposal or design. This usually takes the form of a thesis, dissertation, or grant proposal. Once the proposal is developed and approved, the actual implementation of the research plan can take place. This involves objective techniques identified in the proposal to collect and inter-pret the data obtained. Once the data are on hand, they need to be interpreted correctly. This may take the form of some narrative presentation, with or without examples; statistical comparison; or a computer printout of information. It is always possible that some of these three steps, namely, organization, implementation, and interpretation, as initially set up are not adequate. Even a well-organized proposal (prospectus or design) may not be implemented effectively, resulting in insufficient data. Both organization and execution must be of the highest order. There are instances where both organization and implementation are very objective, but the interpretation leaves much to be desired. All three steps, logical organization, objective implementation, and precise interpretation, need to be of the highest standards possible; they form the essence of the research proposal or design. (The process of formulating a research proposal will be discussed in the next chapter.)

It hardly seems necessary to mention that the investigator is crucial to the success of all research. You as the investigator must be both critical and inquisitive, as well as able to determine what type of research is most feasible for you, as Barzun and Graff so clearly point out.[43]

To the musician largely trained in nonverbal left-brain, right-hemisphere skills, the idea of undertaking research may seem extraneous to his or her training and musical development. Musicians often have been accused of failure to follow the logic of a researcher and thus have neglected to take advantage of research that can provide practical answers to some of their problems. In addition, many musicians have not been trained to think logically and apply concepts of the scientific method. The scientific method is central to the thought process of the physicist, the mathematician, the empirical researcher, and others whose training has been in the physical or social sciences. Leedy directly relates the scientific method to problem solving.[44] Mason and Bramble report that the purpose of utilizing the scientific method is to obtain knowledge to make valid decisions.[45] In a similar vein, McMillan and Schumacher write, "*Scientific inquiry* is the search for knowledge by using recognized methods in data collection, analysis, and interpretation."[46]

Precepts of the scientific method, which is a way of thinking, were initiated and originally utilized by researchers in the natural sciences. These principles now have been applied to research in almost all disciplines. Unfortunately, music educators have at times believed that the scientific method should be used only with certain types of research. This misconception evidently has been due to a misunderstanding of what the scientific method connotes. Each of the six types of research discussed in this book should incorporate the concepts of the scientific method with the understanding, of course, that some modifications may be necessary.

There is no mystery about the scientific method. It is not always a situation where one closets oneself in a laboratory to shut out the outside world and conduct some top-secret experiment. With tongue in cheek, musicians should be used to "the closet" because many hours have been spent by most of them in small practice rooms blowing, pressing, bowing, striking, or using whatever technique is needed to produce sounds. This type of seclusion is neither the method of science nor the scientific method. What the term "scientific method" means is that the methods of science developed by Bacon and others in the seventeenth century and later have been adapted by other disciplines. The scientific method emphasizes controls as strict as possible within the particular method being used. Both the music philosopher who examines and compares ideas and the behavioral music researcher who compares variables in an experimental or quasi-experimental situation can use the concepts of the scientific method.

Stated in its simplest terms, the definition of the scientific method preferred by these writers is: *any investigation that is logically organized, objectively implemented, and precisely interpreted.* Almack succinctly defines the scientific method as the precise search for knowledge.[47] Brennan points out that even in science, reasoning and observation are necessary to obtain valid answers.[48] A more complex definition, one more acceptable to behavioral scientists, is given by Kerlinger, who says that scientific research is a very carefully organized and critical investigation of the hypothetical relationship among various factors under review.[49]

Borg and Gall report that the scientific method as found in the natural and social sciences is based on the philosophical concept of positivism. In positivism, verification of knowledge is obtained through some type of direct observation by the researcher.[50] Vockell writes that the scientific method is "emphasis on using objective, factual data in a hypothetical-deductive fashion to make inferences."[51] According to Mason and Bramble, the scientific method entails a series of procedures which are independent and extend over one another to systematically obtain knowledge. To put it another way, it is a thought process for doing research.[52] The philosophers Cohen and Nagel also emphasize the importance of the scientific method for research.[53] Munro defines the scientific method from the standpoint of the genetic approach to psychology, as distinct from the usual explanation of a work of art in psychological terms, which might not be adequate because the identity, form, or potential value of that work cannot be understood clearly and subsequently appreciated. He points out that a careful thought process—application of the scientific method—can enable a person not only to understand the creative and appreciative process, but also to determine how aesthetic productions are either good or bad.[54]

Best and Kahn write that the terms "research" and "scientific method" are considered to be synonymous by some educators. They then identify the scientific method as consisting of "an informal application of problem identification, hypothesis formulation, observation, analysis, and conclusion."[55] Although all the foregoing definitions are slightly different, they have in common the idea that some type of careful thought process is necessary to carry out the research, regardless of the techniques used.

It is noteworthy that all the references just cited place emphasis in the scientific method on *an objective thought process*. The onus is upon you to organize your study so that objectivity will be the foremost and ultimate goal. Objectivity for a philosophical study obviously will not be the same as it will be for an experimental study, but it still is possible to obtain a certain degree of objectivity in a philosophical study. The scientist's basis for objectivity originally stemmed from certain assumptions regarding natural phenomena. The philosopher, as well as the scientist, might regard these "natural phenomena" as "common sense" assumptions. The German word *wissenschaft*, which literally means "knowledge" and "science," is a good illustration of this application of the scientific method. A train, bus, or airline timetable contains the "science" facet of *wissenschaft* because the information is organized and verifiable in the structural method of science. "Knowledge," however, does not occur until it is verified that these means of transportation did indeed depart or arrive on schedule. Unless this is done one cannot have "knowledge," and can only assume that these modes of public transportation will be punctual. To give another oversimplified example, the scientist and philosopher assume that the sun will rise and set at certain specified times on any given day in the future because of past experience. They cannot prove, however, that these will take place in the future. An assumption can be made only because these phenomena have happened in the past. In designing and producing a machine, manufacturers normally do not demonstrate beforehand that every piece of machinery will respond in the way it should if certain conditions relative to its operation are met. They can only assume that such will occur in view of previous experiences with this machine under comparable testing conditions. Such assumptions are valid and may serve as the focal point of departure for researchers using the scientific method. You have to accept the validity of these assumptions, comments Van Dalen, if your research is going to be conducted in accordance with the precepts of the scientific method.[56]

Even the music educator who finds the realm of science to be an anathema would have no difficulty in applying the scientific method. Many researchers in music actually have been using some of these concepts, perhaps without realizing that they were based on the "scientific method." Science and philosophy are compatible in regard to the premises on which knowledge is based, even though their respective techniques for obtaining data are often different. Unfortunately, the philosophical aspect of the scientific method has not been used as widely in music education as it should be. Note these simple illustrations. How many students who write exercises in conventional four-part harmony understand the philosophical and acoustical reasoning behind the axiom prohibiting parallel fifths? Students may write exercises that are technically perfect, but do they understand why they sound good? Again, do bassoonists who are trying to develop a "resonant" tone really understand the scientific ramifications of timbre? Their teachers may give them certain practical suggestions for reed adjustment or for embouchure development that result in a significant improvement in tone quality, but they still may be unable to analyze why this transformation took place. Some music educators will argue that the development of practical skills must come first. Then, if there are time and inclination, philosophical and theoretical concepts may be introduced. In the natural and physical sciences, where reflective thinking and an "intellectual" approach normally are an adjunct to instruction, the scientific method is not strange to graduate students who initiate a research project. Observing the desirable fusion of skills in theory, Good states that "science without philosophy is blind, while philosophy without science is empty."[57] Now that many schools, even at the elementary level, are placing mini-computers in the classroom, one can anticipate that the logical and creative skills of future graduate students should be at a higher level than is the case in the late 1980s and the early 1990s.

Music is a skill; consequently, the graduate student in music education who has spent countless hours in the practice room often is intellectually handicapped. Yet if research is to be successful, some intellectual activity is necessary. The intellectual process is referred to as "critical" or "reflective" thinking. In an article in a state music educators association publication referred to earlier, the senior author states that "critical or reflective thinking is associated with logic and the scientific method, since all these terms relate to obtaining information through metempirical rather than empirical means."[58] *Metempirical* is a philosophical term that refers to obtaining information solely through reasoning, whereas observation and measurement characterize the *empirical* method. Take the example of a hypothesis, one of the benchmarks of experimental research. A hypothesis just does not suddenly appear; it is normally formulated for testing as the result of reflective or critical thinking; otherwise the rationale for the hypothesis may not be valid. Yes, the behaviorist too must use logical or reflective thinking.

As already observed, logical thinking is necessary if you are to develop, implement, and report on research. Logic is not a popular subject in most schools and the subject usually is reserved for those who plan a career as a philosopher, mathematician, or religious leader. Why should musicians be exempt from using logic? As pointed out earlier in this chapter, a good research project depends on the logical development of a problem which then can be effectively implemented and reported in an objective manner. Among the reasons for the importance of logic in the development of a research problem, these four listed by Searles are the most important:

1. It enables you to understand the deductive and inductive processes of logical inference,
2. Logic makes it easier for you to differentiate between emotional appeal and rational conviction,
3. It assists you to critically appraise assumptions and presuppositions which serve as the bases for your arguments, and
4. Logic assists you to focus on the ambiguity of words, thus resulting in your more effective use of linguistic symbols.[59]

Gorovitz, Hintikka, Provence, and Williams stress the importance of logic for researchers, pointing out that logic is both a developing and an imaginative field for studying the behavior of humans.[60]

Reflective Thinking

You have already read that it is necessary to use reflective thinking to formulate a problem into a pliable and workable form.

This initial phase of research unquestionably is one of the most important, yet it frequently is treated perfunctorily. Several educational researchers, including Mason and Bramble, aver that the ultimate success of a research project is often related to the way the problem is formulated.[61]

Concepts of reflective thinking may be traced as far back as the deductive method used by Aristotle (384-322 B.C.) and other early Greek thinkers. *Deduction* is reasoning from the general to the specific (or particular). This type of reasoning marked one of humanity's earliest attempts to think through problems. As an example of deduction, note the choral conductor who hears some unusual sounds coming from the group and tries to determine what causes them. It turns out that the altos were singing E♭, not E; the tenors forgot to sing F#; and the accompanist was one measure ahead of the group. Deductively, the choral director in this absurd example has observed problems and then has been able to correct them by identifying specified weaknesses. In the research design, to be discussed in the next chapter, the process of delineating a general problem statement and then formulating specific components, or subproblems, is analogous to deductive reasoning.

Syllogism is another example of this Greek concept of deductive problem solving. In categorical or formal syllogism, the most common form of syllogism, the formula of an argument consists of three propositions. The first two, known as major and minor premises, are assumed to be true, and lead to the third proposition, known as the conclusion. No attempt is made to prove or disprove the major and minor assumptions. It is important to remember that the major and minor premises must be accepted as being true without question; otherwise the conclusion cannot be valid. An example of categorical or formal syllogism follows:

> *Major premise:* All musicians are talented.
> *Minor premise:* Conductors are musicians.
> *Conclusion:* Conductors are talented.

In examining the logic of this syllogism one assumes that the musicians concerned are talented or they would not be musicians and that the conductors could not conduct unless they had had musical training and were musicians. The conclusion is then obvious. Characteristic of any categorical syllogism is the identification of three factors, each of which is repeated twice. In the aforementioned example, "musicians," "talented," and "conductors" each appears two times. Of course, because of the acceptance of faulty assumptions, some syllogisms do not result in valid conclusions. Consider this example:

> *Major premise:* A trombone is a brass instrument.
> *Minor premise:* A brass instrument has valves.
> *Conclusion:* A trombone has valves.

The major premise obviously is true; the minor premise is only partially true. Most brass instruments contain either piston or rotary valves; however, the trombone (with the exception of the largely obsolete valve trombone) does not. The conclusion, therefore, is not tenable.

There are many classic anecdotes about those who dared to use logic different from this deductive method as late as the seventeenth century, and who were reprimanded severely. Observe the announcement by Galileo (1564–1642) that while searching the heavens with his new telescope he had discovered four moons revolving around the planet Jupiter. This announcement was received skeptically by many of his peers. One fellow professor even stated that since Aristotle had not mentioned these moons, they could not possibly exist. Others declared that since the moons were not visible to the naked eye they did not exist at all. Such was the stranglehold the Greek system of Aristotelian logic had on scholars up to the late sixteenth century, the time of Francis Bacon (1561–1626), who disagreed with the prevailing concept of blindly accepting deductive theories merely because they were passed on as truth by the authorities.

This uncertainty about the truth of a generalization led Bacon to develop the type of thinking known as *induction*, or reasoning from the specific (or particular) to the general. It was assumed that reasoning based on specific items would result in more valid generalizations. On the basis of these specifics, generalizations could then be made about similar or related but unobserved facts or events. This type of reasoning is used occasionally by music teachers. A band director in a rehearsal may conclude that the group will perform badly after observing several specific deficiencies *before* the group starts to play. First, it may be evident the oboists do not have their reeds completely inserted in the casing, which will result in intonation that is consistently flat. Some of the French horns obviously are using the E♭ slide even though the music is written for F horn. The percussion section may have the wrong music in front of them. This example, like the previous one, is preposterous, but it illustrates that this music teacher observed specific deficiencies and then was inductively able to generalize that an unsatisfactory sound would result if the musicians performed under the conditions just described, even though they yet had not played one note of music. Researchers who are formulating a research design may have in mind specific components to be researched, but then they must inductively derive the general problem statement, or the *gestalt.*

More recently much research has been predicated on a combination of the two concepts; this is commonly referred to as the "deductive-inductive" process, but it also is known by the term "general-to-specific-to-general." Charles Darwin (1809-1882) is generally acclaimed to be the first to combine successfully the idea of Aristotelian deduction with that of Baconian induction. According to Best and Kahn, Darwin, in stating his theory of the origin of species, formulated through deductive-inductive procedures a process that now serves as the basis of the scientific method.[62] A simple illustration: after hearing a beginning string class perform badly, a music teacher analyzes the performance of the students, inductively observing deficiencies and correcting them when necessary. Finally, as a result of the inductive diagnosis of each student's performance, the teacher may deduce what will result if changes are not effected. Ary, Jacobs, and Razavieh indicate that Darwin's approach, the deductive-inductive process, is in accord with the scientific method, the most appropriate for obtaining information.[63] Application of the deductive-inductive process will place an investigator in a much more favorable position to formulate adequately a research topic and then implement the research. This concept of logic makes it relatively easy to organize research reflectively.

Sowell and Casey are among the several research textbook writers who use as the basis for reflective thinking and the scientific method the five steps originally proposed by John Dewey (1859-1952).[64] Research leaders in virtually all fields of education generally hold this distinguished educational philosopher in high regard. Dewey's five steps, as paraphrased, are (1) recognition of need, (2) isolation of the problem, (3) postulation of a solution, (4) accumulation and codification of data, and (5) confirmation and experimental substantiation of hypotheses.[65] To these original five, other educational philosophers, such as Kelley, have added another: appraisal of the solution in light of future needs.[66] Not only do these six precepts form the basis for the delineation of a problem, but they also may be employed for implementation of the research. In view of the current healthy emphasis on disseminating research findings, resolution and completion of the research suggests an additional step, dissemination of the data, which might be proposed as a seventh step. Unfortunately, many excellent reports are of no value to the profession because the investigators have been either unable or unwilling to share their results. Research that is worthy of the name certainly ought to be worth disseminating. Even research of a superficial nature has value for potential researchers because it may point not only to topics needing more investigation but also to mistakes and pitfalls to be avoided. These seven steps, in essence, form the basis for the *formulation, implementation*, and *promulgation* of a research topic. In other words, they constitute a "method" for research in a general sense.

Students in some of the authors' classes have often asked this question: "If the hypotheses are rejected in a study employing directional hypotheses does this mean the research is invalid?" The answer is not necessarily no. You can learn from a situation such as this. It may mean that your level of significance was too restricted for comparison of the variables used in the study. On the other hand, negative information can be used to point up weaknesses in logic or method. If you are looking for a relationship between some variables, to cite an example given by Tuckman, and no relationship is found, the weakness may be in the methodology employed rather than in what is hypothesized.[67]

The scientific method and reflective or critical thinking should not alarm a researcher in music education; rather, these concepts need to be understood and used. Today, when so much emphasis is placed on research in all fields of study, you can ill afford to proceed with a project that is not *logically organized, objectively implemented*, and *precisely interpreted*. You may need considerable assistance and guidance to realize these objectives, especially if your undergraduate training has emphasized "skills" at the expense of the "systematic" and "intellectual" approach to learning. A college or university that does not provide intelligent and perceptive leadership to give graduate students the kind of information and stimulation they need for research is derelict in its duty to train today's and tomorrow's leaders in music education. This does not imply, of course, that advisers should do all the planning for their advisees, nor does it infer that any graduate students who comply with certain academic requirements will automatically receive their degrees. The determining factor simply should be whether or not an individual has been able to produce a piece of research that at least meets the minimum standards prescribed by the institution granting the degree. You are entitled to competent advice and guidance to reach your goals.

Formulating the problem is unquestionably the most important initial step in research. It was mentioned earlier in this chapter that a problem based on reflective or critical thinking is much easier to bring to a satisfactory resolution than one that is not. The most profound as well as the least significant problems may prove to be disconcerting to music educators, but if ways are found to resolve these dilemmas, their teaching should be more effective. The realization that many problems still remain for the researcher in music education has both good and bad aspects. Most impelling, perhaps, is the negative connotation, because it suggests that conditions, however they may be defined, could be better for those concerned if solutions were forthcoming. On the positive side, graduate students frequently may become unduly apprehensive and consequently apply themselves in an overly diligent manner lest someone else "preempt" their topic and complete the research first. Such misgivings usually are needless because, as most research studies bear out, the same problem could be approached differently by other individuals. In addition, when one problem seems to be solved others appear that were not apparent previously.

Even though research activity in music education recently seems to have reached an all-time high, and although solutions to many previously disturbing problems have been obtained by an ever-increasing number of investigators, there are other perplexities in which the explanations obtained have been either inconclusive or unconvincing. Perhaps it is one of the ironies of research that indecisive answers frequently result when a researcher fails to give enough thought to the organization and formulation of the problem. In the desire to begin collecting research data as soon as possible, investigators begin the actual research process before comprehending its significance. An unorganized accumulation of data can be the result of this kind of impulsive action. In an article in a professional journal, the senior author did call attention to this dilemma.[68] More than one adviser has had to remand students to the reflective or critical thinking stage because they had begun to collect disparate data with no reason other than it was interesting to do so. Research data by themselves are virtually worthless unless there is a rationale for interpreting and using them. Commenting on the importance of circumspect attention to the problem, Borg and Gall relate that the distinction between an outstanding project and one that is unscholarly does not rest on how much work you do, but rather on how much thought you give to the selection and definition of your problem.[69]

Involvement in research can be a most absorbing and gratifying experience, especially if an understanding and application of the concepts of reflective or critical thinking as embodied in the scientific method are uppermost in the mind of the researcher. Since the setting for research actually begins with a problem that may need to be clarified or refined before it can be solved, a discussion of this initial phase of research will be deferred until the next chapter, for it is of such importance as to warrant a separate, in-depth treatment.

Initial Considerations in the Selection of Appropriate Literature

It is incumbent on you, as already indicated, to familiarize yourself with the literature in your field. Many advisers continue to be distressed by the inordinately large number of students who come to them for advice regarding a "red-hot" idea before they have examined the literature to determine whether the proposed study is feasible. A preliminary literature search would eliminate many projected topics, leaving the students free to devote their energies, and those of their advisers, to topics within the realm of possibility. It is conceivable that two individuals may be proceeding with the same topic unbeknown to one another. Although the likelihood of this happening is slim, Good and Scates give an account of two music-education research studies conducted on the same national organization, although they were not done at the same time. The projects were completed in different sections of the country even though the institutions were only three hundred miles apart, but the initial study, which was finished five years before the second, could easily have been located by the second investigator in *Doctoral Dissertations Accepted by American Universities*.[70]

Fortunately for music educators, the Council for Research in Music Education, you will recall, has published an annual *Directory of International Music Education Dissertations in Progress* which identifies ongoing studies by author, category (higher education, string instruments, etc.), and institution. Also included are the following indexes: name of investigator, institution of investigator, category. (The 1989 *Directory*, in addition to universities in the United States, lists studies from these foreign countries: Sweden, Bulgaria, Poland, Austria, Norway, South Africa, and Australia.) Other sources for topics include *Dissertation Abstracts International (DAI)* and *Comprehensive Dissertation Index (CDI)*. Consulting these sources should make it easier to avoid the duplication of topics. The question may be raised, why is it necessary to avoid the duplication of topics? It is considered to be a violation of research ethics to deliberately duplicate a study which already has been completed unless it is a replication study, characteristic of the physical and medical sciences.

After your topic has been tentatively approved by your adviser, you should carefully consider and make a projection of the methods, techniques, equipment, and instruments (if any) you will use to bring your study to successful completion. This list might involve the use of aesthetic or philosophical inquiry techniques, questionnaires, or certain standardized tests, instruments of your own devising, or special equipment, such as computers, synthesizers, or other devices. Need for these items will be determined partially by the methods or techniques you choose. An investigation using the qualitative method might use techniques such as interview, case study, or even philosophical precepts. A true experimental study would not use the questionnaire technique; a quasi-experimental topic might use this instrument.

A study which has a historical, philosophical, aesthetic, or even a qualitative basis would call for information that may be obtained from various repositories (libraries, museums, archives, historical societies, private collections, etc.). Since historical research procedures will be treated in detail in chapter 9, mention will be made here only in passing. You will need to know where specific items are located. If visits are involved, you must plan them according to such considerations as financial resources, time available, and hours the repository is open. Frequently, it is next to impossible to conduct systematic and exhaustive historical research without this kind of planning. Field studies, in the form of visits to schools, colleges, or universities, often are necessary in a descriptive study when comparisons are being made between curricular offerings or programs of music education. To determine why a string program may be successful in one school system but not in another can hardly be done properly by means of a questionnaire only. Questionnaires, interviews, and personal visits may be needed to garner enough information to make valid statements when comparing schools or school systems. Specific reference to these techniques will be made in chapters 6, 7, and 8.

Formulating the Research Problem

When you have a general subject in mind it is necessary to proceed through several steps before you reach a point at which your research topic is well defined as well as practical and capable of implementation. Almost every research textbook offers excellent suggestions relating to formulating the research problem. Wiersma avers that good research is not possible without asking the right questions.[71] The most important considerations in pursuing a research problem, according to Rummel, are personal interest, personal capability to pursue the topic, significance of the topic, and data which are available.[72] Almack indicates slightly different points, including what already is known and what needs to be learned, evident inconsistencies, and suggestions for implementation received from various sources.[73] Leedy states that it is imperative that you *"formulate a problem that is carefully phrased and represents the single goal of the total research effort."*[74]

You may ask yourself certain questions about the problem you have under consideration. The answers will go a long way toward determining whether you should proceed with the plan, modify it, or discard it entirely.

By posing and answering general questions you may then proceed to more specific items in an attempt to delineate your problem even more clearly. You might, for purposes of illustration, begin with a topic like "A History of Music in the United States." At first glance, the subject may appear to be a good one for a graduate student, especially at the doctoral level. Before proceeding, however, you would need to ask such questions as: "Will this study cover all phases of instrumental, vocal, opera, symphony, chamber music, music education, etc.?" "Will it be concerned with performance, teaching, or both?" "What years will serve as the limits of the study?" "What kinds of information will I seek?" "Where may I best obtain the desired information?" "How will I interpret the phrase 'Music in the United States'?" "Will the study involve only native-born American musicians?" "Will it include the role of music publishers?" "Will the compositions mentioned be analyzed or only identified without comment?" "Will the study include artists and performing groups from other countries who may have performed in the United States?" "What distinction, if any, will be made between amateur and professional groups?" "Will I collect and catalog manuscripts or facsimile copies of works by American composers?" "What attention will I give to reviews of performances presented by artists in various cities?" "How will I determine what gaps still remain in American music history?"

Almost immediately it should be apparent that "A History of Music in the United States" is a subject that consists of many components, each of which might be a topic worthy of investigation. This matter of delimitation, or focusing on a workable topic, is very important for successful research, yet investigators in music education sometimes do not accord it enough attention. While there are certainly enough topics to go around, graduate students sometimes are unduly apprehensive about the possibility that all areas in which they are interested soon will be fully explored, as was mentioned earlier in this chapter. It bears repetition to remind you that a study well organized and implemented in depth can make a much more significant contribution to human knowledge than one so broad that its generalizations result only in superficial information.

The following fourteen steps are suggestive of those you might keep in mind as you attempt to focus your attention on the hypothetical research problem on American music just noted. The feasibility of any topic may be determined only after similar procedures have been followed. In other instances the impracticability of a plan as originally conceived will be apparent earlier. After revisions you may need to repeat the same procedures until you have developed a satisfactory proposal and then implemented the research. This process—of continually returning to the beginning and repeating the steps until satisfactory results are obtained—is reminiscent of the looping techniques used in certain phases of programming for the digital computer, where a program is repeated in successive steps until the desired information is received. In both instances the same questions may be asked over and over again, but with different objectives in mind.

The fourteen sequential steps in the actual formulation and implementation of a problem are to (1) determine an area of need to which answers are not obvious; (2) ascertain whether or not the idea contains more than one basic problem; (3) delimit the subject to a topic that may be solved according to your background and training; (4) develop basic assumptions and/or hypotheses; (5) locate existing information relating to your topic; (6) ascertain what instruments, tools, or equipment will be needed and whether such items are readily available or may be devised expeditiously; (7) postulate tentative conclusions; (8) implement the plan and accumulate preliminary data; (9) reconstitute and revise the research plan in view of inaccuracies appearing as a result of the preceding steps; (10) accumulate and assimilate additional data; (11) interpret the data; (12) draw up conclusions, recommendations, and suggestions for additional research; (13) obtain an evaluation of the research from peers and associates; and (14) disseminate results to the general public.

In regard to the first point, *area of need to which answers are not obvious*, developing questions may seem to be redundant, but it is only through this type of intellectual inquiry that you really can decide whether you have the basis for your proposed research topic. Answers to questions are frequently available in many sources, although you may be unaware of them. However, the need for a detailed study of a research concern may not be as critical as you had originally believed. Let us say an instrumental music teacher is interested in obtaining background material on Berlioz to serve as motivation for introducing a high-school orchestra to the composer's *King Lear Overture*. This person hardly needs to go beyond Jullien's biography or Boult's *Berlioz's Life as Written by Himself in His Letters and Memoirs*, to cite two important sources. The attempt to locate some new or little-known facts of the composer's life, although it could prove interesting, would hardly be worth the time and effort necessary to prepare for this orchestra rehearsal and might prove to be fruitless. If, on the other hand, you were concerned with one specific aspect of Berlioz's life, then the research, although time-consuming, might result in a noteworthy contribution, such as Barzun's publication of some previously unknown Berlioz letters.[75] Experienced researchers like Barzun usually find it easier to obtain data because they know what they are seeking, whereas inexperienced researchers often do not. Hillway is among the many writers who stress the importance of investigators' approaching research with a good idea of what they hope to find out.[76]

After addressing the second point, *whether the idea contains more than one problem*, it may be ascertained that an initial idea can be subdivided into several problems, each of which might constitute a topic in itself. "A History of Music in the United States" obviously needs to be divided into several topics before it can be considered feasible and practical. It has already been observed that it is very difficult to apply the techniques of solid research to a topic that is too broad in scope. Such a subject disperses your energies in several directions. Figure 1 serves as an illustration of this process of delimitation.

Thirdly, to *delimit the topic to your background and training* can be accomplished as a result of successive delimitations. "The Development of Municipal Professional Symphony Orchestras in the State of Florida from Earliest Times to 1965" is a subject for research that a student with appropriate background, training, and motivation could undertake. The final title not only confines the study to certain objectives but also enables the investigator to proceed with research once the *modus operandi* has been established. The term "professional," as used in this illustration, might be defined differently for Florida from the way it would be for New York City, but the study could be just as valid in either instance if the research were properly constituted and implemented.

After tentatively determining the feasibility of the topic and *developing basic assumptions or hypotheses*, the fourth step, you must then consider whether *basic assumptions* and/or *hypotheses* are needed. (These terms will be discussed in greater detail in later chapters.) It should be noted, however, that assumptions and hypotheses could serve as the core of a study. A basic assumption refers to what an investigator assumes to be true, and thus does not need to be confirmed or rejected by experimentation.

The fifth of the fourteen steps, *knowledge of relevant information*, is a most important step. After you have examined various resources, both published and unpublished, and find that your proposed topic already has been adequately investigated, you should either recast the problem or abandon it altogether. A paucity of information might suggest fertile topics for investigation. On the other hand, a lack of information may suggest the research does not need to be done. Moreover, a wealth of material might enable you to concentrate on a more specialized phase of the problem. Your methodology will be governed to some extent by the kind of data you seek. An experimental project, which would have as its end result formulating and drawing conclusions to controlled observations, would necessitate the quest for a different type of data than would a historical study, which might rely heavily on original manuscripts or documents found in archives. In either instance the information sought must be pertinent to the topic at hand.

Experimental, quasi-experimental, and descriptive studies, in particular, frequently make use of *tests, statistics, special equipment, interviews, or questionnaires*. In this sixth step it may be

Figure 1
Delimitation of a Research Topic

Tentative Title	How Delimited from Previous Listing
A History of Music in the United States	
A History of Instrumental Music in the United States	Delimited to instrumental music
A History of Instrumental Music in the Southern United States	Further delimited to one region of the United States
A History of Instrumental Music in the Southern United States from Earliest Times to 1965	Additional chronological delimitation
The Development of Municipal Symphony Orchestras in the Southern United States from Earliest Times to 1965	Slight change of title and further delimitation to specific form of instrumental ensemble
The Development of Municipal Professional Symphony Orchestras in the State of Florida from Earliest Times to 1965	Additional delimitation to exclude amateur groups but to include a specific state of the United States

necessary to devise and validate tests or to develop special equipment with the specific purposes of your research in mind; in others standard items may be used. Almost without exception, investigators devise questionnaires to fit the needs of a particular study which is usually descriptive or qualitative. Unlike a test, which may be validated or standardized, a questionnaire rarely can be used by more than one researcher unless another one is investigating the same problem under comparable conditions. You may use standardized tests to supplement those you have devised yourself. When tests, equipment, or instruments are not available, you must develop them yourself, adapt existing tests—with permission, of course—for purposes of your study, or revise your methodology to use those in existence.

The seventh step, the *postulation of tentative conclusions*, helps you to anticipate the results of your research. To paraphrase a cliché, if you do not know what information you are seeking, how will you know when you have obtained it? Tentative conclusions essentially are postulated from the hypotheses initially formulated.

In the eighth step, it is through the *implementation of the plan and accumulation of preliminary data* that you can begin to test your hypotheses. You are then in a position to know whether and to what extent your research plan needs to be revised. If *revisions are necessary*, the ninth step, it is imperative to *accumulate and assimilate additional data*, the tenth step.

Mere accumulation of data, however, is not enough. The eleventh step calls for these data to be *interpreted in light of objectives of the study*. It may be of little practical value, for instance, to find out that there are two hundred school-owned oboes in the public schools of a certain state. More important is knowledge about whether or not these instruments are in good playing condition, how many of them are being used and by whom, and the proficiency level of the students playing them. Moreover, the accumulation of additional data may be necessary in order to make logical and valid interpretations.

The important twelfth step, *conclusions, recommendations, and suggestions for additional study*, commonly consists of grouping these data together in the final chapter of a research report. Final conclusions, although they may be similar to the tentative conclusions identified earlier, are deduced after the data have been accumulated and interpreted. Recommendations and suggestions for additional research then follow in normal sequence after the conclusions have been drawn. The recommendations usually include topics that, as you reflect on the project, you believe might have been either approached differently or pursued in greater depth. On the basis of these, you offer suggestions for the benefit of future researchers. Often the final chapter in a research report is the most vital one to someone searching for a topic, for it is here that you may suggest topics that are in need of study.

An *evaluation of the research by peers and associates*, the next to the last of the fourteen steps, can be most helpful. If you wish to avoid the usual redundancies that characterize the creative efforts of many persons you should welcome the opportunity to have an outside observer examine the completed project objectively and impartially. Because of a natural preoccupation with your project, you seldom can do this. Critique of research by peers and associates is fairly standard practice in research in medicine and in the physical sciences, but in music and other areas of education and the humanities its use has been rather limited. It is for this reason that additional members, who are not familiar with the research, are usually added to a doctoral candidate's examining committee at the time of the final oral examination, when the student must defend his or her research. This also holds true for many master's programs.

As a final point, a serious weakness in music education has been *the dissemination of research results to the general public*. Most completed doctoral projects in music education eventually are listed in *Dissertation Abstracts International (DAI)* or some other database, but only a very small percentage of the musical public who might be able to use these findings has access to them. Some research reports do appear in the *Bulletin of the Council for Research in Music Education*, which has been edited by Richard Colwell; in the *Journal of Research in Music Education*, edited by Rudolph E. Radocy; and in other reports published in various national and state educators' or research journals, although usually only as a result of the investigator's initiative in preparing an abstract of the research for publication. (While this chapter was being written it was learned that Richard Colwell would be leaving the University of Illinois to become Director, Center for Research in Music Learning and Teaching at the University of Northern Colorado in Greeley. In this new position Colwell will be responsible for the publication of a new research journal, *CRIMLAT Quarterly*. The *Bulletin of the Council for Research in Music Education* will continue to be published by the University of Illinois under the editorship of Marilyn P. Zimmerman.)

The studies listed in *Dissertation Abstracts International*, as the name implies, consist only of a limited abstract of a few hundred words. Those appearing in the *Journal of Research in Music Education* and in the *Bulletin of the Council for Research in Music Education* contain both an abstract and an article describing the research. Other publications featuring research in music education and therapy include *Bulletin of Historical Research in Music Education*, *Journal of Music Therapy*, and *Journal of the International Association of Music for the Handicapped*. Several state music educators' associations publish specific research bulletins; among them are Iowa, Missouri, Pennsylvania, and Ohio. In other states a section on research is included in the state music educators' journal. One example is the column "Research in North Carolina," formerly edited by Thomas W. Goolsby, a coauthor of this book. In this column abstracts of recently completed dissertations or theses in music education appear in each issue of *The North Carolina Music Educator*. At the time of this writing the column is being edited by Patricia Sink.

If you are planning to do a historical research study, two recent sources should be of assistance to you: Heller's *Historical Research in Music Education: A Bibliography*,[77] and Humphreys' "Bibliography of Theses and Dissertations Related to Music Education, 1895–1931."[78]

Much useful research, as observed earlier, remains unknown because researchers either do not take the time to write an interesting account of it or believe that their responsibilities have been discharged once the project has been completed. This final step in the research process deserves much greater emphasis than it has received up to the present time. If greater efforts are made to disseminate research results, then some of the better master's theses in music education could be made available to the musical public. On a more limited scale, *Master's Abstracts*, containing brief accounts of research by master's candidates, is a companion to *Dissertation Abstracts International*, but circulation is largely limited to libraries.

In an attempt to make research results more attainable and useful, *Update—The Application of Research in Music Education* began publication in the fall of 1982, under the editorship of Charles A. Elliott of the University of South Carolina in Columbia. *Update* now is published twice a year and is available from the Music Educators National Conference.

It is encouraging to note that many music educators are distressed by the sparse amount of research information disseminated in a form palatable to the general musical public. Petzold urges that the results of research be shared with the

> practicing music teacher, using terminology that is readily understandable, so that any implications the study may have for practices in music education are evident. The teacher is seldom enthusiastic about reading an article presented in the typical research jargon that contains an overwhelming amount of technical information. He wants, and deserves, the *Reader's Digest* approach which summarizes the essentials in a straightforward manner.[79]

The finished research project should be the result of careful planning and implementation on the part of the investigator. Emphasizing this, Koefod states that the researcher must make it perfectly clear that he has come up with a most worthwhile idea and has nourished it from birth to maturity.[80]

Efficient Library Use

It hardly seems necessary to suggest that you should first acquaint yourself with the general floor plan and holdings of the libraries you are planning to use. This is not to suggest that you will need to examine every listing in the card catalog before you select a topic. Instead, you should become familiar with the library's card catalog (either manually or through a computerized system), general and special collections, reference rooms, and facilities for the reproduction of materials.

General collections include books, periodicals, government documents, and other publications, of both recent and older vintage. Special collections might consist of such items as writings, diaries, programs, letters, manuscripts, and other personal effects of an individual or group. For instance, a researcher investigating the role of music in the life of Georgia-born poet-musician Sidney Lanier (1842–1881) might examine holdings of the Lanier Room at Johns Hopkins University in Baltimore, Maryland. Uncataloged materials in special collections are often a lucrative source of information.

The reference room contains standard sources of general information, such as encyclopedias and dictionaries of all kinds. Finally, because you may wish to have an item reproduced by some photographic process rather than copy it by hand, especially if the material is extensive, it would be well to know what technical processes are available at the library, how much they cost, and how long it will take for duplication.

A general overview is necessary to determine how many of the source materials you need are housed in a given library. Should it be necessary to look elsewhere, you still must find out where such materials may be found. Professional colleagues, library staff members, and advisers are the most likely sources of such information. They eventually may direct you to another library to repeat the same procedures of acquainting yourself with its holdings and facilities, examining the materials, and so on, until the needed information is found. You should check *Subject Headings*[81] before consulting the card catalog in a library that uses the Library of Congress system of classification. A comparable compilation is available for libraries using the Dewey Decimal Classification.[82] These lists are helpful because they specify what subject headings are used in the card catalog. Another good source of information is *Books in Print*.[83] Also useful is *Forthcoming Books*, published by Bowker six times a year, containing subject headings, author index, title index, and publishers' and distributors' abbreviations.

The library card catalog (computerized or otherwise) undoubtedly is one of your most significant single sources of preliminary information. It hardly seems necessary to discuss this useful tool in detail; however, there are certain cards that are important to you. The most important one is the *main entry* card. On this the local library's call number is inserted by the library staff, unless it already is on the printed cards which are available from several library supply houses. This card contains the essential information, such as author, title, publisher, and other important data. The *title* card lists the same information as that contained on the main entry card, but lists the title of the publication printed in red at the top of the card; the *subject* card contains "tracings" or other headings under which the item is listed in the card catalog. Subject headings appear in red or black capital letters (sometimes both), depending on local preference, to distinguish them from other added designations. Regardless of which card is used, it is important for you to copy everything in a call number exactly, line for line as it appears on the card. Note that the author's complete name, the correct title of the publication, the edition, the publisher, and the place and date of publication are all significant information to be included in a bibliography. The author's dates become important when you are concerned with writings from a certain historical period, as would be true for most aesthetic, historical, and philosophical research studies. Other headings, as shown in tracings, can be very helpful in locating additional sources relevant to a topic. If you know that the name Lundin is associated with the psychology of music, by checking the subject heading "Music—Psychology" you can find that there are other materials on that subject in addition to the 1985 third edition of Lundin's *An Objective Psychology of Music*.

Obtaining Items from Other Libraries

Sometimes important materials are not available locally. It is necessary then to acquire them by other means, either through a computerized system, through interlibrary loan, or by some photocopying process, keeping in mind possible copyright restrictions.

Interlibrary loan is a relatively easy way to obtain items from another library if one is not in a hurry to receive them. It usually takes two to four weeks to get such materials, so "emergency" situations would suggest that this procedure not be used. The computerization of libraries makes it possible to obtain printouts of the desired studies you want at a reasonable cost, or at no charge at all, depending on the library, and more importantly, almost while you wait. When you request sources on interlibrary loan you must know where they can be obtained before you ask your local library to order them (though the librarian also may advise on locating materials). (The computerized systems have this advantage over the interlibrary loan procedure: you do not necessarily need to know where the library is that contains what you desire.)

For the interlibrary loan process a nominal fee to cover postal charges both ways is normally the only charge. Materials obtained through interlibrary loan often do not circulate and therefore must be used in the library requesting them. A two-week maximum period for using items should be anticipated, with extensions possible if there is no demand for them by the sending library. Several states, through a statewide circulation system, have procedures whereby books from any library in the same state may be retained for a more limited period of time. Rare books and items regarded as irreplaceable if lost rarely, if ever, are obtainable through interlibrary loan. You may request a copy of noncirculating materials on a microform or some type of photocopying process.

Photocopying Materials

Various types of photocopying are available to reproduce items in either full-size or microtext format. Full-size copies, either positive or negative, are available through many processes. The photostat, one of the earliest to be used for music, is expensive for extensive copying and often takes considerable time to obtain. More recent processes, such as Xerox™, Verifax™, and Diazo™, to name some, have the advantage of providing a copy more rapidly and at a lower cost than the photostat.

Microforms, both positive and negative, are of four kinds: microfilm, microcard, microfiche, and ultramicrofiche. Microfilm is an inexpensive and practical way to procure copies of resource materials that might otherwise be unobtainable. A microfilm reader has become standard equipment even in the smallest libraries, private or public, so little difficulty should be experienced in locating equipment to read microfilms. When a copy of an entire graduate project, rare book, or collection of musical manuscripts is needed, microfilm, in either 16 or 35 mm, provides a very practical and economical way to secure it. Portable microfilm readers are available for home use from many libraries.

Microcards received considerable acceptance in the United States during the 1960s and 1970s but now have largely been replaced by the older European microform called microfiche. Microcards require special equipment to enlarge the positive image contained on the 3" × 5" cards. The number of pages on a single card may vary from forty to sixty, depending on the size of the item reproduced. Many of the items formerly published on microcards have now been reprinted on microfiche.

Widely used in Europe, the microfiche and ultramicrofiche are now becoming very popular in this country. Microfiche copies of documents, which are less expensive than microfilm, also may be obtained in many libraries having equipment to read and print copies of them. Research studies available through the Educational Resources Information Center (ERIC) of the U.S. Office of Education are obtainable in either hard copy or microfiche. Microfiche also comes in either positive or negative. A microfiche is essentially a piece of film (3" × 5" or 4" × 6") containing frames of microfilm. The 4" × 6" microfiche will accommodate up to eighty pages of textual material. Because microfiche frames are easier to locate and store, the process, although requiring a microfiche reader, has an advantage over microfilm for both researcher and librarian. Portable microfiche readers are now standard equipment in many libraries, and you may sign one out for a specified period, often a week. Ultramicrofiche, a piece of film 4" × 6", can accommodate up to three thousand pages of text. Ultramicrofiche still has not been widely accepted for some sources because most of those items would not contain enough pages for ultramicrofiche to be cost-effective.

Even though you may have a preference for one microform over another, the availability of items in microfilm, microcard, microfiche, or ultramicrofiche will determine which will be used.

Resource Materials

To provide a listing of all resource materials to meet the needs of every graduate student would obviously be ludicrous and impossible. Resource materials generally fall under two categories: print or literary, and nonprint or nonliterary. Under the former are included sources obtained from libraries, archives, and other repositories. Nonliterary sources include questionnaires, interviews, experiments, and observations, to name a few which will be discussed in subsequent chapters.

There are many source lists which you should utilize. The numerous data banks and research materials guides available still do not obviate the necessity for you to do some individual "hand searching." Most large libraries now have computerized card catalogs, as already mentioned. The one at New York University, for an example of one at a private university, is called "Bobcat." This system also interfaces with other private and publicly supported universities in the New York metropolitan area. A state-supported system called "Lincnet," housed at North Carolina State University in Raleigh, ties together the indexes at the sixteen campuses of the University of North Carolina system. Most of these computerized systems enable one to obtain, via computer printout, items which are housed in libraries throughout the system. These on-line processes can save many minutes of looking as well as give you more time to search for other sources, since a computer can search a database in fractions of seconds. A computer can search by author, journal or book, and, in the case of dissertations and government projects, by sponsoring institution and other data. Some databases provide abstracts in addition to bibliographic citations. Among the databases music students would need to use are *CDI (Comprehen-*

sive Dissertation Index), from 1861 to date, with approximately 650,000 citations from many disciplines, including music. *CDI* provides a subject, title, and author guide to doctoral dissertations accepted at universities in the United States and Canada, and some overseas. *RILM Abstracts (Répertoire International de la Littérature Musicale)*, from 1972 to date, contains about 22,000 entries. Covered in this database are historical musicology, ethnomusicology, instruments and voice, performance practice and notation, theory and analysis, music pedagogy, music liturgy, and interdisciplinary studies on music and various other fields related to music.

How about literary sources housed in other locations? In most cases you will have to write to the archive, agency, or unit housing the desired materials, or telephone, to find out whether or not the items you are seeking are available for scholars to use. Archives often contain historical information necessary for many graduate studies. These usually involve a personal visit, as do private collections. Private collections also can provide needed source materials and usually entail personal contacts with the estate executors or family members. No one rule holds for access to these sources; each must be worked out on an individual basis.

Any research depends to a certain degree on the utilization of bibliographic techniques. Some types of investigation require more extensive use of source materials than others. Historical research, aesthetic and philosophical inquiry, and qualitative research will likely rely more heavily on data to be found in libraries and archives than will descriptive, quasi-experimental, and experimental research. It is in the library that preliminary information often is found to confirm the feasibility of pursuing the proposed topic. It is there, also, that you can get much of the information you eventually will use in your preliminary and final bibliographies. Yet it is paradoxical that many graduate students, embarking on the initial stages of thesis or dissertation planning, are still unfamiliar with some of the most fundamental techniques of efficient library use.

Reference Materials for Music Education

Some sources in music education most likely to be beneficial to you are suggested in the section that follows. It must be remembered, however, that new items appear regularly, and no compilation can be completely comprehensive, so you need to be continually alert for new sources that might be of assistance. If you seek specific information on a restricted topic relating to both music and music education you might find Duckles and Keller's *Music Reference and Research Materials: An Annotated Bibliography*, 4th edition, extremely helpful. This new edition includes reference and research tools available on computers as well as a section on women's music. Information on procedures for locating resource materials and on technical matters relating to music research may be found in Druesedow's *Library Research Guide to Music: Illustrated Search Strategy and Sources*.[84]

In addition to the many dictionaries and encyclopedias on music with which you probably are familiar, general references such as *Encyclopedia of Educational Research, Handbook of Research on Teaching* (three editions), *Dictionary of American Biography*, and *Who's Who in American Music*, to name a few, should be perused.[85]

Periodicals in both music and other fields often prove to be one of the most valuable sources of information. Of general interest, the Educational Resources Information Center (ERIC), in 1969, began publishing *CIJE* (*Current Index to Journals in Education*), covering more than seven hundred major journals that relate to various disciplines in the field of education, including music. *CIJE*, a monthly publication, contains the following kinds of entries for journal articles: source journal index, subject index, entry index (article listed by EJ identification), author index, journal contents index, and thesaurus additions and changes. There are sixteen clearinghouses which are responsible for abstracts included in *CIJE*. Many libraries publish a list of the serials they subscribe to, identified by an acronym such as New York University's UNISEC (Union List of Serials Computerized). You can save considerable time also by referring to such periodical guides as *Education Index* (1929-),[86] *Jazz Index* (1977-), *Music Article Guide* (1966-), *Music and Music Education: Data and Information* (1984), *Music Index* (1949-), *Music Therapy Index* (1976-), *Music Psychology Index* (1983-), and *Popular Music Periodical Index* (1973-). Under different subject headings all these indexes list author of article, name of periodical, volume and issue of periodical, date, and inclusive pages of article. Most of these guides are up-to-date within a few months. In addition, many journals indicate on the inside title page in which indexes they are included. An annual index, frequently the last issue of a volume, also appears in most journals. Many of these journals are now on-line, so a computer search can make your work easier as you look for specific information.

Music journals vary widely in objectives and contents. Refereed journals, such as the *Bulletin of the Council for Research in Music Education*, the *Journal of Research in Music Education*, and the *Journal of the International Association of Music for the Handicapped*, to give three examples, are those which depend on an editorial board to determine which articles are to be published. If an editorial board is not listed at the front (or in some other place) of the journal, chances are it is not refereed, which usually means that the editor prints what is sent in, often without regard to its contents or quality. Don't overlook periodicals and journals in other fields also. Some of those you might want to examine are *American Educational Research Journal, Journal of Aesthetics and Art Criticism, Journal of Educational Psychology, Journal of Educational Research, Oral History Review, Phi Delta Kappan*, and *Review of Educational Research*, to identify a few.

Yearbooks of the Music Educators National Conference and its predecessor, the Music Supervisors National Conference, published annually from 1910 to 1940, are especially valuable if you are interested in reviewing philosophical and curricular trends in music education. *Music Education Source Book* [I], initially published in 1947; *Music in American Education: Source Book Number Two*, 1955; and *Perspectives in Music Education, Source Book III*, 1966, are successors to the yearbooks. *Proceedings of the Music Teachers National Association*, containing addresses and papers presented at the organization's annual conventions, was published from 1876 to 1950. Other important items include *Proceedings of the National Association of Music Therapists, University of Iowa Studies in the Psychology of Music*, and *Yearbooks of the National Society for the Study of Education*.[87] In 1973 the American Educational Research Association began to publish an annual sourcebook entitled *Review of Research in Education*. CEMREL, now McRel (Mid-Continent Regional Educational Laboratory), published a series of yearbooks entitled *Research in Arts and Arts Education.*

Since the vast majority of research in music education at present consists of reports that culminate in a graduate degree, you should consider bibliographical compilations of these items to be a prime source. William S. Larson compiled two listings of master's and doctoral projects entitled *Bibliography of Research Studies in Music Education*. The first, covering the years 1932 to 1948, appeared in 1949. The second, published as the Volume V, Number 2 (Fall 1957) issue of the *Journal of Research in Music Education*, includes studies from 1949 to 1956. Roderick D. Gordon continued the

Larson bibliography of completed research but restricted the listing to doctoral studies. *Doctoral Dissertations in Music and Music Education 1957-1963*, compiled by Gordon, was published as the Volume XII, Number 1 (Spring 1964) issue of the *Journal of Research in Music Education*, and supplements appeared in the same journal as follows: 1963-1967, Volume XVI, Number 2, Summer 1968; 1968-1971, Volume XX, Number 1, Spring 1972; and 1972-1977, Volume XXVI, Number 3, Fall 1978. *Doctoral Dissertations in Musicology* (edited by Cecil Adkins and Alis Dickinson, 1984), includes doctoral dissertations in musicology completed and musicological works in progress, and lists over three thousand American doctoral dissertations and works in progress or completed and more than fifteen hundred from other parts of the world. The 1984 edition is the seventh North American edition and the second international edition.

Reference has already been made to *Dissertation Abstracts International (DAI)* and *Comprehensive Dissertation Index (CDI)*. The latter contains a listing by title of all dissertations accepted by United States and many Canadian institutions from 1861 to 1972, with annual supplements.[88] If you are starting to select a topic for investigation, this should be a standard reference to identify titles of completed dissertations. *CDI*, used with *DAI*, should provide both titles and abstracts of doctoral dissertations completed. Music and music education dissertations are listed under the monthly A Series (Humanities volume) in *DAI*. This has been broken down into these categories: IA—Communications and the Arts; IIA—Education; IIIA—Language, Literature, and Linguistics; IVA—Philosophy, Religion, and Theology; and VA—Social Sciences. This means music and music education abstracts will most likely be found under Sections IA and IIA, respectively. However, the other sections should not be ruled out completely because they may contain abstracts of dissertations that are related to music or music education.

DAI does not go back as far as *CDI* but may be even more useful than *CDI* because it contains either 600- or 350-word abstracts, depending on when the abstracts were filed (350 being more recent). Most of the bibliographic listings which have been reported in preceding paragraphs merely identify titles of graduate research; you can obtain photographic copies of completed dissertations (either 6 1/4" × 8" or microprint) from those filed with University Microfilms. University Microfilms, Inc., began publishing doctoral dissertations in 1938. With two or three exceptions, all institutions of higher learning in the United States and Canada that have doctoral programs send their dissertations to University Microfilms. DATRIX Direct (Direct Access to Research Information), a computerized data-retrieval system for doctoral studies, operated by University Microfilms, can provide you with titles of dissertations completed in music education and other fields. It is important to work with your reference librarian to make sure you use the correct key words to obtain the information you are seeking; otherwise your printout may show nothing, or a conglomeration of studies that are not relevant to your research. You will recall that for research in progress, the Council for Research in Music Education, which has been under the leadership of Richard Colwell, has published an annual *Directory of International Music Education Dissertations in Progress*. This is a must for music-education researchers.

Since November of 1966 *Resources in Education (RIE)*, formerly *Research in Education*, has been appearing monthly under the sponsorship of the Educational Resources Information Center (ERIC), of the U.S. Office of Education. The sixteen ERIC clearinghouses acquire, select, catalog, abstract, and index the documents listed in *RIE*. Useful in conjunction with *RIE* and *CIJE*, mentioned earlier, is *Thesaurus of ERIC Descriptors* (11th edition, 1987), which contains all subject headings or descriptors used for retrieval of documents in the ERIC collection.[89] As an example of the types of studies handled by clearinghouses, Kenneth D. Goodman's *Music Analysis: Applications to Reading Instruction* was published in 1973 by the ERIC Clearing House in Reading and Communications Skills, at the University of Illinois in Urbana.

One of the prime repositories of information for music education researchers is the Music Education Historical Research Center, established in 1965 at the University of Maryland in College Park. Also housed in the same library is the American Bandmasters Collection. Curator of these collections at the time of this writing is Bruce Wilson. You can examine manuscripts, letters, speeches, scores, papers, textbooks, and other items, many of them irreplaceable, by leaders in music education both past and present. Also included are yearbooks, minutes from meetings of music educators, state music-educators association publications, early instructional method books, and various publications in the field of music education.

If you are interested in finding out who has prepared bibliographies of a composer's works or articles in various areas of music for use with information-retrieval systems, you might consult the

International Repertory of Music Literature (RILM), mentioned earlier in this chapter. It is a computer-indexed international bibliography containing short abstracts of scholarly works about music published since 1967. It has been under the direct editorship of Barry S. Brook, of the City University of New York.

Studies of a historical or aesthetic nature may make it necessary to examine manuscripts, writings, and other artifacts in libraries or archives, some of which are not open to the general public. If you are interested in studying the compositions of New England composers Charles C. Perkins (1823–1886) or James C. D. Parker (1828–1916), to cite two examples, you almost certainly would need to visit the Harvard Musical Association in Boston to examine manuscripts housed there. For one interested in early Moravian music, the collections of the Moravian Archives at Bethlehem, Pennsylvania, and Winston-Salem, North Carolina, contain prime source materials, not only musical but narrative.

Unlike public libraries, archives frequently are open only by invitation. Researchers, however, are usually granted the privilege to make visits for research purposes if they follow the protocol governing such matters: (1) ask permission to examine a certain collection or collections at a time convenient to the archivist; (2) state purposes and objectives of the visit; and (3) obtain sponsorship from an institution of higher learning or recognized scholar in the field who is interested in the research. Authorities in the field and advisers usually can give excellent advice relative to the repositories most likely to contain information you are seeking.

Other sources of information include questionnaires, interviews, case studies, experiments, etc., all of which will be discussed in detail in subsequent chapters where they relate to the appropriate methodologies.

After your topic has been delineated and approved, the next step in the research process is to develop and implement a research proposal. These processes will be discussed in chapters which follow. You should be aware by now that the research plan can be one of the most significant steps in your research process and should not be taken lightly.

Problems for Review and Discussion

1. What is research? List steps necessary for solid research.
2. Discuss factors important in the selection of a research topic.

3. Why is logic important to the development of a research problem?

4. The formulation of a research problem is dependent upon what general steps or procedures? What are some of the specific questions you might ask as you give consideration to your problem?

5. What is the difference between *pure* and *applied* research? Give synonyms for each of these terms.

6. Differentiate between *qualitative* and *quantitative* research.

7. In succinct terms, what does the phrase "scientific method" imply? Why is the scientific method so important for music-education research?

8. Discuss reflective thinking. What differences exist between the deductive and inductive methods of reasoning? How do they differ from deductive-inductive reasoning?

9. What is a syllogism? Why is a syllogism significant to research?

10. Name and discuss the seven steps of reflective thinking presented in this chapter.

11. Why is the library card catalog an important source of preliminary information?

Supplementary Sources

Adkins, Cecil, and Alis Dickinson, eds. *Doctoral Dissertations in Musicology*, 7th ed., Philadelphia: American Musicological Society, 1984.

Almack, John C. *Research and Thesis Writing*. Boston: Houghton Mifflin, 1930. Chapters 2, 4.

Ary, Donald, Lucy C. Jacobs, and Asghar Razavieh. *Introduction to Research in Education,* 3rd ed.; New York: Holt, Rinehart and Winston, 1985. Chapters 1, 2, 3.

Asher, J. William. *Educational Research and Evaluation Methods*. Boston: Little, Brown, 1976. Chapter 1.

Barzun, Jacques, and Henry F. Graff. *The Modern Researcher*, 4th ed.; New York: Harcourt Brace Jovanovich, 1985. Chapters 2, 4.

Best, John W., and James V. Kahn. *Research in Education*, 6th ed.; Englewood Cliffs, N.J.: Prentice-Hall, 1989. Chapters 1, 2.

Beveridge, W. I. B. *The Art of Scientific Investigation*. New York: Vintage Books, 1950. Chapters 1, 3, 4, 7.

Borg, Walter R., and Meredith D. Gall. *Educational Research: An Introduction*, 5th ed.; New York: Longman, 1989. Chapters 1, 4, 5.

Brickman, William W. *Research in Educational History*. Norwood, Pa.: Folcroft Editions, 1975. Chapters 3, 6.

Burke, Arvid J., and Mary A. Burke. *Documentation in Education*, 4th ed., rev.; New York: Teachers College Press, 1967. Chapters 2, 3, 5, 10, 15-22.

Chambers, M. M. "Selection, Definition, and Delimitation of a Doctoral Research Problem," *Phi Delta Kappan*, November 1960, 42,2:71-73.

Cohen, Morris R., and Ernest Nagel. *An Introduction to Logic and Scientific Method*. New York: Harcourt Brace, 1934. Chapters 1, 11.

Cook, David R., and N. Kenneth LaFleur. *A Guide to Educational Research*, 2nd ed.; Boston: Allyn and Bacon, 1975. Chapter 1.

Davis, Gordon, and Clyde Parker. *Writing the Doctoral Dissertation: A Systematic Approach*. Woodbury, N.Y.: Barron's Educational Series, 1979. Chapter 5.

Dewey, John. *How We Think*. Boston: D. C. Heath, 1933. Chapter 7.

Drew, Clifford J., and Michael Hardman. *Introduction to Designing and Conducting Behavioral Research*. Elmsford, N.Y.: Pergamon, 1985. Chapter 1.

Druesedow, Jr., John E. *Library Research Guide to Music: Illustrated Search Strategy and Sources*. Ann Arbor, Mich.: Pierian Press, 1982.

Duckles, Vincent H., and Michael A. Keller. *Music Reference and Research Materials: An Annotated Bibliography*, 4th ed.; New York: Macmillan, 1988.

Engelhart, Max D. *Methods of Educational Research*. Chicago: Rand McNally, 1972. Chapters 2, 3, 4.

Fox, David J. *The Research Process in Education*. New York: Holt, Rinehart and Winston, 1969. Chapters 2, 4.

Gage, N. L., ed. *Handbook of Research on Teaching*. Chicago: Rand McNally, 1963. Chapter 2.

Gay, L. R. *Educational Research: Competencies for Analysis and Application*, 3rd ed.; Columbus, Ohio: Charles E. Merrill, 1987. Chapters 1, 2.

Good, Carter V. *Essentials of Educational Research: Methodology and Design*, 2nd ed.; Englewood Cliffs, N.J.: Prentice-Hall, 1972. Chapters 1, 2, 3.

Griffiths, Daniel E. *Research in Educational Administration: An Appraisal and a Plan.* New York: Bureau of Publications, Teachers College, Columbia University, 1959. Chapter 1.

Hillway, Tyrus. *Introduction to Research,* 2nd ed.; Boston: Houghton Mifflin, 1964. Chapters 1, 2, 7, 8, 17.

Hopkins, Charles D., and R. L. Antes. *Understanding Educational Research: A Structure for Inquiry,* 3rd ed.; Itasca, Ill.: F. E. Peacock, 1990. Chapters 1, 2, 4.

Jones, Ralph H., ed. *Methods and Techniques of Educational Research.* Danville, Ill.: Interstate Printers and Publishers, 1973. Part I, pp. 35–48.

Kerlinger, Fred N. *Behavioral Research: A Conceptual Approach.* New York: Holt, Rinehart and Winston, 1979. Chapter 1.

_____. *Foundations of Behavioral Research,* 3rd ed.; New York: Holt, Rinehart and Winston, 1986. Chapter 1.

Koefod, Paul E. *The Writing Requirements for Graduate Degrees.* Engelwood Cliffs, N.J.: Prentice-Hall, 1964. Chapter 1.

Leedy, Paul D. *Practical Research Planning and Design,* 4th ed.; New York: Macmillan, 1989. Chapters 1, 2, 3, 4.

Madsen, Clifford K., and Charles H. Madsen, Jr. *Experimental Research in Music.* Raleigh, N.C.: Contemporary, 1970. Chapters 1, 2.

Manual of Music Librarianship. Ann Arbor, Mich.: Music Library Association, 1966. Chapters 5, 10.

Mason, Emanuel J., and William J. Bramble. *Understanding and Conducting Research: Applications in Education and the Behavioral Sciences,* 2nd ed.; New York: McGraw-Hill, 1989. Chapters 1, 2, 3.

McMillan, James H., and Sally Schumacher. *Research in Education: A Conceptual Introduction,* 2nd ed.; Glenview, Ill.: Scott, Foresman, 1989. Chapters 1, 3, 4.

Mouly, George J. *The Science of Educational Research,* 2nd ed.; New York: Van Nostrand Reinhold, 1970. Chapters 1, 2, 3, 4, 5.

Petzold, Robert G. "Directions for Research in Music Eduction," *Music Educators Journal,* January 1964, 50,5:39–42.

Phelps, Roger P. "Critical Thinking: A Prerequisite for All Sound Research," *The New York State School Music News,* March 1978, 41,7:31–32.

_____. "The Doctoral Dissertation: Boon or Bane?" *College Music Symposium,* Fall 1978, 18,2:82–93.

Rainbow, Edward L., and Hildegard C. Froehlich. *Research in Music Education: An Introduction to Systematic Inquiry.* New York: Schirmer Books, 1987. Chapters 1, 2, 3, 4.

Rummel, J. Francis. *An Introduction to Research Procedures in Education,* 2nd ed.; New York: Harper and Row, 1964. Chapters 1, 2.

Runkel, Philip J., and Joseph E. McGrath. *Research on Human Behavior.* New York: Holt, Rinehart and Winston, 1972. Chapter 2.

Sax, Gilbert. *Foundations of Educational Research,* 2nd ed.; Englewood Cliffs, N.J.: Prentice-Hall, 1979. Chapters 1, 2, 3, 4.

Simon, Julian L., and Paul Burstein. *Basic Research Methods in Social Science,* 3rd ed.; New York: Random House, 1985. Chapters 1, 2, 7.

Smith, P. L. "On the Distinction Between Quantitative and Qualitative Research," *CEDR Quarterly,* Fall 1980, 13,3:3-6.

Sowell, Evelyn J., and Rita J. Casey. *Research Methods in Education.* Belmont, Calif.: Wadsworth Publishing Co., 1982. Chapters 1, 2.

Travers, Robert M. W. *An Introduction to Educational Research,* 4th ed.; New York: McGraw-Hill, 1978. Chapters 3, 4.

_____, ed. *Second Handbook of Research on Teaching.* Chicago: Rand McNally, 1973. Chapter 1.

Tuckman, Bruce. *Conducting Educational Research,* 3rd ed.; New York: Harcourt Brace Jovanovich, 1988. Chapters 1, 2, 3.

Van Dalen, Deobold B. *Understanding Educational Research: An Introduction,* 4th ed.; New York: McGraw-Hill, 1979. Chapters 1, 2, 4, 7.

Van Maanen, John, ed. *Qualitative Research Methods.* Newbury Park, Calif.: Sage Publications, 1986, 1987 (a series of seven books).

Vockell, Edward L. *Educational Research.* New York: Macmillan, 1983. Chapters 1, 16, 17.

Watanabe, Ruth T. *Introduction to Music Research.* Englewood Cliffs, N.J.: Prentice-Hall, 1967. Chapters 1-12, 16, 17.

Whitney, Frederick L. *The Elements of Research,* 3rd ed.; Englewood Cliffs, N.J.: Prentice-Hall, 1950. Chapters 1-4 and Appendix 3.

Wiersma, William. *Research Methods in Education: An Introduction,* 3rd ed.; Itasca, Ill.: F. E. Peacock, 1980. Chapters 1, 3, 12.

Williamson, John B., David A. Karp, and John R. Dalphin. *The Research Craft: An Introduction to Social Science Methods.* Boston: Little, Brown, 1977. Chapters 1, 2.

Wise, John E., Robert B. Nordberg, and Donald J. Reitz. *Methods of Research in Education.* Boston: D. C. Heath, 1967. Chapter 1.

Wittrock, Merlin C., ed. *Handbook of Research on Teaching*, 3rd ed.; New York: Macmillan, 1986. Chapters 1, 31.

Yarbrough, Cornelia. "A Content Analysis of the *Journal of Research in Music Education*, 1953-1983," *Journal of Research in Music Education*, Winter 1984, 32,4:213-222.

PART TWO

WRITING THE RESEARCH PROPOSAL AND THE RESEARCH DOCUMENT

Components of a research proposal, research plan, or whatever the guide for the research proposal is called are discussed in this section. It also includes a discussion of collation of data, interpretation of data, and presentation of data—or, what was done, what was found, and what it means.

2. The Research Process

Undoubtedly the most important part of any research study is the development of a viable research plan or guide for the research project. This is usually called the *proposal* (and will be referred to as a proposal in this text). Although there are deviations in research requirements from one institution to another, especially in format, there are many elements to the research process which are common. As mentioned in the previous chapter, most successful research is dependent on the logical development of a topic, a research problem, the development of procedures to solve the problem, successful implementation of those procedures, and then the careful interpretation of the results. This five-phase process cannot be emphasized too much.

There is a great deal of truth in the old adage, "When the problem is clearly identified, the problem is half-solved." All too often graduate students are sufficiently impressed with a sophisticated statistical analysis or a research technique, such as the Delphi technique or discriminant analysis, to become adamant on formulating a research problem to fit the methodology or statistical analysis. Needless to say, pursuing the research process in reverse order seldom results in a valuable or useful product. Another problem common to graduate-level research stems from the many theses and dissertations which appear to be the product of a "fishing trip"—that is, the lack of a manageable topic or a well-thought-out purpose, from which the problem is defined, from which a methodology is determined, and for which specific and appropriate procedures are followed. And there are those students who begin collecting data before the proposal is completed and invariably attempt to make the proposal fit the data. Again, the profession will be better served if a logical and time-proven research process is followed. The words "thesis" and "dissertation" are often used to describe the graduate research documents completed in partial fulfillment of the master's and doctoral degrees, respectively. In some schools they are used interchangeably for the document which is completed as part of the doctoral degree only. In this section of this text, the word "thesis" will be used to refer to the research document completed for either the master's or the doctorate—in short, a thesis is a thesis, and a dissertation is a thesis.

The importance of logical thinking and careful, reflective thinking cannot be stressed enough. The first stage of "simply" determining a topic on which one will conduct research is very time-consuming. It is also very frustrating. Any graduate student who plans to write his or her paper over the spring break is enrolled in a mail-order graduate school or is due to be sorely disappointed. As one begins to define a specific problem and develop procedures, the problem is usually refined and the topic narrowed and focused. One major problem is that most students know very little about research when starting graduate school. In some ways, starting the thesis is like starting a novel in a foreign language just after finishing the first-semester freshman-level course in that language: patience is a necessity.

Regardless of what the research plan or guide is called, the purpose of the proposal is the same: to indicate systematically, in writing, the plan you propose to follow in order to collect, organize, and interpret the information necessary to provide an answer or solution to the research problem. Further, the proposal often serves as a contract of sorts. After numerous revisions resulting from reading related literature, and guidance from the graduate student's thesis committee members, a formal meeting is held to question the student in order to determine if (a) the research project is worthwhile, and (b) the student is capable of completing the project. The proposal, as a contract, then indicates that if the student follows the guidelines or procedures specified in that document, the thesis requirement will be fulfilled. Often the meeting is merely a formality if the student has carefully chosen committee members based on their experience and willingness to provide guidance, and if the student has wisely solicited and followed their wisdom and experience in developing and writing the proposal. All of the committee members cannot be expected to be experts in all areas of music research. The selection of a thesis adviser and committee members may also be dependent on the research problem. The formal defense of the thesis consequently is usually a hearing on the interpretation of the results.

These potential problems—selection of an inappropriate research problem, lack of appropriate procedures designed to provide a solution to the problem, lack of following an approved proposal, and/or not following the advice of the committee members—frequently have contributed toward making the thesis component of a graduate degree a less than pleasant experience. The most obvious evidence of this is the paucity of research in music beyond the level of doctoral theses, which is usually most scholars' initial attempt at conducting formal research.

After the proposal is officially approved by the committee, it functions as your guide for completing the research project. Further, when the verbs are changed from future tense to past tense, the proposal is used as the basis for the first chapter of the actual thesis: "Introduction, Problem, and Procedures." Best and Kahn consider the research proposal to be analogous to the architect's blueprint, which must be prepared before construction can begin on a building. The clearer and more detailed that the blueprint is, the more refined the finished product will be.[1]

Even after the research proposal is officially accepted, it should not be considered completely immutable. Occasionally changes in procedure will be required when the actual data collection proceeds. One would hope these changes will be minor, such as a slight change in title. Sometimes, unforeseen circumstances will require major revisions, such as adding or dropping a subproblem. If extensive changes are required after it has officially been accepted, it is well worth the trouble to file an addendum to your proposal reflecting such changes so that the committee remains aware of what you propose in order to evaluate what you complete.

As an illustration, subsequent to the acceptance of a thesis entitled "An Experimental Study to Determine the Effectiveness of Computer-Assisted Instruction for Beginning Violin Students," it might be advisable to change the title to "An Experimental Study to Determine the Effectiveness of Computer-Assisted Instruction for Beginning Class Violin Students." The change obviously seems a minor one. In the original title, however, no suggestion is given that the instruction will be in a class situation, even though it may have been delineated in the procedures of the proposal itself. The subsequent revision clearly indicates this classification. The research title, described later in more detail, needs to be a succinct and direct statement of the exact nature of the proposed study.

Other changes may assume greater importance to the research proposal, such as a radical change in methodology. In the titles contained in the preceding paragraph, neither is explicit as to the methodology. It is implicit, however, that some type of comparison is suggested. It is in the actual proposal itself, specifically in the methodology or procedures section, that the radical changes in the methodology were made. These changes in turn may suggest some modification of the title. An example: an investigator, having determined that it is not feasible to conduct an experimental study to compare the effectiveness of computer-assisted instruction (CAI) in class violin teaching, decides to randomly select intact beginning violin classes with what Campbell and Stanley call the "pretest/posttest nonequivalent control-group decision" and compare them.[2] More will be said about this technique in chapter 8. The specific experimental techniques would involve giving a pretest to both groups of violin students, then introducing an "X" treatment or independent variable to one group, that is, the CAI program. A posttest would then follow to measure any changes in learning (the dependent variable) for both groups. The scores for each group would be compared to determine if CAI made a difference and the *extent* of this difference, that is, whether it was a "significant" difference.

Thesis formats, as indicated earlier, differ from graduate school to graduate school. Some schools, for example, require the section labeled "Related Literature" to be placed in an appendix. Some condense this section and use it as introductory material leading to the problem statement. Most devote a separate section to related literature. Just as the formats for theses vary among schools, the formats for proposals also vary. Plus, the specific problem investigated in a study may require deviation from a particular school's traditional format. The proposal format outlined in Figure 2 is a "sample" format. This plan merely *suggests* the kinds of information that are usually included in a research proposal. The schema of Figure 2 is flexible, so that the kind of research undertaken will largely determine which of the components will be utilized. The requirements (even if based only on tradition) at a particular graduate school will determine their exact order. Modifications and changes are necessary and completely justified when and where the occasion demands.

Figure 2
Format for a Research Proposal
Title
Introduction (often concluding with an overall "purpose")
Problem Statement (often including an overall "purpose")
Subproblems
Definition of Terms
Delimitations
Procedures
    Methodology
    Treatment of the Data
Need for the Study
Organization of the Study
Related Literature
Bibliography
Appendix (e.g., test or questionnaires)
Vita

The Research Proposal

A research proposal should be long enough to clearly indicate what you propose to do and how this is to be carried out, but not so verbose that it appears to be the proposal and dissertation combined in one document. Often the most difficult section to write for the proposal is the Related Literature section. Ideally you will have read copious numbers of articles, theses, and books related to the research problem, and any attempt to summarize each and every one would be a mammoth undertaking (as would reading the section). This section of the proposal should be limited in ways discussed below. Its primary function in the proposal is to demonstrate that you have "done your homework," that you have an extensive knowledge of the problem, of previous research completed in that area, of other studies utilizing identical or similar procedures which are appropriate for seeking a solution to your problem, and especially, a knowledge of any research on which your study builds. The music-education profession, in general, is in need of research which builds upon previous research findings. The replication of previous studies seems to be intentionally avoided in music, whereas in the natural sciences, replication is essential to establish theory.

You should be able to include all the necessary elements of your proposal in a document no longer than fifty double-spaced typed or word-processed pages, exclusive of the Bibliography, Vita, and

Appendix material. Extraneous material from the research proposal should be reserved for the thesis. A discussion of each of the components of the research proposal with examples for consideration follows. The outline of the following section is contained in Figure 2. Since selection of a topic was discussed in chapter 1, it will not be included in the following discussion.

Title

Rarely does one actually decide on the title this early in the research process. While this is an important aspect of the process of producing the final research document, it is usually one of the final aspects of the process, although a working title is very helpful . . . and subject to change.

The working title is a broad but accurate account of the scope of the study stated in a clear conceptual or cognitive form. The final title may reflect some element of the procedure (e.g., survey, quasi-experiment, or meta-analysis). These authors have reviewed far too many studies in which the final title and the problem statement represent two entirely different entities. This can be frustrating to other researchers who receive titles through an information-retrieval system and order those titles that seem appropriate for their research, only to learn that the title is misleading.

Consider the following example of a title which is considerably different from the problem. *Title*: "Teaching General Music in the Classroom: A Comparative Study of Methods." *Problem*: The focus of this research is to review and compare all textbook series which are published for grades 1-5 that are used to teach music in the elementary school. In comparing the title and problem statement there are several inferences, some valid, others not. The reference to "general music" in the title suggests to many that the study will include elementary classes. On the other hand, general music is also found in middle schools and high schools, especially with all the states' basic education plans being implemented. The term "methods" in the title does not refer to ways of teaching, but to textbooks, and is limited to series published for five grade levels.

Problem Statement

The term "purpose" is often used in research as something synonymous to the problem statement. In this text, the problem will state *what* you wish to find out, and the purpose will state *why* you wish to find this out, or an indication of how the results of the research may be *useful*. Consequently, the purpose and problem

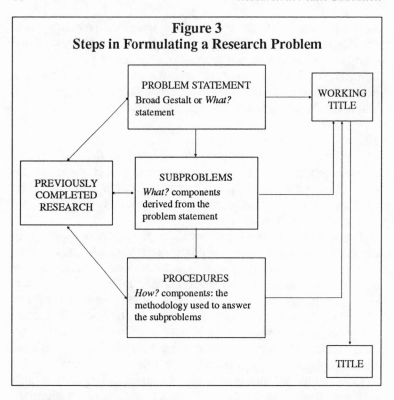

Figure 3
Steps in Formulating a Research Problem

statement can and often do appear in the same sentence, causing researchers to confuse the two.

A flowchart of the steps involved in the formulation of a research problem is found in Figure 3. In this flowchart you may proceed deductively from the broad problem statement to the specific subproblems and then to the more specific research questions. By the time this thought process has been completed satisfactorily, your research proposal should be evident. Note that the subproblems are derived from the problem statement. These subproblems are normally stated as questions. The answers to the subproblems provide concrete evidence toward providing a solution to the problem statement. The procedures are determined by the subproblems and are comprised of the methodology used to answer the specific questions. In short, the procedures are how you will answer the subproblems, which ask specific questions about the broader problem statement.

This deductive process is necessary for the successful development and eventual execution of a research proposal. Again it is absolutely essential that you read completed theses in conjunction with this text. Thus far in this chapter numerous terms and concepts have been used that most college graduates do not understand, terms that graduate-school graduates, however, commonly use and whose meanings they take for granted. The same process applies to reading theses. Much may be incomprehensible to you now; when you complete this text, perhaps less will be incomprehensible.

Subproblems

Sometimes referred to as subordinate problems, specific problems, or research questions, the subproblems focus the investigation to specific aspects of the problem statement (as indicated in Figure 3). In other words, the statement of the problem is broken down deductively into more definite components that can be managed by appropriate research methodology. While the subproblems can be in declarative or interrogatory form, most universities utilize the interrogatory form by tradition. Writing the subproblems in the form of questions makes the presentation of procedures, results, and conclusions easier.

Subproblems are expressed in cognitive or conceptual terms and, unlike the statement of the problem, specifically indicate what you plan to do or find out. Subproblems are the *what* questions; the procedures which follow are *how* the questions will be answered.

Subproblems should be written in logical order because they indicate the direction that the research will take; that is, they guide the procedures and determine the research methodology used. You must find answers to these questions in order to resolve the problem statement.

For purposes of illustrating the reflective process involved, the following example will be developed into a working title, problem statement, and subproblems. Also, in developing a problem statement and subproblems, the researcher must be very open-minded and accept criticisms and suggestions of his or her adviser, committee, and colleagues.

> The nocturne, a character piece for piano, was introduced by John Field (1782–1837). As applied to a somewhat melancholy or languid style, with an expressive melody over a broken-chordal accompaniment, the term "nocturne" has been used by many composers, but perhaps the individual who adapted the idea most successfully was Frédéric Chopin (1810–1849). Interestingly, both Field and Chopin wrote

eighteen nocturnes. As a pianist you decide to examine the
development of the nocturne to assist in your performing
nocturnes by various composers.

A title derived from this illustration might be "The Nocturnes for
Piano by John Field and Frédéric Chopin." A title as broad and general
as this, however, usually benefits from a subtitle to indicate the focus
of the study, such as "The Nocturnes for Piano by John Field and
Frédéric Chopin: A Stylistic Comparison for Performance." A worse
title would be "The History and Development of the Nocturne" or
"Performance of Anglo and Slavic Nocturnes." The latter gives no
indication of what the study is about; the former reads like the title of
a lengthy paragraph in a music-appreciation textbook.

Since the statement of the problem should be a clearly worded
indication of the focus of the study, it should be more specific than
the title. For our illustration, possible problem statements might be
as follows.

1. To determine the extent that the nocturnes of John Field and
   Frédéric Chopin are stylistically the same because of their
   designation as "nocturne" [requiring both *style* and *nocturne*
   to be defined in Definition of Terms].
2. To determine the extent that the nocturnes for piano by John Field
   are comparable musically to those by Frédéric Chopin. [This one
   is far more general and demonstrates the need for subproblems
   to provide even greater focus and guidance for the study.]
3. To compare the stylistic elements of the eighteen nocturnes
   for piano by John Field with those by Frédéric Chopin as an
   aid to their performance. [Again, the Definition of Terms
   would clarify several of these concepts.]
4. The purpose of this study is to compare stylistically the
   eighteen nocturnes of John Field with those of Frédéric
   Chopin as an aid to their performance. [This one combines
   the problem statement from No. 3 with the purpose: *Why?* To
   enhance performance. Beginning the problem statement with
   the word "purpose," however, is often misleading to readers.]

Of these examples, the clearest may be the third one because it
encompasses the important ideas that are necessary to a clear
understanding of what the researcher proposes to learn (the problem), when compared with the original source material and title,
and simply avoids the word "purpose." The first statement has
problems. For example, it suggests that all compositions designated

as "nocturnes" are the same. The second statement gives no indication of what is to be compared. Unfortunately, the term "music" is one of the vaguest terms in the profession—only when encountered in the plural is its meaning possibly further confounded: "musics." The fourth problem statement is essentially identical to the third one. While the purpose is indicated in the phrase "as an aid to their performance," the problem can be obscured. The third statement, then, is probably best because it incorporates more of the information contained in the original statement than any of the others.

Using our hypothetical third choice from above as our problem statement, examine each of these subproblems: (1) What system of harmonic analysis can be used to analyze the nocturnes of John Field and those of Frédéric Chopin? (2) What type of evaluation can be used to determine the rhythmic complexity of the nocturnes of John Field and Frédéric Chopin? (3) What types of similarities and differences are apparent in the nocturnes by Field and Chopin? (4) What measure of aesthetic value can be used to determine the musical worth of the nocturnes by Field and Chopin?

All four of these subproblems are inappropriate. All four of these questions are answered in the Procedures section, *not* as a result of *completing* the procedures. Also, the direct answers to the first two and the fourth subproblem contribute *nothing* to the problem statement (i.e., enhancing performance) and the third subproblem is merely an even more vague restatement of the problem.

Another set of subproblems might be: (1) Is the texture used in the piano nocturnes by Field similar to that used by Chopin? (2) Are there similarities in the rhythmic complexities in the nocturnes by Field and those by Chopin? (3) Do the piano nocturnes by Chopin deviate from diatonic harmony to a greater extent than the piano nocturnes by Field? (4) Do the nocturnes by Chopin have as many notated expression markings as the nocturnes by Field?

Again, all four of these subproblems are inappropriate. While each of these subproblems deals with elements that contribute to style, each can be answered with a simple yes or no. Second, while these subproblems indicate the type of information that will provide a solution to the problem statement, they still are not focused.

A better set of subproblems would be: (1) To what extent is the texture used in the eighteen piano nocturnes by John Field similar to the texture used in the eighteen piano nocturnes by Frédéric Chopin? (2) To what extent is the rhythmic complexity used in the eighteen piano nocturnes by John Field similar to the rhythmic complexity used in the eighteen piano nocturnes by Frédéric

Chopin? (3) To what extent do the eighteen piano nocturnes by John Field and the eighteen piano nocturnes of Frédéric Chopin deviate from common-practice or traditional harmony? (4) To determine the extent that the expression markings notated by Frédéric Chopin in his eighteen piano nocturnes are similar to those used by John Field. (The last subproblem was intentionally written in a declamatory rather than interrogatory form to demonstrate that style of subproblem.) With this set of subproblems, you can see how the procedures would explain *how* the subproblems will be answered. Specific answers and interpretive comments would then provide information toward the resolution of the problem statement which would facilitate the purpose.

One last comment regarding subproblems: the wording of the last set of subproblems contains a bit of redundancy. Redundancy is a dilemma of thesis research which is very difficult to avoid. Occasionally there is so much redundancy that the final thesis appears to be something issued from the "Department of Redundancy Department." The advantage of redundancy in moderation, however, is that there is no question in anyone's mind what you intend to investigate (and how and why).

Definition of Terms

You must define any terms used in the title, problem statement, subproblems, procedures, or results if they are ambiguous, technical or part of the "common wisdom" of the profession, or terms on which few individuals completely agree (e.g., sight-reading). This is not to suggest that you have license to manipulate a definition to meet the purposes of your study or to use one that is not generally accepted by authorities in the field. The sole purpose of including this section in the proposal is to bring about clarity.

A well-balanced Definition of Terms section may contain direct quotations as well as paraphrased terms from the professional literature. You should not make the mistake, however, of taking the easy way out and only using direct quotations to serve as definitions. It demonstrates a greater intellectuality to intermingle direct quotations with paraphrased ideas. Paraphrased sections are also more easily read.

Definitions may be conceptual (clearly and concisely indicating *what* the concept means) or operational (for instance, indicating what tool, instrument, or technique will be used to obtain the desired information). A case in point: a researcher provides a cognitive definition of "creativity" and will be operationalized by using an instrument such as the Torrance Tests of Creative Thinking (TTCT).[3]

Moreover, you must neither offend your readers by defining terms that are obvious, nor assume that all of your readers are as familiar and as well versed in your subject as you are. It is this desirable balance for which you must constantly strive. Referring again to our illustration, for the last set of subproblems, you would need to define *style, nocturnes, texture, rhythmic complexity*, and *expression markings*.

Delimitations

A research plan that is open-ended will rarely result in the most expeditious accumulation and interpretation of data. In their understandable enthusiasm and zeal to make a significant contribution to the world's knowledge (and as quickly as possible), researchers who are conducting a study that is too broad occasionally delimit their study to a greater extent than the subproblems require. At this point a distinction should be made between "limitations" and "delimitations." Limitations represent a circumscription imposed upon a researcher due to external circumstances. For example, certain documents that you need may be unavailable because they have been destroyed by some catastrophe, are lost, or are inaccessible because they are classified as confidential material. Delimitations are circumscriptions that you as a researcher place on your own study. They are often necessary to eliminate ambiguity and to exclude certain inferred items that you do not intend to include. Delimitations and limitations can both be cognitive, conceptual, or *what* statements, and often necessitate a rationale for their inclusion. Some factors that might determine the extent of your delimitation include time and money available or the availability of special equipment or tools needed for the project.

One of the most important of these is time. This is not to imply that you should delimit your topic to the extent, ostensibly because of the pressure of time, that your design is virtually emasculated before the study has begun. The delimitations must be those that will enable you to organize your study in such a manner that you can effectively and efficiently obtain the most complete data possible. By contrast, there are not many occasions when you will find it necessary to expand your topic.

Delimitations may be *negative*, prescribing categories in which a study will *not* venture, thus giving you a better idea of what you hope to effect; or *positive*, succinctly and clearly circumscribing limits of the study from an affirmative standpoint. Positive delimitations are not found as frequently as those stated negatively because it is easy to confuse them with objectives of the study.

Once again, referring to our illustration, delimitations may include an explanation that since the original manuscripts of the nocturnes are not available, only specific editions of the works will be used. Identifying and briefly describing the editions may have important ramifications for comparison of "style" since articulations and expressive markings may be added, deleted, or changed by editors. An example of such a statement might be "The first printed edition of the nocturnes of Field and Chopin will serve as the basis for comparison because the original manuscripts evidently are no longer available" (if indeed this be the case). Note: By definition, the first portion of this statement is a delimitation and the second portion is a limitation; usually all are included in Delimitations.

If you were to decide to compare only certain nocturnes by the two composers instead of all eighteen, then this would be a delimitation. The term "selected nocturnes" would be used in the working title, the problem statement, and each subproblem. The introduction to the proposal may include the reason or basis for selecting certain nocturnes. The procedures would present clearly and in detail the basis for selecting the particular nocturnes studied in the investigation.

Procedures

Two parts normally comprise the Procedures section: Methodology and Treatment of the Data. The Methodology section includes the procedures used to compile the information required to answer the subproblems. In short, the "what" is indicated in the subproblem, and the "who," "how," "when," and "where" are provided in the methodology.

The Methodology will include a description of (1) the kinds of data needed; (2) any technical equipment used or developed (as in a study using computer-assisted instruction); (3) a description of subjects if used; (4) a discussion of instruments used for data collection (questionnaires, standardized tests, or rating scales); and (5) the literature searched or analyzed. In short, the Methodology reflects all sources of information required to answer each subproblem and a detailed explanation of every facet of *how* this information will be attained. The overall methodology (historical, philosophical, experimental, or descriptive) used to answer the subproblems will determine specifically what should be included in the procedures.

The Treatment of the Data section reflects what you will do with the information collected in order to answer the subproblems (i.e., how you will deal with it and present it). This section may include statistical treatments if appropriate, the way historical data are authenticated, verified, and presented and/or interpreted, how questionnaire data are transferred to a computer, or how the information gleaned from the analysis of a musical composition will be treated and presented. Many times, the way that the data presentation is explained is clearer by providing examples; these may appear in Treatment of the Data or in an Appendix.

The singular purpose of the Procedures section is to let your reader know how the information is collected and what will be done to and/or with the data after they have been obtained to make them appropriate for answering the subproblems. This section may well be the most essential component of the research proposal. It requires not only careful critical thinking, but a knowledge of research methodology to determine what approach is most appropriate for gathering information with which to seek answers to the subproblems.

Need for the Study

This section is sometimes included at the beginning of the proposal as introductory material, sometimes immediately following the Definition of Terms and/or Delimitations, and sometimes found at the conclusion of the proposal. The location of this section varies according to each school's format. In this section, you must clearly and briefly set forth why you believe your proposed study is needed, why it is worthwhile, and how the results may be used to benefit the profession. You must be realistic enough to realize that your thesis probably will not win a Nobel Prize (although subsequent publication as a monograph or in a journal article or series of articles is always possible and something you should explore) so you should include nothing that remotely resembles an apologetic approach. For instance, the use of such phrases as "interest of the writer," "encouragement of the writer's peers," and "the writer's desire for musical growth" are not very persuasive, scholarly, or appropriate for the profession's benefit, no matter how true all three may be.

To lend validity to your assertions, you should use citations from the literature and from individuals who share your convictions about the need for such a study. The more convincing the evidence for need is, the less likely a reviewing panel or the committee will ask, "So what?" after reading the proposal. You should indicate the significance of the proposed study for music education and/or other members of the profession. This evidence may be based on critical thinking, personal correspondence, or telephone interviews, or obtained from documented literature. The presence or absence of corroborating and supporting declarations, however, is not always sufficient affirmation that the proposed study is needed. To be significant, a proposal must rest on its own merits; the substantiation of others is additional support.

Organization of the Study

Most proposals include a section explaining how the completed thesis will be organized. The most common organization is to include the introduction, problem statement, and procedures in the first chapter of the thesis (including Definition of Terms, Delimitations, and Need for the Study; the first chapter is commonly the proposal itself with verb tenses changed). The next chapter of the thesis often is devoted to related literature. A separate chapter may be devoted to the instruments used or developed for measuring a variable, the setting for observations, or a historical setting, or the background and explanation of a particular philosophical technique.

A chapter, or several chapters, containing results then follows. Depending on the amount of information and number of subproblems, a separate results chapter may be included for each subproblem. The concluding chapter is traditionally Summary, Conclusions, and Recommendations for Further Study. References and then appendix material conclude the thesis.

Related Literature

One of the most important steps in the preparation of a research proposal is the review of related literature. Undoubtedly, it is among the most difficult sections to write. A genuine problem extends from the fact that logically, it often seems that the related literature should be used as an introduction since it is the background for everything, from the problem statement to the Procedures to the Need for the Study. Another problem is your dilemma as to what belongs in the proposal, what to "save" until the related literature becomes a separate chapter, and what to ignore completely; clearly, no related literature contains a reference to every item encountered or read by researchers pertaining to their topic. When used as introductory material, it is somewhat meaningless to the reader (unless the reader knows what you're driving at) and forces the reader to wade through pages and pages of information before arriving at your problem statement.

There are obvious reasons for the Related Literature section: (1) to avoid the duplication of efforts (which is not the same thing as replication); (2) to narrow down the problem into a manageable one; (3) to determine what areas could benefit from further investigation and build on previous studies; and (4) to apply new methods, techniques, or insights to an old problem. Undoubtedly you will be an expert in your field of research by the time your thesis is completed. Without a careful examination of the literature you will not know what has been investigated and what selected areas require investigation.[4]

In the Related Literature section you include a brief account of your particular area of research, listing some of the most important sources of pertinent information. You should also include concise accounts of any concepts that may be relevant to your topic, such as philosophical, psychological, or social implications.

Often it is difficult for students to determine the organization of the Related Literature section. Concerns include the necessary concepts just mentioned, history of the topic and/or research on the topic, previous studies which used a similar methodology, and previous studies which used similar measures. The organization of each and every Related Literature section will be different. Ideally you will be able to limit discussion to studies on your specific topic that used a similar methodology.

It is necessary to present a brief summary of the significant points found in each source, along with the relevance of each previous study to the proposed study. Sometimes this relevance may be the findings of other research; sometimes only the methodology is relevant. While it is important to present enough information on each source to give an accurate picture of its relevance, verbosity must be avoided lest the section balloon out of proportion to the other sections of the proposal.

The information needs to be presented from both positive and negative points of view. You should point out the positive or useful elements of the previous research as well as any shortcomings upon which you can improve. Some chapters in the completed thesis may include as few as four studies; some closer to fifty previous studies.

Some studies make use of "sources" in addition to related literature. Examples may include questionnaires, personal interviews, telephone interviews, diaries, and musical compositions or examples, among others. Obviously you cannot provide a meaningful summary of these, but their relevance to your study should be included, and they possibly may be included in the Appendix. Since they are important, they also will be listed in the Bibliography.

Bibliography

In the proposal this section may be called or labeled "Preliminary Bibliography" or "Proposed Bibliography." It contains references that you consider to be the most important. No attempt should be made to incorporate every item in the Bibliography in the body of the proposal. As the study progresses, many additional references will be located. The quest for data is an ongoing process, but limits need to be established. In the final document, you may limit the references to the most current bibliographical items relevant to your study (or topic). This bibliographical process continues right up to the time of the completion of the final draft of the thesis (and one would hope, beyond).

Any sources that appear in footnotes should also be included in the Bibliography. There are at least five ways in which bibliographical materials may be presented: (1) alphabetical by author's last name, irrespective of the kind of material; (2) division into primary and secondary sources; (3) division by cited references and "other references"; (4) identification by category of materials (e.g., books, journals, unpublished materials, method books, and musical compositions); and (5) alphabetical by author's last name according to kind of items (i.e., historical, biographical, theoretical, and analytical).

Appendix

An Appendix is optional. It is normally used to contain information used in implementing or clarifying the proposed study. References to these items are made in the appropriate places in the text. Preliminary questionnaires, cover letters, and proposed charts for musical analysis are typical of what is included in an Appendix.

Vita

This section lists your personal qualifications that provide evidence that you are capable of completing the proposed research. It may indicate your formal education, courses taken, and professional and other experiences that may be pertinent to the proposal. In addition, publications or previous research may be included in the Vita as indication of your research ability, but their inclusion is optional. The import of the Vita is obvious. Its main purpose is to show that you have adequate preparation and training to pursue the proposed study successfully. There are instances when committees have questioned the ability of the researcher to carry out the proposed study because certain skills or techniques have not been identified in the vita. It is implicit that you must either already have the skills necessary to carry out the research successfully, or obtain them.

This section is usually only one page in length. At most graduate schools it becomes part of the thesis.

Research Document

It is in your final research document, the thesis or dissertation, that all of your hard work in formulating your research problem, collecting information, and interpreting the data comes to fruition. Just to collect the data is not enough. It would be absurd for you to conduct your research and then hand your adviser a couple of floppy disks and exclaim, "Here's my dissertation. Where do we get measured for the stoles?"

The main purpose of the thesis is to collate and interpret the data, and present the entire research document (regardless of the results). As is true with the formulation of the research problem and its implementation, the interpretation of the data must be accompanied with care and precision. You must report and interpret your findings accurately and without prejudice or bias. If your data indicate that you must reject a hypothesis when you would like to accept it, you must state that you reject it and why ("Results indicate that . . . ") in your thesis. In the section Discussion of the Results, you may wish to expound on why you feel it should have been accepted (a concern based on previous research and not merely opinion), and possibly raise questions on the validity of parts of your study or the validity of previous research. These thoughts are very common to good research and form the basis for the final section of the last chapter, "Recommendations for Further Research." *All good re-search will raise more questions than it answers.*

The format for your final document will vary from school to school and from topic to topic. All schools offering a graduate degree which requires a thesis will publish a manual or handbook that specifies various aspects of format. The components cited in the previous section on proposals will be found in most theses. *All* theses, however, can be divided into three broad sections: *what was done, what was found,* and *what it means.*

What Was Done

This large section of the thesis can be further divided into a prefatory section (title page, abstract, signature sheet, copyright form, acknowledgments [dedication], table of contents, list of tables, and a list of figures), and the first chapter (or two), which is rewritten from the proposal. The material included in the prefatory section is usually specified in great detail by your university's graduate school office. Details will include, for example, exactly what information belongs on the title page, the order of this information, the spacing of this information, the size of the margins, whether or not the date should include the month, and so on. The graduate school guidelines will be specific about which pages should be left unnumbered, which pages should be numbered using lowercase Roman numerals, and where the "regular," Arabic-numeral-numbered pages should begin. They will specify where on the page these numbers should appear, the length of the abstract (usually a 350-word limit since that is the maximum allowed by *Dissertation Abstracts International*), and much more.

Most institutions require the inclusion of a release statement signed by the degree candidate absolving the degree-granting institution from any legal responsibilities that may arise later. Some institutions merely require these forms to be signed and then kept on file rather than included in the thesis itself.

After the table of contents and list of tables and/or figures, each of which will fall under format specifications outlined by the graduate school, comes the main portion of the "what you did" section of the document. This will be in chapter 1 and frequently extended into chapter 2.

As indicated earlier, the first chapter basically includes the proposal with the verbs changed to past tense. It may also include changes in the procedures that were discovered in pilot testing any instruments used in data collection. This introductory section would not include the presentation of any results or their interpretation. When this first chapter is read, the reader should have a clear understanding of *what* you did and *why* you did it, or toward what problem your study seeks a solution; the reader should not perceive hints of what the results or conclusion is. On occasion these authors have encountered studies in which the problem and subproblems have obviously been changed due to the results of the procedures (more commonly, specific hypotheses presented in introductory material appear to have been altered). This immediately indicates poor research and readers cannot help but speculate which sections have been "doctored" throughout the document in an attempt to supply "proof" of some hypothesis. Let us point out again that your thesis is not likely to win a major research prize. The writing of a thesis is an exercise in applied research (not unlike applied music lessons), in which the graduate student applies and uses the techniques and skills learned in research classes. Most graduate degrees indicate advanced scholarship, and scholarship requires research skills. Unfortunately in music education the vast majority of our basic and applied research is confined to master's and doctoral theses.

The first chapter will be organized very much like the proposal. It will normally contain all of the items in Figure 2 through Organization of the Study, possibly in a different order. As pointed out earlier, it is often entitled "Introduction, Problems, and Procedures." A separate second chapter is sometimes used for the procedures, making the first chapter quite short, but more often, the second chapter is entitled "Related Literature." Referring back to Figure 2, the remaining chapters fit between these and the Bibliography.

You will recall that in the research proposal a tentative plan or procedure for conducting research is postulated. Frequently, as the actual research proceeds and data collection begins, and as results are evaluated and interpreted, some modification of the original proposal becomes necessary. It is helpful to wait until a rough draft of the entire thesis is completed before attempting to rewrite the proposal into the first chapter.

The Related Literature section or chapter will probably require extensive revision as new studies are discovered and read. This may reveal that different studies are relevant to your findings and other studies need to be eliminated.

What Was Found

The next chapter (or two, or three, or four) includes the results of your procedures. It is essential to plan and execute this portion of the study meticulously. The material to be presented largely determines the organization of chapters. A common scheme is to devote a chapter to the results for each subproblem, or if the subproblem is written in an interrogatory form, a chapter for the "answer" to each subproblem. This organization applies fairly well to research studies that are quantitative in nature: descriptive (including some studies in aesthetics) and experimental studies. Qualitative studies—historical, philosophical, and some studies in aesthetics—may require a more detailed breakdown of one topic into several chapters. Tables and figures normally appear in the chapters near where reference is first made to them, although there may be instances when incorporating them into an appendix may be more feasible.

It is always helpful to write a summary at the end of each results chapter. While certainly in quantitative studies at least, the results chapters are the easiest to write, they are frequently the most boring to read, especially when they include a large number of tables and narrative description of statistical findings. The summary is beneficial to future researchers who read your thesis to determine its relevance to their own work.

What It Means

This portion of each and every thesis is the most important section. It is incomprehensible how many theses are completed, passed, and filed forever with University Microfilms International where the authors have ignored this section. Possibly, many advisers and committees wade through so much of the data presented in the results that the interpretation of the data becomes confused with the summary of the data.

After the results have been presented and summarized, you should ask yourself (and be prepared to be asked on your defense), "What difference does it make?" In other words: "How can this help the music profession?" Your Need for the Study is an excellent place to begin looking for a response to these questions . . . so is the Related Literature section.

The interpretation of results can appear at the end of each results chapter or in the final chapter, "Summary, Conclusions, and Recommendations for Further Study," as part of the conclusions. The results should be interrupted in view of relevant related literature presented; additional material may be introduced if findings are unexpected and appear to be related to a new and different topic. As an illustration, refer back to our example using the nocturnes by John Field and Frédéric Chopin. The Related Literature section may have included references to previous studies on nocturnes, and it may possibly have included summations of studies using the same analytical techniques described in the Procedures section. In the course of completing the research and presenting the results, just suppose it is discovered that, stylistically, the nocturnes of John Field are more like the mazurkas by Chopin than his nocturnes (they are not, incidentally). You would include references and introduce new material regarding mazurkas in your interpretation of the results and this would lead to "Recommendations for Further Study." Only the *worst* of researchers would have the audacity to return to the first chapter and add a subproblem or reword the problem to include mazurkas and/or add a relevant section in Related Literature (but such happens).

The final section or chapter of the thesis is the one most commonly read by the profession, with many scholars simply reading only this chapter. In this chapter everything comes together concisely into one place. The summary consists of a brief account of the most important items contained in all of the previous chapters. The summary often restates in very succinct terms the problem and subproblems, and the procedures are briefly described. Even if summaries are included at the end of each chapter, it is usually more beneficial to the reader when a single, more comprehensive summary is provided.

Conclusions in many theses prove to be perplexing to the researcher and to the reader because the distinctions between the summary and the conclusions, or between the conclusions and the recommendations for further study, are not clearly defined. When stating conclusions you simply report clear and succinct answers to the subproblems, interpretation of these results, and implications for the profession. Again, the answer to "What difference does it make?" is important for good and useful research. Also, these conclusions or this interpretation of the results may lead to the "Recommendations for Further Study."

Recommendations for additional study are important for potential researchers because (1) related topics needing additional research may be delineated; (2) the investigator may establish priorities for problems needing further investigation; and (3) as mentioned before, all good research should (and will) result in more questions than answers. In view of the intensive research completed and written up in the final document, and the fact that you are now probably one of the world's leading authorities on your topic, you are in an enviable position to make such assessments.

Recommendations may be predicated on conclusions that have validated or refuted hypotheses, or conclusions that were completely unexpected. To follow the chain of thinking: the summary leads indirectly to the conclusions, and the conclusions then proceed logically to the recommendations.

Epilogue

Two parts comprise the Epilogue of the thesis: the Bibliography or References and the Appendix (or Appendices). The Bibliography, which may have been called the "Preliminary Bibliography" or "Proposed Bibliography" in the proposal, now is completed for the thesis. Included are all sources to which reference was made during the course of the research. This is not to suggest that every book or article scanned in hopes of finding something relevant, or every document printed out in a computer search, should be included.

All items in footnotes, end notes, or reference lists must appear in the Bibliography. The same format can be used in the thesis bibliography as was used in the bibliography for the proposal discussed above in the section on proposals.

Appendix materials include important information that impinges on the research but would clutter the format or the flow of the text. Each Appendix used should be indicated by a letter (A, B, C, etc.) and a title. The kinds of data normally placed in the Appendix are lists of individuals or institutions who participated in the study, questionnaires and/or other instruments used to collect data, copies of charters or other legal documents, and other materials too cumbersome to be included in the procedures or results. Musical examples may also be compiled in an Appendix or, if not too lengthy or too numerous, they may appear in the main body of the thesis where reference to them is made (as is customary with figures and tables).

In some theses, those in which the writer is composing or analyzing a lengthy musical work, the final document may be divided into two volumes. One volume would contain the usual prose and the second volume, only the music.

Other Concerns

A thesis virtually always depends on the reader's knowledge of basic aspects of the profession, or what is usually called the "common wisdom." You may safely assume that anyone who reads a thesis in your field will more than likely have a knowledge of basic concepts and principles in your field. Many of these "basic assumptions," aspects of the "common wisdom," principles, or propositions are accepted by the profession without proof. A possible example of this may be the fact that all baccalaureate degrees in music require music theory courses. The profession has assumed that music theory is beneficial to music-education majors, yet no research has been completed to support or refute this assumption.

Furthermore, no university is going to risk the repercussions of an experiment which provides music theory to one group of students and confers degrees on a second group of students without those courses.

Occasionally, however, some basic assumptions must be clarified. This is especially important when the "common wisdom" is not in complete agreement. An example of this might be "sight-reading." Most musicians have a similar idea of what sight-reading is; an exact idea, however, is required for good research. Consequently, this term should be included in the Definition of Terms. Another example: in our illustration using the nocturnes of John Field and Frédéric Chopin, the researcher pointed out in the Delimitations that first editions were analyzed since the original manuscripts were unavailable. He may have considered that one may assume that the first published editions represent the true intentions of the composers as compared to more recent editions. This basic assumption would appear in the Delimitations.

Finally, in our example, the entire study assumes that a detailed analysis of the nocturnes by Field and Chopin will enable a pianist to perform them more effectively. Such a comment is most appropriate in the Introduction of the proposal and/or thesis. The purpose and problem statement are dependent on this assumption. Pertinent comments regarding this assumption may be appropriate in the Need for the Study.

Chapter and Other Headings

Chapter headings usually identify the most important information in the chapter or the largest portion of the chapter. For example, many first chapters are entitled "Introduction, Problems, and Procedures," but may also include subsections of Delimitations, Definition of Terms, Need for the Study, Treatment of the Data (part of procedures), Organization of the Study, and possibly others.

Subheadings within the chapters essentially relate to a flow of ideas within any one chapter. You should refer to your graduate school's thesis handbook for specific format requirements (e.g., you may be required to center the chapter title, then use a marginal heading next in the hierarchy of organization, and underlining may or may not be required). Each order of ideas then becomes identified by some type of heading (center, marginal, paragraph, underscoring, etc.). A popular method of organizing chapters, sections, and subsections in theses in the social sciences is to use an Arabic numeral for a chapter, then that number and one decimal place for the next sections of the hierarchy, then a second decimal place if any of those sections require subsections, and so on.

Some schools require footnotes, some allow end notes, and some require or allow references as specified in the *Publication Manual of the American Psychological Association*. Whichever method is used, consistency is essential, and you must rigidly adhere to the proper format. Many schools today give students a choice; these authors strongly recommend that you determine which method to use from your encounter with previous studies. As you read theses for your present research course and in your search for related literature, notice the different methods of using and citing references; decide which is the most pleasant for the reader and use that format if allowed by your graduate school and your committee.

Problems for Review and Discussion

1. What is the purpose of the research proposal? What changes are permissible in a proposal as the actual research proceeds?
2. Compare the research-design format recommended for use at your institution with the one discussed in this chapter (see Figure 2). Note elements that are common to both.
3. Why is a correct title of your research so important?
4. Using the flowchart found in Figure 3, formulate a problem statement, subproblems, and procedures.
5. Why is the Definitions of Terms section of a research proposal so important?
6. Identify the two parts that comprise the Procedures section and tell how each one is important for research.
7. Why is a review of related literature one of the most important parts of a research proposal?
8. How does the research document differ from the research proposal?

Supplementary Sources

Altick, Richard D. *The Art of Literary Research*, 3rd ed., rev. by John J. Fenstermaker; New York: W. W. Norton, 1981. Chapters 2, 3, 5, 6, 8.
Best, John W., and James V. Kahn. *Research in Education*, 6th ed.; Englewood Cliffs, N.J.: Prentice-Hall, 1989. Chapters 2, 11.

Borg, Walter R., and Meredith D. Gall. *Educational Research: An Introduction*, 5th ed.; New York: Longman, 1989. Chapters 1, 2, 4, 21.

Campbell, William G., Stephen Ballou, and Carole Slade. *Form and Style: Theses, Reports, Term Papers*, 6th ed.; Boston: Houghton Mifflin, 1982.

Davis, Gordon B., and Clyde A. Parker. *Writing the Doctoral Dissertation: A Systematic Approach*. Woodbury, N.Y.: Barron's Educational Series, 1979. Chapters 6–10.

Gibaldi, Joseph, and Walter S. Achtert. *MLA Handbooks for Writers of Research Papers*, 2nd ed.; New York: Modern Language Association of America, 1984.

Good, Carter V. *Essentials of Educational Research*, 2nd ed.; New York: Appleton-Century-Crofts, 1972. Chapters 2, 10.

Gorn, Janice L. *The Writer's Handbook*. New York: Monarch Press, 1984.

Hardyck, Curtis, and Lewis F. Petrinovich. *Understanding Research in the Social Sciences*. Philadelphia: W. B. Saunders, 1975. Chapter 2.

Hopkins, Charles D. *Understanding Educational Research: An Inquiry Approach*, 2nd ed.; Columbus, Ohio: Charles E. Merrill, 1980. Chapters 5, 7, 8, 15.

Irvine, Demar. *Writing About Music: A Style Book for Reports and Theses*, 2nd ed. rev. and enlarged; Seattle: University of Washington Press, 1968.

Keppel, Geoffrey. *Design and Analysis: A Researcher's Handbook*, 2nd ed.; Englewood Cliffs, N.J.: Prentice-Hall, 1982. Chapter 1.

Kerlinger, Fred N. *Foundations of Behavioral Research*, 3rd ed.; New York: Holt, Rinehart and Winston, 1986. Chapter 2.

Leedy, Paul D. *Practical Research Planning and Design*, 4th ed.; New York: Macmillan, 1989. Chapters 1–6, 12.

Mason, Emanuel J., and William J. Bramble. *Understanding and Conducting Research: Applications in Education and the Behavioral Sciences*, 2nd ed.; New York: McGraw-Hill, 1989. Chapters 3, 11.

McMillan, James H., and Sally Schumacher. *Research in Education: A Conceptual Approach*, 2nd ed.; Glenview, Ill.: Scott, Foresman, 1989. Chapters 1, 3–5, and Part V.

Pruett, Barbara J. *Popular Entertainment Research: How to Do It and How to Use It*. Metuchen, N.J.: Scarecrow Press, 1992.

Publication Manual of the American Psychological Association, 3rd ed.; Washington: American Psychological Association, 1983.

Sax, Gilbert. *Foundations of Educational Research*, 2nd ed.; Englewood Cliffs, N.J.: Prentice-Hall, 1979. Chapter 3.

Shafer, Robert J. *A Guide to Historical Method*, 3rd ed.; Homewood, Ill.: Dorsey Press, 1980. Chapter 9.

Sowell, Evelyn J., and Rita J. Casey. *Research Methods in Education*. Belmont, Calif.: Wadsworth Publishing Co., 1982. Chapters 9, 10.

Travers, Robert M. W. *An Introduction to Educational Research*, 4th ed.; New York: Macmillan, 1978. Chapter 4.

Turabian, Kate L. *A Manual for Writers of Term Papers, Theses, and Dissertations*, 4th ed.; Chicago: University of Chicago Press, 1973.

Vockell, Edward L. *Educational Research*. New York: Macmillan, 1983. Chapter 18.

Wiersma, William. *Research Methods in Education: An Introduction*, 3rd ed.; Itasca, Ill.: F. E. Peacock, 1980. Chapters 2, 4, 11.

PART THREE

THE RESEARCH METHODOLOGIES— CONCEPTS AND TECHNIQUES

In this section you will be presented with the concepts and techniques peculiar to six research methodologies: aesthetic, descriptive, experimental and quasi-experimental, historical, philosophical, and qualitative. Examples from the literature are included for each methodology.

3. Philosophical Inquiry: Concepts and Techniques

Presenting a chapter on philosophical inquiry may appear to be an impossible task to many philosophers. Philosophy *is* inquiry, with as many kinds of inquiries as there are categories of philosophy. One could persuasively argue that the content of a particular philosophy is inextricably linked to its underlying method. The method provides a system for uncovering and articulating the meaning of that content. As historical epochs change, so do philosophical interests and contents. From such a standpoint, a methodological account of philosophical inquiry is possible only when presented as a history of philosophy. Historical accounts are numerous and often require multivolume studies. Although this chapter expounds and clarifies several philosophical approaches that can be utilized in research in music education, its scope does not include a comprehensive history of the subject. The treatment of this topic is selective: the approaches chosen for discussion are currently (overtly or covertly) influential; they comprise a broad view of methodology and orientation in philosophy; and the aggregate presented below may enable researchers in music education to direct their research to many varieties of philosophical problems in the field.

Overall, this book attempts to locate the underlying methodological structures of conventional and nonconventional research designs. In traditional research (e.g., experimental, descriptive, or historical), underlying methods are definable and help to demarcate the parameters and ground rules of each of those designs. The underlying method tends to be clearly separable from the content or object of research. On the other hand, in philosophical inquiry (a nontraditional design), content is not easily separable from method. It is necessary to present methods used in philosophical inquiry in concert with their objects of inquiry, that is to say, with content. For that reason, although the focus of this chapter is methodology, some of the contextual meat must remain on the methodological bone. A methodological skeleton cleaned of content does provide a more readily understandable and transferable model. Philosophical inquiry does not lend itself readily to such a distinction between bone and meat, method and content. As the reader works at the separation and digestion of the following methodological presentation, the reader must seek to uncover and define the proposed method in terms of its philosophical content.

A major part of this chapter comprises a review of philosophies of science in this century. As in traditional research designs, models from scientific research can be useful in philosophical inquiry. Accordingly, the protocols and underlying logic in current approaches to the philosophy of science (often written by scientist/philosophers) can provide a ground for philosophical inquiry in music education. However, most traditional texts that present methodological accounts of philosophy deal almost exclusively with logic.[1] While logic is an important research tool in philosophical inquiry, its primacy in the philosophy of science has been seriously challenged within that community. Although this chapter provides a basic account of the nature of logical structures in philosophical inquiry, in following the *current* literature in the philosophy of science, its purview will not be limited to that mode of thinking. The point being made is that the presentation of (1) basic rules of logic (which include inductive and deductive reasoning) and (2) criteria for definition construction are insufficient to prepare a researcher in the use of philosophical inquiry in music education. Limiting the presentation in that way is analogous to giving a nonmusician a basic musicianship course and then suggesting that he or she is prepared to do scholarly analysis of musical works. When read in concert with the chapters on aesthetic inquiry and qualitative evaluation, the combined information of all three will provide a basic outline to the potential use of philosophical inquiry as a design for research in music education. Within this scheme, *philosophical inquiry is being presented as a theoretical base which supports the aesthetic analysis of works of music (chapter 4) and the qualitative analysis of educational contexts in music (chapter 5).*

Purposes of Philosophical Inquiry

Philosophical inquiry is employed to study the underlying principles in any field. One could attempt to develop a comprehensive philosophy that unifies the entire field of music education or argue that such a unification is impossible. Current practices can be studied in order to determine which ones should be retained, abandoned, or modified. Whether an approach is called Suzuki, Kodaly, Orff or Manhattanville, each is directed by a philosophical ground. Sometimes, that philosophical basis is not articulated by practitioners, the clarification of which can impact greatly upon and redirect practice. In other cases, the philosophy of a particular writer in or out of music education can be reviewed and then implemented as a basis for directions in music education. Such a theoretical position might establish principles for music-education practice. Philosophies from seemingly distant fields could be shown to be relevant and fecund for a philosophy of music education. Similarly, one can examine the strengths and weaknesses of existing philosophical inquiries in music education in order further to clarify and develop philosophical bases for the field. Within its use in this text, philosophical inquiry tends to be performed at the levels of theory (i.e., developing and presenting one's own theoretical position) and metatheory (i.e., discussing the theories of others). As such, it is removed from criticism of both musical works (which is a function of aesthetic inquiry) and educational settings (which is a function of qualitative research). Philosophical inquiry remains a foundation for aesthetic inquiry and qualitative research.

In descriptive and experimental research, questions concerning the philosophical basis for research activities are not so overt. Situated in the paradigm of scientific inquiry, the philosophical adequacy of descriptive and experimental studies tends to enjoy an a priori acceptance by researchers adopting those methods. If researchers wish to investigate the philosophical implications of their experimental or descriptive methodologies, philosophical inquiry would be used. Many contemporary debates in research in music education concern the suitability and fashionability of empirical versus philosophical methods.[2] When a researcher defends the adequacy of his or her methodology or attacks that of another approach, philosophical inquiry is often engaged. A resolution of the current debate in the field with respect to whether the basis of theories in music education should be extrapolated from learning theory as developed in psychology or whether that basis should be in philosophies of music and the arts requires the use of philosophical inquiry.

Professionals who demand that philosophical methods in music-education research must be either empirical or philosophical miss the rich possibilities of the juxtaposition of seemingly incompatible and discordant methods. The quantitative results of statistical studies can be enriched and embellished by a philosophical account of the same object of research. In like fashion, philosophical research findings can be clarified, corroborated and tightened by parallel research that generates results in seriational or statistical formats. This suggested interaction of methods for music-education research will be debated at a philosophical level but data supporting that debate will not be limited to philosophical analysis. The systematic and realistic account of the nature and use of data produced by all of the extant research methodologies in music-education research (in texts like the present one) is a first step in bridging data from different research designs. The phenomenological stance of openness toward new and other research approaches will enhance an environment that might support systematic and broad interfacing of research data from divergent approaches.

The purpose of this chapter is to provide an overview of selected modes of philosophical inquiry available to researchers in music education, not to present a philosophy of music education. Therefore, the details of the philosophical debates in music education will not be presented or extended here. In broad terms, the debates pertain to the nature of human knowledge, which is a concern that situates the reader in the marrow of philosophical inquiry. Statistical research is grounded in *objectivism*; research data are accepted as largely autonomous from the researcher, objectified through the use of experimental or descriptive methods. This philosophical position is often broadly termed *realism* because entities in the natural world are believed to be separate or "real" by themselves, prior to human interaction. Realism maintains that through the use of scientific method, a worldless subject (the researcher) can engage subject-free, natural objects. There is an attempt to see things as they "really" are, in fact, without idealization or speculation. From this perspective, research is thought to be capable of providing firm bases for its discipline because research techniques are thought to be independent of the data being studied. Realists generally believe that the methodology of the natural sciences can appropriately be utilized in the human sciences, although they do not consider research results concerning human activities to be as objective as those in the natural sciences.

Contrary to realism, many philosophical approaches are grounded in *historical relativism*; research data in the natural sciences are believed to be relative to the researcher as a member of a community of researchers and as a historical and cultural being. Historical relativists tend to be critical of the appropriateness of scientific method outside of the study of the natural world. They argue against the use of scientific methodologies for philosophical inquiries into the human sciences, history, and the arts. An overview of these two, broad philosophical positions—realism and historical relativism—as well as two middle-ground positions from the current literature on the philosophy of science will help to provide the reader with a context for understanding the grounds for all of the research designs presented in this text.

Realism as a Philosophical Basis for Research

Since the time of Socrates, philosophies have attempted to transcend culture by developing ahistorical and universal definitions, criteria, and theories. The thrust of realism is that through acts of reason, one can uncover pure concepts, theories, or structures that are not spoiled by the subject's biases, the subject's less defined but important cultural prejudices, or even the temporal nature of the subject's knowledge. This philosophical orientation, often termed *rationalism*, is committed to the possibility of pure concepts and theories which provide knowledge that is above culture and therefore is forever certain and unchanging. Universal truths, by definition, exist independently of human perception, which abstracts those truths through sense data (i.e., data collected through the human senses), and thereby provide the foundations for knowledge of reality.

There are many varieties of realism in philosophy today. In the philosophy of science, current realist positions have softened considerably over the past fifty years. With the significant qualification of many of Newton's laws as a result of findings in quantum physics and relativity theory, the notion of transcendental, pure, and eternal truths in science now seems unreasonable, that is, not possible through acts of reason.[3] Some researchers in the philosophy of science have deserted the belief that empirical "verification" of research results is possible and now speak of the more humble possibility of "empirical adequacy."[4] These modern forms of realism provide a useful middle ground between rigid forms of realism and, at the other end of the spectrum, historical relativism. Before moving to that middle ground (and then to historical relativism), a more cogent view of the philosophical roots of realism and a review of realism in its most rigid form, as logical positivism, are necessary. One important point to make now is that many researchers in educational research as well as in the human sciences still adhere to some of the principles of logical positivism.[5] The following account suggests that the positivistic view of science is no longer tenable and that if researchers in music education are to emulate current practices in the philosophy of science, they must look to the current literature for models. *While there are many varieties of realism and antirealism in the philosophy of science, what most current philosophies of science hold in common is a convincing argument against positivism's rigid realist account of the nature of scientific theory and practice.*

At the other end of the spectrum, historical relativists have also been active in attacking positivistic positions. They have done this in an attempt to argue against the suitability of scientific models for research in the social and behavioral sciences, history, and the arts. Some writers presenting a philosophy of music education lean in the direction of historical relativism and its position on the dislocation of scientific methodology from research in music education. The focus of the historical relativists' attack has been on the pitfalls of positivism. That attack is only partially misdirected. Insofar as some researchers have not moved beyond logical positivism to what some call a "postpositivist" basis for research in education,[6] attacks by historical relativists are accurate and congruent to current educational research. However, as will be demonstrated below, positivism does not correctly represent scientific theory or practice nor is it in current use by most philosophers of science. With a newer, softened version of realism prevailing in the philosophy of science, many of the arguments by relativists concerning the appropriateness of scientific method for the human sciences (including educational research) no longer apply. The point is that current philosophy of science is not a rigid realism as presented by logical positivists and as it is often implied in attacks by relativists. Current versions of realism form a middle ground that helps to temper historical relativism. As a result, a rich and rigorous methodology for philosophical inquiry may be available to researchers in music education.

The Philosophical Roots of Realism

Realism can be traced to Plato's desire to discover universals ("forms" or "essences") which are independent of perception and are unchanging and eternal. In Plato's work, *The Republic*, and specifically in the chapter, "The Allegory of the Cave," mankind is metaphorically presented as living in a cave of ignorance. Outside the cave is the light and the basis of knowledge, that is, universal truths and essences. With its back to the cave opening, mankind is chained by leg and neck from childhood and can see only what is in front, the dark inner wall. That wall exclusively presents the "shadows" of the "forms" of the ideal things that pass by the cave opening to the bright outside. The pursuit of the philosopher-king of *The Republic* is to turn his people around toward the light. The allegory clarifies the responsibility of the philosopher-king and any person who wishes to gain "real" knowledge. It also provides a classical example of "rationalism," the hope that through acts of reason one can transcend one's community and culture and reach pure knowledge.

According to Martin Heidegger, at this momentous point in the history of the Western intellectual tradition, Plato caused a dramatic shift for philosophical inquiry.[7] The things outside that pass by the cave opening are not physical things but the "forms" (i.e., essences or ideas) of things. In Plato's view, knowledge requires that the "form" or idea of a thing be understood first, before understanding a concrete and immediate instance of that idea. Accordingly, if one wants to understand and evaluate a particular piece of music one must first have a conception of the pure "form" of such a work. Each individual work is to be approached through and from the idea of that "form." Thus, between the subject and the object is now inserted a concept through which the specific object is understood. Before evaluating a general music program, one must first have a concept or "idea" of a program through which the program under study can be measured.

In Heidegger's interpretation, this basic shift in the nature of human knowledge moves the Western intellectual tradition away from the oneness and immediacy that characterized the manner in which pre-Socratic philosophers—Heraclitus, Anaximander, and Parmenides—experienced phenomena, that is, objects or ideas, in their world.[8] The pre-Socratics presented a highly poetic form of philosophical inquiry marked by a detached interest toward things. In their description of phenomena, there is an attempt to allow things to show themselves more fully and without overt manipulation. An Eastern flavor of oneness with objects permeates the philosophical inquiry of these early Greek philosophers, although some modern thinkers do not grant their often poetic style the status of genuine philosophy. The poetic sense of the meaning of *logos* (speech) as utilized by the pre-Socratics changed to mean logic or concept for modern man. The roots of that shift are in Plato's realism, the need to abstract pure concepts or "logics" of things as the measure of truth. In its more modern form, things are "re-presented" in the mind first by the use of a concept in propositional form. Truth is then measured by the correspondence of a thing to propositions. According to Heidegger, truth as such has been removed from the immediacy of things.

In the seventeenth century, René Descartes further separated the mind from objects with his famous dictum, "I think, therefore I am." Like Plato, Descartes sought to discover universal principles. Through his method of systematic doubt, Descartes seems to have bifurcated the mind from its own body.[9] He separates the inner world of consciousness from the outer world of objects (including one's own body as part of the outer world). With this separation of perception from what is perceived, an important basis for scientific methodology is established. In classic realist fashion, scientific method is placed between the researcher and the data in order to control the subject and free the object for pure, empirical inspection. With Descartes, philosophy was placed upon the "secure path of science." With the strength of scientific methodology, and specifically by coupling philosophy with mathematics and logic, philosophy could claim to provide apodictic or certain knowledge. Scientific axioms transposed into philosophical directives control the researcher's cultural, historical, and personal biases when pondering philosophical issues, just as the scientist places his or her biases in abeyance during experiments. After all, the Newtonian image of the world was that of a perfectly running clock.[10] According to the conventional wisdom of the eighteenth and nineteenth centuries, eventually science would catch up with and explain every element of this wonderful machine called the universe. By the end of the nineteenth century, the same wisdom suggested that the human sciences would share this methodological control over the nature of human knowledge and actions. This evolving scientific culture insisted that anything that is not grounded in strict, scientific method is relegated to sophistry, prejudice, emotionality, and illusion.

Logical Positivism

Perhaps the most extreme form of realism in philosophy was logical positivism.[11] This school of thought, with roots in the nineteenth century, overtly blossomed in Vienna in the 1920s and 1930s and, with less fanfare, continued for at least two more decades. While the tenets of logical positivism have been largely abandoned, some of the details of that theoretical position continue to serve, in some form or another, as criteria for the evaluation of educational research. True to its other name, "logical empiricism," logical positivism accepts the principle of "verifiability": a statement is meaningful if and only if it is, in principle, empirically (i.e., observationally) verifiable. Meaning is dichotomized into cognitive and emotive categories. When a statement can be verified by sense experience (i.e., through one of the senses), positive knowledge is obtained, and that knowledge can be said to be cognitive or rational. On the other hand, statements that deal with emotion or feeling are categorized as "metaphysical" (i.e., beyond or above the physical and consequently not empirically verifiable) and are judged to be meaningless. Metaphysical statements are not, in principle, empirically verifiable and hence there is no way to determine the truth or falsity of such statements through direct experience. According to logical positivism, no empirical experience could support Susanne Langer's insight that music is expressive of life. For the logical positivist, scientific method of the most strict kind is the only source for pure knowledge about reality. Philosophical inquiry must therefore emulate this severe image of science through the use of logic and mathematical reasoning or be relegated to the status of mysticism.

According to logical positivists, philosophical language must be as precise and literal as language used in scientific inquiry. Positivists envisioned language's becoming a form of calculus. Once formalized by philosophers, language would be neutral and pure. A neutral philosophical language could distinguish between real problems and pseudoproblems. It would distill metaphysical positions to reality or show that such positions were meaningless and inconsequential.

What logical positivists missed was that their own philosophy was equally rooted in a metaphysical position (which is the case in any philosophy). Logical positivists believed (or accepted on faith) that human rationality, as a human construction, facilitates only the observation of nature. It follows that for positivists, rationality or reasoning, in itself, reveals nothing. Appearance alone is "real" for the positivist. There is no rationality in nature; rationality remains a human construct. Logical positivists concluded that the image of nature as a rational machine is the result of the incorrect projection of the model of human rationality onto nature. Thus, theories based on logic and reasoning were viewed as instruments or means for the observation of nature in a systematic and rigorous manner. Human intelligence and rationality is merely a neutral instrument for the observation of nature. The image of scientific inquiry was thus relegated to the administration of neutral techniques for the purpose of pure observation. Logic was used to provide order and system. There was no allowance for imagination or leaps of theoretical insight in this view of scientific inquiry. As sociologist Max Weber proclaimed, the image of the world as presented in positivism is that of an intellectual and bureaucratic "iron cage" filled with "sensualists without heart" and technicians without vision.[12]

Logic as a Tool in Philosophical Inquiry

In their discussions of the use of philosophical inquiry, many researchers in music and music education have accented the rigorous methods, precise terminologies, and logic that have made science so successful in explaining, predicting, and thereby controlling the environment. Edward L. Rainbow and Hildegard C. Froehlich clarify the use of "scientific process" in philosophical inquiry and present useful rules for defining terms.[13] Milton Babbitt contends that analysis in music must be constituted of scientific language and scientific method in order for it to reach the status of meaningful discourse.[14] One of the best known methods of logic is Carl Hempel's deductive-nomological or D-N method.[15] The D-N method combines descriptive statements that list features that are immediately given to the senses by the object under scrutiny with explanations of the relationships between those features or events that comprise the object. The term "deductive" suggests that descriptive statements progress logically to the explanations and finally to the ending or conclusive explanatory statement, termed the "explanandum." Thus, deduction is based on logic.

Logic is the analysis of the structure of reasoning in the form of arguments. In formal logic, an argument is a set of sentences, one of which claims to be a conclusion that follows from the others. In the syllogism

A1) All Americans are human beings
A2) John is an American
A3) (Therefore) John is a human being

A3 is a conclusion that is based on statements A1 and A2. That is to say, from A1 and A2 one can deduce A3. One can also say that the conclusion (A3) and the premises (A1 and A2) are both *valid* and *true*. In formal logic, validity and truth function as two distinct terms. The argument

> B1) All pianists have three feet
> B2) John is a pianist
> B3) John has three feet

is *valid*; the conclusion (B3) follows from the premises (B1 and B2). However, the premise (B1) is obviously not *true*. Thus, validity is an intrinsic characteristic, whereas truth must be corroborated through the explanation of the relationship between the argument and the real world (outside the syllogism) to which the argument points.

While *deduction* involves reasoning from a general truth to a particular instance, as one type of exercise in deduction, *induction* involves reasoning from a part of a whole to a general statement, from individual elements to universals. In logical terms, in deduction one infers the consequent from a conditional statement and its antecedent:

> if X, then Y (conditional statement)
> X is the case (the antecedent is the case)
> therefore Y (the consequent).

In induction, one infers a generalized antecedent from a conditional statement and its consequent:

> if X, then Y (conditional statement with X as a generalization of Y)
> Y is the case (the consequent)
> therefore X (the antecedent as a generalization).

Logic clearly reflects mathematical reasoning. Each statement or proposition is developed to support subsequent premises which culminate in a conclusion. However, as Abraham Kaplan notes, the process of scientific discovery (what he terms "logic-in-use") is quite different from the report of scientific findings (what he terms "reconstructed logic").[16] In science, the object under study cannot always be observed directly. Using laws of physics and rules of logical reasoning, scientists deduce conclusions that are not directly observable. At other times, scientists go beyond accepted modes of mathematical logic in order to extend or revamp established scientific theories. One example was Einstein's extension of physics with relativity theory. In such cases, scientists accept the tenets of rationalism.

Rationalism

For the rationalist, thought is a copy of independent reality. Language (in the form of propositions) is determined by thought and is simply a means of transmitting thoughts, which are independent of language. The truth of a proposition is therefore ascertained by its correspondence to thought, which already conforms to reality. The reality of the external world is always the ultimate criterion because it requires nothing other than itself to be determined. In Aristotle's rationalist (and realist) account, propositions are symbols for thoughts.[17] While propositions may be different among language users, thoughts about reality itself remain the same for all humans. Reality determines knowledge or thought, and language simply carries out the conformity of thought to reality in an impartial and independent manner. Accordingly for rationalists, one can use language and reason to step out of culture in order to examine culture in terms of something (e.g., a Platonic "form") that transcends. In modern-day "structuralism," this rationalist view contends that it is possible to transcend culture and understand "underlying structures" or "culturally invariant factors."

Ludwig Wittgenstein's early philosophical output provides an important source in rationalist philosophy. Often one reads about the "early" and "late" Wittgenstein(s) because of the dramatic turn away from earlier positions in his later writings. The key book in his early period is the *Tractatus*. This work presents a rationalist account of propositional truth, stating that language is a picture of reality.[18] Like a photograph, language represents or mirrors reality in a one-to-one correspondence. Thus, reality *is* its presentation in language. One can see the shift from an empiricist view, in which observation of the physical world must be the final place in which to decide truth, to a form of rationalism, in which one need only study language (which includes the languages of mathematics, physics, and geometry), not physical reality, to decide truth. If this rationalist account of propositional truth is to be successful, it must be shown that the structures of propositions (linguistic premises) are isomorphic (i.e., picture copies) to the structures of the facts (in reality) to which they refer. The writings of the early Wittgenstein and Bertrand Russell ascribe to this "copy" theory of the relationship between language and reality.[19] In such a view, philosophical language must be distilled to the most simple and literal terms. This purifies the propositions that constitute philosophical inquiry. Just as reality is built on simple objects, language must also be reduced to the most basic terms or "atoms." This position on the use of basic, literal, and precise philosophical language (as noted above, a position shared by logical positivists) is referred to as "logical atomism."

Research in music education under the methodology of the early Wittgenstein and Russell's logical atomism would shift the study of conditions and ideas in the real world of music education to an analysis of *statements* about those conditions and ideas. As such, philosophical inquiry becomes a methodology for the clarification of language. Most current philosophies of science do not ascribe to logical atomism. In addition, and as noted above, scientific inquiry often goes beyond the confines of inductive and deductive reasoning. The primacy of logic and the requirement of strictly literal language in philosophical inquiry have been strongly contested and in many instances abandoned by philosophers of science during the last thirty years. In fact, some support for that abandonment is from Wittgenstein's later work.[20] Researchers in music education who still adhere to antiquated positivistic and logical atomistic views of scientific method and philosophy are in the unenviable position of embracing a methodology that has largely been deserted in the field (science) to which they look for models and methods.[21] That positivistic view does not correctly represent the scope of research in music education. A firm middle ground between the strict realism of logical positivism and historical relativism (which tends to have an antiscientific agenda) can be found in the current literature in the philosophy of science. This middle ground more correctly (than logical positivism) captures the spirit of research activities in music education.

Current Realist Philosophies of Science

Current realists in the philosophy of science do not adhere to the inactive and passive conception of man's part in knowledge-gathering that permeates logical positivism and its attempted mathematization of philosophical inquiry. Within logical positivism, in the pursuit of "pure" knowledge, the "knower" can be made to disappear. Removed by an objectifying method, only the objects and results of research remain. In the proposed middle ground, there is an attempt to account for the presence of the researcher or knower.

The archetypal figure Immanuel Kant presents an early middle ground. His realist position is much less rigid than the extreme position of logical positivism. The main difference is that in logical positivism, the researcher is believed to be absent from inquiry; only the method and the object of research remain. In Kant's form of realism, man plays an active part in philosophical and scientific inquiry. Like Plato, Kant was committed to the possibility of pure reason. And like Descartes, Kant hoped to provide universal criteria for knowledge of universal principles; to that end, he remained committed to the development of "transcendental reason." Philosophy was to be the judicature that would assess claims made by a culture. Yet, unlike Plato and Descartes, Kant placed man's consciousness overtly at the center of all knowledge-gathering.[22] Kant rejected David Hume's rigid realist model of man's mind as a passive response mechanism that comprehends things in themselves as they exist, separate from consciousness.[23] A philosophical rationale for the twentieth-century stimulus-response behaviorist model of "mind," Hume's premise was that man discovers knowledge as a passive reactor to information given by autonomous, external objects. In such a view, there is no "knower" (no researcher), only the "known."[24] Contrary to that view, according to Kant, external objects must be mediated by concepts that have been formulated by a knowing subject. Objects "conform to the conditions of one's knowledge." While this places the subject at the center, Kant believed that through a transcendental method based on pure reason (note his Platonic roots), one constitutes the objects of observation in a purely formal manner, thereby saving objectivity. Thus for Kant, the human mind, as a proactive (not reactive as in Hume) mediator of experience, is capable of transcending its ordinary subjectivism and securing pure knowledge. This is an early and important middle ground between (1) a rigid form of realism that dislocates the presence of the researcher in acts of research and (2) historical relativism which, as discussed later in this chapter, tends to call into question the suitability of any scientific method for inquiry in disciplines like music education.

In this century, and particularly during the last forty years, realists have developed a middle ground that dispels the rigid, empirical requirements of logical positivism for the philosophy of science.[25] At the same time, they do not accept the more subjective stance of historical relativists concerning the nature of knowledge and research activities in science. If a researcher follows the positivistic demand of empirical verifiability, the parameters of his or her database are greatly restricted. As noted already, the *ontology* of logical positivism—ontology is defined as what is accepted as "real" and worthy of research—accepts only those theoretical positions that are, in principle, empirically verifiable. Current realists have been principally engaged in ontological problems and have discredited the positivistic view that theories which cannot be confirmed through observable evidence do not qualify as scientific theories. This relates to the realists' attack on the Humean view of causality that undergirds positivism. In traditional terms, "causality" refers to the relationship between A and B in which whenever A happens first, B succeeds as a result of A. Hume suggests that there is no element of necessity between these two (A and B) events. The only thing that a researcher can perceive is that B follows A; the researcher cannot successfully theorize that B necessarily must follow when A occurs (such a move would project human rationality on nature). Thus, for Hume and the positivists, a researcher's ontology is limited to observable facts.

Current realists point out that in the practice of science, scientists regularly "conceive" what they cannot immediately "perceive" in order to explain and predict. Rom Harre, a scientist and philosopher of science, contends that while perception is at the heart of scientific research, so are conception and imagination.[26] Many scientific explanations are the result of conceiving without perceiving. Harre maintains that there are at least three realms of scientific research: the first realm is marked by ordinary perception;[27] in the second realm, perception can catch up with conception, i.e., there is a promise of technological development (with increasingly powerful microscopes and computers) through which researchers will eventually be able to "see" what they only conceived as the probable explanation;[28] and in the third realm there are genuine theoretical acts of imagination that will never be directly perceived, i.e., empirically observed or verified.[29]

Harre further substantiates the view that positivism has been shown to be unrealistic in relation to scientific practice by almost all current philosophers of science (realist or not) in the United States and Britain. Rather than attempt to define theoretical language through observational terms, thereby reducing or discarding them, *theoretical language is understood as the means by which observable entities can be explained in the first place. There are no theory-free observations in the processes of scientific inquiry. All methods, scientific or otherwise, are theory laden.* One cannot escape a theoretical position that supersedes or transcends what is immediately verifiable. While observation remains important in scientific inquiry, rationalism (which functions in what Harre called the second and third realms of scientific inquiry) is at the heart of much current scientific inquiry.

Further clarifying the relationship between theoretical and observable data, Mary B. Hesse notes that a positivistic view of the use of *models* in science is not in keeping with actual scientific practice.[30] Conceptual models in science are often in the form of analogical descriptions of unobservable data which have a causal relation to observable data. Theoretical conceptions often must be used to ground and explain observable or perceivable entities. In positivism, the relegation of such models to the status of psychological aids is not in keeping with actual scientific practice. Finally, and as noted earlier, Hesse also holds that scientific theories are not always developed through the canons of logic. One could never limit the development of scientific theories to strict logic. Harre concludes that the validity of formal argument is not primary in science or the philosophy of science. Rather, metaphor and simile are the core cognitive processes in scientific practice.[31] Thus, researchers in music education utilizing traditional and nontraditional designs need not delimit the structure of their theories to the canons of logic or to the observable. In taking imaginative license they can be confident that they are emulating scientific inquiry in the natural sciences.

The current realist position in the philosophy of science provides a much more fluid sense of scientific practice, method, and theory construction than in the positivistic vision. Within that more recent view, *most realists also maintain that research in the human sciences, history and the arts must be considerably more relativist than in the natural sciences.* For example, in natural science, that real blood flows through a subject's veins need not be understood as a "relative" truth. This is a truth in Harre's first realm of perceivable (observable) data and, therefore, no one can seriously doubt that real blood actually flows. However, conclusions in areas outside of the natural sciences are not so apodictically, concretely, or perceivably true. Truth, in the social and behavioral sciences as well as in the arts, is not so definite. In research in music education, one may lean more heavily toward a relationship between objects of study and subsequent theoretical formulations that are analogous to Harre's second and third realms of scientific research, where perception may catch up to conception or may never become observationally corroborated. Simply put, in accordance with a current realist philosophy in science, theories utilized in all modes of music-education research cannot always be corroborated through observational means and such a test may not be a useful, realistic or fruitful criterion for theory construction.

A Middle Ground Continued: The Antirealist "Social Constructionists" in Science

In the philosophy of science, a camp that competes with realism can be termed *social constructionism*. Some of the principles of social constructionism resemble those in historical relativism, yet social constructionists do not tend to "deconstruct" the history of scientific thinking, as do many historical relativists. In this context, social constructionists comprise a large group of current philosophers of science who contend that knowledge generated by the natural sciences is based largely on social construction, not individual objectivism. Scientific knowledge presupposes a paradigm, or overall theoretical orientation, that is shared by a community of practicing scientists. Scientific knowledge and truth are therefore always relative to a particular paradigm and community. Unlike the realists, social constructionists contend that inquiry in the natural sciences cannot be performed independently of social influences or one's cultural and professional community. This constitutes a shift from the realist assertion that nature is prior to research and that researchers can transcend cultural and professional assumptions, thereby attaining objective knowledge in the natural sciences. Social constructionists argue that knowledge generated by any science (whether natural or human) is founded upon and composed of social practices.

Thomas Kuhn—with training in physics—points out that a scientific paradigm is rarely engaged or challenged by scientists.[32] For example, the paradigm of Newtonian physics reigned for centuries in science, with scientists working within a common view that Newtonian laws were eternally correct. In periods of scientific revolutions, as in the Einsteinian qualifications of many of Newton's laws, scientists critically examine the underlying theoretical framework or paradigm in which they are working. However, as a new paradigm (for example, Einstein's relativity) takes hold, the community of scientists pulls back from its metatheoretical concerns and engages in more specific and normal matters of research that presuppose the correctness of the new paradigm. Thus, when scientific findings are disseminated to a scientific community, they are always understood in terms of and through the orientation of both a background paradigm and an overall scientific community. As Hilary Putnam notes, rationality inside and outside of science can be defined only in terms of local cultural norms.[33]

Nobel laureate in physical chemistry Michael Polanyi contends that all knowledge in science is marked by the personal element of the scientist.[34] Individual scientists perform research from a personal and communal standpoint. The distinctive mark of the idea of the "personal" for Polanyi is the scientist's commitment to being responsible for his or her belief in the reality of nature as his or her theories define it. Polanyi maintains that because understanding the rationality of nature (an antipositivistic position) is always mediated by the individual scientist (a Kantian notion) within a community of scientists (a Kuhnian insight), the rationality of nature cannot be independently verified.[35] This points to Harre's second and third realms of scientific inquiry. However, Harre's middle-ground realism differs from Polanyi's social constructionist account because Harre accepts a bedrock connection between a scientist's perception and nature so that the scientific community is not sealed off from nature. As in Kant, for Harre and the current realist school of science, this connection between scientific practice and nature saves objectivity in the practice of the natural sciences. But for Polanyi, both the personal and the communal aspects of scientific research are marked by a historically conditioned consensus. Like Kuhn, Polanyi suggests that scientific truth is relative to the community of scientists who accept it and to their underlying paradigm. Thus, their antirealist positions are grounded in the notion of scientific knowledge being relative to the community of professionals that generate and evaluate such knowledge. Accordingly, truth in the natural and human sciences is relative to its social construction.

While the debate continues in the philosophy of science as to the objectivity of knowledge generated by the *natural sciences*, no debate exists in the literature concerning objectivity in other fields of endeavor. As noted earlier, the idea of objective knowledge generated outside of natural science is considered a myth. Accordingly, the respective impacts of realism and social constructionism as models for *philosophical inquiry* in research in music education are similar. Both middle-ground camps discredit the high stature given to logical structures as the essence of scientific discourse by logical positivism. While logic has its place in scientific discourse, much scientific thinking makes little explicit use of logical structures.[36] Current philosophical research in science—from both the realist and the social constructionist standpoints—would conclude that all research in music education is relative to theoretical assumptions, test biases, cultural presumptions, and the practices and beliefs of the community of researchers who generate knowledge. No current position in the philosophy of science places any credence in the notion that studies in the human sciences can have the objectivity of the natural sciences. This was the Comtean[37] dream of logical positivism, a dream that has been shown to be a delusion.

Historical Relativism

It is clear from the middle-ground positions in the philosophy of science that axiomatic structures like those in the realist version of the natural world cannot be discovered outside of the natural world. The outcome of such a philosophical position for research in music education is a (measured) relativist position. Historical relativists have clarified that position quite well. Nevertheless, many historical relativists present theories that simply deconstruct traditional notions of objectivity and methodology for the sake of such a deconstruction; no alternative methodology is offered.[38] The assumptions of historical relativists will be reviewed here only for their positive insights into the nature of language and knowledge in research.

Hans-Georg Gadamer has concluded that researchers utilizing different modes of philosophical inquiry cannot suspend their biases or, more broadly, the horizons of their existence.[39] There are no universal truths that can enable man to cross cultures or historical epochs purely. This does not produce a radical relativism in which every belief is as good as every other. Instead, historical relativists maintain that knowledge generated by all research is always in terms of the accepted procedures of justification held by a particular culture, society, or professional community. The search for objectivity is replaced by an effort to establish intersubjective agreement, a consensus among cultures, or what Gadamer terms a "fusion of horizons." As Richard Rorty suggests, instead of seeking the creation of a pure form of discourse, one can only recognize that there is a plurality of discourses and that rigorous discourse itself is a key goal of philosophy.[40] Method is not strictly possible in the natural sciences or in the human sciences because one cannot establish an essence in nature or in man.[41] The best that one can achieve is interpretive discourse, but never in any absolute way.[42] While sharing some tenets with social constructionists, this attack on the nature of knowledge and methodology is more extreme than the position of social constructionism.

The abandonment of the Platonic quest for absolute philosophical truths by historical relativists is marked by Heidegger's view that truths must always be understood within the context of one's historical and cultural horizon. Explicit knowledge in research is always understood in relief to a background of a shared paradigm or disciplinary matrix. This was Kuhn's great insight concerning the relationship between scientific knowledge and scientific paradigms. Heidegger's analysis of the ground for shared beliefs and practices goes much deeper. When one converses with another person, acquired social techniques come into play that remain in the background of such a conversation. Heidegger points out that such inherited cultural practices cannot be made explicit in theories because these existential modes of human being (i.e., *being* human) are so pervasive that one could never define them sufficiently to make them objects of explicit analysis.[43] One cannot transcend this primordial dimension of understanding. Heidegger contends that all knowledge gathered by traditional research methods in the natural and human sciences is ultimately circular. Verification or corroboration of results takes place within the confines of the theory that structures that research project. While the social constructionists in science have demonstrated circularity by showing that research conclusions are dependent on the accepted practices, theoretical assumptions, and biases of their research community, Heidegger asserts that the entire theoretical activity of formulating and verifying hypotheses is parasitic on the background of cultural practices and the "life-world" (*Lebenswelt*) that constitutes the overall ontology of any cultural people.

Within the historical relativist perspective, all research is marked by historical pre-understanding. The temporal present is part of a stream of history that moves from the past into the future. One's historical tradition is the basis for pre-understanding anything. Understanding is the fundamental manner in which historical man engages his world. Researchers cannot fully suspend their tradition or its underlying biases. However, rather than cause a negative result in research, according to Gadamer, such historical biases are necessary and are a positive force in research; without historical and cultural contexts, research would be buoyless and incoherent.[44]

Gadamer claims that any sense of method based on the natural sciences is inappropriate for research in the human sciences, history, and the arts. Yet, there is another methodological avenue. *Rhetoric* provides a claim to truth that at once defends the probable, is based on ordinary reason, and is not limited to that which can be tested or observationally demonstrated.[45] Gadamer traces rhetoric from the Greeks and through the humanist tradition in order to provide a vehicle that will free researchers from the model of scientific method. He notes that rhetoric has been applied systematically for centuries in the fields of law and theology, using principles of authoritative example, precedent, and customary standards of evaluation and modes of speech.

According to Gadamer, the traditional understanding of the terms "subject" and "object" can be turned on its head. The object of research can become the subject and the researcher the object. Within this context, the researcher responds to questions posed by the research object. Consequently, data are not dominated by methods that can suffocate different levels of meaning. Experimental research may tell very little about the nature of the rapport between teachers and their students. As discussed in the chapter on qualitative research (chapter 5), ethnographic methods allow researchers to be involved in the fullness of the educational setting in which research is being conducted. Only by remaining open to issues raised within that setting can the researcher be responsive to different types and levels of meaning. While one would not go so far as to accept that "no method is the best method," the researcher must recognize that the use of any method automatically places conditions on what the object of research can mean. The following paragraph is a short philosophical inquiry into the nature of objectivism and subjectivism in research activities. It is offered as an example of what philosophical inquiry from the standpoint of historical relativism might be like.

The suggestion that the use of a method places the researcher in a dominant position over the work may seem overstated. But if one closely examines the nature of methods, one discovers that the result of using highly objective methods of research may be an extreme form of subjectivism, writes Ferrara.[46] Methods prescribe the tasks that researchers must perform. Each method delimits what can be known about a research object based on the nature of its tasks. The researcher follows the protocols of a selected method to

ensure that research is systematic, logical, corroborable, understandable to a shared community of professional colleagues, and
(though less overt) objective to some degree. Traditional methods
in research are placed between the researcher and the database in
order to control both the integrity of the data *and* the researcher.
The method not only controls for the potential inconsistency of data
collection and treatment but also helps to avoid unacceptable levels
of subjectivity in research. Research is considered objective when
a method controls bias and prejudice. However, that same method
may radically and uncompromisingly prescribe what the research
object can mean. While the researcher presents the appearance of
objective distance from the data, the method subjugates the data
because data can only mean and show what the prescribed tasks of
one's method allow data to mean and show. In transferring the
subjective role from the researcher to his or her method, the impact
on the data is not less subjective or dominating. Thus, objectivity is
not achieved through the use of traditional research designs. That
is to say, *the idea of "objectivity" is for the object, not the subject.*
To be objective means to protect the object from dominance of any
kind. In focusing on the dangers that result from a researcher's
subjectivism, philosophical accounts of traditional research designs
have not registered a parallel subjectivism in methods. Hence,
historical relativists are cautious of methods in general.

What is left? One answer is a responsive approach to the nature
and fullness of the database. Heidegger suggests that truth in
research must be understood as freedom.[47] In order to understand
the truth about some object it must be given the freedom to show
itself. Real objectivity, to the degree that such an idea is plausible,
marks research in which analytical tasks engender freedom for
research entities to show themselves in any mode of appearance and
meaning. Methods of research from this standpoint would have to
respond to what research entities can and might mean. In such a
paradigm, the tasks of research focus on the needs and questions
posed by research entities. As a result, methods will be much more
fluid and flexible, with a less prescriptive role than is common in
established methods. This is not to suggest that established and
traditional methods are automatically dislocated from research
entities. Certainly in the construction and development of such
methods there is a response to the nature of research entities which,
in turn, makes methods *appropriate* to data. The point made here
is that research methods most often *appropriate* and thereby delimit
what research entities can mean without a consideration of the

potential of meanings that can be generated from those same entities. Historical relativists thereby shift the power to appropriate research tasks from the method to the research entity. The shift is never complete. However, the change of the researcher's mode of orientation to greater openness and responsiveness clarifies a research distinction between the philosophical positions that support (1) the nature of traditional research activities and (2) the historical relativist standpoint.

Conclusions

Attacks on the suitability of research practices in the natural sciences for research in the human sciences, history, education, and the arts are often based on the abandoned philosophy of logical positivism. In the current literature of the philosophy of science, research practices in natural science are described as a blending of the use of perception (observation) and conception (theory development), logical reasoning and imaginative vision. The implication is that as one moves out of the natural sciences and into the domains of human social, behavioral, historical, and artistic activities, research can more readily leave the confines of the observable (Harre's first realm of scientific activity) to higher levels of theory and metaphysical assumptions. Such an orientation in research in music education may support interaction between traditional and nontraditional methods. Rather than produce chaos, researchers can be responsive to the rich fullness of research entities. Responsiveness is a form of appreciation. Appreciation does not mean liking or disliking. Instead, it names a mode of inquiry that balances questions formulated through the use of one's method with questions that grow more directly from the research entity. This oscillation between subject and object roles is rooted in a dialogical method in which the researcher remains rigorous and directed yet also follows the lead of the research entity. Researchers utilizing philosophical inquiry remain grounded in logical reasoning but, as in the classical dialetics by Plato, also remain open to where the dialogue might proceed. As in a conversation during which neither party knows explicitly where the conversation will end, researchers in music education can also remain open to questions posed by one's database. Explicit answers to questions posed in the process of philosophical inquiry are rarely available.

One might suggest that an *experimental* research design metaphorically resembles a long metal pipe.[48] The researcher pushes data through from one end to the other. This is preceded by the articulation of explicit hypotheses concerning what will come out (in the form of conclusions) at the other end. Conclusions usually come out in seriational or quantitative form that embodies a precise and parsimonious answer to the predictions formulated in the hypotheses. The experimental design or pipe keeps the data confined, protected and controlled. The data are not allowed to show themselves in any way other than through this cylindrical process. The pipe or design is precisely engineered; its continence is not questioned. What is important is (1) whether the researcher has implemented the pipe in the correct manner and (2) what comes out at the other end in the form of conclusions. It is significant to note that the constitution of those conclusions, *now in quantitative form*, is exceedingly foreign in substance to the original composition of the data that went into the pipe. That is to say, the database has been radically transformed into a mathematical formulation which is exceedingly appropriate and fruitful for certain kinds of research questions.

On the other hand, *philosophical inquiry* is more like a cheese grater. Data are pushed across the sharp, rough, indented surface and flow through the perforated holes. Little data remain through to the end of the grater and there are no neat, quantified results that drop out there. Instead, the results of philosophical inquiry are the steady stream of treated or transformed data that flow through for further separation and interpretation. Unlike the pipe, there is no clear continence and no safely controlled and enclosed research space; the cheese/data can "slip off" the top of the open-ended grater. Philosophical inquiry may be more precarious and less controlled. But in experimental design, one "lets go" of the data after pushing them into the pipe. That is to say, the pipe or design takes over. In principle, the "knower" is left tacit in favor of a method and the "known" (data). However, in philosophical inquiry, the researcher "holds on" to the data. He or she handles the cheese/data, "gripping it" in a way that must be responsive to its constitution. Of course, capturing falling bits of grated cheese can be as disconcerting as trying to grasp and contain sand pouring from a glass. An experimental design, like a pipe, provides constraints which reduce this potential sloppiness and incontinence by the quantitative transformation of the data. In philosophical inquiry, control is traded for the presence of the researcher and the researcher's responsiveness to the database. During his or her dialogue with the data the researcher remains open to the needs of the data. And in so doing, he or she is always and only "on the way" to conclusions.

Problems for Review and Discussion

1. Identify the purposes of philosophical inquiry presented in this chapter.
2. What are some of the distinctions between realism and historical relativism?
3. Trace the roots of realism presented in this chapter.
4. What is meant by the term "logical positivism"?
5. What is the importance of logic to philosophical inquiry?
6. What is meant by the term "rationalism"?
7. How can philosophies of science relate to research which uses approaches of philosophical inquiry?
8. Discuss social constructionism as it is presented in this chapter.

Supplementary Sources

Bernstein, Richard J. *Beyond Objectivism and Relativism: Science, Hermeneutics and Praxis*. Philadelphia: University of Pennsylvania Press, 1983, especially pp. 1-49.

Dewey, John. *Logic: The Theory of Inquiry*. New York: Henry Holt and Co., 1938.

Feibelman, James K. *The Revival of Realism*. New York: Henry Holt and Co., 1938.

Gorovitz, Samuel, Merrill Hintikka, Donald Provence, and Ron G. Williams. *Philosophical Analysis: An Introduction to Its Language and Techniques*, 3rd ed.; New York: Random House, 1979.

Harre, Rom. *The Philosophies of Science*, 2nd ed.; Oxford: Oxford University Press, 1985.

Margolis, Joseph. *Pragmatism Without Foundations: Reconciling Realism and Relativism*. Oxford: Basil Blackwell Ltd., 1986.

Nagel, Ernest, and Richard B. Brandt, eds. *Meaning and Action*. New York: Harcourt, Brace, 1965.

Reimer, Bennett. *A Philosophy of Music Education*. Englewood Cliffs, N.J.: Prentice-Hall, 1970.

Schwadron, Abraham A. "On Relativism and Music Education," *Journal of Research in Music Education*, Fall 1965, 13,3:131–135.

Schwadron, Abraham A. "Philosophy and Aesthetics in Music Education: A Critique of the Research," *Bulletin of the Council for Research in Music Education*, Summer 1983, 79:11-32.

4. Aesthetic Inquiry: Concepts and Techniques

Aesthetics is a branch of philosophy devoted to studies of the arts. Simply put, the term "aesthetic inquiry" is the operational form of the term "aesthetics." That is, aesthetic inquiry names a variety of methods that one can use to study the visual arts, literature, music and the theater arts.[1] It is necessary to read the preceding chapter, "Philosophical Inquiry: Concepts and Techniques," prior to reading this chapter. Philosophical inquiry remains a theoretical basis for aesthetic inquiry. Accordingly, one would not be incorrect in suggesting that aesthetic inquiry is a type of philosophical inquiry. However, the field of aesthetic inquiry and its various modalities are so vast that a separate chapter is necessary in order to make such a presentation manageable and clear.

Many students in music education with strong backgrounds in performance or composition utilize musical works as a primary database. This is often the case in dissertations for the D.M.A. but can also occur in certain institutions in dissertations for the Ed.D. and the Ph.D. In these instances, students need methodologies that will enable them to analyze musical works. While philosophical inquiry bears upon this research, aesthetic inquiry can more specifically and aptly provide methods for research. Moreover, the simple adaptation of a traditional method of music analysis (for example, Schenkerian analysis) is insufficient to support a theoretical basis for studies of this kind. Students should be aware of competing analytical methods and various approaches to aesthetic inquiry. This chapter will provide the necessary groundwork for such a metatheoretical position. This should enable students to articulate the inherent strengths and weaknesses of their overall research design (aesthetic inquiry) as well as the specific mode or modes of inquiry that they are utilizing for data collection and treatment. Students are then in a position to defend the appropriateness of their method(s) to the database.

As in any chapter of this kind, selection and delimitation of materials is required. There are at least six approaches in aesthetic inquiry: formalist, psychological, phenomenological, institutional, sociological, and anthropological or ethnographic. The first three are frequently used in research studies. Methods for the last two, sociological and anthropological, are presented to some degree and therefore overlap with the chapters on case study (chapter 7) and qualitative research (chapter 5). Those chapters, which accent educational contexts, do not bridge methods to musical works. Nevertheless, the methods, as presented there, are transferable. In addition, there is a rich existing literature in the sociology of music[2] and in ethnomusicology.[3] Consequently, sociological and ethnographic approaches to aesthetic inquiry will not be presented in this chapter. The novel institutionalist approach will be reviewed along with the first three: formalist, psychological, and phenomenological. In each case, the underlying logic that supports and directs each modality of aesthetic research will be uncovered.

The overreaching goal of this chapter is to understand the inherent strengths and weaknesses of the selected methods of aesthetic inquiry which impact on their ability to be responsive to musical works. As a form of philosophical inquiry, aesthetic inquiry requires the "handling" of the data. If one's method is to be successful, it must be responsive to levels of musical significance. As noted in chapter 3, methods automatically prescribe the tasks that a researcher can perform. Those tasks, in turn, delimit data collection and treatment. In defending the use of a particular method of aesthetic inquiry, the researcher must clarify the levels of musical significance that the selected method permits the researcher to uncover and report. Given the multidimensional thrust of musical significance (a thrust that supports methods as divergent as the six listed earlier), the direction of this chapter will be toward the construction of an eclectic method. The presentation of the four approaches to aesthetic inquiry will be followed by a short overview of theories of musical significance. That review will provide data to establish a working definition of the levels of musical significance. With the presentations of the four approaches and a clarification of the levels of musical significance, a sufficient theoretical basis for the construction of an eclectic method will be accomplished. An explanation of the steps of the eclectic method for music analysis completes the chapter. The use of such a method should allow researchers to respond more comprehensively to several strata of musical significance.

Four Approaches to Aesthetic Inquiry

Formalist

In a *formalist* approach, a researcher limits inquiry to the structural elements in an artwork. In music, such an approach might result in a series of Schenkerian graphs. In visual art, elements such as lines, shapes, colors, and the presence or lack of balance could be discussed.[4] The implementation of a traditional method of formal analysis can bypass the articulation of its underlying assumption. One such assumption in formalism is that the analysis of musical form (which will be termed musical syntax) is the most appropriate way to understand music. This traditional approach suggests that methods cannot be formulated that will support the systematic and corroborable analysis of musical reference. Thus, formalists do not respond to levels of musical significance that include Susanne K. Langer's conception of "virtual feeling" or Martin Heidegger's account of the "life-world" of the composer.[5]

With a philosophical ground in what Rom Harre calls the first realm of scientific inquiry,[6] formalism is committed to the analysis of data that can be collected through observation of the score and thereby can also be readily corroborated by other researchers. Corroboration requires a neutral analyst. As in the image of classical scientific inquiry, formalists leave their presence tacit in the research process. Their presence is substituted by the use of a method that allows for the systematic collection and treatment of musical data. While it would be unappreciative to label formalist approaches "positivistic," one must recognize the covert delimitation of the style (one does not report data in the first person) and substance of the "knower" or researcher in formalist analyses. For the sake of the security attained in research activities described in Harre's first realm of scientific inquiry, referential dimensions of musical significance have been eliminated. In fact, formal accounts of musical significance can be as imaginative as referential accounts. Moreover, formalists very often disagree on the results of formal analyses. Corroboration is never verification. Upon closer inspection, the nature of analyses of referential meanings in music may not be so distant from formal analyses. What is distant, however, are the data that each approach permits and enables the researcher to collect.

Psychological

In another overall approach, one can direct a *psychological* method toward works of art. There are many subvarieties of psychological approaches to art. The Freudian approach is probably the most venerable. In this type of inquiry, the researcher subjects the artist, through the works that the artist has created, to psychoanalysis.[7] Another psychological approach in aesthetics is presented by Rudolph Arnheim.[8] Arnheim's method is not Freudian but utilizes theories of perception and some principles of phenomenology (see below). Arnheim's works provide a systematic application of physical and psychological insights into visual perception to works of art. His overall mission is the recognition that visual thinking can be as powerful as thinking in ordinary languages. He contends that the Western cultural tradition has neglected the experience of the senses in favor of a reliance on language. The sense of sight, which he considers the primary means by which one perceives the world, has been particularly devalued. Unlike Freudian approaches, the theoretical basis for Arnheim's work is gestalt theory. Arnheim's works, like many Freudian analyses, are distinctive because in addition to the presentation of a theoretical basis they present actual analyses of works of art which implement the underlying theoretical base. This writer is not aware of any comparable researchers in music analysis that have presented such a developed and substantive application of psychological principles to a broad range of musical works.[9]

Phenomenological

In addition to formalist and psychological approaches, *phenomenology* is a major force in aesthetics. Phenomenologists, like their formalist and psychologist colleagues, have many subvarieties from which to select. Phenomenology will be presented more fully later in this chapter. For now, perhaps the most efficacious way of distinguishing phenomenological inquiries from the other approaches is to state the motto of phenomenology: "Back to the things themselves."[10] Phenomenology was conceived as a "science of essences" and enables the researcher to suspend theoretical positions in favor of the purely empirical descriptions of the object under study.[11] In this mode of responsiveness to research entities one also balances the impact of one's own involvement with the thing under study. Phenomenologists overtly attempt to account for the presence of the researcher in all acts of inquiry. They maintain that all acts of knowledge-gathering are marked by an "intentional relationship" between consciousness and the object to which it is pointed or directed.[12] Ordinary objects become "phenomena" when consciousness is intentionally directed toward them. This intentional correlation can be presented as follows:

consciousness (a subject) : phenomenon (an object)

Psychologists tend to focus on the left side of the correlation; they provide accounts of how a subject perceives a work of art. Formalists wish to function only on the right side of the correlation; they accept the prescriptions of formal methods which replace and therefore displace the "subjective" presence of the subject, focusing instead on the structural attributes of works of art. By contrast, phenomenologists describe artworks in light of the necessary interaction of a subject with a phenomenon. While some phenomenological schools focus primarily on one side of the correlation or the other, what distinguishes phenomenology from most other approaches in aesthetic inquiry is the balance of their claim to "get back to the things themselves" (the right side of the correlation) while holding on to a knowing and mediating subject (the left side of the correlation).

Institutionalism

A relatively new, nonconventional approach called *institutionalism* can also be utilized in aesthetic inquiry.[13] As orchestrated by George Dickie, an institutional analysis of art locates the essential and defining characteristics of an artwork not in consciousness (the left side of the intentional correlation) or in the artwork (the right side) but in the institutions in which works of art are presented.[14] Dickie wishes to provide a definition of art. However, he will not define art in terms of the subject because he maintains that discussion of the place of a "knower," the subject in art experiences, lands aesthetic inquiry in psychology. Dickie concludes that psychological approaches to art are not relevant to aesthetic inquiry.[15] In so doing, he eclipses any possible discussion of a subject's consciousness in art experiences. Dickie also accepts Morris Weitz's dictum that art is not definable.[16] Weitz and Dickie assert that there are no common characteristics intrinsic to *every* work of art. If common characteristics or elements were found that could connect all artworks, such essential characteristics or elements would constitute a definition of art. But ever-present and essential characteristics elude most aestheticians' attempts at a definition for all of the arts. Thus, Dickie will not define art in terms of the art object.

Early in Dickie's book, he stipulates two criteria that must be satisfied for a thing to be given the status of a work of art: artifactuality and the "conferred status of candidate for appreciation."[17] Artifactuality refers to the fact that some person must have worked on the object and altered it in some way. Thus, at this stage of Dickie's book, natural objects cannot be artworks. The second criterion, conferred status, addresses the condition that some person (not necessarily the artist) acting on behalf of the "artworld" places an object in an art institutional setting and thereby confers a status of "candidate for appreciation" on that object. The artworld, in Dickie's view, is made up of a related set of persons including musicians, writers, directors, critics, museum-goers, theater-goers and *any person* who considers himself or herself a member of this art community.[18] Apparently this is not a very selective club. In fact, only one person need confer the status of candidate for appreciation on an artifact. Thus, if a child draws a picture and a parent hangs it on the wall, for Dickie, it is an artwork. The first criterion for an artwork, artifactuality, has been satisfied by the child, for the child produced the drawing. Dickie goes so far as to suggest that artists themselves can, by hanging their own work on the wall, satisfy the second criterion, candidate for appreciation. Thus, the five-year-old, in hanging his or her drawing on the bedroom wall, has satisfied both of Dickie's criteria and thus has produced an artwork. Dickie refuses to deal with the evaluation of art. Consequently, there is no mechanism within his theory that can help to distinguish any differences between the five-year-old's drawing and a Rembrandt hanging next to it. Both are artifacts. And both have become candidates for appreciation because both are hanging on a wall. Dickie notes that a wall, like a theater or museum, is an institutional setting. Persons in the artworld (which includes just about anybody who has ever aesthetically appreciated anything) understand the aesthetic context that such institutions set up for works of art. If a dancer is performing on a street corner for donations, viewers do not walk through his or her performance space. They walk around the dancer because the corner is an art institution. In allowing this place its continence, they confer upon the performance the status of candidate for appreciation. The dancer makes the dance an artifact. But once again, in Dickie's institutionalism, there is no way to distinguish between the dance on the street corner and a dance in the New York State Ballet Theatre.

The bottom drops out of Dickie's theory when, a few pages later, he suggests that the first criterion, artifactuality, can be circumvented. Thus, if one finds a piece of driftwood on the beach, picks it up and nails it to the wall, that piece of driftwood becomes an artwork.[19] That is to say, Dickie contends that natural objects can be artifactualized without the use of tools by simply becoming candidates for appreciation. Within Dickie's theory, anything—a hat, a glove, a paper bag—could be an artwork by simply placing it in an art institution. Dickie argues that if paintings done by Betsy the chimpanzee from the Baltimore Zoo were hung in the Chicago Art Institute they would, with such a conferred status by the museum director, be artworks.[20] Few aestheticians are willing to place themselves on the same philosophical limb.

How could such a theory become so discussed in aesthetics that one could hardly read an issue of the *Journal of Aesthetics and Art Criticism* from the late 1970s through the mid-1980s without encountering an article about Dickie's institutionalism? Dickie's insights are interesting because they call attention to the institutions in which works of art are presented. What is the impact of place on the manner in which listeners experience, appreciate, and understand a violin performance inside Carnegie Hall or on the street corner slightly to the right of that building? Music critics, analysts, and researchers rarely report the impact of the institutional setting in a systematic and compelling way. Dickie's theory suggests that art institutional settings are fertile grounds for research. As part of a larger eclectic system, a step that permits the discussion of the institution in which a musical work is being performed could provide valuable data. The failure of institutional analyses is that they bypass the art object. In doing a purely institutional analysis of *Rigoletto* at the Met in New York City, one would not discuss the music at all but would concentrate on the institutional setting that, according to Dickie, defines the music as an art object. Without the aid of other steps in an eclectic method that would permit a report of the music itself, institutional analyses remain dislocated from both the artwork and the subjective experience of that work.

The Aesthetic Object and the Art Object

Perhaps a reason for the ultimate failure of Dickie's institutionalist approach is that he does not adequately distinguish between aesthetic objects and art objects. Any object can be made into an aesthetic object. Making a tree into an aesthetic object requires a responsiveness to the tree. The viewer must be intimately involved and yet reasonably "distanced" from the tree in order to give it the "freedom" to show itself.[21] A second-grade teacher could take a class outside to "appreciate" trees, that is, to let them "be." Such an appreciative description might respond to a tree's rough, bumpy surface, its broad and strong trunks, its delicate and colored leaves, and its insertion into the landscape and the blue sky. This responsive approach to the aesthetic qualities in the tree is markedly different from a utilitarian approach in which second graders are informed about the *uses* of trees: as the stuff out of which to produce paper, maple syrup, building materials, and firewood. As an aesthetic object, the tree is allowed to show itself on its own terms. As a utilitarian object, it is subjected by the viewer to a predisposed context of use. Thus, when a meteorologist views a cloud formation, a scientific matrix is inserted between the meteorologist and the cloud formation that utilizes the clouds in order to predict their impact on the weather. On the other hand, that same meteorologist could sit back and take an aesthetic view toward the clouds. This view would generate data that describe the cloud formation's white- and grayness, its fluffiness, its shape and movement. In all cases, the cloud formation and the tree remain the same; the viewer's mode of orientation toward those objects creates aesthetic objects or objects for use.

Are all art objects automatically aesthetic objects? No, because like non–art objects, art objects can be made into objects of use also. Imagine someone listening to Beethoven's Ninth Symphony, undeniably an artwork, in order to stay awake while driving a car late at night. Within this context, the driver/listener is not being responsive to the work, but is using it. No report of the work's extraordinary aesthetic qualities in the form of syntax, orchestration, or referential message is conveyed to the listener. One could conclude that the Beethoven art object has not been allowed to function as an aesthetic object. Thus, while many aestheticians would say that the performance of the symphony remains an art object, the listener's mode of orientation, marked by the "use" of the music rather than a "responsiveness"to it, has not allowed the symphony to be an aesthetic object. *Not all aesthetic objects are art objects* (both a tree and a Picasso can be made aesthetic objects by the viewer). At the same time, *not all art objects are aesthetic objects* (viewers and listeners can decide not to appreciate an artwork's aesthetic qualities).

Aesthetic Inquiry and Musical Significance

Earlier in this chapter, four overall approaches—formalist, psychological, phenomenological, and institutional—that might be utilized in aesthetic inquiry were briefly reviewed. The "intentional correlation" was introduced in order to clarify the differences between several of those approaches. It graphically illustrates the importance of one's consciousness, as the vehicle for one's overall mode of orientation, in acts of aesthetic inquiry. Thus, if one's mode of orientation is marked by a formalist approach to music, it can show only its formal elements. Data that might be of interest to the psychologist, anthropologist, sociologist, institutionalist, and phenomenologist tend not to be reported. This points to an important principle in aesthetic inquiry: *Each approach, in defining the parameters of data collection and treatment, functionally defines the music object; music can mean only what the method allows it to mean.* Methods are often evaluated on the basis of their clarity of purpose, internal coherence and consistency, ability to deal with details, and so on. The test of a method's adequacy to those criteria is not on the basis of the method's responsiveness to the multilevels at which music can function. Methods can develop or evolve in ways that are substantively different from certain levels of musical significance. Perhaps it is unrealistic to suppose that any method could be responsive to a database that generates information so varied that researchers from such divergent approaches as psychology, anthropology, phenomenology, formalism, and so on can each find a dimension or aspect for study. Only an eclectic method could move in the direction of a more comprehensive report. While such a method might not satisfy all of the possible approaches to musical objects, it may begin to interface approaches that have heretofore been dislocated from each other.

In order to construct a method of aesthetic inquiry that can be responsive to the multileveled thrust of musical significance, one must be in command of the theories of musical significance that undergird it. Answers to questions concerning musical significance traditionally have been thought to lie within two broad theoretical structures: formalism and expressionism. In formalism, as noted earlier, musical significance is limited to musical structure or syntax. In expressionism, theorists have concluded that in addition to musical syntax, human emotions and cultural insights crystallized and symbolized in some musical works must also be reported in aesthetic inquiry. A review of the plethora of theorists in each camp is beyond the scope of this chapter. However, delimitation is not so difficult. Certainly no formalist music theorist is more noteworthy than Leonard B. Meyer; likewise, Susanne K. Langer is probably the most-cited expressionist in music-education writings. Therefore, an overview of their theories of musical significance will be presented as models for the respective formalist and expressionist schools. As a counterpoint to that theoretical base, a section will follow on phenomenology and its uses in aesthetic inquiry. With this measured review of selected theories of musical significance, several levels or strata of musical significance will be identified. This combined theoretical base will then be used as a support for the construction of an eclectic method for aesthetic inquiry in music that will be responsive to the layers of musical significance articulated in the selected theories.

Leonard B. Meyer's Formalism

Meyer strives to explain the manner in which musical syntax causes emotional responses.[22] His interest in emotion may create hesitancy in categorizing his theory as formalist. Don't formalists dismiss emotion in music, while expressionists engage it? Yes, but Meyer's projection into the level of musical feeling is only on the basis of syntax; that is, Meyer is talking about an intellectual emotion. In this way, Meyer's work is analogous to the formalist theory in visual arts by Clive Bell, who notes that the very starting point for formalism in the arts is the experience of a particular emotion.[23] For Bell, that particular emotion is the experience of "significant form," which includes the lights and shadows, the lines, shapes, and sections of a visual work of art. Both Meyer and Bell are formalists who are committed to understanding emotional responses in music and art on the basis of the syntax, or grammar of art.

Meyer's theory of emotion is inspired by John Dewey's writings. Dewey maintains that emotion is aroused when a tendency to respond is interrupted.[24] Musical syntax is codified in different compositional styles. Educated listeners learn the underlying logic that supports that musical codification. Certain syntactical devices—progressions, developments, and so on—can act as musical stimuli and thereby arouse the expectation that a certain consequent musical event—a resolving chord, the return to a key center or theme—will occur. When a work simply follows the norms of the underlying musical system of codification, expectations are satisfied and there is no important emotional response. However, when the usual consequent is inhibited, emotion is aroused. Musical meaning, according to Meyer, occurs specifically when an expected consequent is arrested. Meaning is limited to syntax, however, because it is based solely on the relationship of musical fragments to other musical fragments. As one listens to a musical work unfold, earlier sections in the work provide a logical structure from which the educated listener expects a probable continuation and conclusion. In listening to a Haydn symphony, educated listeners do not expect to hear a twelve-tone row or a Romantic development of the second (rather than the first) theme during the Development section. Parameters of probable consequents are established by listeners as they listen and bring to bear their knowledge of the underlying codification of a style of writing within which Haydn's symphonies fit. Within the work itself, the meaning of a particular fragment is the expectation of a consequent fragment that it causes. When these "hypothetical meanings" are brought to closure as the piece develops, they become "evident meanings."[25] Evident musical meanings allow the listener to reconstruct the work and provide a fuller sense of the meaning of earlier hypothetical meanings based on their syntactical relationship to consequent meanings that have become evident. Thus, as one's intellectual understanding of musical syntax increases, real emotional responses (of an intellectual kind) are possible. Within this theoretical framework, Meyer has sought to undercut the bifurcation between formal and emotional meanings in music from the standpoint and on the basis of formalism.

Susanne K. Langer's Expressionism

Although Langer was highly critical of the excesses in nineteenth-century versions of expressionism (which placed the meaning and import of art in the composer's feelings and intentions), her aesthetic theory is expressionist insofar as her focus is on feeling. She concludes that music resembles the dynamics of human experiences. Music is the metaphorical image of actual life.[26] However, music is not "actual" life or feelings; music presents an image of life and feelings in a "virtual" form. Actual life provides compositional materials of a "proto-musical" kind. In actual life, or what Langer terms "living form," the raw materials for musical expression are available to composers. The cardinal characteristic of living form or everyday life is *rhythm*, which manifests in patterns such as permanence and change, growth and decay, stress, progression, rise and fall, release and rest.[27] Composers crystallize these dynamic proto-musical life-patterns during their compositional processes.[28] They transform the actual feelings and rhythms of life into musical form. Just as one can experience actual joy or grief in everyday life (living form), one can experience "virtual" joy or grief in musical form. Music doesn't present actual life; it is expressive of life. That is to say, music is the symbolic transformation of actual feelings into virtual feelings. Music is not sad. More correctly, music is expressive of sadness because it presents the concept of sadness. Langer's key insight is that in their processes of symbolic transformation, composers transform their knowledge of human feelings into the language of music.

An underlying theme in Langer's works, from *Philosophy in a New Key* (1942) to the third book of her trilogy, *Mind, An Essay on Human Feeling* (1982), is that music, a language system, is rational. At the time of the publication of *Philosophy in a New Key*, the conventional wisdom in analytic philosophy was that music is not a genuine language system because it is not presented in linguistic form. Only forms of knowledge that are expressed in language are truly rational. And since music does not follow the rules of discursivity (grammar) or provide the precision of genuine language systems (as in English, French, etc.), music is not rational. Langer challenged this view by noting that music, just like ordinary language, symbolizes the *concepts* of the things to which it refers. This projective power is inherent in both music and ordinary language. Ordinary language transforms actual things into symbols called words. For example, the word "computer" is not the same thing as a physical computer. The word "computer" is a symbol that anyone (who understands English) can comprehend. One does not need to have a computer present when hearing or reading the word because the word points to the *concept* of the thing represented. Thus, language gives man an abstractive ability that allows him to transcend things in their immediate presence and to refer instead to their analogous or corresponding concepts. Similarly, music, according to Langer, conveys the concept or logic of "living life." Instead of transforming the dynamics of "living life" and feeling into words, however, composers transform this sphere of the ineffable into music. And as noted earlier, in this transformed state, feelings are virtual, not actual.

According to Langer, music, understood as the metaphorical image of life, analogously symbolizes human feeling. This opens a new realm of experience. One can understand and experience the essence of grief in a musical/virtual form without actually feeling grief during a listening experience. This is because music presents only the concept or virtual form of grief, not actual grief. Thus, while ordinary language contains great combinative (grammatical) and literal power, music has the power of greater (than ordinary language) congruence to human feelings. The language of music more closely resembles the "morphology" of feeling. This morphology is exactly what ordinary language is incapable of substantively expressing. And given man's evolutionary power of symbolic transformation, when one symbol system (ordinary language) cannot adequately crystallize a domain of human experience and knowledge, another entrance (music and the other arts) is created and developed.[29] Langer concludes that the rationality of music, like poetry (which, due to its metaphorical nature, is not a genuine or ordinary language system) and the other arts, cannot be adjudicated on the basis of the rules of discursivity. Music, a nondiscursive language system, constitutes rules that are different from the rules of ordinary language.

What are the rules of the language of music? Langer, not a trained music analyst, cannot say in detail. The details of musical syntax must be distilled from a formalist account of music. The many varieties of Schenkerian analysis are currently the dominant type of formalism in the United States. At the same time, formal analyses do not consider music's referential potential to be expressive of the ineffable sphere of "living form." Researchers are faced with a dilemma marked by the choice of a theoretical basis that allows for either formal *or* referential data collection. This situation can be circumvented with a system of aesthetic inquiry that allows both levels of musical significance—form and reference—to be reported. But are there only these two levels of musical significance? There are at least two more levels: one more intrinsic level and one more referential level. Both of these two additional levels are not reported in traditional formal and referential approaches. One school of phenomenology, the Husserlian, provides a structure for describing the additional level of *intrinsic* musical significance, termed the "sound-in-time." A second school of phenomenology, the Heideggerian, is interested in a level of referential meaning that is termed "onto-historical" meaning. The presentation of the theoretical basis for each of these movements in phenomenology will provide a foundation for an eclectic inquiry into the multilevel nature of musical significance. However, given the limitations of space, no attempt will be made to incorporate methods for sociological, anthropological, or institutional analyses in the overall eclectic method constructed at the end of this chapter.

Edmund Husserl's Descriptive Phenomenology

Husserl (1859-1938) introduced phenomenology as a foundation for the natural and human sciences. Phenomenology would provide a methodology based on the absolutely verifiable foundations of immediate, conscious experience. Such an empirical philosophical method would have the rigor of science and would concomitantly have the conceptual means to provide the foundation for all knowledge. In the phenomenologist's direct investigation of phenomena, belief in theories and constructive interpretations are suspended in favor of the immediacy of what is directly given to consciousness. In keeping with his Kantian roots, Husserl maintained that researchers can transcend their own biases and ascertain the essential and necessary characteristics of objects under study.

Where does one's consciousness transcend to? It might be easier to answer first where, according to Husserl, consciousness should not transcend. Husserl attempted to formulate a philosophical position that would undercut both the rationalist account of knowledge (with roots in Plato—see chapter 3) and the idealist version. Like Heidegger, Husserl concluded that the rationalist movement caused a bifurcation between the mind and phenomena under study with the idea of a realm of pure knowledge that is not accessible through the immediate experience of things but only through acts of reason. For the phenomenologist, the rationalist approach dislocates consciousness from phenomena because one must insert a theory or "form" (as in Plato) through and by which phenomena-at-hand can be understood. This separation of the mind from the world culminates in Descartes's famous "mind-body" split. While Husserl hoped to remain close to objects, he didn't want to retreat fully from rationalism. He endeavored to maintain sufficient distance from objects so that his phenomenology would not be accused of subjectivism. Idealism was considered too subjective because in its stipulation that phenomena cannot be experienced separately from consciousness, the idealist position tends to posit a disproportionate focus on the knower as the center of knowledge, rather than the more "objective" realm of pure knowledge. What is interesting is that throughout Husserl's long career, he seems to oscillate between both movements, rationalism and idealism. He never successfully undercuts either position. The result is a phenomenology that derives characteristics from both schools but that ultimately leans more (and, for most philosophers, excessively) in the direction of idealism and its inherent subjectivism.

Husserl's early period of phenomenology (approximately from 1896 to 1905) is an attempt to overcome subjectivism or what was commonly referred to as "psychologism" in turn-of-the-century philosophical circles.[30] Husserl's response to psychologism took the form of his *Logical Investigations* (1900–1901), in which he demanded that researchers get "back to the things themselves" and out of the subjectivistic and psychologistic pitfalls of idealism. However, by 1913, his major work, *Ideas*, seems to fall into the very psychologism from which he tried to extricate philosophy in his earlier turn-of-the-century period. The focus of *Ideas* is consciousness, not things. In this book, Husserl presents his famous method of "phenomenological reduction."

The Phenomenological Reduction

There are at least two stages of the phenomenological reduction. The first stage is called the *epoche* or transcendental reduction; the second, the *eidetic* reduction. In the first stage, one must transcend ordinary perception and examine oneself perceiving. This act of abstraction is not difficult. Imagine playing in a baseball game and, during the game, thinking about the game and your perception of it. In the transcendental reduction one thinks about what one is perceiving at that instant. This shifts one's mode of orientation away from what Husserl calls the "natural attitude."[31] The natural attitude is marked by (1) a kind of animal faith in the fact that things are simply as they appear, requiring no special interest or description and (2) the habitual proclivity to be predisposed to things. This "natural" disinterest and prejudice toward things is suspended in the transcendental reduction. One turns inward toward consciousness and examines it. Distinguished from the psychological act of introspection, one engages one's process of conscious activity and phenomena that are engaged by that conscious activity in a realm or field termed the "transcendental ego." It is to transcendental consciousness that Husserl wishes the researcher to move. This is not the transcendental realm of pure concepts, divorced from consciousness, as in Plato's rationalism. There is a subject who is very present. But all sense of "mine" is, according to Husserl, canceled. The world has not changed; instead, the natural orientation that makes it "my" world has been bracketed. For Husserl, this act of transcendence objectifies consciousness by putting one's own subjectivity in check. Through this act of abstraction, one can hold on to consciousness and yet not be mired in its subjective nature. In this transcendental place of abstraction from things and consciousness, a "pure" consciousness or ego engages objects so that the objects can show themselves "purely." The result, Husserl notes, is unencumbered description and apodictic or certain knowledge. Before engaging the notion of the alleged "purity" of phenomenological description, the second stage of phenomenological reduction will be reviewed.

The transcendental reduction sets up a context in which one can carry out the second stage of phenomenological reduction. During the *eidetic* reduction, one performs a kind of free imaginary variation that includes imagining the object under study with and then without certain of its characteristics.[32] Characteristics that can be suspended without destroying the object are considered ancillary and are bracketed out of subsequent variations. Properties of phenomena that cannot be suspended without destroying the object itself are considered necessary or essential to the work. These invariant properties constitute the essence of *eidos* of the object. Thus, the *eidetic* reduction seeks to shed objects of all but their essential and defining structures. And because these essences were described by the transcendental ego, those descriptions are believed to be "pure" and apodictically true.

It is clear that whether one calls the activity of the mind "consciousness" or "transcendental consciousness," one is still working within one's own mind. Can one ever completely and purely transcend and thereby overcome one's own subjectivity? As demonstrated in chapter 3, even with the precise methodologies of science and a database comprised of the natural world, such purity and certainty of knowledge is probably not possible. One can agree that the power of abstraction in man allows him to transcend the immediacy of things. It is that very power of transcendence that is the ground for Langer's notion of symbolic transformation—the power to abstract from and transform experience into discursive and nondiscursive languages. But Langer never stipulates that symbolic transformation is pure or forever certain. No matter what level of abstraction one can bring to the study of anything, and regardless of whether one is doing research in natural science or music, it is doubtful that the power of immediate and empirical perception of data will reach Husserl's promise of immaculate perception.

Even if one accepted Husserl's notion of pure perception in principle, in the practice of aesthetic inquiry it would prove to be unattainable. That is the case because any research activity must ultimately be articulated to a readership in a language. Language forces consciousness out of its allegedly "pure" or transcendental ego status and into the role of mediator and transformer. At best, Husserl's phenomenology might allow a researcher to intuit phenomena purely. But the purity of that experience will be contaminated as soon as one translates it into language. Husserl's transcendental consciousness is ultimately trapped within itself. The knowledge it generates is not pure, but like knowledge generated in the natural sciences, is relative to one's method, the overall theoretical structure or paradigm that informs and grounds one's perception and methodology, the community of professionals to which one writes and subscribes, and ultimately, the limitations and interpretations that abide in the use of language.

For Husserl, the ultimate ground for all understanding is the transcendental ego. In spite of the power of abstraction, this realm remains in the subject. In Husserl's last period of writing (approximately from 1928 to 1938), he attempted to overcome what his critics interpreted as an unacceptable solipsism (a position that maintains that one's consciousness is the underlying justification for all knowledge). In his book *Cartesian Meditations,* Husserl answers that criticism with a formulation of how one's consciousness encounters other consciousnesses. Husserl concludes that one discovers one's own ego first and, through abstraction and empathy, one accounts for "others." Husserl's response to the indictment of solipsism is that one analogically accounts for "others" as "alter egos," grounded in one's *perception* of the reality of other egos and bodies.[33] But this account does not satisfy the critics because there is still only one real ego, "mine." All other egos are derived from "my" ego through association. So long as other egos remain derivative and dependent on one's own ego, the Cartesian image of the isolated monad, cut off from the world and even one's own body, remains the ground for Husserl's phenomenology. Can this approach still be of use to researchers in music and music education? Yes, it is useful because of Husserl's many insights concerning the impact of one's mode of orientation on knowledge-gathering activities and his writings on time.

A Phenomenological Account of Time

In 1905, Husserl provided an extensive description of time as experienced in consciousness.[34] Consciousness "intends" or directs its awareness toward things in time. The nature of temporality as it structures experiences is different from simple chronological time. When viewing a sculptural work from moment to moment, one accepts that the work remains the same work; one does not question its cross-temporal identity. According to Husserl, this is because consciousness retains past images of the piece of sculpture and, on the basis of those past images, expects that it will continue to be the same work of art. Husserl coins the terms "retention" and "protention" to name the respective acts of retaining and anticipating. Objects remain consistently the same in consciousness because (1) they actually remain physically the same in reality and (2) "protentions" are continuously being verified in consciousness as a result of congruence with past "retentions" concerning the same object.

Husserl utilizes the concepts of retention and protention to describe the inner flow of time that occurs when listening to a melody. He uses the metaphor of a comet traveling through space. The glistening tail of the comet represents past notes of the melody that have been retained in one's memory. The present is represented by the head of the comet, and the trajectory or "projectory" of the comet is analogous to "protending" or predicting where the comet or melody might go. During the playing of any melody (as in Meyer's concepts, "hypothetical" and "evident" meanings), during any "now" instant or point in the melody, notes heard earlier are retained in consciousness while one anticipates further development and closure. Thus, for the Husserlian phenomenologist, the manner in which sound occurs in time is of great importance in music analysis. One does not hear a melody as successive, dislocated notes but as a whole melody that is being constituted by consciousness in time. As one progresses through a melody (or work), protentions (future notes or phrases) become less and less protensive, then become present as "now" points and finally recede into the past. Perhaps most important is that during this entire experience of musical time, one experiences a melody (and an entire work) as one enduring whole.

Martin Heidegger's Interpretive Phenomenology

Heidegger was an assistant to Husserl at the University of Freiburg just after World War I. He embraced many of Husserl's phenomenological insights as articulated in *Logical Investigations* (1900—1901). However, like many other philosophers, he considered Husserl's most notable work, *Ideas*, to be a relapse into psychologism. In Heidegger's view, one does not begin with consciousness. One begins in the world, as a cultural and historical being.[35] From the horizon or context of one's world, one discovers and defines oneself. There is no transcendental realm in the world or in consciousness to which one can move for pure or perfect knowledge. Knowledge will always be relative to one's world. Hence, while Husserl contends that the phenomenological reductions enable investigators to describe phenomena purely, Heidegger denigrates the very notion of a pure description of anything. Instead of description, Heidegger notes that investigations are always interpretations that are relative to one's historical and cultural world, termed the "onto-historical" world. Husserl's attempt to transcend one's cultural biases through transcendental consciousness is viewed by Heidegger as another footnote to Descartes's bifurcation (into subject and object) of nature.

Heidegger provides a working definition of art that can be useful for aesthetic inquiry.[36] He suggests that all works of art have two fundamental elements: "earth" and "world." Earth represents the materials that constitute an artwork: the paint in a painting, the stone in a sculpture, the metal in an architectural work, the sound in music. Without materials, there would be no work of art. In his essay on the nature of art, Heidegger analyzes an ancient Greek temple. His description of the stone or earth in this temple does not report lines, balance, symmetry, or geometric shapes; earth must not be confused with artistic form. The earth of this temple is the "stoniness" of the stone and is more fundamental than form. Heidegger draws his concept of earth from the early Greek term *physis*. According to his interpretation, "physis," or the physical, is not comparable to the modern version of physical, inanimate nature. For the pre-Socratic Greeks, the physical earth was described as that which is emerging and rising within itself.[37] From this perspective, the work materials of art are described as emerging and rising up through the work. Paint is not neatly dissected into shapes and forms in Heidegger's brand of aesthetic inquiry but moves in the direction of a step back to the nature of work materials in artists' creative processes. During the creative process, the raw work materials are emerging and erupting with potential for the artist. That potential in the work materials to emerge and rise up remains in the finished artwork, according to Heidegger, although rarely do critics and researchers uncover this dynamic element in art. In fact, Heidegger maintains that the presence of an emerging and dynamic character of a work's materials is one prerequisite for something to be called art. This is to say, it is one of the essential and defining characteristics for art to be art. Accordingly, during aesthetic inquiry, one must not look or listen beyond this level of artistic and musical significance. In music, this level of significance is close to what Husserlians term the "sound-in-time," as presented above.

An example may be helpful. Imagine that you are walking up a long path toward a Greek temple. In your path there are a few rocks that you push out of the way without serious thought. On the path, there is a stone bench upon which you sit for a few moments of rest. Again, there is no active engagement of the nature of the stone in the bench; you simply use the bench for sitting. Finally you arrive at the Greek temple and you are captivated by the stone that constitutes this great edifice: this is stone that has been durable for more than two millennia and that preserves this place of religion and art. Further imagine that the stones in the path and the stone in the bench were of the same type as that in the temple. Why is it that the viewer appreciates the stone in the temple but not in its other forms? Dickie would say that it is because of the institutional setting: people are trained to appreciate artworks and disregard the aesthetic qualities of ordinary stones and benches. Dickie's point is well taken. But Heidegger claims that there is something else at work in artworks. The emerging and "rising up" character of the work materials is preserved in the work of art because of a second element, the world.

By world, Heidegger means the onto-historical world of the composer or creator of the artwork. If the world were only that of nature, one could simply call it "the world." Because mankind brings meaning to the physical world, the world is marked by significance. The onto-historical world is the cultural and historical reality that contextualizes persons who make up that world. The onto-historical world is not some physical entity. It is the ideational space in and through which people live and relate. That ideational context or "ontology" is ever-changing. As events unfold in history, they often have a great impact on the manner in which people define and understand themselves. The French Revolution and World War I are events that dramatically changed the respective ontological settings for Western culture. Heidegger's insight is that in manipulating work materials (the earth), a composer sets a sense of his onto-historical world into his work. Thus, for Heidegger, art can disclose the most profound realities of an onto-historical people. And as in his depiction of earth, Heidegger describes the world as a dynamic happening that occurs in works of art. His statements on "the world worlds" or "the world worlding" convey the inner energy and synergy in art in which the world of the composer erupts through the earth as a dynamic event. The world is characterized as an "openness" and a "spaciousness"; it is not a physical entity. Unlike the physical earth, the world of the composer as set into the work of art is ideational. Thus, Heidegger's use of "world" in art refers to the setting in the artwork of a sense of the onto-historical context that surrounds the composer and is in the spirit, mind, value system, and meaning of that historical and cultural people. Without grounding in art, as that onto-historical world changes, it is lost. Thus, artworks "hold open" the "openness" of the world of the composer. Art "makes space for" the onto-historical world and thereby preserves it in the physicality of the work's earth.

While the earth sustains and makes durable the world, the world is responsible for opening up the earth and letting it be an earth, that is, material that can be experienced as emerging and "rising up." Recall the example of the stones in the path and the bench. Those materials remained closed to inspections because they were utilized simply by kicking or sitting. However, in the case of the temple, the world of an ancient Greek people which has been erected in that artwork caused the viewer to see the stone as stone for the first time. The stone has not been "used up" in the temple but has been "opened up." As a result of the onto-historical world set into the earth materials, those materials "come forth for the very first time."[38] Thus, there is a marriage of earth and world in works of art in which the earth provides durability and sustenance for the ideational and finite world and the world provides an openness that allows the earth to come forth as a "rising up" and emerging material. The earth grounds the world and the world juts up through the earth, with each carrying the other further than each alone could have gone. It is this dynamic interaction between these seemingly opposite elements that causes a work *to be* a work.

According to Heidegger, the coming together of the ideational world and the physical earth is marked by a "strife"instigated by the work of art and preserved by the viewer/listener. It is in that strife that each element, the earth and the world, moves beyond its isolated potential. Ordinary materials have the proclivity to close to inspection because they "disappear into usefulness" when persons engage them in the ordinary utilitarian or what Husserl calls natural ways. At the same time, the world of meanings and significances that mark any historical people is not confined to some physical space but remains in the ideas (that is, in the ideational realm) of that people. Given Heidegger's definition of art, both elements are radically altered in the artwork. The earth is forced to "open" by the openness that characterizes the world and the world is forced into the physically confining space of the work materials or earth. This is a strife that is never brought to closure but that lives in the work and generates its dynamic character. Thus, for Heidegger, the nature of art is that it is a "happening," an active and propelling event in which the earth and the world struggle against the imposition of each on the other. Consequently, the term "art" in this usage changes from the name of a static category or a collection of a certain type of physical objects to the underlying dynamic process unleashed by the strife between earth and world. The statement, art *happens* in the work of art, conveys this active and dynamic definition of art.

For *art* to happen, it must be appreciated. A painting hanging in a darkened museum or music used to stay awake in a car are not works of art under Heidegger's definition. The strife between the earth and the world is possible only if an appreciating person allows that strife to show itself. A method of aesthetic inquiry must enable the researcher to engage these levels of significance. Such a method would not stop at formal elements but would step back to a report of the earth understood as the "sound-in-time." Moreover, researchers must allow themselves to be transported into the world of the artist. In so doing, a researcher stands in the "openness" of the work and thereby preserves the world of the artist.[39] However, that transportation will be relative to one's own cultural and historical world. Researchers keep their feet in the Western cultural world of the late twentieth century as they remain open to other onto-historical worlds. This act of "preserving" the work of art by its appreciators is judged by Heidegger to be as essential as that of the creator. Without composers there cannot be musical works. But *art* cannot *happen* in the artwork unless art is preserved in a way that allows both its earth and world to be experienced in their dynamic strife. This definition of art as a dynamic happening signals the need for an eclectic method that is responsive to the multidimensional thrust that music is capable of providing.

An Eclectic Method for Aesthetic Inquiry into Music

It may be helpful to recapitulate the levels of musical significance uncovered during the review of theories of musical significance above. One level of musical significance is form or syntax. Another level, termed the "sound-in-time," is investigated and described by phenomenologists of the Husserlian school.[40] For this level of significance, the structures of musical time can be examined in terms of properties such as duration, level structure, temporal modes, articulation, and organic relationships.[41] Heidegger's insights into the earth of musical works also help to identify and clarify this level. A third level of musical significance (one that tends to be obvious) in program music can be called "representation." At this level, music can represent events that are extrinsic to the music. A specific piece of music that presents an obvious level of musical representation is Tchaikovsky's *1812 Overture*. Langer uncovered the fourth level in her discussion of virtual feeling. For her, music captures the conceptual essence of human emotions symbolically transformed into sound and syntax. Heidegger provides still another referential level, one that has been termed the "onto-historical world." Thus, there are at least five levels of musical significance—the "sound-in-time," syntax (form), representation, virtual feeling, and onto-historical world—that the proposed eclectic method must effectively engage. Additionally, there are many other strata of musical significance—sociological, ethnomusicological, and institutional—that will not be included. Any system of inquiry for musical significance can provide the researcher only with a partial view of that significance.

The first step in this method is to place the piece and the composer in music historical time. One should present an overview of the life of the composer, his or her overall corpus, and the relationship of the composer's works to other works during that period, and finally move toward a presentation of the work or works that are the focus of the study.

The second step is called "open listenings." During these initial listenings and readings of the score, one becomes oriented to the various levels of musical significance in a preliminary manner. Whenever the word *listenings* is used in the remainder of this chapter, it is understood to indicate listening both with and without the score. This step helps to satisfy the phenomenological principle of allowing the work to show itself. One responds to any level of significance that unfolds. At this point in the method, the historical data reported in step one are suspended (through step seven) to whatever degree that is possible. No attempt is made to compare the work under study to any other works until step eight of this method.

In step three, a method for formal analysis (for example, Schenker, LaRue, Piston, Reti, or Meyer) is implemented. The choice of method will depend on the researcher's expertise and the requirements of the piece under study. The language used to explain musical syntax must be within the guidelines of the formal system: graphs for Schenker, Roman numerals for Piston, time lines for LaRue, and a literal narrative style when providing prose statements. Nonformal data (the "sound-in-time" or any level of musical reference) that was reported during step two must be temporarily (but not absolutely) suspended during step three in order to maintain the integrity of each formal system. The researcher should endeavor to disallow phenomenological data from bleeding into the formal analysis at this point in the method. Although later there is interfacing of data, the initial formal analysis must remain strictly syntactical.

In step four, one performs a phenomenological description of the "sound-in-time." One attempts to suspend non-phenomenological data collected in the previous steps. Husserlian phenomenologists do not collect referential data. Instead, they deal directly with what they consider to be the empirically verifiable "sound-in-time." No attempt is made to engage the onto-historical world of the composer in phenomenological description of the Husserlian type. The nature of the language used in phenomenological analysis can be more poetic than in the literal language of formal analysis. Thus, within the overall eclectic method, there is a loosening, during step four, of the literal and mostly direct sign language (graphs and Roman numerals) that characterizes step three. To hear the "sound as such" is something like the suggestion by Roman Ingarden that one stratum of significance in a literary work of art is constituted by pure "word sounds."[42] In hearing words as unalloyed phonemes, one attempts to ignore referential meanings and step back to a point that is more fundamental than syntax. Unadulterated "word sounds" may give the literary critic a sense of the flowing quality or perhaps the jagged texture of a text which would not be evident without such a hearing. This kind of listening may have been more the domain of very highly trained and sensitive musicians. Great performers carefully attend to the sound of their tone. They are able to distinguish between syntax (the sound in form) and the "sound-in-time." When performers monitor their sound within the flow of musical time, they approach the exclusive momentary suspension of a sense of syntax and reference. This kind of listening is close to the manner in which a descriptive phenomenologist listens and then describes. Unlike a musical performer, who moves simultaneously through many levels of musical significance, during steps three and four, the researcher must focus on a single stratum of significance. This permits that stratum to be what it is more purely (but not apodictically). The resultant explanation of musical syntax (in step three) and the description of the "sound-in-time" (in step four) have greater clarity and focus because of the demarcation and restriction of the type of data being collected in each step.

In step five, the first of three levels of referential meanings is investigated. Some musical works have no obvious representation, as in abstract forms such as the sonata. One would simply report that in the work under study (perhaps a Mozart symphony), there is no program or obvious representation. However, while obvious representation tends to be the least compelling level of significance, it is necessary to report its presence in the analysis of program music. A program may have been preliminarily reported in the open listenings of step two but during those listenings the analyst remains open to any level of significance. The program may require more systematic analysis. Step five ensures that if a program is present, it is fully reported. During this step, if the work has a text, a suitable method of literary criticism is implemented. A method of literary criticism is particularly crucial if the text is a poem. Ingarden[43] and E. D. Hirsch[44] offer helpful approaches.

Musical representation is located at this point in the eclectic method because it functions at a referential level of meaning. After step two (open listenings), steps three (formal analysis) and four (phenomenological description) each deal with *intrinsic* data. That is, form and the "sound-in-time" are intrinsic dimensions of music. As such, these levels of data can be corroborated empirically. However, as one moves to referential levels, the strength and clarity of empirical corroboration tend to become strained. Of the three referential levels singled out in the eclectic method, representation is the easiest to corroborate. Hearing the French national anthem during the *1812 Overture* is a clear representation of the presence of the French army. Not all representations are that obvious, but this remains a level of reference that is less thorny than the interpretations of "virtual feeling" and "onto-historical world."

Step six calls for the report of virtual feeling. Music can express happiness, joy, sadness, excitement, anxiety, turmoil, tranquility, and so on. In interpreting virtual feelings, the researcher must be careful not to dominate the work. The actual feelings that one experiences when listening to a work are secondary. It is the apprehension of knowledge of the symbolic transformation of feeling into the language of music that is the mission of this step. It is easy for a researcher to submit to his or her feelings. In order to guard against the potential undue subjectivism in this kind of data collection, the researcher must attempt to ground, that is, corroborate, each referential insight concerning virtual feeling in the "sound-in-time" or the syntax. It is not enough to speak of excitement; one must ground that feeling in an intrinsic level of musical significance. That is to say that one must be able to discover what, in the intrinsic elements, are the reasons for the proposed expression of a virtual feeling. Only intrinsic levels of significance can provide a sufficient measure of empirical adequacy. These acts of corroboration, in the form of bridging referential meanings to intrinsic elements, provide the first systematic interfacing of levels in the overall eclectic method. Data from steps two, three, four, and possibly five become the basis for clarifying and retaining referential data collected in step six. The style of the language utilized continues to be poetic but is also mixed with the literalness of the formal data from step three, which are used to support the referential findings in step six.

In step seven, the researcher engages the presence of the onto-historical world of the composer. If one accepts Heidegger's definition of art, one must respond to the potential in musical works to exemplify and ground a composer's "world." The musical work makes a "new space" in sound for the composer's knowledge and experience of his or her world. The literary style of the report can be highly poetic during this step. Insofar as works of art are metaphorical, their significance is not limited to sound or syntax but radiates outward into musical reference. Indeed, symbolic power is substantiated by the referential meanings that grow from a work. Insofar as the work is a symbol, the researcher must look through it to its referential messages. Given this metaphorical nature and strength of music, analyses of referential levels of musical meaning must also have the power to project. A purely literal language style cannot adequately respond to referential meanings because it lacks the projective power of metaphorical or poetic language. Just as a musical work's symbolific mission is to project meanings into an ideational space, so must the analysis radiate out beyond the confines of literal language. In the dual projections of the musical work and the analysis, both may *intersect*. That intersection is the principal criterion for evaluating referential analyses. That is, an analysis of referential meaning in music is successful to the degree to which it intersects with the work's projective (i.e., referential or metaphorical) meanings. One cannot stipulate that analyses of referential meanings are correct or incorrect with the precision acquired by the use of formal systems. The most positive metacritical evaluation that one could direct to analyses of referential meanings is that the analyses are expressive of and congruent to those meanings.

Flights of fantasy must be avoided during step seven. It is easy for an analyst to "image-process" away from the work and simply use the music to substantiate or clarify some social, political, or historical account of the world that surrounds the composer.[45] If these extramusical data in fact grow from the music itself, then they should be reported in this step. However, a difference in one's mode of orientation is noteworthy: in one approach, music is used as a paradigm example; one imposes on the work a prescribed picture of the world that surrounds its creation. In the second approach, one allows the music to show itself first. Then, on the basis of that responsive involvement, the researcher reports onto-historical data. The first approach is marked by dominance of the work, the second by responsiveness to the work. As in step six, interfacing data from previous steps continues. Each onto-historical datum must be grounded in the "sound-in-time" or the syntax and can be informed by insights into virtual feeling reported in step six as well.

Step eight is marked by a return to the open listening process. As in step two, any level of musical significance—"sound-in-time," syntax, representation, virtual feeling or onto-historical world—can be reported. In addition, the researcher can bring historical data collected in step one to bear upon the analysis. One permits all of the strata to interact but there is a notable difference between these open listenings and those in step two. As a result of the systematic analysis of each stratum (during steps three through seven), each level of musical significance features a degree of autonomy, clarity and fullness that was not the case in the earlier open listenings. At the same time, they all remain a part of the whole piece. This innate circularity in the eclectic method is a strength because after separating the levels of the "sound-in-time" and syntax, according to the protocols of the respective methods, a partial synthesis of all levels begins with the analysis of virtual feeling (step six) and onto-historical world (step seven). But in steps six and seven, the focus remains on referential levels. In step eight, all of the levels are more freely allowed to interact. Referential insights enrich and make more profound syntactical data as the latter ground and clarify referential meanings. Like the voices in a fugue, each level is independent yet dependent and homogeneous with the others. In this set of open listenings, the work can present itself as a polyphonic texture of dimensions of musical meaning. Each level remains perceptibly distinctive, yet interweaves with the others as part of the enduring, whole work.

In step nine, a performance guide is presented. The researcher need not have to be an accomplished performer in order to write such a guide. The systematic analyses of the multilevels of significance that precede this step in the eclectic analysis provide the researcher with a broad and yet detailed account of the work. From that perspective and knowledge base, the researcher is in a strong position from which to suggest performance interpretations. If the researcher is an accomplished performer on the instrument for which the piece is composed, then he or she can also suggest technical and physical approaches and insights that might make his or her interpretive insights more easily implemented. But that performance accomplishment is not mandatory for the execution of step nine.

Step ten is entitled "metacritique." Here the researcher must discuss the impact of the inherent strengths and weaknesses in the eclectic method of the first nine steps of the analysis. The criterion of technical correctness may be brought to bear concerning the historical data presented during step one and the syntactical data presented in step three. However, to the degree that music functions as a symbol, the articulation of a quantitative correlation of correspondence truth between musical metaphor and a poetic analysis is not forthcoming. The evaluation of analyses of referential levels must utilize other criteria: organicity and fecundity. An analysis is *organic* if it remains grounded in the work itself. Referential data must grow from the soil of musical "sound-in-time" and syntax. Moreover, if the analysis spawns further insights into and understanding of this work, it is worthwhile or *fecund*. Step ten requires the researcher to study and evaluate his or her own theoretical position in order to extend and improve it. Such a metacritical stance toward one's own theoretical position as it impacts on the practice of musical analysis is an instance of theory and practice at its best.

As a summary in outline form, the foci of the ten steps in the eclectic method are as follows:

1. Historical Background
2. Open Listenings

3. Syntax
4. The Sound-in-Time
5. Musical and Textual Representation
6. Virtual Feeling
7. Onto-historical Context
8. Open Listenings
9. Performance Guide
10. Metacritique[46]

Conclusions

There are a number of different methods of aesthetic inquiry. Each is predisposed to one level of musical significance. Insofar as methods must prescribe the tasks that a researcher performs, each method automatically delimits musical significance to the level that is the focus of those tasks. Those tasks are most often for the sake of the method, not for a comprehensive and multilayered report. This places the researcher, through the method, in a dominant position over and against the musical work. In order to "switch roles," one must allow the music to direct the questioning. Aesthetic inquiry can provide researchers with methods that enable them to be responsive to music yet remain rigorously systematic. Although the motto of phenomenology, "back to the things themselves," points to a responsive methodology, Husserlian phenomenological accounts of music (as in the other approaches discussed in this chapter) focus on a singular dimension of significance, the "sound-in-time." Heidegger's aesthetic inquiries are an exception to that singularity, in that he reports two levels of significance. His definition of art responds to the dynamic relationship between musical sound and reference, between the "earth" and the "world." However, he does not adequately account for musical syntax or a factualist (as distinguished from an ontological) historical overview. Only an eclectic method can begin to be responsive to the multidimensional thrust of musical significance.

The eclectic method proposed in this chapter has undergone steady development by Ferrara[47] and has been implemented in many studies.[48] The formulation and evolution of this method concretize the attempt to balance responsiveness with methodological prescription. The researcher must carry on a genuine dialogue with the work. This dialogical process is marked by being open to the musical object. Nevertheless, the eclectic method delineates what data will be collected, when they will be collected (within the overall method), and how they will be collected. As a broad construct, this method structures historical, syntactical, phenomenological, formal, representational, virtual emotional, and onto-historical data collection and treatment. Several categories of data are omitted: sociological, psychological, ethnomusicological, and institutional. Thus, even the proposed eclectic method delimits data. The ambition of this chapter, however, goes beyond the specific eclectic method presented. The assertion of the need for methodological eclecticism in response to the requirements of musical significance is the key message in this chapter. Eclectic methodology will support aesthetic inquiry marked by the *balance* of technical control and responsiveness, perception and conception, logical reasoning and the imagination.

Problems for Review and Discussion

1. What is the meaning of "aesthetics"? Of "aesthetic inquiry"?
2. Give the meaning of and characteristics of these approaches to aesthetic inquiry: formalist, psychological, phenomenological, institutionalism.
3. What is the difference between an art object and an aesthetic object?
4. What constitutes Leonard B. Meyer's concept of formalism?
5. What is the crux of Susanne K. Langer's concept of expressionism?
6. What is the focus of Edmund Husserl's descriptive phenomenology?
7. How does Martin Heidegger's interpretive phenomenology differ from Husserl's descriptive phenomenology?
8. Identify the ten steps of the eclectic method for aesthetic inquiry into music, as discussed in this chapter. Give an example of each one.

Supplementary Sources

Beardsley, Monroe C. *Aesthetics: Problems in the Philosophy of Criticism*. Indianapolis: Hackett Press, 1981.
_____. *The Aesthetic Point of View*. Michael J. Wreen and Donald M. Callen, eds. Ithaca, N.Y.: Cornell University Press, 1982.

_____. "Understanding Music," in Kingsley Price, ed., *On Criticizing Music, Five Philosophical Perspectives.* Baltimore: The Johns Hopkins University Press, 1981.

Budd, Malcolm. *Music and the Emotions: The Philosophical Theories.* London: Routledge and Kegan Paul, 1985.

Coker, Wilson. *Music and Meaning, A Theoretical Introduction to Musical Aesthetics.* New York: The Free Press, 1972.

Cook, Nicholas. *A Guide to Musical Analysis.* New York: George Braziller, 1987.

Dufrenne, Mikel. *The Phenomenology of Aesthetic Experience.* Edward S. Casey, trans. Evanston, Ill.: Northwestern University Press, 1973.

Epperson, Gordon. *The Musical Symbol: A Study of the Philosophical Theory of Music.* Ames: Iowa State University Press, 1967.

Ferrara, Lawrence. *Philosophy and Music Analysis Bridges to Sound, Form, and Reference.* Westport, Conn.: Greenwood Press, 1990.

Goodman, Nelson. *Languages of Art.* Indianapolis: Hackett Press, 1976.

Gurney, Edward. *The Power of Sound,* 1893; New York: Basic Books, Inc., 1966.

Hanslick, Edward. *The Beautiful in Music,* 1891; Gustave Cohen, trans. Morris Weitz, ed. New York: The Liberal Arts Press, 1957.

Ingarden, Roman. *The Work of Music and the Problem of Its Identity.* Adam Czerniawski, trans. Jean Harrell, ed. Berkeley: University of California, 1986.

Kaelin, Eugene F. *Art and Existence: A Phenomenological Aesthetics.* Lewisburg, Pa.: Bucknell University Press, 1970.

Kivy, Peter. *The Corded Shell, Reflections on Musical Expression.* Princeton, N.J.: Princeton University Press, 1980.

_____. *Sound and Semblance, Reflections on Musical Representation.* Princeton, N.J.: Princeton University Press, 1984.

Lipman, Matthew. *Contemporary Aesthetics.* Boston: Allyn and Bacon, 1973.

Margolis, Joseph. *Art and Philosophy, Conceptual Issues in Aesthetics.* London: The Harvestor Press, 1980.

Merleau-Ponty, Maurice. *The Visible and the Invisible.* Alfonse Lingus, trans. Evanston, Ill.: Northwestern University Press, 1968.

Meyer, Leonard B. *Music, the Arts and Ideas.* Chicago: The University of Chicago Press, 1967.

Smith, F. Joseph. *In Search of Musical Method*. New York: Gordon and Breach, 1976.

———. *The Experiencing of Musical Sound, Prelude to a Phenomenology of Music*. New York: Gordon and Breach, 1979.

Spiegelberg, Herbert. *The Phenomenological Movement, A Historical Introduction*. The Hague: Martinus Nijhoff Publishers, 1982.

Weitz, Morris. *Philosophy of the Arts*. New York: Russell and Russell, 1950.

5. Qualitative Research: Concepts and Techniques

Educational research is built largely on research paradigms associated with experimental psychology. However, over the past three decades, qualitative research paradigms have steadily gained entry into educational research. Qualitative research is known by many names, including *ethnographic, naturalistic, subjective*, and *postpositivistic*. Method for this approach has its roots in the ethnographic research designs developed by anthropologists and sociologists. Ethnographies are reports about cultural contexts or groups. They report, as comprehensively as possible, the totality of the database from the viewpoint of the subjects under study. Assuming the viewpoint of the group being studied requires that the researcher empathize with that group. Ethnographic research is empirical and takes place in the setting under study; data are acquired firsthand. Statements by subjects are often taped, transcribed and then studied critically in order to uncover patterns or themes that are congruent to the actual living context from which they were extrapolated. Consequently, most of the data collection in qualitative research is performed during fieldwork.

Qualitative research utilizes two primary data-gathering tools for fieldwork: participant observation and interview. Both tools are marked by the centrality of the researcher as a data-gathering and -analyzing instrument. In response to that centrality, the first topic covered in this chapter is a consideration of the uniquely explicit prominence of the researcher in much qualitative research. Next, an overview of some of the basic strategies involved in field research will be presented. This is followed by more detailed accounts of the research techniques involved in participant observation and interview. After collecting data in the field through observation and interview, the researcher must make sense of his or her notes. To that end, guidelines for analyzing data and drawing conclusions are presented in the next section of this chapter.

An additional but optional step in qualitative research is indicated by the code word *evaluation*. Evaluation connotes specific protocols that do not have to be addressed in qualitative research. For example, most qualitative evaluation studies require a judgment and recommendation as to whether the program or data site should continue to operate or exist. This is not the case with qualitative research, which tends to limit its purview to data collection, description, analysis and the development of theory. Thus, qualitative research and qualitative evaluation are not necessarily synonymous. Clearly, all research studies include some element of evaluation, but this use of the term is so generic that it misses the specificity of the term as it is used in *qualitative evaluation* in education. One can suggest that qualitative evaluation is subsumed under qualitative research. Evaluation is based on the collected data, descriptions, and analyses in qualitative research. But to repeat, "evaluating" the educational setting for the purpose of supporting or rejecting its continuance, or in order to suggest tactics for improving activities performed by an organization or group, is not required in qualitative research. This step is associated with qualitative evaluation.

Consequently, after presentation of guidelines for analyzing data and drawing conclusions in qualitative research, some of the protocols associated with qualitative evaluation are presented toward the end of this chapter. Finally, several remarks about the relationship between quantitative and qualitative research complete the chapter. Accordingly, the following topics will be covered:

1. The Researcher as Instrument
2. Strategies for Field Research
3. Participant Observation
4. Interview
5. Data Analysis
6. Drawing Conclusions
7. Qualitative Evaluation

The Researcher as Instrument

Within qualitative research is a tradition whereby the principal research instrument is the researcher. It is unusual from the viewpoint of quantitative designs to think of the researcher as the primary instrument for data collection and analysis. Egon Guba and

Yvonna Lincoln suggest several characteristics that qualitative researchers manifest in their role as primary instruments:[1]

1. Responsiveness
2. Adaptability
3. Holistic Emphasis
4. Knowledge-Base Expansion
5. Processual Immediacy
6. Opportunities for Clarification and Summarization
7. Opportunity to Explore Atypical or Idiosyncratic Responses

Guba and Lincoln point out that the phenomenological character (see chapter 4 of this text) of qualitative data-gathering can be seen in the characteristic of *responsiveness*. Responsiveness is a mode of orientation toward data that is distinguished by the phenomenological stance of "letting an object show itself for its own sake." However, this is not the neutral phenomenological attitude espoused by Edmund Husserl. Instead, qualitative researchers must *interact* with data. If one is studying a group of high-school teachers, for instance, not only must one respond to their signals, suggestions, and motives; one must also provide prompts and suggestions to the group. One interacts with the group in order to create the necessary atmosphere in which the group can give its own account of its situation on personal terms. Within this dynamic interaction with the group under study, the qualitative researcher does not seek to exert precise methodological controls.[2] Thus, the demand for a neutral researcher, in both classical phenomenology (of the Husserlian brand) and many conventional methods of educational research, is repudiated. Responsiveness, more in keeping with a Heideggerian interpretive stance, is based on interaction, not neutrality.

Adaptability, the second characteristic, indicates the capability in the human instrument of adjusting spontaneously and creatively to different types of data. Guba and Lincoln note that, while conducting an unstructured interview, the researcher may uncover ancillary data that may be of considerable importance in understanding the person or group being interviewed. During such an interview, the researcher may register the aesthetic tastes of the respondent(s) by viewing their room(s), office(s), or general environment.[3] The researcher is not limited to the specific data collected in the interview; auxiliary data are limited only by the researcher's sensitivity to their presence and potential weight. Accordingly, the researcher simultaneously must deal with the multiplicity of levels of direct data. Adaptability points to the multipurpose character of qualitative researchers. This quality is paramount. Much qualitative research does not begin with a specific hypothesis. One often enters the research process with a methodology, a chosen data site, and a general sense of where that research may go. Adaptability is necessary in order for the researcher to investigate a context until issues and patterns become concretized.

The third characteristic of the qualitative researcher as primary instrument, *holistic emphasis*, is related to adaptability. The limit of testing constructs in the human instrument is measured by the inventiveness of both the researcher and the respondents.[4] Holistic emphasis points to the ability to see beyond a delimited topic to its overall context. Respondents in a study are interpreted from the standpoint that they are part of a world that provides a context which defines the meanings of their activities and lives. Data that might be collected in response to holistic emphasis are analogous to the levels of "virtual feeling" and "onto-historical world" discussed in chapter 4 in this book (see the section on "Aesthetic Inquiry and Musical Significance"). Traditionally, educational researchers tend to dislocate these contextual and existential aspects of research entities because of the near impossibility of managing the inherently confounding variables in such data, that is, of exerting some control. However, in the qualitative researcher's responsive approach, if such data are collected in the field, then he or she must adapt the research design to that more holistic context. As in the eclectic method presented in the previous chapter, more directly observed data (which might be analogous to musical syntax as well as the "sound-in-time") can be enriched and embellished by a responsiveness to their overall emotional and onto-historical context (described as eclectic musical analysis). Similarly, more directly observable data may help to define and ground these less conventional and somewhat existential areas of the database. Interfacing of directly perceived and conceived data types can enrich the study, although the researcher may risk losing precision and control as he or she moves from directly observable entities to existential concerns. To carry the analogy with eclectic music analysis further, as the researcher moves through the investigation of several levels of musical significance and reaches the eighth step in the method, "open listenings," he or she is able to respond to the multiplicity of levels of musical significance simultaneously. Each level stands out independently because of the earlier individual analysis of each level. Moreover, the orientation of "openness" on the part of the researcher enables each level to interact with the others as parts of a whole. A similar multiplicity of dimensions of meaning can be achieved by qualitative researchers if their responsive attitude provides a research setting that allows them to adapt to the observation of several levels of data simultaneously. This would result in the kind of holistic emphasis that Guba and Lincoln prescribe.

Guba and Lincoln also suggest that holistic emphasis points to the ethnographic demand for the researcher to understand statements and issues articulated by the respondents within their own frame of reference. However, they retreat from the requirement of sociologists and anthropologists, who have formulated ethnographic procedures, to become a living part of the culture in which the research is being performed. Thus, an educational researcher conducting research in an inner city slum may not have to live there in order to achieve effective qualitative research. Instead, he or she must keep within sight the life-world of the educational setting. In so doing, the more directly observable educational phenomena may be enriched by the holistic context in which they occur.

Another quality is the ability to investigate subconscious experiences; that is, what Guba and Lincoln term *knowledge base expansion*, their fourth point. Discursive or propositional knowledge is usually defined as that knowledge which can be articulated through speaking or in written language. Many writers, including philosopher Michael Polanyi,[5] have explored a realm of knowledge that is pre-propositional. Anyone can recall an experience of knowing something intuitively without explicitly articulating that knowledge in language. Guba and Lincoln note that qualitative researchers must be open not only to their own "tacit knowledge" but also to that of their respondents. Responding to this realm of knowledge may enable the researcher to connect propositional data to the life-world that helps to situate the holistic context of the database.

Guba and Lincoln's fifth characteristic, *processual immediacy*, is the researcher's power to process data instantly as received, screen the data and, as a result of that instantaneous distillation, make an almost immediate modification or variation in the direction of the investigation.[6] Guba and Lincoln note that such decisions for modification are best made at a distance from the site of data collection. However, given the relative flexibility in the human instrument, in comparison to formal tests in more traditional research designs, data collection processes and directions are often refined in the field. While conventional questionnaires cannot be changed in midcollection, qualitative researchers often alter their inquiries based on clearly determined evaluations (albeit qualitative) that provide justification for such changes. This allows them to accommodate data that cast a new light on the overall database. Guba and Lincoln assert that the ability of the human instrument to redirect inquiry increases the reliability and validity of qualitative research. The ability to immediately process and respond to data through adaptation to the database is a great strength of the researcher as primary instrument. While there is a clear connection between processual immediacy and adaptability, they remain distinct. As a result of the ability to *process* data instantaneously, one may choose to adapt the inquiry to new themes, issues and patterns.

When performing an interview, the researcher has *opportunities for clarification and summarization*, the sixth point. When a respondent makes a statement, the interviewer can ask the interviewee to clarify or embellish it. In this way, during an open or unstructured interview, a qualitative researcher can examine and penetrate the meaning of a respondent's answers. This is not so practicable when utilizing written questionnaires which, by their construction, do not allow for any meaningful modification of the inquiry based upon the responses received. Summarization, according to Guba and Lincoln, serves three purposes.[7] First, it allows the researcher to check his or her data collection with the interviewee. Second, summarization is a way to "get the informant on record." The informant can choose to take issue with previously collected data or not. Of course, summarization does not guarantee that informants are being honest; it just increases the chance of expressing their intent. Nevertheless, this tactic can add credibility to such data. Finally, information that has been neglected (by the respondent) or excluded (by the researcher) can be added to the compilation.

Guba and Lincoln cite L. A. Dexter, who notes that standardized interviews and typical surveys handle atypical responses statistically.[8] There does not seem to be a way for standardized tests to *explore atypical or idiosyncratic* (or "elite") respondents effectively, Guba and Lincoln's last point. The human inquirer can obtain "inside" information more effectively than a test by placing himself or herself in a position that allows for the observation and/or interview of atypical, special, or "elite" respondents. Such data may be entrapped by the formulistic structure of a standardized instrument. The data collected from such individuals may significantly enlarge or alter the boundaries of the inquiry. With the strength of a responsiveness (that written survey questionnaires may not have) to such deviations in the database, one can, through processual immediacy, instantaneously modify the direction of the inquiry. Through such adaptation, the researcher as instrument broadens the boundaries of his or her inquiry in a manner that will accommodate the need for holistic emphasis in qualitative research.

Strategies for Field Research

John Lofland and Lyn Lofland delineate several aspects of qualitative field research.[9] Many of those aspects, which in some cases define steps in the process, are summarized below. While the following section—comprised of a delineation and description of those seven steps—uses much of Lofland and Lofland's overall format, the discussion is not limited to their purview. These steps are as follows:

1. Selection of a research topic
2. Selection of an appropriate data site
3. Gaining access to the data site
4. Getting along with the members of the group under study
5. Recording data
6. Validating data
7. Analyzing data

Often, the *selection of a research topic* is based on one's current or past concerns. These concerns may relate to one's profession, social class, personal preferences, and so on. Starting the research process on the basis of where one is in one's life provides a genuinely personal and emotional commitment to the chosen topic. Potential methodological and ethical problems can be averted with the use of strict research operations.

Once a research topic has been established, one must *select an appropriate data site*, the second step. If one were interested in doctoral programs in music education, the list of potential sites will tend to be limited to institutions that grant the doctorate in music education. Geographical and practical aspects of the site must be weighed. Familiar institutions (for example, one's alma mater) can be tempting. However, the overall criterion for the selection of a data site is the extent to which it will provide the richest and most meaningful data. Data collection in the field means direct contact with the group under study. This points to the need to consider one's relationship to the setting. Will you be welcome? Can you gain the trust of the respondents? Will you be able to maintain sufficient scholarly distance?

When the site has been selected, one must work on *gaining access*, the third step. Studying open or public settings offers no real problem. Someone studying the life performances of fifth-grade bands can simply attend those performances. In closed settings, the researcher must decide whether to keep his research activities a secret or make himself and his work known to the group. In the latter instance, the researcher makes his intentions known, secures cooperation, and in some cases acquires formal permission. He must identify the decision makers who will grant or deny permission. The presentation of oneself as a candidate for performing research should balance knowledge about the importance of the data site with a self-portrait that conveys a desire to learn more about the setting. Marked by courtesy, one's style and delivery to decision makers can be, sometimes, the most important element in a presentation. Also important is that in qualitative research, the promise of anonymity is assumed. The researcher must assure the decision makers that real names of persons, and possibly places, will be excluded from the research report.

A thorough, written explanation of the proposed research should be submitted to persons who will take part in the decision as to the use of a given data site. The National Endowment for the Humanities has a research outline that is useful for fieldwork proposals.[10] The key headings are as follows:

History

The proposal opens with the history of the project in conjunction with a review of similar projects. What is the theoretical or methodological tradition that undergirds this type of research?

Purpose

This can be divided into short-range and long-range purposes. The short-range section delineates what will be accomplished during the time of the proposed research (perhaps a few months to a few years). The long-range section explains how the proposed research might fit into a broader research problem, issue or development in the researcher's field.

Significance

There is some overlap with the purpose section when articulating the significance of the proposed fieldwork. This section should answer questions that include: Why should this field research be performed? How will it contribute to knowledge in the field? and Will it strengthen theory or enhance practice?

Product

The researcher should identify the product of the research. There is some overlap between this section and the delineation of short-range purposes.

Dissemination

Who will the consumers of this research be? How will research results be made available to that community of scholars, practitioners, businesspersons, and so on?

Plan of Work

What are the methodology and field techniques? The researcher should establish that he or she can extrapolate traditional or nontraditional methods from the literature and articulate their potential use in the research.

Other Addenda

All of the previous sections may generate notes, bibliography, and appendices, which are listed at the end of the proposal.

Once one has gained entry into the data site, one must *maintain a positive relationship with the members of the group*, the fourth step. The field researcher treats every member as a potential consultant. The reception may be enthusiastic, but Werner and Schoepfle warn field researchers to be wary of overly enthusiastic "natives."[11] One can quickly become inundated with requests and responsibilities that may be beyond the scope of the designated research. Most often, according to Werner and Schoepfle, the immediate response by the group to the researcher is benign neglect. As time passes, the field worker's activities may make stronger commitments possible with group members. Of course, complete rejection by the group is also a possibility. In rare instances, a hostile group will cause the researcher to leave the site and move back to step three (see above) in this process.

Many insights on how to get along with respondents are delineated at the beginning of the current chapter under the heading "The Researcher as Instrument." What is important to note is that relationships in the field are a dynamic affair in a continuous state of change. Lofland and Lofland subdivide that overall living dynamic into three tasks.[12] First, one must get along with oneself. Personal problems can arise as a result of a new environment, isolation, lack of privacy, fear of disclosing certain reported information, "loathing" the people in the group, or the temptation to lose one's critical distance and simply be in the group. A major part of the dynamic is, obviously, getting along with the "natives." Lofland and Lofland accent the need to engender a relationship of trust with respondents. There should be an absence of threat. Moreover, the qualitative field researcher must balance his or her knowledge of the setting between an appropriate investigator role and that of an inquiring student who wishes to learn as much as possible about the data site. One must decide whether to stay aloof during internal debates within the membership or to align oneself with one faction. In educational contexts, Lofland and Lofland note that when factions develop, field-workers usually align themselves with either teachers or students but not both simultaneously. Some members of the group may attempt to exclude the researcher from certain aspects of the database. In these instances, the researcher may need to make use of "allies," who might be some of the people who were approached in step three (gaining access to the data site). The third subdivision of the field research dynamic consists of dealing with ethical questions posed by one's own conscience and colleagues. Many questions arise as a result of the first two subdivisions: Is it ethical to take sides with factions? Is it ethical to use allies to gain entree? Is it ethical to study people whom one hates or with whom one has developed strong emotional ties?

Recording data, the fifth step, is a process that occurs in concert with the next two aspects: validation and analysis of data. The research proposal will guide many decisions on what data to record and what data to neglect. Nevertheless, reporting data can be rather open-ended in qualitative design. One is always open to new hypotheses and modifications of direction and accent. The chief sources of data are the words and activities of the group under study. However, Werner and Schoepfle accent the reflexive observations of the researcher's own internal states as another important source of data. They suggest that there are two broad types of observations: observations of the outside world and observations of one's inner world. They recommend that the researcher keep two journals: one for outside data and one for introspective accounts.[13] Data are recorded by using handwritten notes, audio and video tapes, photographs, and, in some cases, documents. The data log should be duplicated immediately so that future modifications and deletions can be measured against the original, unedited version. At least one copy should be in chronological order. In the field, jotted notes and memory can be used to "fill in the cracks." When one has returned from the field, immediate review of field notes is strongly recommended in order to facilitate recall and understanding of written or taped data.

Validating the data, the sixth step, occurs both in the field and in the act of rereading field notes. Validity is the degree to which the reported data clearly represent a given situation. This establishes some measure of reliability and replicability, though not to the degree of precision associated with quantitative studies. Marion Lundy Dobbart suggests that qualitative researchers are more concerned with validity than replicability because there may be more than one valid account of any social situation.[14] While researchers may be able to agree on what actually occurred, they often disagree on the meaning of the underlying patterns in those happenings. Moreover, human situations are always changing. A second researcher returning a year later to replicate the study may discover a modified data site. In fact, the original study may have caused modifications in behavior. Validity can be enhanced when field researchers utilize several research methods. These include varieties of participant observation and interviewing which are presented later in this chapter.

Lofland and Lofland provide seven helpful criteria (in the form of questions to pose) by which the validity of recorded data can be checked:[15]

1. Is the account built on direct perception or were the data gathered by secondhand or even less direct means? If the basis for the account is less than direct perception, one must accept it with caution and seek further validation.
2. What was the spatial location of the researcher? Is his or her proximity to the occurrence a factor in accepting the account?
3. What is the impact of the social relationship of the researcher and the respondent on the possible validity of secondhand

data? Might the respondent be intentionally distorting or embellishing this account?

4. Is the researcher himself being self-serving or biased? Is he making everything fit neatly with his original plan? Has she neglected information that conflicts with her developing hypotheses or her sense of the patterns and issues that characterize the data site?

5. What is the history of errors in previous written field notes? Has the researcher himself distorted information? Has the particular respondent under validation been dishonest, inaccurate, self-serving?

6. Is the recorded account internally consistent or are there contradictions?

7. Does the recorded account have external consistency? Is it consistent with other reports of the same occurrences? Has the researcher made sufficient efforts to validate problems that have occurred in the first six criteria?

As implied in the earlier account of processual immediacy (as conceived by Lincoln and Guba), observing, note-taking, validation, and analysis are often simultaneous activities in qualitative field research. This results from the fact that although field researchers enter a data site with methods of data collection prescribed in their written proposal, they often modify their techniques and strategies based on the nature of the data that are being collected. Therefore, data collection and analysis are intimately linked to the emerging quality of field research. Nevertheless, there is an overall movement that, while not strictly chronological, tends to proceed from observation/note-taking to validation and then to analysis and the formulation of conclusions. Thus, after validating the large collection of data, one must *analyze the data*, the final step.

During the process of analysis, a chronological copy of field notes can act as the master file. A duplicate copy is then organized into categories of interest. A biographical cross-file can be composed for each of the individuals consulted in the study. Events can also be categorized by type. One can then begin to understand why certain events occurred as they did. As a result, linkages and patterns will begin to develop among the various files. For example, the researcher may discover that the performances of an austere band director were of a particular type, while another, more gregarious director's performances were markedly different. Studying cross-files can result in coding field notes in many different ways and under different categories. This process is closely related to the largely inductive strategies of natural-history method. In providing narrative analyses of the meaning of field note descriptions, the researcher carefully uncovers linkages and patterns as well as relationships between variables.[16]

Having provided an overview of the role of the researcher and general strategies in qualitative research, a more detailed account of techniques of data collection (observation and interview) and treatment (analysis, drawing conclusions, and evaluation) are presented below.

Participant Observation

A cardinal technique for data collection in qualitative research, *participant observation* is traditionally connected with field research.[17] This method is the process by which researchers gain some level of membership in the group under study.[18] In anthropology, an observer's participation in the activities of a group of persons usually requires learning their language and values. Moreover, most field research demands at least one year of living within the context in which research is being performed. Usually, these requirements are adjusted in educational research. The need to "speak the language"is most often met by educational researchers doing fieldwork in their own countries. Nevertheless, a researcher doing fieldwork in a distant part of the United States may have to learn indigenous habits of speech. A study in jazz education might require understanding an idiosyncratic use of language. In the case of an ethnomusicological study of American Indian music, traditional ethnographic directives, including the assimilation of the native language, would have to be satisfied. But even in cases not so ethnographically distinct, matters of language and empathy remain important. For instance, researchers studying high-school students in a concert band must be empathetic toward their idiosyncratic use of language.

As participant observers, educational researchers engage in the activities of the group and then re-create those activities and interactions in field notes written during the activities or as quickly as possible after their happening. Researchers try to draw from the group its sense of reality, its patterns and issues. One collects stories, anecdotes, and myths in order to formulate the important concerns of the group.[19] At times, the articulation of themes and beliefs by the group might not be congruent with the observed behavior of its members.[20] Often, the behavior of individuals in the group or the group as a whole is at odds with stated intentions and goals. In some cases, participant observers become more actively involved with the group by informing that group about the discrepancies between its stated goals and behavior observed by the researcher. Responses to the observer's insights and possible modifications in behavior may become the subsequent focus of the research.

Sometimes,the researcher perceives reasons to conceal her observer status. The observer may conclude that if she presented herself as a researcher she would be rejected. Alternatively, she may conclude that her status as an observer will cause the group to behave differently from its usual habits. This reactive behavior modification might disallow an accurate reconstruction of the dynamics and activities of the data site. In these instances,the observer "infiltrates" the setting and becomes a member of the group.[21] She poses as an individual interested in joining the group. She might become a teacher in a school system under study. The concealed participant is in a better position to build friendly trust so that members of the group more readily "open up."[22] In spite of the research advantage in concealed participation, some researchers have rejected it on ethical grounds as an invasion of privacy.[23] In addition, Raymond Gold notes that methodological problems arise in such complete participation observation because the researcher, as a concealed and complete member, may lose scholarly perspective.[24] Moreover, the researcher may be reluctant to ask "too many" questions for fear of being exposed, causing a potentially harmful delimitation of data. The same fear can inhibit taking on-the-spot notes, a most important part of data collection.

It should be clear that there are various possible degrees of direct participation in the activities of the group. At one end of the spectrum, the researcher is involved completely. This does not require that one's identity be concealed. One can be involved completely, and concomitantly known as a researcher to the group. In studying high-school orchestras, one might play in the violin section, eat lunch with the group and interact with orchestra members before, during, and after rehearsals. At the other end of the spectrum, one minimizes participation with the group. Walter Borg and Meredith Gall refer to this type of observation as "nonparticipant."[25] While observing in the field, the nonparticipant observer endeavors to achieve an impartial, neutral orientation. The observer positions himself or herself in the most unobtrusive place possible within the field setting. Nonparticipant observation often entails minute-by-minute accounts of the activities of the group. Borg and Gall cite P. J. Pelto and G. H. Pelto's recommendation that the nonparticipant observation method should be interfaced and validated with more interactive methods such as participant observation and informant interviewing (see below). Although one gains greater precision and focus in the more neutral stance of nonparticipant observation, one loses many of the creative and spontaneous strengths and qualities of the researcher as instrument.

J. P. Spradley distinguishes three types of field observation: *descriptive, focused,* and *selective.*[26] *Descriptive observation* is usually all that is possible in the early stages of a fieldwork project. One tries to capture "everything," clearly an impossible task. While a more systematic approach is favorable to the "shotgun" approach in descriptive observation, greater systematization requires developed focus and selection of data. The researcher must become oriented to the new data site and remain open to most forms of data. In so doing, the researcher observes and describes (in field notes) virtually everything and anything. The most common problem with open descriptive observations is that the researcher becomes mired in unessential details. Nevertheless, such a shotgun approach can uncover data that might be missed by focusing and selecting too early in the process.

A second type of field observation delineated by Spradley, *focused observation*, results from the cognizance of patterns and issues that allow the researcher to concentrate on certain data while ignoring others. It accents the observation and report of types or categories of activities and the development of taxonomies and other semantic structures.

Finally, according to Spradley, *selective observation* requires a further sharpening of one's focus. Distinguished from focused observation, which tends to scrutinize types or categories of activities, selective observation concentrates on the "attributes" of those types of activities performed by the group. Instead of generating taxonomies, selective observation may provide folk or inveterate definitions of the structures that were identified in focused observation. Spradley also notes that all three observational stages are directed by the original proposal, the researcher's developing comprehension of the data site, and views expressed by the respondents.

Furthermore, concentration on certain aspects of the database may result from negotiations with the group under study.

Goetz and LeCompte provide a framework that synthesizes observational matrices frequently used in field research.[27] Participant observers tend to watch and listen for answers to the following questions. Field researchers are not required to address all of them. Instead, Goetz and LeCompte provide this synthesis in order to delineate important areas of potential observational focus:

1. *Who* comprises this group or setting? What is their total number? How does one acquire membership? Are the characteristics of and types in the group relevant to the study? Who is (are) the researcher(s)?

2. *What* is occurring? What do the group members do and say to each other? What is the research problem or task?
   a. Are there repetitive or irregular behaviors? What resources are required in activities, and how are they disseminated? Are activities coordinated, categorized, taught, and justified? Are there different social contexts?
   b. What is the rapport between group members? How do they participate and interact? What is their connection? Are there evident differences in status and role within this interaction? What is the process of organization for interaction?
   c. What is the nature of the meaning and matter of their discussions? Are there common subjects? What stories or anecdotes are reportable? Are means of communication comprised of verbal and nonverbal languages? Are conversations rooted in beliefs? Do conversations follow formats? Do some people talk while others only listen?

3. *Where* is the group or setting? What are the physical contexts in that scenario? What natural resources are there? Are technologies created or utilized? How are space and physical objects allocated for use? What things are consumed? Are there any products that result from the activities of the group? Within the context of the group's usage, are there salient sights, sounds, smells, and feeling sensations?

4. *When* does the group meet and interact? What are the length and frequency of these meetings? What is (are) the group's

position(s) on the use and distribution of time as well as the relationship of the present within the context of the past and the future?

5. *How* are the elements identified above connected? Are there patterns of interaction? Is the perspective of those connections and patterns the researcher's or the group's? Is there stability? Is change possible and, if so, how is it handled? How does the group govern itself: through rules, norms or mores? Are there extrageneric relationships with other groups or organizations?

6. *Why* is this group in existence? Why does it function as it does? Is that function and existence congruent with the group's history? Are there symbols, traditions, values, and cultural views that can be discovered in the group?

Interview

An interview with a member or members of the group may be quite structured or unstructured, or at some point between those extremes. In a strict sense, *interviewing* differs from *observation*: observation leans more heavily toward listening and seeing; in an interview, the researcher takes a more active role by prompting a consultant with questions. As discussed earlier, however, observation is not always neutral. While demarcating lines might be easier to draw between nonparticipant ("neutral") observation and interviewing, in participant observation the researcher may take an active role in the group by prompting, showing, manipulating, infiltrating, or otherwise intervening in the data-gathering process. In practice, therefore, participant observation overlaps with interviewing techniques; there are numerous degrees of active participation in observation. A similar spectrum of strategies is found in interviewing. Interviews can be highly structured surveys in which the researcher poses the same prepared questions to all consultants. Unstructured (open-ended) interviews may have a list of areas of concern without a specified chronological order or formulated questions. Spradley describes interviews in fieldwork as friendly conversations in which the researcher incrementally inserts new issues in order to acquire a fuller sense of the database.[28] When such interviews take on the complexion of unstructured conversations with members of the group, it may be difficult to distinguish them from similar techniques of participant observation.

Before presenting several strategies that may be used in interviews, three types of interview will be discussed. According to Goetz and LeCompte, whether interviews are structured or unstructured, they generally fall into one of the following types: *key-informant interviewing, career or life histories,* and *surveys.*[29]

Key-Informant Interviewing

Key informants are members of the group who have special knowledge, status, or ability to communicate. One reason for interviewing a key informant is that he or she may have access to information otherwise denied the researcher. If one were doing a study of choirs in junior-high-school settings, student members might be potential key informants. Students may have insights into perceptions of a data site that are considerably different from those of an adult music teacher or administrator. As Borg and Gall note, criteria for selecting students as key informants include whether they are (1) in leadership roles; (2) brighter than and more mature than other students; and (3) willing to be interviewed.[30] Goetz and LeCompte stress that, as atypical individuals, care must be used in choosing them and in integrating their knowledge. While key informants may add valuable insights, they can also manipulate the researcher and confound otherwise developing patterns and meanings in the collected data.

Career or Life Histories

Career or life histories are interviews that encourage narrative accounts of the subject's professional or personal life. In attempting to formulate a description of successful chamber music instruction, an investigator could interview renowned chamber teachers and elicit data that might provide a detailed account of their training, the development of their methods, modifications in their teaching practices, and other aspects of their working environment. Goetz and LeCompte note that career histories are more common than life histories in qualitative research of educational settings. Career information that is collected from professionals may significantly impact on the researcher's understanding of the educational setting, its values, important issues, and practices.

Surveys

Survey instruments are used for highly structured interviews. Surveys are used when large amounts of data are needed from many respondents through a uniform and systematic instrument. In traditional educational research, surveys are used to collect quantitative data. In collecting numerical tabulations of some variable, the quantified results from a survey of a sampled population can be generalized to the entire group. In qualitative research, surveys are usually implemented subsequent to collecting data through less formal interviews and participant observations. When sufficient background information has been gathered, the survey instrument can be constructed and implemented by the researcher. Goetz and LeCompte explain three forms of surveys that are used in qualitative studies: *confirmation instruments, participant-construct instruments*, and *projective devices.*

Confirmation surveys assess the validity of earlier reports. These surveys are questionnaires that verify key-informant and other kinds of data in terms of the entire group. Their purpose is to show the degree to which the group shares beliefs and behaviors. Confirmation surveys facilitate, and make manageable, investigations in which the group is comprised of a large number of members. In such a data site, it may be impossible to follow up with individual confirmation interviews. Goetz and LeCompte also note that the questionnaire in confirmation surveys provides easy storage of data for examination and possible replication of the study by other researchers. However, surveys in and of themselves lack the corroborational strength of observation. Participant observation is marked by direct, empirical data collection. When observation techniques, unstructured interviews, and surveys are used in concert, such triangulation of methods provides an eclectic ground that is most supportive of (1) capturing the holistic context while responding to details; (2) having defined directions yet being able to adapt to new issues and meanings; and (3) interfacing and thereby validating data which are gleaned from both formal and informal techniques.

Less structured than confirmation surveys, *participant-construct surveys* are used to understand how respondents structure their social and physical worlds. Researchers attempt to determine a set of underlying structures that the group can agree upon as important and real. Participants may be asked to delineate all of the members or entities that comprise a particular category of things. In studies in music education, one might ask participants to enumerate all types of repertoire performed by the group. One might ask students in an elementary school band to compose two lists that specify respectively what they think they and their teachers can do during rehearsals. Goetz and LeCompte note that in an analogous study carried out by LeCompte, a typology of children's thoughts concerning their roles and those of their teachers was developed.[31] The parameters of categories that respondents use to structure their world and the means they use to determine those categories are clarified through interviews. It is possible to formulate sociograms in which respondents arrange the names of other members of the group following any logical set of criteria. For example, respondents (teachers, students, administrators, or any member in the overall study group) may be asked to categorize students in a fifth-grade band based on whether they take private lessons outside of the school, whether they own their instruments, the level of their performance ability, their popularity, their dress, or their maturity.

Projective techniques are used when the researcher cannot observe the behavior of members of the group in actual situations involved in the study. This may be the case when eliciting information about home practice habits of junior-high-school orchestral players. In this instance, photographs, drawings, or games may be used to draw out opinions and reactions in order to determine patterns of behavior that are unobservable in the natural setting.[32] Goetz and LeCompte note that many researchers use ambiguous or indirect stimuli to acquire information about the respondent's values and self-image. These can be helpful in assessing the impact of different degrees of authority structures in classrooms upon one's self-image. Projective techniques must be combined or triangulated with other techniques of field research in order to corroborate the meanings that respondents extrapolate from their environments.[33]

Interview Techniques and Guidelines

Preparing for the Interview

Werner and Schoepfle stress the importance of the pre-interview or "contact" stage.[34] The early contact stage begins before the researcher arrives at the site of the interview. The selection of potential consultants may be ad hoc, opportunistic, based on the potential consultant's expertise or social standing, or according to a systematic sampling plan.[35] B. Tymitz and R. L. Wolf urge the researcher to contact personally each prospective consultant.[36] The introduction to the interview should be courteous and informative. Letters of introduction, friends, and colleagues can be used in order to urge the potential consultant to agree to the interview. The researcher should acquire as much background information on the interviewee as possible. The entirety of this data should facilitate in the formulation of preliminary questions and topics. Consultants should be informed in writing of the time, date, and place of the interview. An estimate of the time needed and a short description of the study are also helpful. A confirming telephone call one day in advance of the scheduled interview is advised. Researchers should dress in accordance with the surroundings of the data site and interview.

Leonard Schatzman and Anselm Strauss point out five components involved in the logistics of preparing for interviews.[37] The details of these components must be clarified and, in the case of the first four, communicated to the respondents prior to their interview.

1. *Duration* indicates the length of each session.
2. *Number* refers to the sum of individual sessions needed to complete the interview process.
3. *Setting* refers to the location of the interview.
4. *Individuals involved* is a descriptive list of the interviewer(s) and respondent(s) involved and who will be present at each separate session.
5. *Respondent styles* indicates the indigenous ways in which the group communicates.

Werner and Schoepfle delineate areas that require preparation for an interview. First, one must list topics and ensure that they are appropriate for the respondent. During the initial contact with a potential consultant, the researcher should discuss potential topics for the interview. One should acquire some sense of the interviewee's expertise. During the first formal interview, field researchers usually apply a "grand tour" style that accents broad issues rather than highly focused and detailed ones. In preparing for the second interview, broad topics that were discussed earlier can be focused further so that the interviews can move from a "grand tour" status to a more detailed "mini-tour" status. Potential topics and questions are listed in an interview guide. Questions can be placed on individual index cards to allow for flexibility in ordering. Or, questions can be entered on a computer, easily reordered, and printed in new sequences. However, although the ordering of index cards is performed manually, it may be preferred because it allows a spontaneous or on-the-spot adaptation of question sequence during the interview.

A second category to check in the preparation for interviews is equipment. It is a good idea to have a checklist of all of the items in this category. Few occurrences are more disruptive to an interview than a malfunctioning tape recorder, camera, or video camera. The field researcher should carry at least two of every essential piece of equipment, including batteries, wires, and cables. If one is recording musical performances, one should make certain that the audio capabilities of the equipment will do justice to the performance. The researcher should ask for permission to record the proceedings. While setting up the recording equipment, one attempts to keep that activity and its subsequent presence as unobtrusive as possible.

Performing an Interview

In *structured interviews*, problems are defined by the researcher in advance and the respondent is expected to answer in terms of the interviewer's framework and problem statements. The interviewer seeks answers within the context set by his or her own hypotheses. This kind of interview is closer to the end of a spectrum demarcated by the questionnaire, with the unstructured interview at the opposite end. Each respondent tends to be asked the same questions although, as noted earlier, the order of questions can be adapted for varying reasons. The object of structured interviews is to gain largely representative or "typical" responses that will enrich the researcher's frame of reference. Guba and Lincoln accent the *unstructured interview*, a much freer form that allows the respondent to shape the focus and direction of an interview more so than in structured interviews.[38] Key-informant interviews tend to be unstructured because the interviewee is usually in command of special knowledge of the data site. In such instances, the "atypical," "elite," or "key" informant is given as much license as possible to shape the researcher's data collection. This may generate data of great depth because the respondent probably knows considerably more about the topic than the interviewer; the depth of knowledge concerning the issues at hand should not be limited to the interviewer's ability to formulate defined questions about those issues. Often, unstructured interviews are necessary when a researcher is suddenly confronted with unsolicited data. For example, if a group member in a data site unexpectedly pulls the researcher by the arm and initiates a conversation concerning another member of the group, the researcher cannot tell the group member to hold on to that information until appropriate questions are formulated. The researcher allows the subject to supply information. Often, such data have great value and may lead to new issues, relationships, insights, and meanings. All information, whether elicited from formal or informal interviews, must be subjected to validation and analysis. Generalizations as to whether data gathered from structured interviews are more valid than data from unstructured interviews cannot be drawn.

Common courtesies are important during the interview. The interviewer, properly dressed, should arrive a few minutes early. A telephone call is a must if one is going to be more than five minutes late. Dexter advises that after introducing oneself, the researcher should briefly summarize the project. This is followed by a succinct explanation of the interviewer's role in the study.[39] The physical surroundings of the interview should permit the interviewer to be at ease. Eye contact is necessary between interviewer and interviewee and there should be no others present unless that has been previously discussed and agreed upon. Guba and Lincoln stress that extreme courtesy and value-neutral behaviors are essential to a successful interview. A value-neutral orientation does not delimit gentle prompting by the interviewer. The rhythm and ambience of the interview should resemble an interesting conversation in which both conversants are actively involved and concerned. All writers on this subject concur that the single most important skill the interviewer must acquire is empathy. Interviewers must place themselves within the world view of the interviewee. Even if one is conducting a highly structured interview, one must still understand the interviewee's conception of the meaning of the dialogue. This point does not circumvent the fact that the researcher's empathetic understanding will, to some degree, place the collected data within the researcher's own frame of reference.

Constructing questions is an activity of fundamental importance to the researcher. Clearly the nature of these questions will depend on the expertise, intelligence, and maturity as well as the social and professional status of interviewer and interviewee. Guba and Lincoln provide ten useful types of questions that may be posed.[40]

1. *Hypothetical* questions start with a "what if" phrase.
2. *Pose the ideal* questions prompt the consultant to respond to a hypothetical situation.

3. *Devil's advocate* questions confront the respondent with an opposing frame of reference or view.
4. *Interpretive* questions propose the meaning of events for a response and consideration by the consultant.
5. *Suggestive* questions may elicit open-ended discussion.
6. *Reason-why* questions probe the respondent's explanation of an event.
7. *Argument-type* questions attempt to provoke the respondent to reveal data that might not be accessible without such provocation.
8. *Source* questions bring to light the grounds for information or supporting data and documents.
9. *Qualified yes-no* questions measure the determination and earnestness of a respondent's feeling or belief concerning a particular aspect of the data site.
10. *Filter* questions require the respondent to create or modify categories, classes, or kinds for the database.

When the interviewer needs further information or more critical thinking about a particular response or issue, he or she may utilize different types of "probes."[41] According to Herbert J. Rubin, silence itself can be a useful probe.[42] Rubin notes that probes can provide reasons why certain reported actions took place. Guba and Lincoln list several kinds of probes:

1. *Clarification* probes require the interviewee to make a previous response less ambiguous.
2. *Critical awareness* probes ask the consultant to reflect upon, evaluate, or exemplify an issue or an interpretation.
3. *Amplification* probes seek to draw further information.
4. *Refocusing* probes cause the respondent to draw new relationships or seek alternative answers.

Another aspect of questioning to consider while interviewing is sequencing. Guba and Lincoln suggest three ways to sequence questions.[43] First, the *funnel sequence* orders questions from the general to the specific. Questions must follow each other logically so that there is coherence in the overall interview guide or list of questions. Each question, building on information secured from the previous answer, requires a narrowing of the topic. Starting with general questions helps to keep directions and concentrations in the interview open to different foci. Second, the *inverted funnel* begins

with specificity and moves to more general issues. This sequence
dynamic can be an aid in encouraging hesitant or unwilling respondents to become more at ease with subsequent questions that are
more expansive.

Third and finally, the *quintamensional method* starts with questions requiring "descriptive-awareness" responses, then shifts to
those eliciting value judgments and the expression of personal
feelings or attitudes toward that issue or topic. For example, a
question requiring descriptive response might be, "Did you know
that even though the repertoire requirement in the concerto competition was open to all styles, the conductor preferred to select
someone playing a Mozart concerto?" That question could be
followed by, "Did that knowledge cause any resentment by com-
petitors who prepared concerti by other composers and in other
periods?" "Specifically, who was angry?" "What did they say?"
And then in order to probe the personal intensity of the respondent's
part of this issue, "How do you feel about this issue?" "Do you
think that the conductor should have delimited the repertoire to
Mozart concerti?" "Does the fact that the winner happened to be
the only person who prepared a Mozart concerto have an impact on
your feelings concerning the competition . . . the winner . . . the
conductor . . . the orchestra?" As demonstrated in the sequence of
these questions, the quintamensional method starts with questions
that do not require emotionally charged answers but ask for descriptive responses. However, those descriptive responses open the door
to a topic about which the researcher would like to probe the
consultant's feelings. As one moves the respondent in that direction,
questions should intensify and thereby elicit data that reveal the
depth of the respondent's feelings toward that issue.

Interview Guidelines to Remember

Goetz and LeCompte provide a large number of sources concerning rules and guidelines for interviewing by qualitative researchers.[44] The original sources are listed after each entry. The
guidelines are:

1. Pose questions in language that is understandable to respondents.[45]
2. Use open-ended questions for qualitative responses.[46]
3. Use closed questions in order to secure enumerative answers.
   Answers to closed questions tend to be more precise and
   defined.[47]

4. During early or exploratory phases of the study, use ambiguous questions to increase variations in responses and in order to determine underlying meanings in responses without leading the respondent.[48]

5. Generally avoid asking leading questions[49] unless deliberately implementing techniques like "devil's advocate" questions.[50]

6. Generally, pose singular questions that incorporate a single idea. A question that is comprised of a string of questions can confuse the respondent.[51] However, carefully presented multiple questions can be used in order to allow respondents greater freedom by choosing the aspect of the question he or she wishes to answer.[52]

7. If one uses questions beginning with the word "why," make certain that there is a clear purpose, e.g., to elicit cause-and-effect-relationship responses.[53]

8. Use probes for amplification of the database.[54]

9. Use questions that ask for "who," "what," "when," "where," and "how," in order to prepare and support subsequent probes into those issues.[55]

10. Generally, try to speak less than the respondent.[56]

11. Run trial or pilot sessions of interviews to practice posing questions in advance of the actual interview.[57]

12. Make very clear assurances of anonymity and protection to respondents.[58]

13. Begin the interview with a short summary of the purpose of the research and your role.[59] During the interview, inform the respondent about shifts in focus and topic so that he or she has a clear sense of the direction and coherence of the interview.[60]

14. Sequencing questions ensures scope and prevents redundancy, which may result in interviewee boredom.[61]

15. Reserve difficult or complex questions for later periods in the interview after a rapport of trust has been established.[62]

16. During the post-interview period, immediately fill in incomplete statements, cues and key words utilized in the interview notes.[63]

17. Use quotation marks around all exact quotations and word-for-word statements in the interview notes in order to differentiate them from personal remarks and summary notes.

Data Analysis

Regardless of the form of data collected through the observation and interview techniques described above, they must be transformed into facts that can aid in the systematic, clear, and concise understanding of the meaning of those data. Analysis is synonymous with interpretation of data. Data analysis is a continuous process that runs through the period immediately following each data-collection segment (individual participant observations and separate interviews) and continues after fieldwork is completed. Data analysis can take the form of written thoughts regarding emerging questions, patterns, and themes. The *analytical memo* is performed at this stage to build links between observational notes. These links may develop into patterns and themes that add a conceptual structure and logic to the data and to the meaning of the activities in the data site. This aids in planning each new observation and interview session because it is based upon what has been previously analyzed. In this regular review of observation notes and interview "write-ups," analyses provide a reconsideration of data that might locate contradictions or conflicts regarding the perspectives of reality between the researcher and the group. The following steps may be utilized in order to focus themes from field notes:

1. Recurring ideas should be the basis of tentative categories for organizing the field notes or log.
2. Categories can be clarified by comparing them to early thoughts concerning the meaning of the data that might have initially been written in the margins. Category construction and filing are the means by which raw data are distilled into manageable divisions.
3. New categories are developed by examining the congruence of the categories developed in step 2 to initial thoughts which were articulated in analytical memoranda as marginalia, etc.
4. Direct quotations from participants are filed under appropriate categories in order to link them firmly.
5. Added data in the categories might generate new themes and patterns.
6. The researcher's own biases and frame of reference are brought to the forefront for analysis.
7. Data are validated by reconsidering the categories and themes in light of the potential impact of biases held by the researcher and participants.

Robert C. Bogdan and Sari Knopp Biklen distinguish analysis in the field from analysis that is performed after data collection is completed. They provide several helpful suggestions for executing the former.[64] Some of these directives overlap somewhat with the list immediately above.

1. Plan future data-collection sessions based on what is found in previous observations. Build new directives and issues on the insights developed from analyses of previous field notes.
2. Write many "observer's comments" on the field-note pages in order to analyze the data. Do not hesitate to speculate about the meanings of recurring words, events, ideas, and topics.
3. Write self-memos about what has been learned thus far.
4. Test self-developing ideas and analytical insights on members of the group. Utilize the services of key informants for this purpose. Do not defer to their opinions completely. Balance personal insights with key informants' evaluations of them.
5. Utilize metaphors and analogies. Try to raise actual events to higher levels of abstraction. Try to capture the spirit of the particular setting and happening.

The final analysis can begin by reviewing the original research proposal. Even though by this point the research may have diverged from the proposal, it is important to understand new problems, questions, and directions in terms of the original plan. Next, one must reread raw data and the initial and intermediary analyses. The investigator should question data in a way that is similar to the manner in which respondents were questioned.[65] While reading through the data, certain words, phrases, patterns, or events should be underscored as they come to mind. These sets of information become "coding categories" and provide a way of sorting data.[66] Notes can be written in the margins, as undertaken during earlier stages of analysis. They become the ground for further organization, abstraction, integration, and synthesis of the database. Furthermore, they can be formed into a preliminary outline which sorts the data. This procedure begins with a search for regularities and patterns across the data. These patterns and regularities become the basis for categories. The process is like putting together a jigsaw puzzle. The raw data are analogous to all the pieces in a big pile, without form, pattern, or meaning. After sorting and filing, patterns begin to develop; a clearer picture of what the puzzle or field notes might represent emerges. Written summaries should accompany every significant constitution of a new pattern or category in the developing puzzle. Justifications for fitting data together are derived both from the investigator's insights and from statements made by participants that have been recorded in field notes.

The sorting and filing of data can be extremely daunting. Bogdan and Biklen provide several "coding families" or types which can be helpful.[67]

1. *Context codes* are codes within which very general data concerning the setting, topic, or subjects can be filed.
2. *Definition of the situation codes* clarifies the manner in which subjects define a setting or issue. It is a place to file participants' world views. Data filed in this unit should answer questions such as What is important to participants and what are their goals?
3. *Participants' perspectives* include data that shed light on the shared rules and norms of the subjects.
4. *Participants' perspectives about other people* uncover how subjects understand each other.
5. *Process codes* refer to words and phrases that cut across sequences of events or time. The researcher views persons, groups, or events over time and attempts to perceive change occurring within that sequence.
6. *Activity codes* signify regularly occurring types of activities.
7. *Strategy codes* refer to the means by which members accomplish objectives.
8. *Relationship and social structure codes* consist of patterns of behavior by members who are not officially defined as part of the organization. These might include friendships, romances, enemies, and cliques.
9. *Methods codes* separate data that bear upon research procedures.

During continued data analysis, initial categories become building blocks or units for larger categories. Goetz and LeCompte stress that broad categories or divisions must be congruent to the natural setting described by the raw data.[68] Categorization requires tasks that include comparing, contrasting, aggregating, and ordering.[69] This supports indications with respect to the relationship among smaller units and how they can be linked to form larger categories. Bases for sorting items into categories include the spatial, the physico-temporal, the conceptual, the linguistic, or the social.

When investigating similarities and differences in the developing categories, the researcher must articulate the manner in which each unit is used and identify their respective significances. Properties of each category are uncovered by delineating the ways in which all of its units are alike and different from units that constitute other large categories.[70] These properties form the core of abstract definitions for each category. Some properties of units may be common to units which are in different categories. Analytical searches for similarities between units tend to occur first. This kind of data analysis permits the specification of category characteristics. Searches for differences between units are accented in the later stages of analysis. These analyses provide further elaboration and qualification of the categories. On the basis of discovered common and differing properties, new subcategories are devised and former categories may be abandoned.

Validating data is a continuous activity in qualitative research. Guba and Lincoln suggest four methods for establishing the credibility of data.[71]

1. Host Verification
2. Triangulation
3. Independent Observer Analysis
4. Phenomenon Recognition

Host verification entails matching the researcher's experiences against the understanding of members of the group. This can be executed by selecting "facts" in the field notes which articulate the understanding of the group members or by including several members in the analysis of the data's validity. *Triangulation* corroborates findings by utilizing other methodological techniques and measures. *Independent observer analysis* questions whether another independent observer would have made similar observations and would have drawn similar conclusions. Finally, during *phenomenon recognition*, the researcher encapsulates a picture of the "reality" of the data site as he or she understands it and asks members whether it is congruent to their own perception and understanding.

Drawing Conclusions

It may be a wrenching experience for researchers to transcend their study sufficiently to make definitive statements about the significance and profundity (or lack thereof) of several months or more of field research. Drawing conclusions requires an interpretation of the meaning of the data in contexts that can go beyond the immediacy of the data site and study. Old categories may be refurbished and new linkages may be constructed. It is an opportunity to consider the strengths and weaknesses in the chosen methodology as well as in the overall plan and to consider the impact of those strengths and weaknesses on the collection and treatment of data. Conclusions can be made concerning the appropriateness of the chosen methodology for the study and the application of that methodology to other studies.

Conclusions are descriptive constructions in prosaic or graphic form that specify the attributes of the properties, distinctions, characteristics, and idiosyncrasies of the database. The significance of the collected data and analyses must be placed within the perspective of the questions asked in the proposal and during the study. Moving beyond the immediate subject, the researcher can use metaphor and simile in order to enrich the final picture of his or her work. While these linguistic tools are used freely in philosophical and aesthetic inquiry, some researchers may be reluctant to take such a projective leap. Nevertheless, the similarities between arts criticism and curriculum criticism have become a *leitmotif* in works by many qualitative researchers, Elliott Eisner most prominent among them.[72] These similarities are apparent within the context of chapters 6, 7, and 8 in this text. Just as the significance of a musical work cannot be reduced to syntax and its accompanying literal, descriptive language, so educational settings must not be so reduced. Literal descriptions of musical syntax remain a necessary step in aesthetic inquiry, as are literal descriptions of observations and interviews vital to understanding educational settings. Language use in qualitative evaluation, particularly during conclusions, must be capable of achieving resonance and confluence with the holistic reality of the data site. The projective power of metaphor and simile provides the linguistic thrust necessary to send one's narrative in an intersecting course with the meanings that emanate from any human living context.

Goetz and LeCompte recommend that Conclusions sections of qualitative research reports be presented in four stages:[73]

1. Summary presentations of data
2. Interpretation of data
3. Integration of findings
4. Significance of findings

A *summary presentation of the data* is comprised of a descriptive narrative that might utilize graphs in order to delineate the characteristics of the data site. Data may be organized into categories based on exhibited attributes. The descriptions are supposed to be empirically based and deal specifically with the data at hand; no attempt is made to suggest comparisons between the data site and other related but extrinsic phenomena.

Interpretation of data clarifies the meaning of the data *in relation to the questions posed in the study*. The researcher explains relationships between phenomena and draws comparisons between categories described in the preceding "summary of data" section of the report. This part of the report continues to limit its purview to intrinsic relationships. That is, no attempt is made to provide comparisons to extrinsic phenomena or categories.

The *integration of the findings* pushes the interpreted meanings of the data into broader and related areas of interest. The findings of the report can be correlated with findings of other reports in order to uncover harmonious or discordant correspondence. At a metatheoretical level, theory spawned by the study can be placed in a polemic with alternative theories for the purpose of embellishment, corroboration or refutation. This may cause a most fruitful working back to the "interpretation of data" and "summary of data" sections in order to ground theoretical statements more concretely in the data.

The *significance of the findings* can begin with a recapitulation of the preceding interpretation and integration of data sections within the perspective of why those insights are significant. In this final stage of the report, one should delineate how the research results promote, aid, increase, improve, or clarify the body of knowledge that relates to the study. Potential applications of the findings can be specified and recommendations for further study can be made.

Qualitative Evaluation

Bogdan and Biklen distinguish qualitative research and qualitative evaluation.[74] They note that in evaluation studies, the researcher is often hired by a contractor to assess a particular program in order to improve it or provide grounds for its continuation or termination. Certainly there is overlap between qualitative research and qualitative evaluation. One could not carry out an evaluation without first having performed qualitative research. Therefore, for the purposes of this book, evaluation will be considered an optional step in the overall process of qualitative research. The position of evaluation in the overall qualitative research design is that step immediately following "data analysis." Its main impact on qualitative research occurs in the conclusions of the written report.

Borg and Gall describe differences between research and evaluation.[75] First, evaluation studies are set in motion for the purpose of making a decision. On the other hand, the purpose of qualitative research studies tends to be the acceptance or rejection of hypotheses about the data site that were formed early in the study or generated at later stages. A critical difference is that qualitative research can stop at the testing of the hypotheses, and qualitative evaluation must continue to the point of making practical decisions. A second difference, according to Borg and Gall, is that evaluation may have a limited purpose, with findings bearing only upon the actual site that was studied. As a result, external validity may be limited. In contrast, researchers tend to be more concerned with discovering wider applications to the theoretical underpinnings and methodological structures of their work. Certainly, the differences are not so black and white. Some qualitative evaluation studies may have wide theoretical appeal and applicability. Borg and Gall note that they provide only a general sense of the differences.

Borg and Gall also provide a helpful list of several tasks associated with qualitative evaluation.[76]

1. *Identify the stakeholders* by preparing a list of anyone who is part of the program being evaluated. Ignoring a stakeholder can cause grave problems, from potential sabotage to a discreditation of the results.
2. *Decide what is to be evaluated.* Delineate distinguishing program characteristics.
3. *Delineate resources and procedures.* Resources include people, equipment, physical space and other cost items needed to run the program. Procedures are the strategies used with the resources in order to realize program goals.
4. *Describe the program management system.* Who runs the program? Are they efficient?
5. *Identify evaluation questions.* There are two phases for selecting questions: the divergent phase entails creating a large list

of questions, issues and concerns that may be studied; the convergent phase requires a reduction of the divergent phase list to a manageable number.

6. *Develop an evaluation design and a time line.* Will there be internal evaluators? These are members of the program who might be utilized in the evaluation process. The researcher is considered an external evaluator or third-party evaluator. The evaluation design is constructed in order to deal with questions formulated in the convergent phase.

7. *Collect and analyze data.* This will utilize the research processes of qualitative research.

8. *Generate an evaluation report.* This is the final report. A condensed version, often termed the "executive summary," is often expected as well. A *meta-evaluation* is expected to be a part of the final report. In that section, a presentation of the strengths and weaknesses in the research design and their impact on the study are considered.

Borg and Gall list four criteria that should be satisfied in order to meet the requirements of a "good evaluation study."[77] An evaluation has *utility* if it can be employed by the persons in the program. A study has *feasibility* if the evaluation is suitable to the setting and the design is cost-effective. *Propriety* is satisfied if the rights of all persons affected by the evaluation are protected. *Accuracy* refers to the level of congruence between the report and the activities and occurrences in the data site.

Bogdan and Biklen caution evaluators concerning several potential problems.[78] First, *ownership of the data* can be a problem. Contractors usually assume that the data are theirs. However, the researcher must promise anonymity to subjects. Can researchers trust the contractor to protect their right to privacy? *Making the program goals the object of the study* can cause problems because qualitative research usually is not conducted in order to answer prescribed and specific questions. However, the researcher can follow the protocols of qualitative research fully and then bring the accumulated database and analyses to bear upon the evaluation of the program. *The hierarchy of credibility* refers to the tension caused when members of lower status are allowed to evaluate members of higher social or political status. For example, if students are asked to be internal evaluators of the activities of teachers or administrators, the contractor may complain that the students' credibility is not acceptable, given their place in comparison to the hierarchy enjoyed by teachers and administrators. Needless to say, students can provide valuable data concerning teachers' and administrators' activities. Researchers will have to establish that their design enabled them to sufficiently control for bias and the students' lack of hierarchical status.

Finally, an additional source of friction between the qualitative evaluator and the contractor can occur when a program is particularly poor. In this case, the evaluation report might *overly criticize* the program, that is, point out the predominance of weaknesses in the program, for lack of apparent strengths. In such an instance, if the contractor has a vested interest in the continuance of the program, an overly critical report may cause a particularly thorny problem. As Guba and Lincoln point out, evaluation studies can disrupt the prevailing political balance for the members of the program as well as the contractor/organization members.[79] The resolution to these kinds of strifes between the evaluator and the contractor must be balanced by the ethical responsibilities of the researcher to reconstruct as fully as possible, and to the best of his or her ability, the data site. An evaluation based upon reliable qualitative research cannot be adjusted to the expectations or needs of the contractor.

Conclusions

Qualitative and quantitative research designs have distinguishing philosophical foundations and strategies that make them appropriate for investigating certain questions and inappropriate for examining other questions. Qualitative design places great emphasis on the researcher as a data-gathering instrument. This can cause problems with bias and lack of consistency in data collection. However, those weaknesses are balanced by the ability of the data collection tool to adapt almost immediately to emerging questions and to emphasize the holistic qualities of the setting. Reduction of the database for the purposes of controlled variables is not of great concern. Instead, the researcher interacts directly with the data in order to give them a fair and full description. As a result, data are rich and "real." Another advantage in qualitative research is that field reports preserve the chronological flow and rhythm of the data in the natural setting. Successful qualitative reports are like verbal film documentaries of the data site. With a comprehensive description that reconstructs the data site, field notes can be analyzed through systematic means in order to interpret patterns and meanings in the database. Thus, in qualitative design there is interfacing of a great number of details with broad conceptual, philosophical, and sociological topics. Theoretical insights and new hypotheses are grounded in observational data collected in the actual setting. The possibility of unexpected theoretical leaps abounds. The fact that researchers are required to maintain an interested detachment during observation is part and parcel of the great empirical tradition. Moreover, the researcher can deal effectively with atypical data that conflict with hypotheses. When a researcher wishes to provide a full and observationally grounded report of the details and breadth of the data site, qualitative research design provides a powerful alternative to quantitative designs. This does not diminish the strength of quantitative designs to be responsive to other types of research questions.

Of course, disadvantages in qualitative research abound as well. Collecting and analyzing qualitative data are extraordinarily laborious and time-consuming. Receptiveness to the fullness of a database has its obvious merits but such a responsiveness can overload the researcher's data-collecting capabilities; there are too much data from which to choose. Consequently, qualitative methods do not provide the controls and precision that mark quantitative designs. Validity and replicability are not easily measured in qualitative studies and it is difficult to measure the degree to which observer and respondent biases distort findings. Given all of these drawbacks, qualitative researchers see the inherent reductionism in quantitative designs as the greater evil. Is there an answer, or must this current dilemma of the dislocation of quantitative and qualitative research designs continue?

One answer is an eclectic approach that mixes qualitative with quantitative methods. There is a notable tradition in the extant literature concerning research methods for the social sciences that attempts to converge the two methodologies.[80] Qualitative data can be used to enrich and enliven quantitative data. Conversely, quantitative data can ground and clarify the other. When several designs are triangulated or combined, validity is often increased, because of added observational and seriational interfacing. However, preparing graduate students to be experts in a multiplicity of research methods may be an impossible dream because the (usual) comprehensive overview of available methods and the subsequent thorough grounding in one design require significant time and energy. The movement in educational research that, over the last thirty years, has called into question the fecundity of quantitative studies will not wane in the near future. Steadfast also will be the often-justified disapprovals by critics of qualitative methods for their lack of acceptable levels and measures of validity and replicability. But the swinging of the pendulum may indeed be inevitable in all things. And if countermovement is inescapable, as the forces on either side of the quantitative/qualitative debate exert increasing opposition, when the pendulum finally changes direction there will be a great collision at some central point. After the dust settles, perhaps researchers will find themselves fully in methodological eclecticism.

Problems for Review and Discussion

1. What are the principal data-gathering tools for obtaining information in qualitative research?
2. Discuss the characteristics that qualitative researchers manifest in their role as primary instruments.
3. What strategies are important for field research?
4. What criteria may be used to check the validity of data?
5. Discuss techniques necessary for successful participant observation.
6. How does an interview differ from an observation?
7. What is the meaning of the term "key-informant interviewing"?
8. When should a survey be used to collect data?
9. Discuss steps necessary for a successful interview.
10. What procedures may be used to sort data?

Supplementary Sources

Calhoun, Craig J., and Francis A. J. Ianni, eds. *The Anthropological Study of Education*, The Hague: Mouton, 1976.

Cook, T., and C. Reichardt, eds. *Qualitative and Quantitative Methods in Evaluation Research*, Beverly Hills, Calif.: Sage Publications Inc., 1979.

Filstead, William J., ed. *Qualitative Methodology: Firsthand Involvement with the Social World*, Chicago: Markham, 1978.

Garfinkel, H. *Studies in Ethnomethodology*, Englewood Cliffs, N.J.: Prentice-Hall, 1967.

Goodman, Leo A. *Analyzing Qualitative/Categorical Data*, Cambridge, Mass.: Harvard University Press, 1978.

Gorden, Raymond L. *Interviewing: Strategy, Techniques and Tactics*, Homewood, Ill.: Dorsey, 1975.

Green, Judith L., and Cynthia Wallat, eds. *Ethnography and Language in Educational Settings*, Norwood, N.J.: Ablex, 1981.

Guba, Egon. *Effective Evaluation*, San Francisco: Jossey-Bass, 1981.

Jacobs, G., ed. *The Participant Observer*, New York: George Braziller, 1977.

Johnson, J. *Doing Field Research*, New York: Macmillan, 1975.

Kreuger, Parri J. "Ethnographic Research Methodology in Music Education," *Journal of Research in Music Education*, Summer 1987, 35,2:69-77.

Spindler, George D., ed. *Doing the Ethnography of Schooling*, New York: Holt, Rinehart and Winston, 1982.

Strauss, Anselm L. *Qualitative Analysis for Social Scientists*, Reston, Va.: Music Education National Conference, 1987.

Tait, Malcolm, and Paul Haack. *Principles and Processes of Music Education*, New York: Teachers College Press, Columbia University, 1984.

Willis, George, ed. *Qualitative Evaluation, Concepts and Cases in Curriculum Criticism*, Berkeley, Calif.: McCutchan Publishing Corp., 1978.

6. Concepts of Quantifying Research Data

Many students feel that the greatest difference between qualitative and quantitative research is that quantitative research has to do with quantities, or "numbers of things," such as twenty-four subjects in a sample, while qualitative research has nothing to do with numbers (especially statistics), and therefore its name is derived from "quality research." This distinction obviously is made tongue in cheek. In reality both often deal with numbers and clearly both can be quality research.

One important distinction has to do with the treatment of the data in addition to the type of data. In most instances, *quantitative* research will deal with numbers of "things" or measurement of things on an objective scale. Quantitative researchers also, however, diligently strive to maintain a cautious distance from the data to avoid having any influence on the data, data collection, or data treatment and manipulation. Quantitative researchers view themselves as an undesirable variable in the research process and work toward collection of unbiased and uninfluenced information in their attempt to be objective. Most quantitative researchers also use some type of statistical treatment to analyze the information. Unfortunately much of this caution against bias often results in being overly cautious when interpreting results.

Referring back to chapter 2, being overly cautious is one possible reason that so many quantitative researchers fail to interpret their results and merely present the results, letting the reader supply his or her own interpretation. *Implications for the profession should be the first and last elements of good research*: "What difference does it make?"

In conducting *qualitative* research, however, the researcher is completely subjective—he or she becomes not only the one who actually treats the data, deciding which are worthwhile and which can be ignored, but also the one who actually collects and compiles the data. Quantitative researchers, on the other hand, always desire more data from more subjects. As a qualitative researcher, you rely on your intuition and emotion as well as your intellectual judgment during data collection. Consequently, interpretation is usually much easier and obviously more subjective than in quantitative research. As a qualitative researcher you interpret your findings as you perceive them, which may or may not be as they really are (which is a primary criticism of qualitative research).[1]

Borg and Gall point out one difference between qualitative and quantitative research in terms of the relationship between the researcher and those who are the object of study.[2] When conducting quantitative research you attempt to secure a good, close, and trusting relationship with those individuals with whom you work and/or investigate. In order to collect objective data, however, a relationship that is too close can be an extraneous variable and damage the validity of the study. One means toward collecting unbiased information is the use of valid and reliable instruments for data collection. The term "test" is used frequently and will be used appropriately as a "catch all" term for all types of standardized tests, questionnaires, rating scales, and similar instruments of objective measurement. Through objective study, quantitative researchers believe that results of carefully controlled investigations can be generalized to other individuals who are similar to the individuals selected for study. That is, if the researcher is careful not to allow himself or herself to have any influence on the variable under investigation, then the results of the study can be considered applicable to all members of the population from which the subjects under study were selected: for example, all fifth-grade students in the United States. This premise assumes that there are underlying principles of behavior that are common to all members of a specific population with a normal and measurable variance (terms which will be discussed later in this chapter). This behavior is present in the population and present in the same measurable amount in any selected subgroup of this population. Consequently, quantitative researchers study *samples of populations*.

Qualitative researchers, on the other hand, if investigating individuals, as opposed to historical or philosophical topics, usually establish a personal relationship and maintain close contact with those individuals being studied. Qualitative researchers usually attempt to determine and investigate the feelings or the perceptions of those individuals rather than overt behavioral characteristics. In order to gather information on subjects' personal feelings and perceptions, it is essential that researchers establish a close relationship with the individuals being investigated.[3] As a result of this need, qualitative researchers are likely to study only one or a very few individuals. These researchers feel that each individual, each community, and each small group of people (such as a single chorus) will have its own unique values, perceptions, responses and beliefs, which can only be determined through close observation and interaction with that group within the context of their society or subsociety. Qualitative researchers are extremely cautious about generalizing to any other individuals. This results in the criticism that generalizing to a population is the very reason for undertaking research in the first place.

The concepts introduced in this chapter are common to most quantitative research. Some of the concepts are also found in qualitative studies. The foremost difference between the two types has to do with the *kinds* of data that you obtain in your research. Both types of research can utilize tools described in this and the following chapters in gathering data. Research is conducted to explain *what was*, *what is*, and *what will be*. Historical research is frequently used to examine what was; quantitative methods are usually used to investigate what is (descriptive research) and what will be (experimental research).

Variables

The use of the word "variable" is prevalent in all quantitative research. *Variables* can be virtually any class of any phenomenon that can be measured, that is, anything for which a number can be used to differentiate specific elements of that phenomenon. The speed of an automobile can be a variable and people's weight can be a variable. A category such as gender can also be considered a variable; although it does not require "measurement" to determine gender, a number can be assigned to each gender.

Some variables are called *constructs*. Researchers use this term to specify certain variables that cannot be directly measured, but that most people agree really do exist. Intelligence is a construct; talent is a commonly used construct in music. While it may not be directly measurable, a construct directly affects behaviors, which can be measured in order to provide an indication of the degree of presence or absence of that construct in an individual. For example, a researcher can use a performance test, a pitch identification test, a melodic-memory test, or a combination of these as a measure of an individual's musical talent.

Independent and Dependent Variables

The two primary types of variables used in quantitative research are independent variables and dependent variables. *Independent variables* are those that a researcher believes may have some effect on the *dependent variables*. Suppose you design and conduct an experiment to determine which of two methods of teaching the oboe has the greatest effect on the students' ability to discriminate pitch. Teaching method is the independent variable, and the students' scores on a pitch discrimination test would be the dependent variable. The dependent variable "depends" on something; in this case it is the method of teaching oboe. Researchers often use the independent variable to predict or determine how the dependent variable will be changed due to any changes in the independent variable, intentional or not.

In experimental research, the independent variable is the one that is altered or manipulated, such as the method of teaching oboe. In descriptive research the independent variable may be some fixed facet of society. If you conduct a descriptive study to compare the attitude toward a band of students from three different socioeconomic statuses (SES), by race, gender, and grade level, for example, then SES, race, gender, and grade level are all independent variables and the scores from the "attitude test" are the dependent variable. The study is designed to determine the degree to which "attitude" *depends* on students' SES, race, gender, and grade level. It may be easy if you remember that the dependent variable is the outcome and the independent variables are the "other" ones.

Populations and Samples

A *population* is a group of any size in which the members share at least one identifying characteristic. One population, for example, is all the human beings living on the planet earth; another population is all seventh-grade students in Farmville, North Carolina. In quantitative research you identify the population to which you would like to generalize your research results, keeping in mind that the more individuals to whom your results can be applicable, the more valuable your study may be. Suppose you conduct an experiment to study the effects of three methods of music-reading instruction on fifth-grade beginning string students and, due to generous funding from the federal government, you are able to include in your study every fifth-grade string student in the country. In this case, you would be studying an entire population: fifth-grade students in the United States who begin on a string instrument.

Sampling

Quantitative researchers are seldom so generously funded, so they *sample* the population; that is, a sample of subjects is selected from the population as representative of all members of that population. In order to compare the effects of these methods of teaching music reading for fifth-grade beginning string players, you would sample the population and then generalize the results of the study to the entire population. Leedy avers, "The sample should be so carefully chosen that through it the researcher is able to see all the characteristics of the total population in the same relationship that they would be seen were the researcher in fact, to inspect the total population."[4]

After the population has been identified, there are four types of sampling used to select subjects from a population: random sampling, stratified sampling, cluster sampling, and accessible sampling. *Random sampling of subjects* is a simple concept; it means that every person in the population has an equal chance of being selected. Subjects are selected in one of several ways: drawing names out of a hat, flipping a coin, throwing dice, or using a table of random numbers, which can be found in most statistics books (see Figure 4). A table of random numbers is used in the following manner: (1) assign all members of a population a number; (2) turn to the table and select a row and column number; (3) proceed across the row or down a column, using the numbers to select the members of your sample.

The advantage of a random sample is that if the sample is of sufficient size, then the results of your study are accepted as being applicable to the total population. In other words, you would achieve the same results if you gleaned the same information or conducted the same experiment with all members of the population as you did with the randomized sample. The extent or degree to which you can generalize your results to the actual population can be determined using statistics (i.e., a margin of error can be calculated).

Stratified sampling of subjects is used when it is important that the sample be comprised of the same proportion of subgroups as

Figure 4
Random-Numbers Table

Column

Row	1	2	3	4	5	6	7	8	9	10
1	57292	80180	26582	14731	42844	08790	74765	94622	66615	30544
2	28725	34391	05300	70258	50713	97703	39478	48601	04379	96678
3	84847	17645	87466	24680	77634	49611	86766	04635	99743	45801
4	00380	63719	44701	58093	81069	27526	15031	71057	20560	19386
5	45671	29073	90157	31942	69805	50358	41983	17846	82196	04739

the population. In our study of fifth-grade beginning string players, for example, we measure and find that the population consists of 60 percent violin players, 5 percent viola players, 25 percent cello players, and 10 percent bass players. And we think that the instruments played may be important to music-reading skills. If you sample at random, the resulting sample may not have the same proportion as the population, so we determine the size of the sample we want and then the number of each instrument required for the sample to be balanced in the same proportion as the population. In stratified sampling, our population would be divided into groups by the instrument played; then the proper number of subjects would be selected at random from each of these four groups.

Cluster sampling of subjects is when groups are selected instead of individuals. In our study, we may randomly select towns across the United States, then include all fifth-grade beginning string students in those towns as members of our sample.

In most research in the field of music education, it is impossible to obtain any of these types of samples from a large population. First of all, the populations to which you may wish to generalize your results can seldom be randomly sampled. Obviously, it is impossible to compile a list of all the names of the fifth-grade beginning string students in the United States in order to draw names from a hat. Instead researchers use an *accessible population*, such as all of the fifth-grade beginning students in Columbus, Ohio, and a sample from that population. With a manageable population, it becomes feasible to generalize from your sample to the accessible population. In order to generalize from the accessible population to the true population you must gather and provide demographic information on the accessible population. Characteristics of the accessible population in Columbus, Ohio, such as socioeconomic status, gender proportion, instrumentation, ethnic groups, and the like, may be generalized only to urban fifth-grade beginning string students. Even then the population to which you may generalize your results is a large number of students in this country. If your accessible population includes the suburbs surrounding the city of Columbus, then the results of your study may be generalized to the larger population of urban and suburban fifth-graders.

A second major problem in true random sampling is that if any subject declines to participate in the study, then it is no longer considered a true random sample, because all of the members did not have an equal chance of being included in the sample—even though it was that subject's decision not to participate. As an illustration, a quantitative researcher may want to survey famous opera singers to determine when they began voice lessons. After defining "famous," the researcher is able to compile a list of all living singers who meet that criterion, and randomly selects a large number of that population as the sample. The researcher then mails a short questionnaire to his or her sample to be completed and returned. It is unlikely that 100 percent of those receiving the questionnaires will return them completed. Consequently, the quantitative researcher must realize that there is a difference between those individuals who took the time to complete the questionnaire and return it and those who did not—and that those who responded no longer truly represent a random sample. They are *volunteers* of sorts. Consequently, true random sampling is virtually impossible in music-education research.

Volunteers as a Sample

Almost all basic and applied research in music education is conducted with volunteers. Further, numerous studies indicate that volunteers are a biased sample and different from nonvolunteers in many ways. Borg and Gall present an excellent discussion of these differences, compiled from previous research.[5] The differences between volunteers and nonvolunteers may make it difficult to interpret results and generalize to a population, but not always. Referring back to the hypothetical study of opera singers, if your questionnaire contained a question regarding their yearly income, then differences between volunteers and nonvolunteers would probably affect your results (since volunteers normally are from a higher socioeconomic level than nonvolunteers). If, on the other hand, you were more interested in performance anxiety, then the differences between volunteers and nonvolunteers might have little effect on your results, since research shows that there is little difference in anxiety between these two groups.[6]

In soliciting volunteers for conducting research there are many ways to enhance the appeal for volunteer subjects which may provide a representative sample of your true population (pay, for example). Borg and Gall present at least ten suggestions for improving the pool of volunteers.[7]

While it is a fact that true random sampling from a large population is virtually impossible, and most research is limited to a volunteer pool of potential subjects from an accessible population, it *is* possible to make *random assignment* for conducting experiments. Under this method, all of the volunteers are assigned at random to one of the groups participating in the experiment. This method has greater constraints than random selection. Instead of every member of the true population having a equal chance of being selected, constraints result in a situation where a volunteer from a limited population will be assigned to one of two or three groups. Consequently, it is possible that one or more of the groups could end up different from the true population on variables that could affect the outcome of the experiments. These differences become less likely as the size of the sample increases.

Matching Subjects

Another way that differences between groups can be avoided is to use *matching* for group assignment rather than random assignment. Matching is predicated on assigning subjects to groups based on their scores on a test or some other characteristic which is believed to be important or could possibly have an effect on the outcome of the experiment. A subject who has a certain score is paired with another subject who has exactly the same score on the test. One is assigned to a group by the flip of a coin and the matched counterpart goes to the next group. Subjects who cannot be matched are eliminated from the study.

Matching results in several problems. First, eliminating subjects is a very costly procedure for any research—a general rule of thumb for any and all research is *the more subjects, the better the research*. Second, it is difficult to match students in any research design that makes use of more than two groups. Third, it is impossible to match subjects on every characteristic that could have bearing on the results of the study. And finally, it may simply be impossible to find a match; when teachers are studied, for example, there may be only a dozen teachers in the school district which comprises the accessible population. These teachers will most likely have completely differing styles of teaching.

A method similar to matching is *ranking*. Using this procedure, the potential subjects are ranked according to test scores (or whatever variable is used); then a coin is flipped to assign the highest-ranking subject to one group, the next subject goes to the next group, and so on until all subjects are assigned to a group (alternating down the list). No subjects are eliminated and the groups are "close" to being matched.

Random Assignment

A term that is used with increasing frequency in research studies is "random assignment." While random selection of subjects from an identified population is usually impossible, it may be possible to randomly assign subjects from an accessible population. Suppose you identify the population as ninth-grade choral students and your accessible population is the ninth-grade choral students in Dallas, Texas. While it is impossible to be assured that the ninth-graders in Dallas are representative of ninth-graders throughout the country on every characteristic that influences their musical achievement, random assignment of these students to two groups for comparison will at least result in comparable groups.

It must be pointed out, however, that random assignment of subjects means that *each* subject must have an equal chance of being assigned to either of the two or more groups. If Dallas, Texas, has six thousand ninth-grade choral students that can be randomly assigned, then the subject pool is quite large. If intact classes are randomly assigned to one of two (or more) groups, then n = number of classes, not the number of individual students.

Size of Sample

The most basic rule of thumb for all quantitative research is *the larger the sample size, the better*. If, for example, one could study an entire large population, it would be fantastic. But most research in music education must be practical. To determine the minimum number of subjects you must have in your sample, there are several considerations: (a) How reliable do you want your study to be, or, how accurately do you wish to be able to generalize your results to the total population? and (b) To what extent does your population vary on their scores on the dependent variable (which is pretty tricky since this measure is usually not made until close to the end of the study)?

Determining the size of the sample required for a study is not an easy task. Often, studies that have the potential to make a significant contribution to the profession result in unreliable results because the sample size is too small—and this is often due to the experimenter's simply not having access to a sufficient number of subjects. If you wish to conduct an experimental or correlational study, but are limited to a set number of subjects (the band students in your school, for example), then you should perhaps begin the research process all over—that is, select another topic. The sample size must fit the design of the study, which is designed to "solve" the problem. When you attempt to design a study or select a topic to utilize a certain group of subjects, then you are asking for frustration (a bit like "putting the cart before the horse"). The exception here is when the "select group of subjects" comprises the total population, or when the study is intended to investigate characteristics of that select group of subjects (e.g., a single high-school band). The "Catch-22" is that the study then could *not* be generalized to any other group of people, so it is likely to benefit no one but the researcher who completes his or her degree.

Considering the elegance and ideal situation of being able to randomly select subjects from a total population, with the reality of time and financial limitations that accompany graduate school, here is a practical way of determining an adequate sample size (additional considerations are mentioned later when tests for differences are discussed). The Review of Related Literature will provide useful information in determining a sample size. Critical evaluation of previous studies will indicate which studies would have found significant differences if the sample size had been larger. Considerations also include how strong the treatment to be used is (compared to the treatments used in previous studies), the length of the study (for example, two methods of teaching ear-training are more likely to make a difference over a twenty-six-week period of time than a two-week period of time), and the variance of the subjects who have been tested or measured on your instrument for measuring the dependent variable. Regarding this last consideration, a published test will indicate in the manual how previous groups who have taken the test cluster about the average score; if scores on a given test are usually fairly close together for a given age group, then there is little variance, and fewer subjects may be needed. For example, suppose you compare two methods of ear-training with two groups of sixth-graders. If the published test you use to measure their ear-training ability at the end of the treatment indicates that scores tend to cluster around the class average, then fewer subjects could be used in each class than if the test manual indicated that scores were fairly spread out. More subjects in each group would be required. In the latter situation, more subjects would be needed in each group due to the overlapping of scores (the higher scores of the "lower" group overlapping with the lower scores of the "higher" group), which lessens the significant difference between groups.

Scores and Observations: Measuring Variables

The basis of all quantitative research is the ability to measure something. At its extreme: any behavior, phenomenon, or concept that is genuine can be measured (we may not know how yet or have the proper instruments, but if it is true, then it can be measured). Clearly, anything that can be taught can be measured; less clearly, anything that can be learned can be measured. Consequently, concern is given to the validity and reliability, which together indicate the accuracy of the instruments used for measuring behavior, phenomena, or concepts. Validity is whether or not an instrument measures what it is supposed to measure. Reliability is an indication of how well the instrument will show the same results under identical or comparable conditions. (Validity and reliability are discussed in the next section.)

While both independent and dependent variables can be measured, most research reports and theses deal only with scores or observations as the dependent variable (remember, the dependent variable is the one that is dependent on your criterion measure). The scores or observations (measurements) are called data, which are simply information.

Types of Data
Data are normally in one of three broad forms: continuous scores, ordinal data, or nominal data. *Continuous data* are usually defined as scores that can fall anywhere on a continuum. In practice they are usually test scores such as intelligence tests, *Scholastic Aptitude Test (SAT)* scores, or scores on a music test that may range on a continuum from 0 to 100.

Ordinal data are the result of ratings. These data often result from rating scales, as when individuals rate an item on a scale of 1 to 5, with 1 indicating "strongly disagree" and 5 indicating "strongly agree." Ordinal data are frequently used in music studies since it is easier and more appropriate for subjects to rank the symphonies of several composers, for example, than to attempt to provide a score from 0 to 100.

Nominal data are categorical measurements. Nominal data can be a true dichotomy (such as male and female), an artificial dichotomy (such as skilled and less-skilled music readers), or in categories (such as violin, viola, cello, and bass players).

Types of data gathered in a quantitative study are important for statistical analysis. Some methods of treating continuous data will not work with ordinal data. Other methods designed for artificial dichotomies, however, can be used for continuous data if a dividing point is established to compile the continuous data into two groups (high and low, for example).

Tests

A thorough discussion of tests and measurements is beyond the scope of a text such as this one. The Supplementary Sources list at the end of this chapter includes several excellent sources for further understanding and selection of tests. Since tests and measurements are so critical to quantifying any information, certain key terms are provided in this section. While most graduate students have a negative attitude toward and perhaps even a dreaded fear of tests, the term can be used to label any instrument used to identify and measure (quantify) any specific behavior or characteristic of an individual, group, situation, or program. An interview can be considered a test, just as the *Graduate Record Examinations* can be considered a test.

Norm-referenced Tests

Most quantitative studies in music make use of norm-referenced or domain-referenced tests. *Norm-referenced tests* are usually constructed over a period of time by an expert, or group of experts, and undergo extensive revisions and changes. At the end of this rather elaborate construction process the test is administered to a large sample of the population for which it was designed. Using information about the population as well as their test scores, a table is constructed for interpreting scores when the test is administered to other samples of the population. Test items generally range from easy to difficult; an individual's (or group's) score can be compared to the "norm." For example, the most widely used norm-referenced music test is Colwell's *Music Achievement Test*. With this test you can compare your sixth-grade classes' scores to sixth-grade scores across the country on major-minor mode discrimination, feeling for a tonal center, tonal memory, melodic recognition, and many other aspects of music that are taught in music education.[8]

Norm-referenced tests determine how a student compares with other students in a particular subject area. These tests do not provide information regarding the student's strengths and weaknesses within that subject area. Consider, for example, the *Scholastic Aptitude Test (SAT)*: while this norm-referenced test provides separate math and verbal scores with which one can compare a student's score to the national average, the score does not reflect if the student did very well in basic multiplication and division and very poorly in algebra, or if he or she did equally well in each area of math skills. In other words, a student who answers all of the basic math correctly and answers all of the advanced math incorrectly could achieve the same score as a student who answers half of the basic math correctly and half of the advanced math correctly.[9]

Domain-referenced Tests

Domain-referenced tests measure one's degree of achievement in one specific area without reference to anyone else's degree of achievement. The results of a norm-referenced test may indicate that a sixth-grade student can better determine if eight-note melodies are the "same or different" than 57 percent of other sixth-grade students. A domain-referenced test may indicate that a student can accurately discriminate "same or different" for 85 percent of one-to six-note melodies and only 40 percent of the melodies which contain eight notes.

Domain-referenced tests use a sample from a limited and very specific subject or performance area. Considering the testing of math skills mentioned in the previous paragraph, a domain-referenced test may be used to determine the student's performance in multiplying two two-digit numbers rather than all types of math functions. And rather than construct a test which is composed of all possible combinations of multiplying two two-digit numbers, a sample of these combinations is used. A domain-referenced test measures the student's performance level in this one specific area (or domain). Thus, the primary difference between domain-referenced and norm-referenced tests lies in the way the test results are interpreted.

Standardized Tests

Norm-referenced tests are usually *standardized tests.* That is they are designed and constructed to yield accurate results if the person administering the test follows specific instructions and guidelines. Standardized tests are usually published with normative data with which scores for students from a specific population can be compared to the population.

A standardized test is not always available to fit the needs of the researcher conducting quantitative research in music. Consequently, construction of a test is often part of a thesis. Whether you select a standardized test to collect data or construct your own test, three concerns that are important when determining the accuracy of the test are validity, reliability, and the standard error of measurement.

Validity

The extent to which a test measures what it is supposed to measure is *validity*. Researchers concerned with evaluation and with tests and measurements deal with five types of validity: face validity, content validity, criterion-related validity, predictive validity, and construct validity. The term *face validity* is encountered in many theses in which the authors construct tests for measuring student achievement. Face validity is a subjective judgment (consequently the least important type of validity in quantitative research) to determine if the test measures what it is supposed to measure. Often the researcher will have members of the committee look through the test to determine if it has face validity—that is, if, on the surface, the test looks like it measures what it claims to measure. *Content validity* is the result of a systematic and objective evaluation (or construction) of the test to determine if it measures what it is supposed to measure. Obviously, in order to determine if a test measures the subject matter or assesses the information for which it is constructed, clear and concise objectives are a prerequisite. Just as sampling is used to select a representative group of a defined population, content validity requires at least a representative sampling of a subject area's content.

For example, if you conducted an experiment to compare two methods of teaching a music appreciation course, you would want an achievement test to measure accurately what is learned. In order to draw conclusions, the test must be representative of the entire content of the course—that is, a high content validity—and not just a test on some aspect of the course, such as names of Romantic composers.

The extent to which a test is able to predict one's achievement in future endeavors is called *predictive validity*. Perhaps the most widely used example is the *Scholastic Aptitude Test*: the *SAT* has high predictive ability of undergraduates' grade-point average; it is used to predict high-school students' achievement in college. *Criterion-related validity* is similar to predictive validity. Predictive validity is determined for a test by giving the test and then waiting for the predicted behavior to take place, measuring it, and comparing or correlating the scores of the two measures. Criterion-related validity is determined by giving the test and then immediately administering another test, and comparing the two scores. For example, Bowles's *Belwin-Mills Singing Achievement Test* was administered to several hundred college music majors who were then given the *Aliferis Music Achievement Test* and the *Watkins-Farnum Performance Scale*. The Bowles test manual publishes criterion-related validity at .81 with the Aliferis (College Entrance Level) and .73 with Watkins-Farnum.[10] As a result of these coefficients, you would know that Bowles's *Belwin-Mills Singing Achievement Test* is a good instrument to determine subjects' ability to sight-read while playing their wind instruments (i.e., what the Watkins-Farnum test purports to measure), although the Belwin-Mills requires subjects to vocalize melodies.

Construct validity is an indication of how well a test measures a construct (discussed in chapter 2). For example, most people believe there is a trait known as talent (a construct). With time and diligence you could compile a list of characteristics of individuals whom you and your colleagues agree are talented in music and then determine which of those characteristics or behaviors could be measured objectively. A test could then be constructed to measure most of those characteristics. The greatest problem when verifying construct validity is in dealing with the construct. For example, talent is used to refer to performance, ear-training, the ability to adapt to new musical instruments quickly, music reading skills, composition, and many academically oriented areas; constructing a single test to measure all of these attributes would be impossible.

Reliability

The degree to which a test is consistent in its measurements is its *reliability*. Numerous methods for calculating reliability coefficients can be used (ranging from .0 to 1.00, although neither of the extremes is ever attained). The most common method used to determine reliability is to give the test to a large number of people, wait for a period of time (a week, perhaps), and then give the test to the same people. A correlation coefficient is then calculated from the two sets of scores. If the test is of sufficient length, a correlation coefficient can also be calculated by comparing scores from one-half of the test (odd-numbered questions) to the responses on the other half of the test (even-numbered questions); this type of method would require only one set of scores from a group. Normally, the longer the test, the more reliable it is.

While validity is subjective in nature, reliability is a statistical, objective measure. Reliable measures are clearly important in quantitative research, but validity is more important. If a test does not measure what it is supposed to measure, then it doesn't matter if it fails to do so with high reliability!

The final concept with which researchers must be concerned is the *standard error of the mean*. No test is perfect; all scores measured by any one test contain an element of error. This error can be due to test anxiety, the students' not reading a particular question carefully, their tiring as the test progresses, or their simply not marking the correct response when the answer is known. The standard error of the mean can be calculated mathematically (it is related to reliability) and results in a range within which an individual's score falls. The standard error of the mean for some intelligence tests is 10; if a student scores 90 on that I.Q. test, then a counselor can be confident that the actual score is between 80 and 100, and most likely closer to 90 than to 80 or 100.

Selecting Tests

In many quantitative studies, there arises the need to measure variables. In experimental and quasi-experimental studies, researchers will most often need a test for measuring the dependent variable (pitch discrimination, for example). In correlation studies, there occasionally is the need to measure several variables (such as self-concept, scholastic achievement, and music achievement). Several sources contain lists of published tests and descriptions to assist researchers in selecting an appropriate test.

The Ninth Mental Measurements Yearbook is probably the most useful guide for researchers. It contains a description and critical review of 1,266 tests of the 6,056 tests it references.[11] A second valuable catalog is *Tests in Print III*. Also introduced to the field of tests and measurements by the late Oscar K. Buros, it lists 2,672 tests.[12] While it does not include reviews of the listed tests, most are cross-indexed to present and earlier editions of the Buros *Mental*

Measurements Yearbooks, where the tests are often described in detail. Researchers should not limit themselves to the present *Mental Measurements Yearbook*, but should also look in earlier editions for music tests of varying types.

Gronlund suggests a systematic method for selecting appropriate tests to avoid arbitrary selection based on availability, convenience in administering/scoring, or some other factor which is not in keeping with the established goals for using the test.[13]

Your first task is to determine specifically what type of information you wish to accumulate through testing. An area as broad as "music achievement" will not be specific enough. Due to the complex nature of music education, tests for the cognitive, psychomotor, and affective domains of music learning may still be too broad; you must determine the area of learning to be assessed, plus how the information will be used (i.e., placement, formative, diagnostic or cumulative evaluative).[14]

After the specific objectives of the test are determined, you may refer to the *Mental Measurements Yearbooks* or *Tests in Print III* (or any appropriate professional journals, such as *Journal of Educational Measurement, Measurement and Evaluation* and *Guidance*) for a published test to reliably measure the objectives of your study. It is conceivable that an unpublished test may be quite valid and reliable. These may be discovered during your review of related literature or more easily and with greater confidence by consulting with the director of the Center for Research in Music Learning and Teaching at the University of Northern Colorado (Greeley, Colorado). This center has the single best collection of published and unpublished tests in music and music education in the world (including the Educational Resources Information Center).

Sample copies of those tests under consideration should be purchased along with the test manual. Unpublished tests are usually secured by contacting the authors or purchasing microfilm or hard copies of previous theses from University Microfilms International in Ann Arbor, Michigan.

Studying the test copies will result in your determining the test or tests which are most appropriate for achieving your objectives. The manuals will reveal the actual uses for which the test authors constructed each. They will indicate how the test is to be administered (any equipment required, time, any special training for the test administrator—for example, some music tests require a piano and at least some degree of piano proficiency) and how to score and interpret the results.[15]

Although thousands of tests are published for educational purposes, in many instances you will be required to construct a test for your specific research proposal. Study of published tests and textbooks designed for test construction is absolutely essential.

The opening paragraph of this section indicated that the word "test" is used for any instrument designed to gather and quantify objective information (and subjective information, in the case of "opinionnaires"), yet the majority of the section was devoted to "tests" as the term is more frequently used: a paper-and-pencil, right-or-wrong examination-type form of assessment. Other types of instruments such as questionnaires are discussed in the following chapter on descriptive research. The importance of objective testing has been emphasized more in this book's edition than previous editions due to the implementation of the various "basic education plans" in all fifty states.

As music and the fine arts are included in basic education, music educators *must* rely on testing to evaluate the status of learning, just as the other basics have done for at least five decades. There are many who feel that testing can ruin "the musical experience" and that the true "aesthetic response" cannot be tested. Regarding the latter, while the aesthetic experience is a construct, most of the physical and intellectual, and many of the emotional, aspects of this experience *can* be tested. Just as pure intelligence cannot be measured, we do test related aspects or components of intelligence—that is, those characteristics that we associate with an intelligent person. Secondly, there is no justification in believing that regular testing should or will "ruin" music. Professional musicians have used tests for years: auditions and recitals (Carnegie Hall may be among the most glorified and aggrandized of all tests for professional musicians). There are probably few methods to motivate an individual that are more powerful than tests. Used on a daily basis, they clearly indicate to students what they are expected to learn. All too often in graduate school, for example, students have to wait until the final examination to discover the objectives of the course.

Basic Statistics

Certain concepts in statistics are fundamental to virtually all quantitative research. Graduate students should have some knowledge of these in order to read and understand articles in professional journals and other theses. Even if you decide to pursue qualitative research, you will be limited in your understanding of an enormous body of research and, consequently, will be limited in assisting your students in their research.

There is little reason to do the mathematical calculations for statistical analyses except as a means to enhance your understanding of statistics. Most college and university computing departments are equipped with statistical packages that do all of the necessary calculations by computer. Programs such as SPSSX and SAS basically require the researcher to provide the data, select what type of analysis is desired, and indicate this analysis by specific commands found in the user's manual; the results of the analysis are then printed.[16] The researcher must know (1) what kinds of data to use in the analysis (e.g., raw data, transformed data, or descriptive statistics), (2) what method of analysis is most appropriate for the procedures of the study, and (3) how to read or comprehend the results of the statistical analysis in order to draw conclusions.

Most people are aware of the expression "Well . . . that's Greek to me" or "Oh . . . that looks like Greek to me" when they encounter something that is totally incomprehensible. Appropriately, perhaps, or maybe only by coincidence, statisticians have traditionally used Greek letters to indicate various terms and concepts. The ideas presented in this section will avoid Greek letters and use very little math.

Kinds of Statistics

The two primary categories of statistics are *descriptive* and *inferential*. Descriptive statistics are used to describe the characteristics of a sample. The characteristics of a population are called parameters. Inferential statistics are used to analyze the data in order to interpret or allow one to infer the results of the study from the sample to the population from which the sample was drawn. Usually inferential statistics are used to test for differences between one group (who may have been taught using an experimental method) and another group (taught using a "traditional method"). These differences are representative of the differences that would occur in the entire population. (Discussion of inferential statistics will be postponed until chapter 8.)

Descriptive Statistics

Two types of descriptive statistics are used to describe the characteristics of a sample: measures of central tendency and measures of variability. *Measures of central tendency* include the mean, median, and mode. Together these statistics describe the "center," or point toward the middle of a group of scores (which is called the distribution of scores). The *mean* is simply the arithmetic average; you add up the scores, divide by the number of scores, and derive the mean (usually indicated by $\overline{X}$).

Suppose you administer a music achievement test to a sample of eight individuals (indicated in tables of research reports as n = 8) and obtain scores of 90, 80, 80, 70, 66, 55, 46, and 41. These scores total 528, and when divided by 8, the mean equals 66 ($\overline{X}$ = 66). The mean is used quite frequently in research. The means for two groups in an experimental study, for example, can give a quick comparison of the average scores for the two groups.

The *median* represents the middle point in a distribution of scores. Half of the scores in a distribution fall above the median and half of the scores fall below the median. For the distribution of scores in the preceding paragraph, the median is 68. Although none of the subjects scored a 68, that score indicates the midpoint of the distribution. Medians are sometimes more useful than the mean for providing an accurate view of a distribution. As an illustration, consider the professors' salaries in a small but "up-and-coming" department of music. In order to draw students and help establish a better reputation, this small department hires a famous violin performer/teacher at an enormous salary ($125,000/year); the other eight faculty members receive salaries which range from $22,000 to $40,000 per year. The addition of that one violinist would make a tremendous increase in the mean salary in that department of music (probably infuriating the rest of the arts and sciences faculty), but would have negligible effect on the median. In this case the median would provide a better picture of the salary schedule than would the mean.

The *mode*, a third measure of central tendency, is the most common score or observation in a sample. In the distribution used to illustrate the mean above, the mode is 80 because more individuals scored 80 than any other score. In a distribution such as 1,2,3,3,3,4,5,6,7,7,7,8, and 9, there are two modes. This *bimodal* distribution has modes of 3 and 7. (Another bimodal distribution of "scores" would be if one were to measure the height of all living adults. There would be a wide range of "scores," say in inches, with those scores tending to cluster around the average height of females and again around the average height of males.)

These three measures of central tendency are used for continuous scores and ordinal scores or rankings. Nominal data are arranged in frequency distributions such as:

Instruments	n	Percentage
violin	18	51
viola	4	11
cello	10	29
bass	3	9
	n = 35	100%

This list indicates the number (n) of observations or "scores" in each category. The percentage column is included simply as an aid to interpreting the number of observations in each category; in this sense, the percentages can be considered "transformed data" or "transformed scores."

Measure of variability, the second type of descriptive statistic, is used to show how a distribution of continuous scores varies or deviates from the mean. The primary measures of central tendency are the *range, standard deviation*, and *variance*. The most obvious measure of variability is the *range*. In our hypothetical distribution of scores for the music achievement test mentioned earlier (90, 80, 80, 70, 66, 55, 46, and 41; n = 8), the range is 49. The range is simply the difference between the highest score and the lowest score. When scores are close together the range is small, so there is little variability. When the scores are far apart the range is large, so there is greater variability. Also, it becomes obvious why a range would be meaningless for ordinal and nominal data.

The most frequently encountered measure of variability is the *standard deviation*. You have probably encountered the term "standard deviation" in virtually every quantitative research report, article, or thesis that you have read. This statistic is an indication of how scores cluster around the mean. The word "standard" is used for this deviation of scores because a mathematical formula is used to calculate this statistic, so that regardless of the particular study you read, or what kinds of continuous data are described (e.g., test scores, number of colleges, or length of eye fixation in milliseconds), you will always know that 34 percent of all the scores or observations fall between the mean and one standard deviation above the mean. Another 34 percent of the scores fall between one standard deviation below the mean and the mean. If, for example, you have a distribution of scores for which the mean is 25 and the standard deviation is 5, then 68 percent of all of the scores will fall from 20 to 30.

This statistic, the standard deviation, is based on the *normal curve*. The normal curve is a phenomenon of nature. Theoretically, if all the heads of adult males were measured for their hat sizes, and these sizes in inches were plotted on a graph where the vertical axis was the frequency of occurrence (or "how many heads were 21.5 inches in circumference") and the horizontal axis was a linear scale of 18 to 26 inches, and each adult male's head size was plotted as a pinpoint on this graph, the resulting millions of pinpoints would run together to form a normal curve. Theoretically the same phenomenon exists for intelligence. The most popular test for measuring intelligence is based on a mean of 100 with a standard deviation of 15. The *Scholastic Aptitude Test (SAT)*, which is administered to tens of thousands of high-school students each year, is revised and adjusted so that the mean is 1,000 and standard deviation is 200 for combined verbal and math scores. If the vertical axis is the number of students, and the horizontal axis is the *SAT* scores ranging from 400 to 1,600, and you plot the number of students who score 400, the number who score 401, the number who score 402, and so on, then "connect the dots," the resulting curve would resemble the graph in Figure 5, with the mean, median, and mode all equaling 1,000.

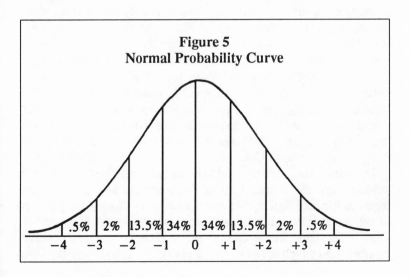

Figure 5
Normal Probability Curve

The normal curve illustrated in Figure 5 shows the mean and the *approximate* percentages of scores that fall within each area of the curve, in relationship to the standard deviations. It is assumed that scores and observations for any variable will fall in a distribution that approximates the normal curve. With this in mind, you may better understand why large samples are better than small samples.

If we apply this curve to *SAT* scores, we find that 34 percent of the scores fall between 1,000 and 1,200; also, 34 percent of the scores fall between 800 and 1,000. Knowing that the mean *SAT* score is 1,000 and that the standard deviation is 200, if you can remember your score you can determine where you stood years ago in relationship to all of the high-school seniors in the United States.

Part of the definition of the normal curve also includes sets of data, or scores or observations, where the median and mode equals the mean.

In our hypothetical discussion of the small department of music that hired a "big-name" violinist to enhance the school's reputation, the mean salary is much higher than the median. This occurs in test scores in all types of research and results in a *skewed* distribution. (See Figures 6 and 7.) In the case with the faculty salaries, the mean is considerably higher than the median, so the distribution is positively skewed and may result in a distribution resembling that graphed in Figure 6.

One other statistic used as a measure of variability should be mentioned; it is the basis of all experimental studies and will be treated in more detail in chapter 8: *variance*. Variance is the very reason for research. As Kerlinger has succinctly stated, if we were all the same, there would be no reason to study anything. All research is conducted to determine *why* things are the way they are—and "things" do differ, whether they are intelligence, oboe playing, teaching methods, or economic status.[17] The word "variance" is used frequently as a specific statistical term (it is the standard deviation squared) *and* in a general sense to describe or discuss how measures of a certain variable differ. For example, you may wish to study the variance of instrumental-music program budgets in the state of Colorado.

Deviation scores are calculated by subtracting the score for each subject from the mean. If all of these deviate scores are added together the total will equal zero. You may try this with any group of numbers. First, calculate the mean, then subtract that number from each score (being careful to jot down which are positive numbers and which are negative numbers); then, add those positive

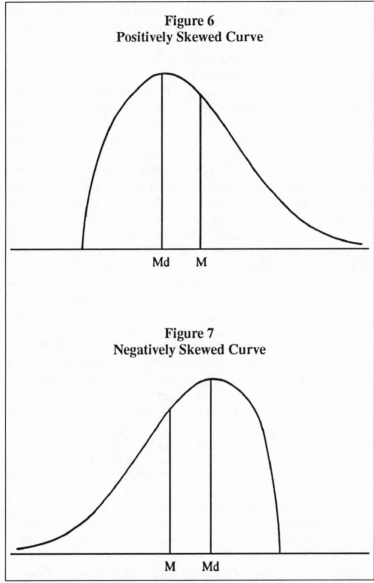

Figure 6
Positively Skewed Curve

Md   M

Figure 7
Negatively Skewed Curve

M   Md

and negative numbers together. The result will be zero, regardless of whether your scores are normally distributed, positively skewed, or negatively skewed. This is actually part of the definition of the word "mean." In order to avoid the dilemma where the total of the deviation scores is zero, those scores are squared to get rid of the negative numbers. Those squared deviate scores are then added together and divided by n (or the number of scores, almost like another mean). The result is the *variance*. The square root of the variance is the standard deviation.

Quantitative researchers are concerned with two types of error variance, or two sources of variance. The first is *error variance* and the second is *systematic variance* (these two are also frequently labeled variance "within subjects" and "between subjects," respectively). *Error variance* results from lack of reliability, which exists in every instrument constructed for testing or gathering objective data. Let us say you were to take the *SAT* today and then take it again in about 48 hours. The odds of your making the same score are pretty slim; your mean score from the two testings might be the best indicator of your true score. The difference between your mean score and the two test scores is error variance. If you administer a pretest and a posttest in an experimental study to a sample of 200 subjects, you can get an idea of how much error variance will exist in each of the 400 test scores.

The other type of variance, *systematic variance*, is the difference in test scores (or scores on any observational instrument) due to changes in a variable as a result of an experimental treatment. For instance, in the experimental study just referred to, if the 200 subjects are divided into two groups, the first group of 100 subjects will be taught pitch identification using an experimental method and the other group of 100 subjects, identified as the control group, will be taught pitch identification using the "traditional method." Other than the course of the nine- to sixteen-week treatment, you would hope to enlarge the systematic variance—that is, you would "hope" that the posttest scores "improved" a great deal between the pretest and the posttest for the subjects in your experimental group and remained about the same for the control group. This systematic variance between groups is due to your new method, and the larger it is the more significant the findings may be.

It is possible to misconstrue your findings because of error variance. One example is that when you administer your posttest, suppose one of the students in your control group happens to get "lucky" and score very high, far higher than the other 99 of his classmates. This subject is called an "outlier" because he doesn't fit in the overall group picture. An "outlier" is a designation for one or more subjects whose scores differ from the mean to such an extent that they *skew* the distribution. What this subject's score does is to add considerably to error variance. Other sources of error variance are due to inappropriate tests for the dependent variable;

the fact that students grow and mature during any experimental program; the fact that observers, no matter how well they are trained, will make mistakes in recording behaviors; and many other factors to be discussed in chapter 8. Some of these extraneous sources of variance can also erroneously increase or decrease the systematic variance.

The goal of all experimental research is to decrease error variance and increase systematic variance. This means that you try to design a study using appropriate sampling techniques, appropriate tests or some other instrument for measuring variables, and appropriate procedures for keeping the error variance as low as possible, while using an experimental treatment strong enough to make a significant increase in the overall variance for the experimental groups. This idea will be further developed as you read on.

Measures of Relationships

Many quantitative studies are concerned with determining the relationship between two or more variables from which predictions are made of varying degrees of accuracy. The descriptive statistics and examples discussed above are concerned with scores or observations from a single variable. Many studies are concerned with investigating the relationship or *correlation* among several variables. An example might be to determine the correlation between the scores of a sample of students on a music test and their scores on an I.Q. test. Correlations may be negative (the higher the music score, the lower the I.Q. score) or positive (the higher the music score, the higher the I.Q. score). The mathematical formulas for calculating correlations result in *correlation coefficients* which vary from -1.00 to +1.00. Perfect correlations of +1.00 or -1.00 are seldom found in research, nor are coefficients of 0.00, which would indicate absolutely no relationship whatsoever.

There are numerous types of correlations that can be used to determine the extent that two variables are related or "correlated." Selection depends on which kinds of data are used: continuous, ordinal, or nominal data. The two classifications of correlation techniques are those which use bivariate methods (one independent variable and one dependent variable) and those which use multivariate methods (several independent variables and one or more dependent variables).

Figure 8 contains a list of techniques for calculating correlations and the types of data for which each type or correlation should be used. Again, due to the availability of computer statistical packages

Figure 8
Correlational Statistics and Appropriate Uses

Bivariate Correlations	Variable 1	Variable 2	Comments
product-moment correlation	continuous	continuous	most often used
Spearman rank-order correlation	ranks	ranks	derived from product-moment
Kendall's tau	ranks	ranks	better than rank-order for numbers less than 10
biserial correlation	artificial dichotomy	continuous	
point-biserial correlation	true dichotomy	continuous	
tetrachoric correlation	artificial dichotomy	artificial dichotomy	
phi correlation coefficient	true dichotomy	true dichotomy	
contingency coefficient	2 or more categories	2 or more categories	usually chi-square

Multivariate Correlations	Dependent Variable	Independent Variable	Comments
multiple regression	ordinal, nominal, continuous	ordinal, nominal, several continuous	indicates effect of each individual variable
discriminant analysis	dichotomy	several continuous	effects on "group membership"
canonical correlation	several continuous	several continuous	indicates effect of each individual variable

which you will probably use to compile and analyze your data, no formulas are given. The computer will do all of the calculations.

As noted in Figure 8, some techniques are for correlating two dichotomies (either true—such as male and female—or artificial—such as skilled and less skilled) and the combinations of these. The only combination missing is ordinal data to continuous data. Researchers handle these correlations by ranking the scores of a measure resulting in continuous data from highest to lowest and then treating those scores as ranks; this allows use of the Spearman rank-order correlation.

Multiple regression is a sophisticated correlation technique; due to the use of computers and available statistical packages all that you as a researcher must do is enter the different variables. Multiple regression is so powerful that it can be used successfully with continuous, ordinal, or nominal data. It not only calculates the relationship of several independent variables to one dependent variable, but it also indicates the separate influence that each of the independent variables has on the dependent variable.

Rogers conducted a study in which 421 high schools representative of all fifty states were selected at random for a survey. The band director and principal were each mailed a questionnaire. A portion of the questionnaire was a rating scale to measure the directors' and principals' perceived value in marching band contests. Rogers's response rate was 77 percent of the band directors and 85 percent of the principals. Sixty-seven percent of the schools surveyed had questionnaires returned by both the band director and the principal. Rogers reported the correlation for the six questionnaire items which were rated by both principals and band directors (using the Pearson product-moment rather than the Spearman). He next investigated these relationships with analysis of variance (which you may critique after reading the next two chapters of this text). Finally, he used data obtained from the questionnaire, such as enrollment, hours spent in rehearsal, and number of awards, as predictor variables for six separate multiple regressions on each of the six "value" items.[18]

Discriminant analysis is similar to multiple regression in that several independent variables or predictor variables can be used to determine the relationship they have with one dependent variable. In this technique, however, the dependent variable must be dichotomous. This technique is becoming increasingly popular in the admissions offices in some universities. Independent variables may include *SAT* scores, class ranking (in percentiles), GPA, socioeconomic status, code variables for specific extracurricular activities, and others. The dependent variable is "accept" and "not accept" (a dichotomy). Multiple regression, on the other hand, could be used with the same set of independent variables and yield the potential students' predicted GPA by entering both the independent and dependent variables for many individuals. After the computer establishes the best possible equation—that is, which variables should be weighted as having the most influence, the second most influence, etc.—then only the independent variables need to be entered to predict the success of the students in college. Each year the data from the previous year's class can be entered into the equation in order to refine the data and make them more accurate.

An easily accessible example of the value of discriminant analysis is Goodstein's study of the leadership characteristics of high-school band directors. Goodstein used a published standardized test to assess a leadership score of 104 successful band directors and a random sample of 104 band directors from the same thirty-seven states. Band directors also completed Goodstein's questionnaire, which was used to quantify demographic data from both groups. A point-biserial correlation was used to determine the relationship of twenty-eight variables from the leadership test and questionnaire to the artificial category: successful or random band directors. Twelve variables were determined to be significantly correlated. Those twelve variables were then entered into a computer program to determine which variable predicted successful achievement most accurately. Interesting results are found in Goodstein's study. He also entered the data from the random sample to determine how many of those directors were "successful." You should review this study to discover how discriminant analysis can be used.[19]

Canonical correlation is among the most sophisticated techniques for determining relationships and/or prediction. Referring back to the previous paragraph for the example of using multiple regression for prediction, the same independent variables could be used, but the canonical correlation could predict students' GPA in their major, their overall GPA, and what they will "probably" score on the *Graduate Record Examinations*.

May made excellent use of this sophisticated statistical technique in his study of musical preferences of elementary students. His study measured audiation achievement of 577 students on a published standardized test. Students also rated twenty-four thirty-second musical excerpts on a five-point scale. Three discriminant analyses were used to investigate the students' ratings on the variables: grade level, race, and gender. May's computer analysis yielded two significant canonical correlations. Both of these very complex relationships accounted for only 26 percent of the students' total variance. Students who did well on the tonal and rhythmic subtests of the standardized test correlated the highest with rock music and lowest with jazz. The second canonical correlation found the closest relationship for students with the best tonal audiation skills to be preference for art music, country and western, and nonwestern ethnic music.[20]

Tests for Differences

Many quantitative studies use some type of statistical test to determine if there is a *significant difference* between statistical tests, because differences are essential in experimental research. They are used less in descriptive research, except for relationship studies, where a researcher may want to see if the correlation between two or more variables is significant.

The basic concept of all statistical tests for differences is a mathematical formula to determine the *probability* that scores or observations of the dependent variable for subjects in two or more groups could have happened by chance.

Probability

An understanding of probability, or at least some understanding of this very complex term, may be apropos. When you flip a coin, the probability of getting heads is .5 ($p = 1/2 = .5$). If you roll dice in a game, the odds of rolling a "2" are .17 ($p = 1/6 = .1666 \dots$). Many individuals will gamble on what "the common wisdom" calls the "law of averages." That is, if you flip a coin ten times and the first nine times it comes up "heads," you can usually get someone to give you pretty healthy odds that you cannot come up with "heads" again. Take their odds. If you flip the coin nine times in a row and you get "heads" each time, what are the odds of getting "heads" a tenth time? Odds are 50/50; $p = .5$ each and every time.

The following is paraphrased from an example brightly conceived by the research pedagogue Fred N. Kerlinger.[21] Assume you wish to conduct an experiment to determine whether making it difficult to get in a group makes that group more desirable and valuable to a sample of yuppies. Your hypothesis is that difficulty of being accepted into a specific group makes that group more attractive to the members of that group. The idea is that the harder it is to be accepted into a particular country club—expensive membership fee, high minimum monthly dinner bills, expensive cocktails, a long waiting list, driving a Volvo or BMW ("maybe" an Acura), submitting a résumé, "hanging-out" with the "in" crowd— the more momentous being a member is to those in the club and the more significance they will attach to their membership in that country club.

Your sample is selected at random and randomly assigned to three groups. Group A will undergo extreme difficulty and adversity in being accepted into a country club. Group B will go through a fairly standard degree of trouble in joining another country club. Group C will be able to join a different country club by simply paying a fee (charged to their Sears credit card) and signing their name. At the end of the experiment you have all of the subjects indicate on a seven-point rating scale their perception of "importance of belonging in your group." You now add the subjects' ratings in each group and divide by the number of subjects in that group. The mean ratings for each group result in: A = 5.6, B = 4.8, and C = 3.4.

These means initially seem to support your hypothesis; that is, the A group rated their club the highest; the C group, who were able to join the club with no difficulty, rated their club the lowest; and B group falls between the two. But is it possible that if you drew numbers out of a hat and assigned them to subjects, by averaging them you could find the same resulting order of A > B > C? Yes, you could, and what are the chances? Or, what is the probability of getting this order purely by chance?

If you drew numbers from a hat, assigned them to subjects, and calculated the group means, there are six possible orders to the three groups:

$$A > B > C \qquad A > C > B \qquad B > A > C$$
$$B > C > A \qquad C > A > B \qquad C > B > A$$

The probability of arriving at your results is the same as rolling a "2" on one die in a game: $p = 1/6 = .17$.

There are two ways to interpret your findings: (1) the results of the experiment agree with your hypothesis, and the chances of getting the same results by chance are $p = .17$; or (2) if your conclusion is incorrect, and the rank ordering of the three groups really did occur by chance, then you could conduct the experiment one hundred times and get this $A > B > C$ about seventeen times. This probability makes it very difficult to accept the hypothesis, if you could bet the same results one out of six times purely by chance.

This is a very simple statistical test for differences (not a good one) to determine the probability of your achieving or compiling or collecting the same results by chance as the results from your experiment. If there had been four groups (A, B, C, D) then there would have been two dozen combinations, and the probability of obtaining $A > B > C > D$ would be 1/24, or .04. With these odds, you could have accepted your hypothesis with confidence. The probability of attaining the same results by chance would be only four out of one hundred times.[22]

Significant Differences

Basically all statistical tests for differences determine the probability that your results could have happened by chance. You as a researcher establish the *alpha level* prior to any calculations for these tests. The alpha level is the level of probability that you establish as the point where you will accept or reject your hypothesis. If you established an alpha level of .20 (that your findings result twenty times out of one hundred purely by chance), then you would have accepted your hypothesis in the example above involving three groups joining the country clubs since your results were at the .17 level. This finding relates to significance level.

In research, an alpha level of .20 is not very stringent. It allows too many cases (twenty out of one hundred) to slip by out of pure chance. In other words, you are saying that there is a one-out-of-five chance that your *significant difference* is really due to luck. Researchers labeled this a *Type I error*: finding a significant difference when one really does not exist. It is really due to luck. Lowering the alpha level to $p = .10$ helps to reduce the possibility of making a Type I error. Lowering it to $p = .05$ helps even more. At this point you would have been forced to reject your hypothesis about the three groups in the three country clubs because those results ($p = 0.17$) exceeded your significance level. If your experiment had made use of four groups in four country clubs and your results were the same, the probability would be $p = .04$, or $A > B > C > D$. Those results would have been significant with alpha set at $p = .05$ and you could have stated that the results were due not to chance, but to the independent variable. Note that many hypotheses are stated in the *null form*. A null hypothesis is rejected when your results appear to be due to the independent variable and not due to pure luck. (We decided to remind you of the null version just in case this chapter started to make sense to you.)

As you might anticipate, where there is a Type I error, there must be a Type II error. A *Type II error* is simply the opposite, the probability of failing to find a significant difference when one really does exist. Type II errors are affected by how "powerful" a statistical test for differences is. Power can be generated in a number of ways. For example, you can increase the power of a test (that is, increase your chances of finding the significant difference) by raising the alpha level from .05 to .10—but this also increases your chances of making a Type I error. Another way is to use more sophisticated statistical tests; analysis of variance is more powerful than a *t*-test. Finally, the power can be increased by increasing the size of your sample. Several mathematical formulas can be used to determine how much power you have in any given statistical test for differences. These are beyond the scope of this text and will not be presented. One important feature, however, is that one of the numbers that is plugged into this formula is n, the sample size. And the larger the sample, the more powerful the test for differences—the less likely you are of making a Type II error.

Summary

The objective of this chapter was to establish a foundation for terms and concepts used in quantitative research. Most graduate students using this text will never use all of the methods and statistical tools described in this and subsequent chapters. Most graduate students as professionals, however, will encounter all of these methods and concepts when reading research. One of the continual problems in music and music education is that research seldom reaches the hands (and minds) of practitioners.

Problems for Review and Discussion

1. Differentiate between independent and dependent variables. Find examples of each in a research document.
2. What is the difference between a population and a sample? What procedures may be used to draw a sample from a population?

3. Find examples in the literature of each kind of sample discussed in this chapter.
4. Explain the difference between norm-referenced tests and domain-referenced tests.
5. Define continuous data, ordinal data, and nominal data. Find examples of each in research literature.
6. What are the five kinds of validity discussed in this chapter? Give an example of each one.
7. What is the difference between descriptive and inferential statistics? How can you determine which kind of statistics would be best for your research?
8. What is the difference between measures of central tendency and measures of variability? How can you tell when each one should be used?
9. Why are measures of relationships important?
10. What is the significance of probability for quantitative research?

Supplementary Sources

Ary, Donald, Lucy C. Jacobs, and Asghar Razavieh. *Introduction to Research in Education*, 3rd ed.; New York: Holt, Rinehart and Winston, 1985. Chapters 5-8.

Asher, J. William. *Educational Research and Evaluation Methods*. Boston: Little, Brown and Company, 1976. Chapters 3, 4, 8.

Berk, Ronald A., ed. *A Guide to Criterion-Referenced Test Construction*. Baltimore: Johns Hopkins University Press, 1984.

Best, John W., and James V. Kahn. *Research in Education*, 6th ed.; Englewood Cliffs, N.J.: Prentice-Hall, 1989. Chapters 2, 4, 7, 8.

Borg, Walter R., and Meredith D. Gall. *Educational Research: An Introduction*, 5th ed.; New York: Longman, 1989. Chapters 6-9.

Brown, Frederick G. *Measuring Classroom Achievement*. New York: Holt, Rinehart and Winston, 1981.

Colwell, Richard J. *Music Achievement Tests*. Chicago: Follett Educational Corp., 1967-1970.

Committee to Develop Standards for Educational and Psychological Testing. *Standards for Educational and Psychological Testing*. Washington, D.C.: American Psychological Association, 1985.

Drew, Clifford J. *Introduction to Designing Research and Evaluation*. St. Louis: C. V. Mosby, 1976. Chapter 4-7.

Fox, David J. *The Research Process in Education*. New York: Holt, Rinehart and Winston, 1969. Chapters 5, 6, 7, 11, 12.

Gay, L. R. *Educational Research: Competencies for Analysis and Application*. Columbus, Ohio: Charles E. Merrill, 1976. Chapters 4, 5, 7.

Gronlund, Norman E. *Constructing Achievement Tests*, 3rd ed.; Englewood Cliffs, N.J.: Prentice-Hall, 1982.

Hopkins, Charles D., and Julian C. Stanley. *Educational and Psychological Measurement and Evaluation*, 6th ed.; Englewood Cliffs, N.J.: Prentice-Hall, 1981. Chapter 7.

Kerlinger, Fred N. *Behavioral Research: A Conceptual Approach*. New York: Holt, Rinehart and Winston, 1979. Chapters 2-5.

_____. *Foundations of Behavioral Research*, 3rd ed.; New York: Holt, Rinehart and Winston, 1986. Chapters 3-12.

Mason, Emanuel J., and William J. Bramble. *Understanding and Conducting Research: Applications in Education and the Behavioral Sciences*, 2nd ed.; New York: McGraw-Hill, 1989. Chapters 6, 8, 9.

McMillan, James H., and Sally Schumacher. *Research in Education: A Conceptual Approach*, 2nd ed.; Glenview, Ill.: Scott, Foresman, 1989. Chapters 6, 7, 8.

Mitchell, James V., ed. *The Ninth Mental Measurements Yearbook*. Lincoln, Neb.: The University of Nebraska Press, 1985.

_____. *Tests in Print III*. Lincoln, Neb.: The University of Nebraska Press, 1985.

Rainbow, Edward L., and Hildegard C. Froehlich. *Research in Music Education: An Introduction to Systematic Inquiry*. New York: Schirmer Books, 1987. Chapters 8-10.

Sax, Gilbert. *Foundations of Educational Research*, 2nd ed.; Englewood Cliffs, N.J.: Prentice-Hall, 1979. Chapters 5, 9.

Sowell, Evelyn J., and Rita J. Casey. *Research Methods in Education*. Belmont, Calif.: Wadsworth Publishing Company, 1982. Appendices.

Travers, Robert M. W. *An Introduction to Educational Research*, 4th ed.; New York: Macmillan, 1978. Chapters 4, 9, 11, 13.

Tuckman, Bruce W. *Conducting Educational Research*, 3rd ed.; New York: Holt, Rinehart and Winston, 1988. Chapters 4-7.

Van Dalen, Deobold B. *Understanding Educational Research: An Introduction*, 4th ed.; New York: McGraw-Hill, 1979. Chapters 3, 5-8.

Vockell, Edward L. *Educational Research*. New York: Macmillan, 1983. Chapters 3-7.

7. Descriptive Research: Concepts and Techniques

As mentioned in the previous chapter, most research attempts to explain *what was, what is,* or *what will be.* This chapter is devoted to *what is.* Descriptive research essentially deals with what exists at the present time. It is a broad umbrella category that can be further divided into several types of methodologies. Each is appropriate for pursuing different types of research—that is, a research design or methodology that is appropriate for one problem and purpose may be completely inappropriate for another problem and purpose.

Descriptive research has traditionally constituted the majority of research completed in music education, as well as the field of education in general. One reason is that graduate students are under the impression that descriptive research is the "easiest" type of research to conduct. This is certainly a false illusion; *good* descriptive research is just as difficult to conduct, if not more so, than any other type of quantitative research. One reason for its difficulty is that you, as a scholar, must interpret the results. The results in good descriptive research provide a clear, substantiated view of *what is,* but some researchers attempt to manipulate those findings into what *should be.* The addition of an unjustified and overly subjective component to an otherwise clearly objective research technique can create problems in the validity of any quantitative study.[1]

Purposes of Descriptive Research

In music education, descriptive research usually is conducted for one of three purposes: (1) to obtain data on the current status of existing phenomena, such as conditions, practices, and situations; (2) to establish relationships among several variables, using the data about the current status to investigate relationships that may provide greater insight into the current status; and (3) to determine developments, trends, or changes by describing variables as they develop over a period of time.

Frequently, it is beneficial to know the current status of a subject area. The state music consultant in most states compiles a list of various aspects or variables from each school district in the state: number of music educators and their area(s) of specialization, highest earned degree, number of students enrolled in each music course, number and kind of school-owned instruments, number and specific titles of music textbooks, etc. When assembled, these data provide an *overview* of at least some components of music education in the state. When this information is compiled graphically, it can be used to indicate trends or changes.

The task of the graduate student, however, is not to simply compile the information, but to investigate relationships that may be discovered through the collection and treatment of these data. The state music consultant may look for *relationships* between the variables, such as the number of general music teachers and the number of students enrolled in general music. He or she may then exert influence in appropriating additional state funds to those school districts that need more general music teachers. Other information may be useful for determining how to upgrade the music program in a school district that may be judged quantitatively to be inferior to the others in terms of the items contained in the survey. It should be apparent that this quantitative, descriptive survey cannot indicate whether the qualitative standards in one school district are better or worse than those in another school district.

The data compiled each year by the state music consultant could also be used to investigate *trends*. Comparison of these data may indicate that an increase in enrolled students justifies and necessitates recruiting more general music teachers. The state music consultant can also use the information resulting from his or her descriptive study to show administrators of growing school districts how other districts changed when they experienced a similar growth.

Kinds of Descriptive Research

There is considerable disagreement among researchers as to what constitutes descriptive research. For the purposes of this book, three broad categories of research will be considered descriptive research: *survey* studies, *relationship* studies, and *development* studies. Some researchers categorize the methodology discussed in chapter 4, aesthetic inquiry, as a kind of descriptive research (depending on the methods used to conduct the study). Others claim that labeling a mode of inquiry "aesthetic inquiry" is analogous to calling descriptive or philosophical studies by their subject matter (e.g., "salary inquiry" or "teaching methods inquiry"). The difference may lie in its unique blend of subjectivity and objectivity in investigation of one of the most elusive constructs that we can accept as real. Aesthetic inquiry, as a blend of descriptive and philosophical methods, is much like the difference in music harmony and music theory. Music theory utilizes subjective interpretation of the composer's intention (hence the name "theory"), whereas harmony is quantifiable—it is either right or wrong to say a B-flat triad is a V chord in the key of E-flat major.

Another category of research that many writers place on the same level as survey studies is *observational studies*. The writers of this text consider observational studies to be a method of collecting data. Observational techniques are often used as procedures for collecting data for survey, relationship, and development studies as well as experimental and quasi-experimental studies. The difference between "kinds" of descriptive research is due to the overall purpose of the study and the treatment of the data. Each kind of descriptive research can use a variety of techniques for collecting data.

The primary purpose of any kind of survey is to obtain objective data regarding the current status of a specific situation or practice. The survey is the single most common type of research in the United States. Surveys are conducted by the television industry, the advertising industry, political organizations, and numerous privately owned public opinion polls. The data are usually used to describe current situations or practices. And they may be used to make intelligent suggestions for improving current situations or practices. The Gallup poll may be the most widely known survey in this country. The oldest continuous survey is the census taken of people living in the United States; that survey has been taken every ten years since the U.S. Constitution was ratified.

Survey Studies

A survey in itself is simply a systematic method of collecting information on one or more variables. Traditionally, data collection has been conducted using a questionnaire or interview. In recent years the use of observational techniques has become increasingly popular. For assessing many behaviors, the questionnaire and interview are inappropriate, since people are not always cognizant of their own behavior. An example might be a study comparing the time in choral rehearsals spent in actual singing to the time spent in listening to the director talk. If you used a questionnaire to determine the percentage of rehearsal time that the director spends talking, whom would you have complete the questionnaire? Most likely, the director would underestimate the time he or she spends talking. On the other hand, the students would probably overestimate the percentage of rehearsal time that their director talks. An unbiased observer, however, could measure those times using two stopwatches to provide accurate and objective quantitative data.

Also, observational techniques can satisfy the criterion of objectivity, essential to good quantitative research. Some individuals answer questionnaires or interview questions with responses that they feel the researcher wants to hear or that they "wish" were true. In a sidewalk interview, for example, if you stopped individuals and asked whether they prefer rock, country-western, or classical music, they might indicate classical music, thinking that this response might appear more sophisticated. If you conducted the interviews wearing cowboy boots and a ten-gallon hat, they might respond, "Country-western." And if you were standing by your van, on which was placed a sign, "HOT & LOUD: WPFG—the louder, the better," then more respondents might answer that they preferred rock music. Such bias is occasionally a problem when graduate students attempt to conduct surveys using music-appreciation students as subjects. While these classes are usually large in number and provide accessible samples of a general student body, many subjects will respond to questionnaires with what they perceive to be the "correct" response.

Observational techniques as a research tool enable the researcher to gather more objective data. Certainly the individual conducting the observations can exert bias, but there are techniques discussed in a subsequent section which can enhance objectivity of data collection.

Survey studies are used to describe situations and practices in all facets of education. Common areas in which educational researchers conduct surveys include school surveys, job analysis, content analysis, public opinion surveys, and curriculum surveys.

Relationship Studies

This type of descriptive research not only collects information regarding the current status of a situation or practice, but uses the data to determine the extent to which a relationship exists between variables. This kind of descriptive study attempts to gain insight into why things are the way they are. Examples of this type of descriptive research are (1) *casual-comparative studies*, which attempt to investigate why the current status exists by making comparisons of phenomena to determine what variables accompany certain practices, activities, or conditions; (2) *correlation studies*, which are used to determine the extent to which two or more variables are related and the extent to which a change in one variable affects the other variables(s); and (3) *case studies*, which are usually considered a qualitative mode of inquiry (discussion as such will be postponed until the final section of this chapter).

Casual-comparative studies compare the incidence of certain factors or conditions and then attempt to show the reasons why they occur. Not only does this type of research investigate present conditions, but it also seeks to determine a causal relationship. Borg and Gall report that this method of investigating causal relationships is gradually being replaced by correlational methods.[2] Traditionally, causal-comparative research has been used in lieu of or as a pilot test to an experimental study.

In experimental research, the investigator is able to exert rigorous control of influences on the dependent variables and manipulate the independent variable to determine the causal relationship within the realm of a predetermined level of probability. In some research problems, however, the investigator is not able to manipulate the independent variable. An extreme example is the causal-comparative research used to determine the relationship between smoking cigarettes and lung cancer.

A primary reason that the use of correlation techniques has been favored over causal-comparative methods is that researchers now have greater access to sophisticated statistics. The *t*-tests and ANOVA discussed in the next chapter have been used by researchers for many years. Other techniques, such as multiple regression and canonical correlation, are relatively new techniques and are part of the computer statistical packages available in virtually every academic computing department of every university that has a graduate school. Both SAS and SPSSX are available for microcomputers, found in almost one-third of the homes in the United States.[3]

The causal-comparative method is normally limited to investigation of the relationship between two variables. Statistical techniques such as multiple regression can determine the influence of several variables on a single dependent variable. Multiple regression can indicate how several "causes" can determine the "outcome," as well as the weight or relative influence of each of those "causes" (independent variables). In most areas of teaching and learning—especially with regard to music—seldom can the "cause" of any behavior, practice, activity, policy, or procedure be limited to one variable. Learning is such a complex phenomenon that the capability to examine several "causes" of one "outcome" is generally going to provide more valuable information than studying a one-to-one relationship.

On the other hand, causal-comparative research is valuable to investigate the relationship of certain independent variables that are very difficult to manipulate. The effect of cigarette smoking on lung cancer was mentioned. An example in music education might be if you wanted to investigate the extent of difference in music-reading ability between freshman string majors in college who started in a Suzuki program and freshman string majors who started in a traditional string class. Obviously, conducting an experiment to investigate this problem would take years, and the attempt to identify a population of future music majors among a group of fifth or sixth-graders would be ludicrous. Causal-comparative methods can be used to investigate this problem by examining past events. For this reason, the method is also commonly referred to as *ex post facto* research, and consequently it is often treated as an entirely separate kind of research. Literally meaning "after the fact," this procedure investigates cause and effect after they have actually taken place, thereby introducing a certain amount of subjectivity into the study. It is even considered by a few researchers to be superior to experimental research because the relationship occurs naturally, without intentional manipulation of the independent variable.

One example of research using causal-comparative techniques is that by Zalanowski, who studied the relationship of several aspects of musical preference (using a rating scale—ordinal data) and left-brain/right-brain "style of thinking" (an artificial dichotomy). Obviously, the researcher could not manipulate subjects' "style of thinking." Few music researchers are able to perform brain surgery to alter the cognitive patterns of a randomly selected sample in order to study left-brain/right-brain perception and cognitive processes, so the causal-comparative method may be the best technique to study these behaviors. Zalanowski presents several tables which contain correlations between scores on these variables. The researcher used the Pearson product-moment correlation to determine the extent of these relationships. You should be able to read this study in the *Journal of Research in Music Education* and discuss how its validity might be enhanced, based on your present knowledge of statistics from the previous chapter.[4]

Another example of causal-comparative research is the study by Cutietta, Millin, and Royse on hearing loss suffered by school band directors. These researchers present evidence that the noise level encountered by many band directors exceeds the safe level set by the U.S. government. Over a period of time this noise may result in permanent hearing loss. Obviously, such research would be impossible with an experimental and control group.[5]

A serious weakness of causal-comparative research and *ex post facto* research is the impossibility of controlling the independent variable in order to replicate the study, since the independent variable must be reconstructed after the circumstance has taken place. Kerlinger lists the primary weaknesses of this type of research as the inability to randomize groups and the difficulty in interpreting the data properly.[6] Referring back to the string class illustration above, since randomization is impossible, can one assume that seven years ago the students who started in a Suzuki method were from the same population as those who started in a traditional string class? Certainly they may be the same in age, but how does geographic location enter as an extraneous variable? Socioeconomic status? Length of time in Suzuki program? Parental influence? And so on. All of these factors make interpretation very difficult, if not impossible.

Correlation studies have become an increasingly growing area of research due to the development of more accurate statistical techniques and their accessibility through computer packages. As already indicated, correlation studies are used to investigate the interrelationships between variables. These techniques can be used to determine the relationships between intelligence and musical achievement, gender and musical achievement, or an adjudicator's ratings and musical achievement.

Notice in the previous sentence that three different independent variables were mentioned as possibly correlated with musical achievement (the dependent variable). If you were to use a test to measure musical achievement which resulted in continuous scores

(0 to 100, for example), there are correlational techniques to determine the relationship of this variable to intelligence (also a continuous measure), gender (a dichotomous measure), and rankings (an ordinal measure). Further, techniques such as multiple regression can be used to determine the effects of all three measures, independent variables, on musical achievement. These various types of correlation statistics are listed in Figure 8 in the previous chapter.

As in causal-comparative studies, correlation techniques cannot be used with confidence for determining cause and effect, but correlations can be used for determining relationships and the degree of those relationships. To use a worn-out cliché, correlations are similar to the "chicken and the egg": it is not always possible to determine which causes the other. A genuine advantage is to use correlations to predict effects and relationships.

Significant Correlations

Correlations are usually used to study the relationship of one independent variable with a dependent variable. Due to advanced statistics and computers it has become relatively easy for you to investigate the relationship between several independent variables and even several dependent variables. This has become important in the last few decades. While it has given teachers and researchers valuable insights to discover how several variables are related, such as high-school GPA and college GPA, it is of greater value to determine how high-school GPA, class ranking, family's SES, amount of scholarship aid, intended major, and years in high-school extracurricular activities affect college GPA. In other words, we can get a clearer picture, and probably a more accurate picture.

To keep matters simple in order to grasp a few basic concepts, we will first discuss correlations of one independent variable and one dependent variable. Suppose you give a music achievement test, Text X, to one hundred subjects. Then you give them an I.Q. test, Test Y. Their scores on Text X range from 30 to 85 and their scores on Test Y range from 92 to 147 (undoubtedly your professor's score got mixed in there on the extreme; which end?). Interestingly, as you pair up those scores for each subject in your sample, you discover that the individual who scored 30 on Text X scored a 92 on Text Y; the subject who scored 31 on Test X scored a 93 on Test Y; the subject who scored a 32 on Text X scored a 94 on Test Y, and so on. Not only could we conclude that Text X has tremendously high concurrent validity, but the two measures result in a perfectly positive correlation of r = +1.00 (correlation coefficients are usually written as "r"). If the pairs of scores "went the other way," the correlation coefficient would be -1.00, indicating a perfect negative relationship or correlation (concurrent validity would still be high).

It stands to reason that if one of these measures can be used to predict the other variable, then they are related. Some researchers will even go as far as to indicate that the variable measured by the predictor test "causes" the variable on the other test.[7] This may be going a bit too far, since we would never know whether high music achievement "causes" a high I.Q. *or* a high I.Q. causes greater musical achievement. Most people would probably be inclined to accept the latter.

One phenomenon of correlation coefficients is that the coefficient squared equals the explained variance in a variable.[8] If you will recall our discussion of variance in the previous chapter, it was loosely defined as "how a group of scores vary from the mean." If an independent variable is correlated to a dependent variable to the extent that the correlation coefficient is .42, then the independent variable explains .1764, or 17.6 percent, of the variance in the dependent variable. This "explained" variance is the reason why many researchers will infer that the independent variable "causes" 17.6 percent of the variance in the dependent variable. Such a conclusion may be true, but it is probably a bit too strong. Correlations are a good way to investigate conceivable cause and effects, which can be verified through experimental research.

Depending on the size of the sample and the size of the correlation coefficient, a correlation may be significant. If you will recall the discussion of probability in the "Tests for Differences" section of the previous chapter, you will remember that this significant correlation would indicate that the correlation is too strong for the coefficient to have resulted by chance (the variables are related too closely). A computer program used to calculate the correlations between independent and dependent variables will also print the probability level of that coefficient resulting by chance. Any correlation coefficient that results in a probability value less than the established alpha level—discussed in the previous chapter—indicates a significant correlation.

Brand, in 1986, conducted a study to investigate the relationship between music in the home environment and musical perception and achievement of second-grade students. This is one of several fine correlation studies completed by Brand. In his 1986 study he surveyed the home environment with one measure, subjects' tonal and rhythmic perception with a published standardized test, and music achievement on formal and informal observational evaluations. Three multiple regression analyses were computer-generated or -calculated. Tonal perception, rhythmic perception, and music achievement *each* served as a dependent variable to determine how that dependent variable was affected by four independent variables: parents' attitudes toward music, parents' concert attendance, parent/child's use of stereo systems, and parents' previous performance experiences. Brand reports descriptive statistics for each independent and dependent variable, and measures of central tendency and variability, and uses a correlation matrix to present the individual correlations of every possible pair of variables. The four independent variables had a significant effect on music achievement.[9]

Due to his rather large sample size, a correlation as small as .16 is significant. This means that in a sample as large as Dr. Brand's, a correlation of r = .16 is a "closer" relationship than would have occurred by chance; more specifically, a relationship that close would have occurred by chance less than five out of one hundred times (with a group of subjects the same size). Since a correlation of this magnitude accounts for, or "explains," only 2.5 percent of the variance ("r squared") in the dependent variable, researchers often distinguish between *statistical* significance and *practical* significance.

Development Studies

This kind of descriptive research collects information on existing situations (like survey studies) and determines relationships (as in relationship studies). Development studies carry the investigation one step further: they examine changes in these variables over a period of time. Development studies include *longitudinal studies*, *trend studies*, and *cohort studies*. The difference in these three types of studies has largely to do with sampling techniques.

Longitudinal studies are normally conducted over a period of time with data collected from the same sample at specific intervals during the study. These measurements indicate change and development. Longitudinal studies are obviously time-consuming and very seldom, if ever, used for thesis research. They are often expensive but still constitute one of the best ways to study human development.

A prime example of the importance of longitudinal studies is the work of Piaget. Virtually every student in any field of education is at least familiar with the theories of Piaget. His work was the result of longitudinal research.

A type of longitudinal study that is used far more frequently is the *cross-sectional study*. Cross-sectional studies are similar in concept to longitudinal studies. Instead of measuring the same sample at periodic intervals, however, different subjects from the same population are measured at the same time. These subjects are then representative of that population at different points in their development. As an illustration, assume that you wish to study a specific characteristic (variable) of a population, and how this variable changes every five years over a seventy-year period. With a true longitudinal design, you would randomly sample the population (five-year-olds) and measure the variable. This measuring (or testing) would be repeated every five years for seventy years (perhaps your grandchildren could deposit your thesis for you). A more reasonable method is the cross-sectional technique, where individuals at the ages of five, ten, fifteen, twenty, twenty-five, etc., are randomly selected from the population and tested. These data are then considered representative of the various stages of growth. The changes in American society and culture during the last seventy years should provide obvious reasons for recognizing the degree that cross-sectional studies may not be as valid as longitudinal studies. Clearly, the environmental influences on preschoolers seventy years ago were quite different from the influences on preschoolers today.

A cross-sectional study was compiled by Cutietta and Haggerty in 1987. These investigators studied the phenomenon of color association with music in 1,256 subjects. The related literature provided evidence of two distinctly different theories. One possibility was that synaesthesia is a naturally occurring response to music in very young children, which is not reinforced while growing up. Consequently, color association would result as a function of "memory" in adult life. A second possibility was that color association with music was a learned behavior as a result of association; that is, listening to certain types of music in the presence of certain colors. If this were the case, then color association with music would become stronger as one approaches adulthood.[10]

Cutietta and Haggerty completed an initial phase of the study by testing students at the elementary, secondary, and college levels. Admirably, since the findings of the first phase were difficult to interpret and resulted in more questions than answers, the researchers conducted two follow-up phases to complete the study. These researchers use the words "trends" in discussing the results of the first phase, as opposed to "conclusions," "proof," or "evidence." Overall, Cutietta and Haggerty compared color association to music in students in grades 1, 3, 5, 7, 9, 11, and college in the first phase, and at ages three, four, five, seven, eight, nine, ten, and eleven in the second phase. In the third phase, subjects were grouped into college-age and those in their twenties, thirties, forties, fifties, sixties, and seventies. Rather than follow the same subjects for a period of sixty-five years, the cross-sectional methodology allowed the researchers to collect data from subjects representative of different stages of the target population. These data were collected at the same time. Since the independent variables were nominal data, that is, age, grade level, or age groups, and the dependent variable was nominal data (six different colors), chi-square tests were used to determine differences (to compare categories with categories).

Longitudinal studies and cross-sectional studies are often called "growth studies." Both types of studies are concerned with changes over intervals of time. Cross-sectional studies determine growth by testing subjects at different stages of development—all subjects tested at the same time—as representative of the growth of the population.

Trend studies are similar to longitudinal studies, except instead of testing the same subjects at different stages of development, the population is sampled and subjects at the same level of development are tested. For example, you could test high-school freshmen in your state every two years to determine music-reading skills of that population (high-school freshmen). Comparison of data over a ten-year period may provide information as to whether high-school freshmen are benefiting from music as part of "basic education."

Trend studies identify or predict what is likely to take place in the future based on what has been happening. One of the best-known types of trend studies is the school census, conducted annually in many school districts. These data help politicians determine when and where to build new schools or close old schools and plan for teacher recruitment or transfers.

The largest and most comprehensive trend study undertaken in the field of education has been the National Assessment of Educational Progress. You should investigate this study, for which data were initially collected in 1974.

Genuine longitudinal or trend studies are seldom conducted in music education. There is a great need for trend studies to help determine the effects of music in basic education. Trend studies could help to determine the effect that music education has had on the education of today's youth. Most parents, administrators, teachers, and politicians are apparently willing to believe that music belongs in basic education, although there is no research to support such a claim. Trend studies are desperately needed to determine if music education is actually enabling students to meet the goals and objectives claimed by music educators.

Cohort studies are a type of longitudinal study that measures an entire population at periodic intervals over a period of time. For example, if Georgia includes music as part of the basic curriculum for grades K through 12 in 1990, then you could use several methods to determine the effects. You could have tested musical achievement of all first-graders in the state of Georgia in 1988, and continue testing all students in Georgia every two years, in grades 3, 5, 7, 9, and 11 (for ten years), to conduct a longitudinal cohort study to determine musical achievement in Georgia's schools over a decade. Or you could test all eleventh-graders in Georgia in 1990, and continue with yearly testing of eleventh-graders for ten years to determine if students show a trend for greater music achievement each year, by comparing the yearly scores. In 1988, eleventh-grade students would not have benefited from the curriculum change; in each subsequent year, students would have had an additional year of music, until 1999, when those eleventh-graders would have had ten years of music education. This, of course, would be a trend study.

Combined Studies. The above descriptions of kinds of descriptive studies may be misleading as you read these descriptions and then read completed doctoral dissertations and journal articles. The word "trend" may appear in a title when the study is obviously not a trend study, the word "cohort" is rarely seen in a title, and few if any of the studies you have read are as "cut-and-dried" as the descriptions contained in this chapter.

Most research will use a combination of the methods presented in the previous chapter or the previous section, in the section that follows, and in the next chapter. "Survey" refers to a type of descriptive research. But longitudinal and trend studies usually use methods of data collection normally associated with surveys. Furthermore, the information collected by these instruments may be tested for differences between groups *and* used to establish correlations to investigate additional relationships.

In reality, every study is at least slightly different, depending on the problem and subproblems. One subproblem may require correlational statistics to determine relationships. Another subproblem in the same study may require that the same data be tested for differences between groups. And yet another subproblem may require no statistics at all, but a narrative description of the data and possibly a comparison with data from a previous study to loosely determine trends.

When you write a proposal, new questions may arise as you develop procedures and outline and refine the treatment of the data. These questions may develop from new methods of treating the data as your research skills grow, and possibly may result in additional subproblems or even eliminating a subproblem. The point is, the procedures are developed from your subproblems. The subproblems will determine the most objective means for data collection and what to do with these data in order to resolve the problem.

Tools of Descriptive Research

The collection of data for various kinds of descriptive research discussed in the foregoing pages is predicated on the use of certain tools, singly or in combination. Those most frequently used are the questionnaire, opinionnaire, interview, rating scale, observation, checklist, and standardized test.

Questionnaire
Perhaps the most widely used tool in descriptive research is the questionnaire. Unfortunately, it also has been abused and misused, with the result that researchers and recipients alike tend to regard the questionnaire as anathema. Far too many graduate students attempt a survey study with the belief that questionnaires can be constructed quickly and easily, and that the individuals to be surveyed have nothing better to do than read through pages of leading questions with poor grammatical construction while trying to figure out what the researcher wants. In most of these projects, it is much less trouble for the recipient simply to throw the questionnaire away.

When an investigator takes the time and thought necessary to construct a sound questionnaire, it may be the most efficient means for gathering large amounts of data that would otherwise be impossible to collect. Borg and Gall outline the primary steps in constructing a questionnaire: (a) determine objectives; (b) decide on a sample; (c) develop individual items for the objectives; (d) construct the complete questionnaire; (e) pretest the questionnaire; (f) write the letter of transmittal; and (g) mail the questionnaire and complete any necessary follow-ups.[11] Occasionally, questionnaires are sent out that appear to have involved only the fourth step, constructing the questionnaire. Those studies usually result in a very poor response rate, which greatly affects their validity (validity, remember, is accurately measuring what you are trying to measure). If a questionnaire is intended to assess information from a sample which is representative of a defined population, but you receive only a few responses, then the study has not measured what it purports to measure. Consequently, validity is reduced.

Objectives. The objectives of the questionnaire are drawn from the problem statement and subproblems. You must list what specific information you wish to collect through the questionnaire, keeping in mind your reasons and how you will treat the responses. There should be a clear reason for each item on the questionnaire and each item should benefit one or more of the listed objectives. Keeping in mind how the data will be treated will also help in defining objectives and in subsequent steps of the process.

Suppose your study is to determine the existing status of high-school marching bands and their participation in marching-band competitions. The first objective may be to determine the percentage of bands that attend competitions; a second objective may be to determine the number of contests entered by these bands. Additional objectives may include information regarding budgets, teacher attitudes toward winning/losing (which would be a difficult area to study objectively using questionnaires), or why directors believe marching-band contests are beneficial. Listing specific objectives will help you to focus the study and make writing the individual questionnaire items easier. It will help keep the questionnaire more focused and shorter. All of these aspects will enhance response rate. Occasionally, reviewing the list of objectives also reveals that some of the information can be obtained from existing sources. Knowing that the response rate is higher with a short questionnaire, you should use other sources of information whenever possible (such as data procured from the state department of public instruction).

Sampling. After the specific objectives have been listed, the population that can supply the information should be defined. In our example regarding marching bands, you may discover from your objectives that band directors can supply most of the information, but some of the objectives would best be determined by band students, band adjudicators, and/or school principals. Those objectives which can best be answered by individuals other than the band directors should be dropped from the list, or an additional population should be defined. Such expansion can result in a more valuable study, if time and money are available to sample several groups. Otherwise, it is best to return to the problem statement and give the study more focus—for instance, the existing status of marching bands as perceived by band directors.

After the population is identified, the entire population can be mailed questionnaires, or one of the sampling procedures discussed in the previous chapter can be used. If the population is high-school band directors in Illinois, the names and addresses are easily obtained from the Illinois Music Educators Association. If the population is music-theory teachers in colleges and universities in the United States, then a random, stratified, or cluster sampling can be conducted from the *Directory of the College Music Society.*

Developing the Items. Questionnaires make use of two forms of questions: closed and open-ended. Closed items, such as checking male or female, make the questionnaire objective, easy to administer, facile in response, and fairly simple to tabulate and analyze. Because of the rigid construction, however, respondents may not be able to express their answers as clearly as they wish. This weakness can be overcome to some extent by providing the opportunity for an alternative answer.

Responses to closed items may be in the form of (1) checking "yes" or "no" or checking the appropriate category, (2) underlining or circling the applicable response, (3) ranking items according to their "correctness," or (4) inserting specific data in a blank or space provided. An example of each of these four types of items follows on page 237.

The open-ended questionnaire enables respondents to reply in their own words, thus permitting them not only to be more candid but also to give reasons for their responses. However, the time necessary to formulate an answer carefully and critically can be discouraging and restricting to a busy respondent. You will also find that data obtained from an open-ended questionnaire frequently are difficult to tabulate, organize, and summarize in quantitative form.

1. *Directions.* Please check the correct response. Your highest completed degree is:

___ none ___ Bachelor's ___ Master's ___ Advanced Certificate ___ Doctorate

2. *Directions.* Please circle the correct response. How would you rate the attitude of your principal toward show choirs?

1	2	3	4	5
enthusiastic	sympathetic	impartial	tolerant	antagonistic

3. *Directions.* Please rank each of the following college courses or programs according to the extent that it has made you a "better" band director. (#1 had the most influence; #6 had the least influence).

___ music theory   ___ music-education courses

___ applied music   ___ student-teaching participation

___ ear-training   ___ performing ensembles

4. *Directions.* Please provide the correct answer in the blank provided. How many full-time music therapists are employed in your institution?

___ .

Many times, while one open-ended question can solicit a wide range of information, the same information or essential elements of that information can be obtained through several closed questions. Borg and Gall suggest that open-ended questions may be given to a small group of respondents, from whose answers the research can develop a closed question.[12]

One of the most difficult tasks in developing items for a questionnaire is to avoid "leading questions." These are items that either reveal some underlying purpose that may bias the responses, or questions that are asked in such a way as to lead the respondent to feel that a certain answer is "correct." Unfortunately, such bias is common in educational research. For example, in the previous discussion under "Objectives," a parenthetical comment was made regarding the difficulty of using a questionnaire to determine band directors' attitudes toward winning/losing. This is because most band directors would respond to a question within this "realm" according to what they would like to believe, not necessarily what they genuinely believe or, more importantly, what they convey to their students.

Problems also arise from questionnaire items which make assumptions. For example, the statement "While marching bands enhance a high school's image, they do little to develop expressive performance" makes the assumption that marching bands enhance the school's image. In some programs, the marching band may indeed work toward expressive and musical playing but do little to help the school's image in the way that many communities view marching bands (that is, by winning contests, although one would hope that the community and professionals would recognize a marching band's expressive performance).

Questionnaire items that make use of an ordinal scale usually contain an odd number of responses so that the middle choice is "not applicable," "unknown," or "impartial" (as in the second example above). Recent research has indicated that an even number of choices may prove more useful, since that does not provide the respondent with a "neutral position." In other words, an even number of responses forces the respondent to lean toward one direction or the other; one would hope this would result in a more thoughtful answer. It is also common to extend ordinal scales in the belief that most respondents do not make use of the extreme ends of a rating scale. With this in mind, the second question illustrated above can be expected to have most respondents indicating "2," "3," or "4" on the five-point scale, with many indicating "3." An even number of responses (1 through 6) would have increased the variance; a scale of 1 to 8 would have increased the variance even more.

Constructing the Questionnaire. The first consideration as to whether or not an individual will complete and return your questionnaire is based solely on cosmetic appearance. In conducting research using a questionnaire, it is worthwhile to have a commercial printer produce your finished product.

Cosmetic attributes include color and quality of paper, color of ink, type size, and the method of reproduction or photocopying. With today's accessibility to desktop publishing and the graphic capabilities of personal computers, it is possible for graduate students to construct a very attractive questionnaire. Subtle details, such as carefully aligned staples, as well as more obvious details, such as typographical errors, will affect the response rate.

Questionnaires should be kept as concise and to the point as possible. Any terms that are ambiguous should be defined or, better yet, avoided completely. Sometimes graduate students become caught up in educational jargon or technical terms that are for the most part meaningless to the population being sampled. Lengthy explanations in the cover letter probably hurt the response rate more than they help.

The most important questions should appear at the beginning of the questionnaire and the easiest questions, or those requiring the least thought (such as indicating gender), at the end. The exception to this is when the most important questions are open-ended and may require thought and time. Respondents may not complete the instrument if the first question requires considerable writing. Directions should be clear and succinct, in italics or bold print, if possible. Any questionnaire that may be potentially confusing should include examples of what is intended.

Additionally, the questionnaire should be honest. In order to solicit some types of information, you must ensure anonymity. A coding system for questionnaires is essential for accurate followups and should be kept subtle. If a code number appears somewhere on the questionnaire or the self-addressed return envelope of a study which solicits very personal information, the respondent may not return the questionnaire or may not answer the items honestly. Potentially embarrassing questions are best left off the questionnaire (if your pilot study sample refuses to return the questionnaire, you know you have problems). Further, if you include a final question asking "Would you like a copy of the results of this survey?" make sure to send it to those respondents who indicate "yes." This question appears frequently and makes those who complete the questionnaire less likely to be disturbed about submitting their name and/or address or school as part of the questionnaire. Unfortunately, this question frequently has been abused as a technique to enhance the response rate rather than as an honest question and means to disseminate research. Such dishonesty and unethical practices have done nothing but impair the work of future researchers.

Pretesting. Prior to sending out a questionnaire, you should pretest it on your peers and on individuals similar to the sample to whom you will send the questionnaire. Not only should you ask those individuals to complete the questionnaire, but you should solicit suggestions for improving the instrument. Their comments and suggestions may indicate which questions should include an "other" response category, which questions should be completely changed to open-ended or to closed questions, which questions may not receive honest answers, and the length of time required for completing the questionnaire (which may or may not be stated in the cover letter to enhance the response rate).

The Cover Letter. The purpose of the cover letter is to explain to members of the sample why they should take the time to complete the questionnaire and return it. This is not an easy letter to write. The letter may include the purpose of the study, its relevance to the profession, its sponsorship, and the date by which the questionnaire should be returned.

Explaining the purpose of the study and its importance to the music profession can either read like the Need for the Study in a thesis, which is usually dry reading, or can make the respondent feel important and feel that he or she is in a position to help contribute to important research. Most people, especially musicians and administrators, are not offended by flattery. A possible exception is when it appears overly done or is on a photocopied form letter typed on a typewriter whose e's appear as smudges and the graduate student didn't bother to close the cover of the photocopying machine when making 200 copies of each page!

Many graduate students have received better response rates when the cover letter was from an administrator, such as a dean or department chairperson, than when it was signed by themselves. Some populations, such as recent graduates of a doctoral program, may respond to an appeal from a graduate student more readily than from an administrator. They may be more inclined to assist another graduate student.

The cover letter need not be longer than three paragraphs. The first paragraph should include the purpose of the research and how the results will be used; the next paragraph should stress the importance of the recipient's information; and the final paragraph should indicate the deadline by which responses are needed.

Although the precise lapse of time before a questionnaire is required to be returned is dependent on several factors (distance of mailing, length of questionnaire, and time of year), a period of two weeks is not unreasonable. Certain times of the year are generally avoided for sending questionnaires to music educators. The Christmas season is generally a poor time to expect responses, as is the beginning of football season for band directors.

A number of studies have been devoted to determining how to enhance the response rate to questionnaires. These studies indicate that cash rewards and the use of Special-Delivery return envelopes enhance the response rate.[13]

Follow-ups. Approximately one week after the deadline for return of the questionnaire, you may send another letter and another questionnaire to those individuals who did not respond. There is little reason to assume the questionnaire is still on their desks. The second letter may be more personal, indicating that you are confident that the individual is willing to cooperate for the "good of the profession" and that the returned questionnaire apparently was "lost in the mail." As many as four follow-ups can be used in attempting to achieve an acceptable response rate. The third attempt may simply be a postcard, the fourth attempt a certified letter.

Some researchers use a telephone interview to secure responses to questionnaire items when the response rate is too low. This technique should be considered as a last resort. Depending on the type of information solicited by the questionnaire, responses may be quite different if asked in a telephone interview.

Although there is no general agreement as to what constitutes an acceptable minimum percentage for questionnaire returns to represent a valid study, in the opinion of Good, the minimum of 90 percent seems plausible.[14] Formerly a minimum percentage of 75 was considered acceptable by many quantitative researchers, but the American Educational Research Association, among other professional groups, has insisted upon and been able to reach a figure of 95 percent. A response rate that high usually is reached only by solid follow-up techniques. Obviously, the higher the percentage of responses, the more valid the study.

Delphi Technique

This technique was developed by the Rand Corporation to predict future defense needs, but it has been used in educational situations to identify problems, establish priorities, and provide solutions to those problems. Merriam and Simpson have included the Delphi Technique as a form of descriptive research falling under the umbrella label "futures research."[15]

The Delphi Technique frequently has been used in conjunction with workshops. When used in this context, the workshop leader usually sends out a list of priorities or objectives. You, as recipient of the list, then prioritize the items and return the list to the workshop leader. A revised questionnaire, or list, is then constructed, based on the results of the first round of responses. The second, revised questionnaire or list is then sent to the same workshop participants. After further refinement of the list, it is sent out a third and possibly fourth time until the priorities or objectives have been agreed upon by all or the vast majority of the respondents. Such a procedure is rather time-consuming and consequently is seldom used by doctoral students. Its strength is that it has all of the advantages of a panel discussion, that is, general consensus of a group of experts in one field, with feedback among participants. It has the added advantage of (a) time to think, (b) the absence of some dominating personality on the panel, and (c) objective structure.

In a school of small or medium size, an entire faculty can be used to determine priorities for guiding a school. Administrators can then use that consensus for requisitioning funds for future budgets.

Opinionnaire

The opinionnaire, often known as an "attitude scale," measures a person's opinion, attitudes, and/or beliefs. While the process is similar to using a questionnaire, the information is subjective in nature and the validity of the statements cannot be verified. Respondents, for example, may conceal their real attitude or provide answers that they think will be most acceptable to the investigator. Respondents may be asked to indicate their degree of agreement or disagreement with certain statements, as in the example on page 243.

Pembrook, in one of his several studies on computer-assisted instruction, assessed college student opinions or attitudes toward

Directions: Circle the number above the description that indicates your opinion of the statement that follows.

1. Instrumental music instruction should be provided for all children in middle school.

1	2	3	4	5	6
Strongly Agree	Agree	Agree with Reservations	Disagree with Reservations	Disagree	Strongly Disagree

2. Show choirs should be limited to six outside-of-school performances per year.

1	2	3	4	5	6
Strongly Agree	Agree	Agree with Reservations	Disagree with Reservations	Disagree	Strongly Disagree

utilizing a melodic dictation computer program. Pembrook's opinionnaire included twenty-three statements regarding the computer
facilities, hardware, software, and their receptiveness on a five-
point Likert scale. Nine additional questions were included, for
which the seventy-five respondents circled responses about their
specific interaction with the computer program (such as, too simple,
about right, and too hard). His last two items were open-ended
responses.[16]

Interview

The interview technique is an oral procedure for collecting
information on a direct person-to-person basis. Frequently interviewers use a questionnaire on which they fill in the responses given
by the subject being interviewed. The interview can also serve to
help determine the validity of a questionnaire. If the answers
received from a questionnaire result in a high correlation with the
information gathered using an interview procedure, then the validity (certainly the reliability) may be creditable.

The steps in developing the interview as a research tool are
similar to developing a questionnaire: the purpose and objectives
must be defined, a sample selected, and the interview itself must be
constructed, including the opening and closing comments and clear
questions. Depending upon the size of the sample, the researcher
may be forced to recruit and train other individuals to conduct the
interviews. This assistance is essential if the researcher is in any
way, shape, or form likely to bias the responses. Finally the interview must be pretested by those who will conduct the interview,
and any refinements made to the instrument as needed.[17]

Interviews may be either *structured* or *unstructured*. In the
former the interview procedure follows a fairly rigid pattern with
regard to the questions asked, the sequence, the anticipated responses, and any ancillary techniques used to motivate responses.
Data obtained from the structured interview are usually easier to
compile and evaluate than those from an unstructured interview.
The unstructured interview, however, is more flexible and informal.
The casual, friendly manner which is a frequent characteristic of
this type of interview often elicits responses that might not be
possible through any other means. However, comparison of data
from various subjects is more difficult.

It is usually possible to obtain more detailed data through an
interview than by an impersonal questionnaire sent through the
mail. In addition, interviewers are able to ask for clarification of

any answer that they may not understand, which is impossible when using a questionnaire. If a subject misunderstands a question, it is also possible for the person conducting the interview to restate the question, which is impossible when using a questionnaire. Follow-ups are not necessary for interviews except in some cases to determine the reliability of the process (that is, to make sure subjects give the same responses the second time).

The greatest advantage of the interview over the questionnaire is that more meaningful material can be assessed in a shorter amount of time. A trained interviewer, for example, can code responses in such a way as to include aspects such as the subject's voice inflection. With training, a careful interviewer can solicit personal information that subjects might be reluctant to put in writing.

The obvious disadvantage is that the interviewer can bias responses, especially when attempting to remain extremely objective. For example, some subjects may wish to ask a few questions of their own. The interviewer, in an attempt to follow a structured interview outline, may ignore the questions or refuse to "chat," leading the subject to misinterpret this objectivity as unfriendliness.

Borg and Gall list a number of common mistakes made by researchers in conducting interviews. These can be categorized as biases of the subjects, such as holding negative feelings toward research in general (as perhaps your class does right now); biases held by the interviewer, such as feeling embarrassed by asking certain questions or a lack of confidence; and problems in the interview guide, such as leading questions (e.g., "Do you believe every child should be made to suffer through eight years of piano lessons?").[18]

If you prefer to use a tape recorder to preserve the comments on magnetic tape you should first obtain permission of each subject. You should not resort to subterfuge through the use of hidden microphones or camouflaged listening devices. A recorded interview can be played back many times to recheck information; generally, recording also speeds up the interview process.

Rating Scale

A rating scale, according to Tuckman, is a tool used by researchers to record quantitative data on specific variables by individual subjects.[19] Although there are many types of rating scales, both published and unpublished, one of the most common is the form developed by Rensis Likert. The Likert scale is by definition

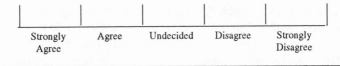

Figure 9
Likert Scale

Directions. Place an "X" at the appropriate place on the
scale below that most clearly represents your
attitude.

Music should be required of all seventh-grade students.

| | | | | |
Strongly   Agree   Undecided   Disagree   Strongly
Agree   Disagree

a five-point intervallic scale from which a score can be determined
(see Figure 9).

The student-evaluation forms that instructors are asked to complete for university placement bureaus or forms used by music-education instructors in conjunction with student-teaching evaluation
frequently involve subjective judgment. A Likert scale, for example, might be used to rate a person's skill in teaching, with 1
representing "superior" and 5 indicating "poor" achievement. In
this instance the middle ground might include 2 as "above average," 3 as "average," 4 as "below average."

Most rating scales used in research have been expanded to a
seven- or nine-point scale at least. When a number of subjects are
rated on a five-point scale, or when a number of subjects use a
five-point scale to rate a variable, there are likely to be many ties.
Since no two people are the same, it would follow that there should
never be a tie on any possible variable. This is not practical, of
course, but it does make good research sense to avoid as many ties
as possible. And as mentioned, the use of an even number of items
on a rating scale forces respondents to lean toward one end of the
scale or the other.

There are some hazards associated with the use of a rating scale.
It is often difficult to determine the specific trait or specific attitude
to be measured—in short, some variables are very difficult to isolate.
Another weakness is the so-called halo effect, in which the ratings
of a specific trait, behavior, or variable are influenced by something
else. This results in unintentional bias. Consequently, a teacher who

gives less homework, for example, might be rated higher by students than a teacher who is very demanding. The halo effect is difficult to control and is more prevalent when subjects are uncertain on where or how to rate a particular variable or person (another advantage of an even-numbered scale).

Observation

Direct observation is obviously the most objective way for you to obtain data for descriptive research; it is also the most subjective method by which information is gathered. As discussed in the previous chapter, it is easy to distinguish between quantitative and qualitative research in some ways, but in other ways, it is virtually impossible for you to draw a line separating the two. While observational methods are the primary tool for much qualitative research (e.g., ethnographic research and case studies) *every* good researcher attempts to make the observations as objective and unbiased as possible. Further, the nature of research in education, *especially* music education, is clearly subjective to a degree, regardless of how diligently you try to remain apart from the study. For example, there are many who argue that questionnaires are more objective than observational methods, since the observer is influenced by his or her own set of beliefs and may record only what he or she "sees" — not necessarily everything that is. Unfortunately, it should be apparent that subjects who complete questionnaires also bring their own individual biases to bear on a study. It can be argued that a descriptive study which utilizes a questionnaire is biased by the subjective responses of perhaps hundreds of subjects, whereas an observational method can be affected only by the bias of the observer. *With careful, honest, systematic observation by trained researchers, there can be a complete and total absence of bias, making observation methods the most objective quantitative research method available.*

When trained observers use a systematic form to record behaviors or variables, pilot tests and systematic analysis of the observational forms can be used to determine the validity of the observations, that is, to ascertain if the observers are measuring what they are supposed to measure. Comparison of the scores or ratings from several observers can be used to determine reliability (that is, the accuracy of the observer). Applying present-day technology, especially the videocassette recorder, should make this research method the most popular technique for data collection during the 1990s.

The most common threat to gathering objective data is the extent to which an observer disrupts the natural setting. Techniques such as making several prior visits to the natural setting (such as a rehearsal) before beginning data collection can reduce this effect. The more unobtrusive the observer can be, the more accurate the information will be. The classic example of an unobtrusive measure is observing the wear and tear of the carpet in an art gallery to measure which painting attracts the most people.

The first task in using an observation to gather information is to precisely determine what kinds of data are to be collected. For example, there is a plethora of studies in music education that are basically the results of "going fishing." These are studies in which young researchers have gone to great length to identify superior and weak band directors or superior and weak choral directors, and then observed behaviors in an attempt to determine how those teachers' rehearsal techniques differ. A more reasonable approach is to first define specifically the variables to be recorded.

Borg and Gall categorize observational variables into three large groups: low-inference variables, high-inference variables, and evaluative variables.[20] Low-inference variables are overt behaviors of which little interpretation is required on the part of the observer. An example of low-inference variables in rehearsal might be each time that a band or choral director uses reference to a color in describing tone quality. Another low-inference variable could simply be each time the teacher says, "O.K."

High-inference variables are those behaviors which require interpretation, or those behaviors which represent deeper feelings. An example might be a study in which the researcher attempts to determine to what degree a new orchestra director is anxious during a rehearsal. The researcher can make a list of high-inference variables which can be observed and from which one can infer anxiety. This list would identify low-inference variables and might include stammering, rubbing one's hands together, stopping and starting again without making a corrective comment, drying the palm of the right hand on one's pants leg, or fainting. Or the researcher may simply have the observers record *any* behavior that they believe is the result of anxiety; these would be high-inference behaviors.

Generally the observers' records differ more when observing and measuring high-inference behaviors than when measuring low-inference variables. Some aspects of good teaching, however, such as degree of daily preparation, self-confidence, and anxiety, manifest themselves through such an extreme range of specific behaviors that observation of high-inference variables is necessary in many studies. Findings in these studies can then be used to compile a list of low-inference variables.

Evaluative variables present an even more difficult task for the observer. In recording evaluative variables, the observer must not only observe and record high-inference variables, but also rate them on some scale as to their effectiveness (such as a Likert scale). There is a paucity of music-education research using this method, yet it provides a superb technique for objectively studying the rehearsal techniques of "better" ensemble directors. For example, a study could identify a number of superior band directors, and procedures could be developed for observing and measuring such low-inference variables as how much time is spent talking versus how much time is spent playing, the amount of time spent in making announcements, and the amount of time spent in warming up, tuning, technical drills, working on concert music, etc. Evaluative variables might be used by observers to record which corrective comments are directed toward technical proficiency, intonation, tone quality, balance, and blend, and also to rate which comments are the most effective. Use of videotapes can make this task easier. Analysis of the most effective comments could lead to improved rehearsal techniques.

A primary consideration when selecting a published observational form or developing a format with which to record observational data is the *type* of data being measured. Borg and Gall have categorized most recording formats into four large divisions based on the method of recording: (a) durations, (b) frequencies, (c) intervals, and (d) continuous observation.[21] Recording of durations has already been discussed. An example is using a stopwatch to measure the time that an ensemble director spends in talking and the time spent in having the group play. A frequency count is used to tally a specific behavior or variable each time it occurs, either low- or high-inference variables. For generations graduate students have amused themselves by keeping such tally marks in their notes to record each time the professor says, "Now . . . "

Interval records are used to record observations of variables at specific time intervals, such as every thirty seconds. The most famous published observational form is that developed by Ned Flanders. In the Flanders Interaction Analysis System, there are seven variables for teacher behavior using low-inference variables, such as lecturing and giving directions, and high-inference variables, such as accepting ideas of students; two variables for student behavior; and one for silence or confusion. The observer records on the form what behavior(s) is (are) taking place every three seconds, using a separate page for thirty-second time intervals.[22] Difficulties in these types of observational techniques include the possibility of several behaviors happening at once, the effect of some "major" event occurring which influences subsequent records, and the essential training and practice required of the observers.

Recording continuously has grown in popularity with the advent of portable videocassette machines. They enable the recording of subjects rather unobtrusively and allow observers to return to view specific events under observation. The primary negative factor is the copious amount of data that are obtained. These observations are quite valuable in ethnographic research, when case studies are conducted, and in qualitative studies for which a narrative of events in their proper order is essential to gain insight into a phenomenon. Videotaped records, however, can be used with any of the above methods to obtain objective and quantified data.

Witt conducted a study in which forty-eight fifty-five-minute rehearsals were observed by an unreported number of observers. The forty-eight rehearsals were divided approximately equally between junior- and senior-high string orchestra and band rehearsals. The directors ranged from first-year teachers to one with thirty-one years of experience. The observers recorded low-inference behaviors: student attentiveness and the use of time "on-task." The rehearsals were also recorded (audio only) for later analysis of the time spent in performance, actual instruction, and other activities. The results of Witt's study are reported using descriptive statistics and narrative. She also compares those findings with previous research results.[23]

Standardized Tests

Standardized tests in music and in other subject areas are often employed as tools for gathering data for descriptive as well as experimental research. Achievement tests in music, for instance, can be used to determine the present level of attainment. Those data might then be used as the basis for survey studies, relationship studies, or development studies.

There are numerous published music tests of various kinds on the market (e.g., aptitude, achievement, readiness, and appreciation) that could be used, for example, with other standardized tests for relationship studies (e.g., interest inventories, measures of mental aptitude, personality tests, and a multitude of others). As in the previous chapter, you are encouraged to peruse the *Ninth Mental Measurements Yearbook* and *Tests in Print III* to gain further understanding of the possibilities of using standardized tests in research.

Case Studies and Ethnographic Research

Case studies are those studies which generally investigate a single individual, group (such as a band), or institution (such as a school or a small community) in great detail. While a case study is descriptive in nature, and the researcher normally attempts to be as objective as possible in his or her intensive examination of the relationships affecting (and resulting from) the subject, most case studies can be considered qualitative in nature. Case studies are included in the quantitative section of this text because the observational methods are generally the same as those used in quantitative descriptive studies (with qualitative techniques used to interpret the data).

Sax lists four purposes of the case-study method: (1) to provide a hypothesis that can be tested under similar circumstances; (2) to determine the availability of unique situations to test hypotheses; (3) to deal with a study that may provide new insights into a problem; and (4) to demonstrate how a theoretical model can be used in a specific situation.[24] In the examination of one person (or one group or one school) you may discover relationships and evidence of why and how those relationships developed; those relationships can subsequently be investigated using correlational studies, and the "why" or "how" of those relationships can be investigated through experimental studies. By examining a single phenomenon, individual, or entity (the case), this approach seeks to uncover the interaction of significant and essential factors that are characteristic of the phenomenon or that make up the phenomenon. The case study seeks holistic description and interpretation.[25]

A case study may profile a person or group for a relatively short time. The medical and behavioral sciences have made extensive use of the case-study technique for many years; recently there has been an increasing interest in applying this concept to the social sciences and humanities (especially music therapy).

Because it is desirable to learn about the total interaction of persons, not only with others around them, but also with situations they encounter daily, case-study research frequently is undertaken by a team of qualified personnel, each a specialist in a different field or discipline. For instance, the investigator who is a musician might elicit the assistance of a physician, a psychologist, and a sociologist to study cooperatively how the last-chair players in the third clarinet section of a high-school band react to the other members seated ahead in the section. This team might, individually and/or collectively—through interview, observation, testing, and the examination of personal written reports, such as diaries, letters, and anecdotal records—render a comprehensive account, offering recommendations for remedial action to assist the subject in making whatever attitudinal adjustments may be necessary. In most school systems the personnel in the counseling (or guidance) departments are the key persons in organizing and implementing studies involving the cooperation of subject-matter specialists from various fields. Music teachers may find themselves assigned to such teams, especially if the subject of the case study seems to do better in music than in other subjects. Case studies that are team efforts may not be any more objective than those by a single investigator, but they are likely to be less subjective than a single researcher's interpretation of the case.

Another reason that case studies are generally considered qualitative rather than quantitative is due to the selection of the subject (or the case) to be examined. A case is never selected at random, but is carefully chosen for specific characteristics in which the investigator is interested (such as an orchestra in a rural community or a unique child in an unusual situation).

Ethnographic research is a procedure that, although developed by anthropologists to study a specific culture, has received considerable attention from educational researchers. The main characteristic of ethnographic investigation is that some special process is used to permit the researcher to maintain continuous observation of a situation so that all things related to the study can be recorded. As such, while ethnographic research uses observational techniques often associated with quantitative research and is clearly descriptive in nature, it is usually considered qualitative research (see chapter 5). Clearly, most aspects of a social, political, and/or economic environment can be quantified and measured, but proponents of ethnographic research insist that the subjective interpretation of those influences on a subject or group, the reaction of the subject or group, and the subsequent effect back toward the influence are what is important. This is similar to the argument for years presented by those who believed that an infant's behavior was determined genetically and by those who emphasized that the infant's behavior was determined by the environment. Research results and opinions were argued back and forth for decades before behavioral scientists began to realize just how great an influence infants themselves have on the environment.

The researcher may use a variety of techniques to record observations. Most of these techniques are borrowed from quantitative research methodology. With development and accessibility of video cameras, ethnographic research has become even more popular in recent years. Often, hypotheses are developed which can then be tested using quantitative techniques discussed in the next chapter.

Ethnographic researchers maintain that studying the total context in which behavior occurs is essential to understanding any behavior, as opposed to quantitative techniques, which may attempt to isolate a particular behavior. These supporters further believe that ethnographic research provides a more accurate picture of the interaction of subjects within their natural society and how they are influenced by that society. Critics of this type of research feel that when the researcher enters the society to be studied, the society is drastically changed, consequently destroying all validity of the study.

Critics also are concerned with the extent to which the results can be generalized to other groups or societies. Among recent music studies using ethnographic methods is Krueger's study of student teachers. She administered numerous quantitative tests to student teachers, made quantitative observations and records, and combined those data with qualitative information, such as the student teachers' personal journals and informal interviews.[26]

Problems for Review and Discussion

1. For what purposes is descriptive research undertaken?
2. Differentiate among survey studies, relationship studies, and development studies. Find examples of each in the literature.
3. How would you know when a longitudinal or a cross-sectional study would be more appropriate to use in a research study?
4. What factors need to be kept in mind in the construction of a questionnaire? Distinguish between the kinds of questions used in a closed and open-ended questionnaire.
5. How may the Delphi Technique be used in music-education research?

6. How does an opinionnaire differ from a questionnaire?
7. When should an interview technique be used? What are the advantages and disadvantages of the interview as compared to the questionnaire? What is the difference between a structured and an unstructured interview?
8. For what purposes is a rating scale used? Indicate precautions that must be considered when this research tool is used.
9. When and why should observation be used as a research tool?
10. When should you use a case study in a research project?
11. What are some of the advantages of using ethnographic research techniques?

Supplementary Sources

Ary, Donald, Lucy C. Jacobs, and Asghar Razavieh. *Introduction to Research in Education*, 3rd ed.; New York: Holt, Rinehart and Winston, 1985. Chapters 11, 12.

Asher, J. William. *Educational Research and Evaluation Methods*. Boston: Little, Brown and Co., 1976. Chapter 6.

Best, John W., and James V. Kahn. *Research in Education*, 6th ed.; Englewood Cliffs, N.J.: Prentice-Hall, 1989. Chapters 4, 7, 8.

Borg, Walter R., and Meredith D. Gall. *Educational Research: An Introduction*, 5th ed.; New York: Longman, 1989. Chapters 11-14.

Drew, Clifford J. *Introduction to Designing Research and Evaluation*. St. Louis: C. V. Mosby, 1976. Chapters 2, 4, 9.

Fox, David J. *The Research Process in Education*. New York: Holt, Rinehart and Winston, 1969. Chapters 15, 17-19.

Gay, L. R. *Educational Research: Competencies for Analysis and Application*. Columbus, Ohio: Charles E. Merrill, 1976. Chapters 1, 5-7.

Gronlund, Norman E. *Measurement and Evaluation in Teaching*, 4th ed.; New York: Macmillan, 1981. Chapters 11-16.

Hopkins, Charles D. *Understanding Educational Research: An Inquiry Approach*, 2nd ed.; Columbus, Ohio: Charles E. Merrill, 1980. Chapters 3, 10.

Keppel, Geoffrey. *Design and Analysis: A Researcher's Handbook*, 2nd ed.; Englewood Cliffs, N.J.: Prentice-Hall, 1982. Chapters 7, 8.

Kerlinger, Fred N. *Foundations of Behavioral Research*, 3rd ed.; New York: Holt, Rinehart and Winston, 1986. Chapters 3, 22-24, 28-32.

Leedy, Paul D. *Practical Research Planning and Design*, 4th ed.; New York: Macmillan, 1989. Chapters 8, 9.

Mason, Emanuel J., and William J. Bramble. *Understanding and Conducting Research: Applications in Education and the Behavioral Sciences*, 2nd ed.; New York: McGraw-Hill, 1989. Chapters 6, 8, 9.

McMillan, James H., and Sally Schumacher. *Research in Education: A Conceptual Introduction*, 2nd ed.; Glenview, Ill.: Scott, Foresman, 1989. Chapters 7, 8, 11.

Merriam, Sharan B. *Case Study Research in Education: A Qualitative Approach*. San Francisco: Jossey-Bass, 1988.

Merriam, Sharan B., and Edwin L. Simpson. *A Guide to Research for Educators and Trainers of Adults*. Malabar, Fla.: Robert E. Krieger, 1984. Chapters 4, 6-8.

Mitchell, James V., ed. *The Ninth Mental Measurements Yearbook*. Lincoln, Neb.: University of Nebraska Press, 1985.

_____. *Tests in Print III*. Lincoln, Neb.: University of Nebraska Press, 1985.

Rainbow, Edward L., and Hildegard C. Froehlich. *Research in Music Education: An Introduction to Systematic Inquiry*. New York: Schirmer Books, 1987. Chapter 9.

Révész, Geza. *The Psychology of a Musical Prodigy*. Westport, Conn.: Greenwood Press, 1970.

Sax, Gilbert. *Foundations of Educational Research*, 2nd ed.: Englewood Cliffs, N.J.: Prentice-Hall, 1979. Chapters 5, 10-12.

Sowell, Evelyn J., and Rita J. Casey. *Research Methods in Education*. Belmont, Calif.: Wadsworth Publishing Company, 1982. Chapters 4, 5.

Travers, Robert M. W. *An Introduction to Educational Research*, 4th ed.; New York: Macmillan, 1978. Chapters 6-8, 11-13.

Tuckman, Bruce W. *Conducting Educational Research*, 3rd ed.; New York: Harcourt Brace Jovanovich, 1988. Chapters 9, 10.

Van Dalen, Deobold B. *Understanding Educational Research: An Introduction*, 4th ed.; New York: McGraw-Hill, 1979. Chapters 3, 5, 6, 10.

Vockell, Edward L. *Educational Research*. New York: Macmillan, 1983. Chapters 3-6, 11.

8. Experimental and Quasi-Experimental Research: Concepts and Techniques

While descriptive research is aimed at investigation of the existing status of a phenomenon, experimental research is used to determine *what will be*. True experimental research is the only method available to determine a cause-and-effect relationship. Relationship studies and even development studies are occasionally used for predictions, but these cannot be completely reliable as evidence of a cause-and-effect relationship. As mentioned earlier, correlational and causal-comparative studies can be used to imply a causal relationship, but experimental research is required to verify a causal effect between variables.

Experimental research is usually regarded as the most objective of the six methods of research discussed in this book. Because of the rigid controls imposed on factors in experimental research it is possible to duplicate this kind of study and receive virtually the same results each time the study is replicated. This is not always the case with descriptive research and is seldom the case with philosophical or aesthetic inquiry. Experimental, laboratory, or empirical research is sometimes regarded as "a glimpse into the future," because it can show what is possible under carefully controlled situations.

Another term associated with this type of research is "behavioral research." Even though researchers using any mode of inquiry often have an idea of what their results will be, with the better controls possible in experimental studies the results are more definitive than in other kinds of research. Research in the laboratory has long been regarded as the "method of science." Experimental studies in music education and in education usually attempt to simulate empirically—as closely as possible—laboratory conditions in the classroom or in the field with individuals or groups rather than the process followed in the laboratory with subjects.

The basic concept of experimental research is that a sample of subjects—the larger, the better—is selected at random from the population identified as that to which the causal results of the study are to be generalized. The subjects are then randomly assigned to one of two groups: (1) the experimental group, which receives the experimental treatment or independent variable; or (2) the control group, which does not receive the experimental treatment. During the experimental period, the two groups are treated exactly the same except for one factor: the *experimental treatment*. After the treatment, both groups are compared by measuring the dependent variable, which is presumed to have been affected by the independent variable (the experimental treatment). These measures are then tested statistically for a significant difference between the two groups, or tested to determine the extent to which the two groups differ and the probability that this difference occurs by chance or the probability that this difference results from the independent variable.

True experimental research is conducted constantly in the health sciences to provide new medicines, medical treatments, and insight into diseases and wellness. Laboratory animals provide a living organism that can be completely isolated from any extraneous variables that in any way can affect the dependent variable; this is called *control*. Researchers maintain rigorous control over the experiment, meaning that as many extraneous variables as possible are eliminated. Psychologists have copied this method of research and have made significant discoveries in animal behavior. Whether the results of the rigorous experimentation of social scientists can be generalized to human beings or are limited to the population of albino rats remains to be seen.

In the medical profession, controlled experimentation often eventually makes its way out of the laboratory in order to use human beings as subjects. Under carefully controlled conditions (frequently regulated by the U.S. Food and Drug Administration), new medications, including vaccines and treatments, are tested to determine cause-and-effect relationships. After years of testing, a new substance is finally released to the public.

The field of education is not so lucky. On the one hand, true experimental research with human subjects is extremely difficult to accomplish (since the cages have to be so large). Seriously, all of the many factors that can affect a person's learning cannot be controlled (assuming an experiment designed to improve learning). On the other hand, attempting to teach several hundred white rats to read using a new experimental treatment is obviously ludicrous. In short, as you gain an understanding of experimental designs you will understand the strengths and weaknesses of attempting this type of research.

Also included in the new edition of this book is a discussion of quasi-experimental designs. In past decades, these designs have appeared occasionally in the literature as some type of "substandard" research design. It is true that quasi-experimental designs do not exert as much rigorous control over experimental research as do experimental designs, but you will find that, clearly, most experimental research in education has been conducted using quasi-experimental designs. Perhaps with better understanding and with increased recognition of these designs, the music-education profession will benefit from *good* quasi-experimental research rather than being so critical of *weak* experimental research.

Concepts of Experimental Research

The concepts of the experimental treatment, the experimental group (or those who receive the experimental treatment), and the control group have already been mentioned. Also of importance is the idea of a pretest and a posttest. These tests are used to measure both groups on the dependent variable before and after the experimental treatment is given to the experimental group. One would probably expect (or hope) that the pretest would indicate that the experimental group and the control group are about equal on the dependent variable before the experimental treatment, and that after the experimental group "receives" the treatment, the posttest indicates that there is a *difference* between the two groups.

Hypothesis
Your expectation, based on facts that are already known and on conditions that are expected to exist, is a *hypothesis*. A hypothesis can be confirmed only by testing the relationship that may be evident between the known and the presumed. Many label an unconfirmed hypothesis a theory—others may label it a myth.

Kerlinger describes a hypothesis rather succinctly as a statement of the relation between at least two variables. Hypotheses are always in declarative form, and they specifically relate variables to variables. The two requirements for acceptable hypotheses are that they are clear statements about the relationships between the variables and that they clearly indicate how this relationship can be tested.[1] Accordingly, hypotheses simply specify how two or more measurable variables are related.

Occasionally, graduate students encounter hypotheses in the literature that use vague constructs—such as "talent"—which require further definition. One source of confusion for some graduate students is the practice of stating hypotheses in the null form. A hypothesis can be a directional hypothesis: "Students who begin a wind instrument in the fifth grade will sight-read more accurately after six months of instruction than students who begin a wind instrument in the seventh grade." Or a hypothesis can be stated in the null form: "There will be no difference in sight-reading accuracy between students who begin a wind instrument in the fifth grade and students who begin a wind instrument in the seventh grade, following six months of instruction." The null form became traditional, as it was derived from early statistical tests; the basis of all statistical tests for differences is that when the mean score of the experimental group is subtracted from the mean score of the control group, the result is zero or null.

Validity

Another concept basic to experimental research is *validity*. Validity was discussed in relationship to testing and was defined as the degree to which a test measures what it is supposed to measure. In experimental research, validity is based on the same idea. *Internal validity* is concerned with the extent that the measured difference between the experimental group(s) and the control group is due to the independent variable (like it is "supposed" to be), or the extent that the measured difference is perhaps due to some extraneous variable that may have made certain students perform better on the criterion measure (dependent variable) than other students.

Internal Validity

Campbell and Stanley developed a schema for conducting experimental research that has become the standard for all educational and social-science researchers and research textbooks.[2] Cook and Campbell, some years later, extended a number of those ideas in another text focusing specifically on quasi-experimental research as a more feasible alternative to true experimental designs.[3] Based on these two texts, researchers recognize twelve factors or extraneous variables that can jeopardize the internal validity of experimental and quasi-experimental studies: history, maturation, testing, instrumentation, statistical regression, selection bias, experimental mortality, interactions with selection, treatment diffusion, compensatory equalization of treatments, compensatory rivalry of control group, and demoralization of control group.[4] Each of these can affect the validity of a study in varying degrees. If it were possible to measure the effect, they could simply be treated statistically as another independent variable (which affects the dependent variable). Unfortunately all of these are considered a threat to internal validity.

History refers to a naturally occurring event that can have an effect on either the experimental group or the control group. As an illustration, suppose a music study was designed which randomly assigned schools to the experimental and control groups, and during the period of experimental treatment a college orchestra performed at one of the schools: this event could have an effect on the students at that one school to encourage or enhance learning or practice.

Maturation is the second factor—the fact that subjects are growing older and more mature due to the passage of time. The time of day that the experiment is conducted, for example, is an important maturation variable. When subjects are hungry or tired they may not perform well on a task. If some of the music students have heard a composition before, their musical taste could have matured to varying degrees and their reaction to repeated listenings of it could threaten validity. The most common form of maturation as an extraneous variable in educational research is due to different schools representing students of different socioeconomic backgrounds.

Testing, the third factor, is the effect that taking a pretest might have on the scores of a posttest. Some students might be reminded of test items as a lecture progresses, resulting in their remembering certain bits and pieces of information, or they may simply do better on their second encounter with a test. While the effects of history and maturation increase with the time over which an experimental treatment extends, the threat of testing is lessened as the time or experimental period is extended.

Instrumentation, the fourth factor, relates to changes in the instrument(s) used to measure the dependent variable between the pretest and the posttest. On an ear-training test, for example, if the procedure for recording the correct answers were changed from oral to written, instrumentation would probably be an affecting variable. This threat is especially a concern when the dependent variable is measured by observers. Individuals who record performance errors on sight-reading tests might be more strict or more lenient on the posttest than on the pretest. Some researchers have videotaped pretest and posttest performances and "mixed them up" to prevent the observer from knowing which was the pretest and which was the posttest (furthermore, audiotapes might be preferred if factors such as physical appearance might create a bias with instrumentation).

Statistical regression, an interesting phenomenon of nature, is the fifth factor. Simply stated, the odds are very favorable that subjects who score the highest on a pretest will score slightly lower on the posttest and the students who score the lowest on the pretest will score higher on the posttest. This tendency, also called *regression toward the mean,* resulted in several "educational companies" making a great deal of money in the 1970s by contracting with schools and parents to raise the weakest students' scores on various achievement tests. Such companies could guarantee raising the scores of the weakest students in the school since, due to this natural phenomenon, the scores would be raised whether those students attended classes or not.

Selection bias, the sixth factor, occurs when an experimenter has previously worked with some of the subjects included in the sample but not with others. It also can be due to the difference in subjects who volunteer. An example might be apparent in an experimental study to compare musical achievement between students who start on string instruments in the fourth grade and students who start on string instruments in the sixth grade. One may assume that the principal who allows the teacher to enter the school to start students "two years early" may indeed be quite different from other principals. Those differences may influence the attitude of both teachers and students in that school.

Experimental mortality is when subjects are dropped from the study for various reasons. This seventh factor can result from a wide variety of reasons, such as students moving or simply being absent from school on the day the posttest is administered. Also called "attrition," loss of subjects can be a serious problem in many experiments, especially those in which subjects could possible drop a class due to the experimental treatment itself.

Interactions with selection is the eighth factor. These may be a variety of interactions with the subjects who participate in the experiment. The most common is the *selection maturation interaction.* This may occur in the previous example where beginning string players are started in the fourth and sixth grades: the sixth-graders selected for the study may be more mature than the fourth-graders and, compounding the problem, the fourth-graders beginning on a string instrument may be among the most mature fourth-graders. A *selection × history* interaction can present a threat to internal validity when subjects are selected from volunteer groups in several geographic locations. Events occurring in one city may affect just the participating subjects in that city. Another interaction which commonly threatens validity is *selection × instrumentation*. This problem exists when the test chosen as a pretest and posttest is inappropriate for the subjects selected for the study. In some cases the test might be too easy or too difficult, and in other cases it may be inappropriate due to factors such as socioeconomic background, teacher biases, or hundreds of other possible characteristics of *part* of the sample. Or the test might be easier for some subjects in the sample than for the other subjects composing the sample.

Treatment diffusion, a ninth factor added by Cook and Campbell to the eight identified by Campbell and Stanley, is due to the experimental treatment's appearing as "attractive" to members of the control group. For example, if a new method of teaching class piano is used for several sections of freshman music majors and the remaining sections are taught using the "traditional method," it is quite possible that by the end of the semester the students in the control group ("traditional method") will have learned some of the techniques of the new method. It is also possible that some of the "traditional method" teachers will see the experimental sections progressing more rapidly and "borrow" a few techniques to "enhance" their own teaching.[5]

Compensatory equalization of treatments, the tenth factor, occurs when administrators or parents intervene in an experimental setting to provide a control group with what they perceive to be necessary in order to "even out" the educational experience. This has occurred when politicians observed or were led to believe that an experimental treatment provided an unfair advantage to a select few. In music-education research in the 1990s, it is likely to occur in experiments designed to test the effectiveness of computer-assisted instruction. If parents or administrators become concerned that their students (the control group) are "falling behind" or not getting their "fair share," they will intervene; as a rule, parents will go to any length to secure what they believe to be equal treatment for their children.

Compensatory rivalry of control group, the eleventh threat to internal validity, results when the control group "tries harder" to perform as well as the experimental group. This problem, known for years as the "John Henry Effect" (after the legend of the steel driver vs. the steam machine), occurs when subjects are aware of the experiment.

Demoralization of control group is virtually the opposite of compensatory rivalry. When subjects are aware that they are participating in an experiment, they may become passive or "bummed out," or angry and "outraged." This twelfth factor can result in experimental mortality or, worse, a posttest score of subjects ranging in attitude from apathy to anger to despair to despondency.

External Validity

While all twelve of the above-mentioned factors could threaten the internal validity of a study, the experimental research is also concerned with threats to *external validity*. Threats to internal validity affect the extent to which the experiment measures what it is supposed to measure. Campbell and Stanley identify four threats to external validity, or the extent to which the results of the experiment can be generalized to the target population. Or, to maintain the same wording, the extent to which the sample participating in the experiment remains representative of the population that it is supposed to represent. These four factors are reactive effects of testing, *interaction effects of selection bias × the experimental treatment,* reactive effects of experimental arrangements, and multiple-treatment interference.[6]

Reactive effects of testing are very similar to the testing threat to internal validity. Threatening external validity, the reactive factor implies that the results of the experiment may not be generalized to the population, since the pretest enhanced the effects of the experimental treatment. The results of the experiment can then be applied to the population only if the entire population is given the "pretest" before a new teaching method.

A second source of external validity is the *interaction effects of selection bias × the experimental treatment.* This threat to external validity becomes apparent when any type of selection bias enhances the effects of the experimental treatment. It is similar to the threat of selection bias to internal validity. If the subjects are selected in a biased manner (whether intentional or not), the results of the experiment cannot be generalized to the population with any degree of confidence.

Reactive effects of experimental arrangements, the third factor, refers to the artificiality of the setting for much experimental research in education when students are aware that they are participating in an experiment. Also known as the "Hawthorne Effect," after the experiments at the Hawthorne plant of Western Electric (near Chicago) described by Elton Mayo which claimed that workers would produce more as long as someone paid attention to them. The foremost music-education researcher, Richard Colwell, has remarked on several occasions that if students will perform better if they think they are part of an experiment, then teachers should utilize the "Hawthorne Effect" as frequently as possible.

While the extent of these reactive effects cannot be measured, their presence can be determined within a safe margin of reliability. Many experimenters use a placebo, for example, a setting where subjects supposedly in the experimental group are actually in the control group or some subjects in the control group believe that they are in the experimental group. The placebo has been used effectively for decades in the medical profession; in the field of education its use is usually limited to self-instructional programs, such as computer-assisted instruction.

The fourth threat to external validity is *multiple-treatment interference*. This is the result of several experimental treatments given to the same subjects without sufficient time for each separate treatment to "wear off" before the next treatment is provided. In these cases, it is impossible to determine which individual treatment or which combination of treatments is responsible for any change in the dependent variable.

One final concept prior to a discussion of experimental designs is the strength of the experimental treatment. As mentioned in chapter 6, the larger the sample, the better; by similar convention, the stronger the experimental treatment, the better. Treatments seem to be stronger when extended over a longer period of time than when attempting to produce significant differences during a few days.

Experimental Designs

Pilot Study

As mentioned in the previous chapter, you are strongly advised to pilot-test questionnaires and other instruments used to gather data for a descriptive study. In experimental research, it is virtually essential to conduct a *pilot study* to determine whether the relationship hypothesized between the independent and dependent variables will materialize in a situation comparable to the one proposed for the actual study. It is also essential to determine if your method for testing that relationship is possible, that is, if you can manipulate and measure the independent variable as intended. Runkel and McGrath point out that a pilot study is used to confirm one's guess about characteristics of a given situation.[7]

In order to determine if you can manipulate the independent variable, it is required that you administer the experimental treatment to a group similar to the sample which will participate in the study. This pilot study will provide an opportunity to refine procedures (such as teaching methods), make any necessary changes in design to establish greater control over threats to internal and external validity or other extraneous variables, make any changes to strengthen the experimental treatment, and practice the data collection process.

A smaller number of subjects is studied in the pilot study. If you propose to use four hundred subjects in your research, your pilot study may involve twenty subjects. In order to establish an estimate of the strength of your experimental treatment, allow the pilot study to extend over the same length of time as the planned study. This also enables refinement of any portion of the procedures or method that may interfere with the research over a period of time.

True Experimental Designs

In addition to identifying threats to internal and external validity of experimental research, Campbell and Stanley outline three true experimental designs, in addition to three "pre-experimental" designs, which are appropriate for pilot studies.[8] Figure 10, adapted from one of their tables,[9] not only outlines these designs, but also indicates potential threats to their validity. The symbol X in the notation for each design indicates where the experimental treatment is given in relationship to the testing, which is indicated by the symbol O. The true experimental designs also use the symbol R to indicate randomized groups, which is required by definition of experimental designs. Dotted lines are used to separate groups for which testing is completed at the same time.

The first three designs on the chart are not appropriate for good research, but are fine for pilot studies: one-shot case design, one-group pretest/posttest design, and static-group comparison. The first design, *one-shot case study*, indicates that the experimental treatment is given to a group of subjects and then a test is adminis-

Figure 10
Designs for Pilot Studies and Experimental Studies and Threats to Validity

<u>Designs</u>   <u>Threats to Validity</u>

A. Pre-experimental or Pilot Studies

<u>Internal</u>: history, maturation, selection bias, experimental mortality

  1. One-shot case design

    X O

<u>External</u>: interaction of selection bias × experimental treatment

  2. One-group pretest/posttest design

    O X O

<u>Internal</u>: history, maturation, testing, instrumentation, interactions with selection and possibly statistical regression

<u>External</u>: interactions of selection bias and testing × experimental treatment

  3. Static-group comparison

    X O (experimental group)

        O (control group)

<u>Internal</u>: selection bias, experimental mortality, interactions with selection and possibly maturation

<u>External</u>: interaction of selection bias × experimental treatment

B. True Experimental Studies (using random assignment of Ss and control groups)

  1. Pretest/posttest control group design

    R O X O (experimental group)

    R O   O (control group)

<u>Internal</u>: none

<u>External</u>: reactive effects of testing and possibly interaction of selection bias × treatment and/or reactive effects of experimental arrangements

  2. Solomon four-group design

    R O X O (experimental group)

    R O   O (control group)

    R   X O (experimental group)

    R   O (control group)

<u>Internal</u>: none

<u>External</u>: none, possibly interaction of selection bias × treatment and/or reactive effects of experimental arrangements

  3. Posttest-only control group design

    R   X O (experimental group)

    R   O (control group)

<u>Internal</u>: none

<u>External</u>: none, possibly interaction of selection bias × treatment and/or reactive effects of experimental arrangements

tered to the group. This design makes it impossible to accurately measure or determine the effect of the treatment.

The second design in the top portion of Figure 10 is the *one-group pretest/posttest design*. This design initially appears to be somewhat more valid than the one-shot case study, since a pretest is used to which the posttest scores can be compared, but this design has more internal problems. The threat of testing becomes important, as do possible threats from instrumentation, such as inappropriate tests indicating a greater or lesser difference between tests. Observers may record answers slightly differently the second time they observe behaviors, or interviewers may become more accustomed to questions and paraphrase items. Statistical regression can also be a problem. If this design, for example, is used to try a new method of teaching sight-reading to the best performers in a band, their performance scores are likely to go down (regression toward the mean) on the posttest. This regression may lessen the true effects of the experimental treatment, the new method of sight-reading.

The final design that might be appropriate for a pilot study is the *static-group comparison*. This design does not use a pretest, so comparison of scores before and after the experimental treatment is impossible. By using two groups, however, it guards against invalidity due to history, testing, instrumentation, or statistical regression, since *both* groups should be affected by those factors presumably in the same way. In this design, selection bias and all of the interactions associated with it are a more serious threat. Since the groups are not selected or assigned at random, there could be significant differences between the subjects who receive the experimental treatment and the subjects in the control group.

All three true experimental designs are based on randomly selecting and/or assigning subjects to either an experimental or a control group. All three designs guard against all threats to internal validity because any of the extraneous factors that may influence the posttest scores of the experimental group should affect the posttest scores of the control group to the same degree. External validity could be threatened in the *pretest/posttest control-group design* by the effects of the test, making the posttest scores higher than if a pretest was not given. The *posttest-only control group design* guards against this particular threat but does not allow a comparison of the pretest and posttest scores. The *Solomon four-group design* has the advantages of both of these. It is a design which falls into a different class, to be discussed below under "Factorial Designs."

Quasi-Experimental Designs

True experimental research, the only form of research to show a causal effect, you will recall, is extremely difficult to conduct outside of a laboratory environment. In the world around us, there are so many extraneous variables that affect what one learns or does, or how one will perform in or rehearse a band, that true experimental research conducted in a laboratory may not be applicable. This argument has been the basis of a great deal of qualitative research, especially ethnographic research and case studies, by researchers who recognize that education is only in part (and a small part at that) dependent on what goes on in the classroom.

In the early 1960s, the term *quasi-experimental research* was first used. Since that time, it has been used most frequently in a negative sense. Because this type of design falls short of controlling all outside factors, it could be considered a weak experimental design. The term was coined by Campbell and Stanley for research experiments that identify independent variables, include experimental treatments, and measure dependent variables, but in which subjects cannot be or are not selected at random and are not randomly assigned to the experimental or control group.[10] The result is that the groups are usually *nonequivalent*. And in quasi-experimental designs, they are always treated as nonequivalent (which is the way groups of people are in the real world).

Most researchers are limited to a relatively small number of intact classes for conducting experimental research. For example, suppose you wish to try a new technique in music appreciation to determine its effect on musical preference. Your university has six sections of music appreciation. You must make the decision of randomly assigning three sections to the experimental group and three sections to the control group (n = 6), or use the individuals in each section as the number of subjects rather than the sections themselves, for a nonequivalent design. In the first case, n = 6 is such a small sample size that the results may be meaningless. In the second, a quasi-experimental design, instead of comparing scores of each section on the dependent variable (the "class average"), you will deal with each individual's pretest and posttest scores, and more may be learned. Certainly more may be inferred from the quasi-experimental design than from the experimental design where n = 6. Hopefully, this will become apparent, after a few more pages.

In the late 1960s and early 1970s a number of leading educational researchers were very critical of the unnatural environment required of experimental research, whether it was conducted in a laboratory or in the field. One of the country's leading thinkers in this area is Richard Snow.[11]

Snow has labeled his alternative research designs "representative designs," a term also used in several research textbooks, such as in the comprehensive text by Borg and Gall.[12] The ideas presented by Snow reflect a strong advocacy for using quasi-experimental designs and techniques over true experimental techniques.

Snow proposes that experimental research in education must be designed as accurately as possible to mirror the natural settings in which teaching and learning most frequently take place and to reflect the natural characteristics of the students. The need for designs other than true experimental designs to reflect these phenomena is based on several propositions: (1) the characteristics of the educational setting are complex and interrelated; (2) students and teachers constantly perceive and digest information (they will not respond apathetically or nonchalantly to experimental treatments); (3) students and teachers will accept, compensate, and settle into the educational setting; and (4) any experimental treatment will undoubtedly affect the students' and teachers' attitudes and behavior toward a wide variety of areas and topics.[13]

The following suggestions were made by Snow to encourage experimental research in schools, since knowledge of cause and effect is so desperately needed, but also to keep the experiments more representative of the natural settings of the students' and teachers' environment:

1. Conduct the research in a school rather than in an artificial setting if the results are to be generalized to a school.
2. Use more than one school in the design of the study in order to generalize more accurately—that is, a stratified sampling of schools in different parts of town or of teachers with varying years of teaching experience may increase the external validity of the study.
3. Maintain accurate records of observational data of subjects (perhaps also questionnaires and interviews) during the experimental treatment to assist in interpretation of the results— attempt to discover the subjects' reaction to the treatment beyond test scores on the dependent variable.

4. Maintain accurate records of events that occur in the school or community in which the experiment takes place, such as concerts, change of principals or teachers, etc.[14]

These suggestions not only will help in interpreting the results of the experiment, but when included as a narrative in the research document will assist readers to understand the extent to which the results can be generalized to the target population. These thoughts, assumptions, and suggestions are important foundations and legitimate grounds for utilizing quasi-experimental research designs to improve education. Succinctly, the greatest problem with true experimental research designs is that they alter the subjects' natural environment. The importance of the natural environment is probably greater in a band, choir, or orchestra than in any other class in public or private school systems. Quasi-experimental designs should be viewed as beneficial, valuable, logical, and a justifiable means toward gaining insight into causal relationships in music education. With regard to the important interactions that are necessary for music-education instruction to excel, quasi-experimental designs are in many ways superior to true experimental designs for experimental research.

Identification of Quasi-Experimental Designs

The point of the preceding discussion was to emphasize that quasi-experimental designs are indeed "good" and a type of research to be respected and used, not criticized. The primary difference between true experimental designs and quasi-experimental designs is based on the inability to randomly assign subjects to groups. Consequently, quasi-experimental designs are our best hope.

Campbell and Stanley outline ten quasi-experimental studies in their monumental handbook of experimental designs.[15] The six most appropriate for research in music education are presented in Figure 11. As in Figure 10, the O represents testing the dependent variable and the X represents the experimental treatment. All four of the threats to external validity discussed in the preceding section are threats in quasi-experimental designs. Compliance with Snow's suggestions listed above can help in drawing conclusions. However, in order to generalize results, keep it only to smaller populations that you as a researcher would prefer. The first three designs in Figure 10, which are considered appropriate for pilot studies, could

Figure 11
Quasi-Experimental Designs and Threats to Internal Validity

<u>Design</u>	<u>Threats to Internal Validity</u>
1. Time series design	
O O O O X O O O O	history and possibly instrumentation
2. Equivalent time-samples design	
X_1 O X_0 O X_1 O X_0 O	none
3. Nonequivalent control-group design	
$\underline{\text{O X O}}$ (experimental group)	interactions with selection
O O (control group)	
4. Counterbalanced design	
X_1 O X_2 O X_3 O X_4 O	none
X_2 O X_3 O X_4 O X_1 O	
X_3 O X_4 O X_1 O X_2 O	
X_4 O X_1 O X_2 O X_3 O	
5. Separate-sample pretest/posttest design	
O X	history, maturation, experimental mortality, interactions with selection and possibly instrumentation
X O	
6. Multiple time-series	
$\underline{\text{O O O X O O O}}$ (experimental group)	none
O O O O O O (control group)	

also be labeled quasi-experimental designs, since random assignment of subjects is not conducted.

The first quasi-experimental design is the *time series design*. In such an experiment a single group of subjects is tested on the dependent variable at periodic intervals. The experimental treatment is provided somewhere between two adjacent tests. The immediately preceding and following tests are analyzed as the pretest and posttest. The other tests are used to verify that extraneous variables did not interfere with the statistical treatment. That is, the dependent variable should remain stable during the testings prior to the experimental treatment. Following the experimental treatment there may be a significant difference in the dependent variable. Subsequent testings could conceivably indicate that the level of the dependent variable continues to rise after the treatment (e.g., learning continues), that it falls to the pretest level after a period of time, or it remains the same as the posttest level. Each of these provides valuable insight into the effects of the experimental treatment.

The *equivalent time-samples design*, the second one outlined in Figure 11, is similar to the time series design. The symbol X indicates the point where the experimental treatment is provided to single group of subjects; X_0 indicates the *absence* of the treatment. The design is outlined for clarity: the alternation of "treatment-test, no treatment-test," etc., should be randomized and not simply flip-flop back and forth. Campbell and Stanley advocate this design when you expect that the effect(s) of the experimental treatment will be temporary.[16] This design controls for history, unlike the time series design (the first in Figure 11), since the several "posttests" can be compared to determine if such extraneous variables affected the tests following X_1.

The most popular quasi-experimental design is the third one, *nonequivalent control-group design*. This is similar to the true experimental pretest-posttest control-group design except that the subjects are not randomly assigned. The primary difference in threats to internal validity is that the quasi-experimental design may be influenced by the interactions of *selection × maturation* or *selection × history*. This problem is most obvious when subjects in separate schools participate as subjects in the experiment. Further, the threat of *statistical regression* is a concern when one group or class is selected for the experimental treatment because they "need" it (i.e., they are low achievers) or because the principal strongly supports music education (which may make the teachers and students in that school have better attitudes and achieve more).[17]

The nonequivalent control-group design was used by Peery and Peery to investigate the effects of exposure to classical music on the musical preferences of preschool children. The experimental and control groups were nonequivalent, because the ten-month experimental treatment was given to children whose parents chose to have them participate in a music-enrichment program. Students in both groups were asked to rate musical excerpts on a five-point Likert scale on which "smiley faces" of varying degrees were substituted for numbers. Eight separate analysis-of-variance tests were run to determine pretest differences between the experimental and control groups on eight different musical selections. The groups did not differ on the pretest scores for seven excerpts. The eight tests for differences on the posttest measure, however, revealed significant differences for four of the six classical selections, indicating that exposure to classical music changes its appeal.[18]

The fourth design outlined in Figure 11 is a *counterbalanced* or *factorial design*. This, like the Soloman four-group design in Figure 10, will be discussed in the section below entitled "Factorial Designs."

The fifth quasi-experimental design is the *separate-sample pretest/posttest design*. In this design two nonequivalent groups of subjects are tested at two different times. The group which may be considered as the control group is shown in Figure 11 as receiving the experimental treatment after the pretest. This treatment is included in the figure for convenience. In reality it would make no difference if that group received the treatment or not; the first group is not tested again. The scores for this "control" group are used for comparison with the scores of the experimental group, which is tested after the experimental treatment. The only advantage of this design over some others is that it guards against the threat of testing and any interaction of testing and the experimental treatment.

This design appears in numerous research textbooks, preceded by an R for each group. The symbol R is used in the experimental designs in Figure 10 to indicate random assignment to groups. Campbell and Stanley included the Rs in their original table that includes the separate-sample pretest/posttest design as an indication that the *time* of the testing can be chosen at random, and *not* for the same reason that the symbol appears in their table of experimental designs.[19]

This design could prove useful in experimental research where true experimental designs are impossible to use and a control group may prove difficult "to control." Cook and Campbell cite the 1975 study by Minton as an example of this design's application.[20] Minton wanted to determine the effect of the television program "Sesame Street" on the scores of a group of kindergarten students' reading-readiness tests. She was able to test a large sample at the end of their kindergarten year. The only group available for comparison, though, were those who were tested several years previously, before the television show was ever aired.[21] The effect of history and instrumentation could be a serious threat to validity in this design. Maturation could also be a factor, since five-year-olds in 1975 may be more mature than five-year-olds tested three or four years earlier.

The final quasi-experimental design, *multiple time-series*, is essentially the nonequivalent control-group design "surrounded" by additional pretests and posttests for the two groups. As mentioned for the equivalent time-samples design, the experimental treatment need not be given in a systematic location within the continued testing, but preferably somewhere at random. This design is preferred over both the nonequivalent control-group design and the time-series design because it guards against threats to internal validity. You are encouraged to review the preceding comments for both of these designs to see how the multiple time series design utilizes the best of both.

While this is one of the more expensive designs to implement, it is perhaps the best quasi-experimental design. Graduate students are strongly encouraged to read chapter 5, "Quasi-Experiments: Interrupted Time-Series Designs," in the text by Cook and Campbell. That chapter contains a detailed discussion of this design and others derived from it.[22]

Factorial Designs

Factorial designs enable you to measure the effect of two or more independent variables simultaneously and to examine their interactions. As an illustration, suppose you wish to compare the effects of notational complexity on the duration of eye fixation of subjects who are sight-singing music. The dependent variable would be fixation durations in milliseconds. The independent variable would be notational complexity: easy melodies and difficult melodies. You hypothesize that the most complex melodies will require longer fixation durations because subjects need more time to process information.

To test your hypothesis, however, you decide that instead of presenting only two melodies to each subject, you may gain further understanding of sight-reading by presenting each subject with four separate melodies, each one becoming more difficult. You now have the same dependent variable (fixation duration in milliseconds) but your independent variable is expanded to four levels of notational complexity.

Your adviser points out that the order in which these four melodies are presented to subjects could affect their eye movement (fixation durations), since by the fourth melody, they might be "expecting" a tough one. Conversely, if the melodies go from difficult to easy, by the fourth one, subjects may expect an "easier" one. You can mitigate against the effect of order by dividing subjects into four equal groups and presenting the melodies in four different orders. Using the same notation as in Figures 10 and 11, you could graph this design as follows.

Group A	X_1	O	X_2	O	X_3	O	X_4	O
Group B	X_2	O	X_3	O	X_4	O	X_1	O
Group C	X_3	O	X_4	O	X_1	O	X_2	O
Group D	X_4	O	X_1	O	X_2	O	X_3	O

Each X is a melody (1-4) and each O is the subjects' performance while you monitor their eye movements and record fixation durations. Turn back to Figure 11 and you will notice that this design is a counterbalanced design. It is also called a *Latin Square* design.

Using a factorial design, not only could you compare the effects of each melody on fixation duration, but you could also compare groups to see if order has any effect on fixation duration. This experiment has two independent variables, or *factors*— consequently it is called a factorial design.

Assume that during your pilot study you discover that the fixation durations of those subjects who can sight-read really well differ a great deal from those poor souls who cannot sight-read the easiest melody very well. Unfortunately this design, as explained by Campbell and Stanley, does not lend itself to a pretest very well[23] because a pretest would pretty much foul up any type of sight-reading study. You were hoping to use a pretest because those scores could then be used to separate the strong and weak sight-readers for additional comparison.

The solution now is to give your subjects a standardized test to determine which subjects sight-read well and which are the weakest. Since the subjects' task will be to sight-sing these melodies, it will be best if your test requires them to vocalize melodies. You go to Buros's *Mental Measurements Yearbooks* to locate such a test. To get two distinct groups, you test dozens and dozens of volunteers until you secure a dozen really excellent sight-readers and a dozen fairly weak sight-readers.

You now have added another factor, sight-reading ability, and you have three-way factorial design: *sight-reading ability* (two groups with twelve in each group) × *notational complexity* (four melodies) × *order* (four orders). It could be charted as on page 277.

You can now compare fixation durations in three ways: (1) by ability level (which group of subjects used the longest fixations?); (2) by melody (which of the four melodies requires the longest fixations?); and (3) by order (which order of fixations requires the longest fixations?). Each of these three independent variables, or factors, can have a significant *main effect* on fixation durations (the dependent variable).

The statistical analysis will also indicate if there are any *first-order interactions*, or *simple main effects*. There are three possibilities: ability level by melodies, ability level by order, and melodies by order. This means that you could find that fixation durations are longer for the *interaction* of ability level and melodies, for example. You might find in such an interaction that the two groups do not differ significantly, but the weaker sight-readers use considerably longer fixation durations on the level 3 melody than the stronger sight-readers, who use longer fixation durations for the other three melodies. Interactions are difficult to interpret.

The example above could have one possible *second-order interaction*, or *simple-interaction effect*: ability level by melodies by groups. Goolsby hopes that you never find a significant second-order interaction without having had a course in statistics.[24]

Schleuter and Schleuter conducted a study to investigate the relationship of grade level and gender with rhythmic aspects of musical achievement.[25] This is an excellent example of a three-way factorial design, which utilized grade level, gender, and rhythmic response as the three factors. It is labeled a "mixed" design because, first, subjects are *nested* in the factors of grade and gender—meaning that each subject could be in only one of the four grade

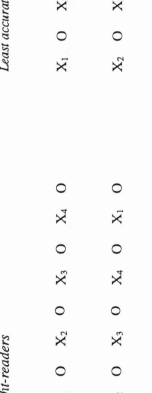

Most accurate sight-readers

Group A X_1 O X_2 O X_3 O X_4 O

Group B X_2 O X_3 O X_4 O X_1 O

Group C X_3 O X_4 O X_1 O X_2 O

Group D X_4 O X_1 O X_2 O X_3 O

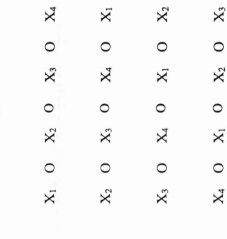

Least accurate sight-readers

X_1 O X_2 O X_3 O X_4 O

X_2 O X_3 O X_4 O X_1 O

X_3 O X_4 O X_1 O X_2 O

X_4 O X_1 O X_2 O X_3 O

levels and in only one gender group. And second, subjects are *crossed* with rhythmic response— meaning that all subjects participated in all three measured rhythmic tasks. In simpler terms, suppose you had one hundred subjects in four grade levels; that might be twenty-five in each of the levels. Then assign them by gender; there would be fifty in each "level." But on the rhythm test, there would be one hundred in each of three subtests. To further complicate matters, Schleuter and Schleuter discovered a significant interaction. You are strongly encouraged to struggle through their article and then to reread it after reviewing the two preceding chapters.

Inferential Statistics: Concepts

The previous two chapters have provided background for a basic understanding of inferential statistics. Descriptive statistics were discussed in the section entitled "Basic Statistics," in chapter 6. The second type of statistics used in quantitative research is inferential statistics. These techniques are used to *infer* results from the sample to the population represented by that sample.

At this point you should have read the previous chapters and enough journal articles and theses to be acquainted with types of scores or measures: continuous, ordinal, nominal (including dichotomies). You should also be at least familiar with the two kinds of descriptive statistics: measures of central tendency and measures of variability. And finally, from the previous two chapters, you should have some idea about what probability means and how correlations indicate the relationship between variables.

Parametric Tests

Parametric tests are used for determining differences between groups when all of three conditions are met: (1) the scores or observations being tested are from a continuous scale with equal intervals (not nominal or ordinal data); (2) the group of scores are close to a normal distribution (mean = mode = median, with 68 percent of the scores falling between one standard deviation above and below the mean); and (3) the variances of the groups being compared are very close to being equal (this condition is called "homogeneity of variance").

t-*tests*

One of the easiest parametric tests to conceptualize is the *t*-test. This test in essence compares the mean of one group to the mean of another group, the mean of the dependent variable for the experimental group to the mean score of the control group. As an illustration, suppose you teach ear-training at a college. You use a "new" method for the experimental group and teach the control group using a "traditional" method. At the conclusion of the semester you administer a standardized ear-training test and, as you expected, the mean for the experimental class is higher than the mean for the control class. Following your logic used in chapter 6 under "Tests for Differences," you know that there was a 50-50 chance of the experimental group's mean being higher than the control group's mean. Consequently, it is difficult to say that your "new" method caused the students to learn more, or to at least score higher.

In order to obtain a significant difference, that difference must be greater than what could have resulted by chance. Using a *t*-test merely involves plugging numbers into a formula. This formula calculates a ratio of the difference between the two groups' means (the systematic variance, of sorts) and the error variance (the spread of scores around the means in each group), to derive a *critical value*.

One simply consults a standardized table for *t*-tests which will indicate, according to the size of the sample, the probability value for the critical value. From this probability value one can determine if the hypothesis or null hypothesis is accepted or rejected according to the alpha level which was established before conducting the experiment.

An excellent example of using a *t*-test to determine differences between undergraduate and graduate students is the 1987 Madsen and Prickett study. Scores were derived from a quantitative analysis of a written essay in which students at both levels of music education were requested to discuss legal and ethical aspects in teaching. This study serves as a fine example of quantifying what would normally be considered a qualitative research topic, as well as the use of a *t*-test for significant differences.[26]

Analysis of Variance (ANOVA)

The *t*-test is useful for determining the differences between two groups. When more than two groups are involved in an experiment, the more sophisticated and more powerful analysis of variance is appropriate. If your experiment involved four groups—labeled A,

B, C, and D—then in order to use *t*-tests, you would have to compare A-B, A-C, A-D, B-C, B-D, C-D. This requires six separate inferential tests, which greatly increases the odds of making a Type I error (discovering a significant difference when one really does not exist).

While several groups can be analyzed simultaneously with ANOVA, they are lumped together as independent variables. Continuing with the previous example, suppose you wished to determine the effects of your new ear-training method on students who have different applied majors: A = winds, B = piano, C = voice, and D = strings. Your independent variable is "student's major" and your dependent variable is "scores" on a standardized ear-training test. There is no control group as such.

Whether you attempt the calculations by hand or use a computer, the basic concept is the same. First, all of the variance for the four groups is lumped together (this variance is how the scores of *everyone* who participated in the experiment vary around the mean for total sample) for the *total variance*. Second, the mean for each of the four groups is calculated and the variance within each group is calculated (this is the *error variance*, the variation of subjects' scores around the groups' means, i.e., within-group variance). Third, the error variance (the within-group variance for the four groups) is subtracted from the total variance to determine the *systematic variance* or *between-group variance*. Finally, a ratio called the *F ratio* is calculated by dividing the systematic variance by the error variance.[27] After you obtain an F ratio, a table of F ratios is consulted. Based on your sample size, the table indicates the probability level of that F ratio.

In ANOVA the error variance is considered the result of sampling error. The systematic or between-group variance is considered the variance due to the independent variable, which in your experiment was a new method of teaching ear-training. The F ratio will be small if there is a great deal of error variance in proportion to the systematic variance, indicating that the differences between groups are the result of chance. If the difference between groups is large enough that the systematic variance is considerably larger than the error variance, then the difference between groups may be significant. That is, the probability of your groups differing as much as they do is less than your alpha level. The F ratio, for example, may indicate that your difference would occur less than 5 percent of the time by chance (alpha = .05).

Analysis of Covariance (ANCOVA)

A statistical test for differences that is related to analysis of variance is *analysis of covariance*. This technique is used to control for differences between groups that were discovered on the pretest. This technique is especially useful in quasi-experimental designs, where random assignment of subjects to groups is not possible.

For example, Colley conducted an experiment using the quasi-experimental nonequivalent control-group design. Eight intact second- and third-grade classes served as subjects. Two classes in separate schools served as control groups while six classes in one school served as the experimental group (using three different methods in two classes each), a procedure intended to reduce the threat of treatment diffusion and compensatory rivalry and/or demoralization of the control group. The experimental group was taught a "new" method in general music for an eleven-week period. A rhythm recognition test, a rhythmic dictation test, and a performance test were used for pretesting and posttesting. Analysis of variance was used to determine if the two groups differed on any of the pretests. Colley discovered that the groups were significantly different on their scores on the rhythm recognition tests. Use of ANCOVA, however, allowed her to control for these pretest differences when analyzing the posttest scores for gains. In effect, ANCOVA adjusts the scores in such a way as to make the groups equal on the pretest by adjusting the posttest scores for subjects in the "higher"-scoring pretest group. She found significant differences on the posttest, indicating superior rhythmic recognition skills for the experimental group as well as significant gains in rhythmic dictation and performance achievement. This study also demonstrates the use of a *Newman-Keuls* test for *post hoc* analysis. The ANOVA, or in this case, ANCOVA, test indicates that the groups differ. A *post hoc* test is then required to determine the difference(s) in the three experimental teaching methods.[28]

Multiple Analysis of Variance (MANOVA)

This parametric test is used when two or more groups are to be compared on more than one dependent variable. This test is very similar to analysis of variance, except that the computer calculates all the variance from several dependent variables in one single test. This test also compares the effect of both variables working together to affect the dependent variable. If a significant F ratio is found, separate ANOVA tests are used to find which dependent variable is different.

Schmidt and Sinor conducted an experiment to determine the effects of children's "thinking style" (as measured by a publisher's standardized test) on several dependent variables: music audiation, creative thinking (both measured by a published standardized test), and gender. In this rather sophisticated study, the MANOVA showed that the data were not normally distributed. Unlike many researchers who would have simply ignored this indication and published invalid results, Schmidt and Sinor used an alternative method: they approached their study as a factorial design and examined differences appropriately.[29]

Nonparametric Tests

Nonparametric tests are generally less powerful than parametric tests. They are appropriate for determining differences between groups when the data are in nominal (categories) or ordinal (ranks) form. Nonparametric tests are also used when the measures from the groups are not normally distributed. Nominal data, for example, cannot be normally distributed; that is, they cannot be plotted on a graph to resemble a normal curve. In some studies, when a measure that results in continuous, intervallic data is used, the resulting scores will not be normally distributed.

Chi-Square

If you will refer back to Figure 8 in chapter 6 you will notice that there is one bivariate correlation to compare or determine the relationship of two dichotomies. Two other methods are used more frequently. For example, if you wished to determine the relationship of men and women to band directors and choral directors in your state, such information usually appears as percentages. For example: 72 percent of all band directors in the state of Z are male, while 84 percent of the choir directors are female. It does not take a great deal of thought to figure out the other percentages. Occasionally, however, there arises the need to determine whether this is a significant difference or a proportion due to chance.

Another example might be a research project to simply determine if students who have had music-appreciation classes in college attend orchestra concerts where a ticket purchase is required. The independent variable is having had music-appreciation classes: "yes" or "no." The dependent variable would be continuous if you asked, "How many?" But probably the vast majority of the responses would be "one"; perhaps there would be a few "twos," and very few "threes" or "fours." So using a simple "yes" or "no" on this dependent variable might be wise.

Chi-square is a test for this type of relationship to determine any significant differences. It is not restricted to two independent variables and two dependent variables. In theory you can use as many of each as required. In practice, however, the fewer the better—or the fewer, the more accurate the test.

This test can be used with any type of data that can be placed in categories using frequency counts. It compares the frequencies for each level of each variable with an "expected" frequency. Using the example above, the independent variable "music appreciation" had two levels: "yes" or "no," and the dependent variable had two levels. The test basically makes the assumption that one variable is not related to, or affected by, the other variable. Consequently, it is often called a test for independence. It does not determine the degree of relationship as a correlation, but yields a probability value of the relationship occurring by chance. As for other tests, you compare the probability value to your established alpha level to determine if something other than chance has affected the relationship.

An example of the use of chi-square is the observational study completed by Kostka, who taped forty-eight piano teachers instructing two students each. The ninety-six piano lessons were observed, and twelve variables ranging from low- to high-inference variables were recorded by a live observer and an additional observer who listened to the tapes. Behaviors of the teachers and students were then recorded and tallied. These frequency distributions were analyzed by chi-square for three levels of student achievement: elementary, secondary, and adult. Almost all of the variables differed across groups.[30]

Mann-Whitney U-Test

This test is similar to the parametric *t*-test, but does not require the three conditions of parametric test. The *Mann-Whitney U-Test* uses ordinal or continuous data (the latter are ranked) for the dependent variable to determine the differences between groups. The *Wilcoxon Rank-Sum Test* is very similar and can be used for the same types of data. The difference is that the Wilcoxon test is used when the groups are related (such as matching subjects).

The Wilcoxon Rank-Sum Test was used to analyze ordinal data in a study by LeBlanc and Sherrill in 1986. Those researchers had

127 students rank male and female vocalists on a scale of "weak" to "strong." An additional analysis was conducted using the Spearman rank-order correlation. That study provides an excellent example of this nonparametric inferential test as well as a graph of the Spearman correlation.[31]

Price used the Wilcoxon Rank-Sum Test to determine differences between the pretest and posttest rankings of "preferred" composers of 187 music-appreciation students. The nonmusic majors rated a list of dozens of composers on a scale of one to ten. The Wilcoxon Rank-Sum Test indicated that students preferred more serious composers at the end of their course.[32]

Kruskal-Wallis Test

This test is the nonparametric equivalent to analysis of variance. It is used when more than two groups of subjects are used in a study (*t*-tests, the Mann-Whitney U-Test, and the Wilcoxon Rank-Sum Test are limited to comparing only two groups).

Rosenthal's study of four groups of music-education majors' performances on their applied instruments is an excellent example of the applicability of the Kruskal-Wallis nonparametric ANOVA. Forty-four music majors studied the same étude. They were divided among four groups which received different types of instruction. One group was allowed to use a taped recording of a superior performance of the étude; one group was allowed to use the recorded tape plus a tape of verbal instructions; a third group was provided only the verbal instructions; and the fourth group simply practiced the étude. The dependent variables were accuracy of pitches, rhythms, dynamics, tempo, and phrasing. A significant difference was found for all dependent variables except phrasing (requiring five separate Kruskal-Wallis ANOVA tests). *Post hoc* tests indicated that the "aural model only" group performed better in every aspect.[33]

Problems for Review and Discussion

1. Why is experimental research usually regarded as more objective than the other types discussed in this book?
2. What is the difference between the declarative and null forms of a hypothesis? Find an example of each one in the literature.
3. What is the meaning of internal validity? What are the threats to internal validity identified in this chapter?

4. What is the meaning of external validity? What are the threats to external validity identified in this chapter?
5. When and why should you conduct a pilot study?
6. What are the true experimental designs identified in this chapter? Find examples of each type in the literature.
7. How would you determine whether to use an experimental or quasi-experimental design?
8. What are the quasi-experimental designs identified in this chapter? Find examples of each kind in the research literature.
9. Why are factorial designs important for experimental research?
10. Identify the kinds of inferential statistics discussed in this chapter and find an example of the use of each kind in the literature.

Supplementary Sources

Ary, Donald, Lucy C. Jacobs, and Asghar Razavieh. *Introduction to Research in Education*, 3rd ed.; New York: Holt, Rinehart and Winston, 1985. Chapters 9, 10.

Asher, J. William. *Educational Research and Evaluation Methods*. Boston: Little, Brown and Co., 1976. Chapters 5, 11, and Appendices.

Best, John W., and James V. Kahn. *Research in Education*, 6th ed.; Englewood Cliffs, N.J.: Prentice-Hall, 1989. Chapters 5, 6, 9.

Borg, Walter R., and Meredith D. Gall. *Educational Research: An Introduction*, 5th ed.; New York: Longman, 1989. Chapters 15, 16.

Cook, Thomas D., and Donald T. Campbell. *Quasi-Experimentation: Design and Analysis Issues for Field Settings*. Boston: Houghton Mifflin, 1979. Chapters 1-8.

Drew, Clifford J. *Introduction to Designing Research and Evaluation*. St. Louis: C. V. Mosby, 1976. Chapters 2, 3, 8.

Fox, David J. *The Research Process in Education*. New York: Holt, Rinehart and Winston, 1969. Chapters 8-10, 16, and Part IV.

Gronlund, Norman E. *Measurement and Evaluation in Teaching*, 4th ed.; New York: Macmillan, 1981. Chapters 11-16.

Keppel, Geoffrey. *Design and Analysis: A Researcher's Handbook*, 2nd ed.; Englewood Cliffs, N.J.: Prentice-Hall, 1982. Sections III, IV, V, and VI.

Kerlinger, Fred N. *Behavioral Research: A Conceptual Approach.* New York: Holt, Rinehart and Winston, 1979.

_____. *Foundations of Behavioral Research*, 3rd ed.; New York: Holt, Rinehart and Winston, 1986. Chapters 13-23.

Leedy, Paul D. *Practical Research Planning and Design*, 4th ed.; New York: Macmillan, 1989. Chapter 10.

Mason, Emanuel J., and William J. Bramble. *Understanding and Conducting Research: Applications in Education and the Behavioral Sciences*, 2nd ed.; New York: McGraw-Hill, 1989. Chapters 3-5, 7.

McMillan, James H., and Sally Schumacher. *Research in Education: A Conceptual Introduction*, 2nd ed.; Glenview, Ill.: Scott, Foresman, 1989. Chapters 3, 9, 10.

Sax, Gilbert. *Foundations of Educational Research*, 2nd ed.; Englewood Cliffs, N.J.: Prentice-Hall, 1979. Chapters 6-9.

Van Dalen, Deobold B. *Understanding Educational Research: An Introduction*, 4th ed.; New York: McGraw-Hill, 1979. Chapters 8, 9.

Vockell, Edward L. *Educational Research*. New York: Macmillan, 1983. Chapters 8-13.

9. Historical Research: Concepts and Techniques

The main focus of historical research for years has been the collection of data to record and interpret past events. Usually labeled "chronological" or "narrative" history, this type of reporting is also referred to as "historiography." Leedy writes that the purpose of the historical method is to "provide a means through which a researcher may deal with problems that arise from events that happened in times past and to interpret what might otherwise be considered merely as the happenstance of blind fortune."[1]

Newer Historical Research Approaches

Recently historians have begun to use more interdisciplinary approaches, with the result that in historical writings terms appear such as these listed by Shafer: psychohistory, comparative history, cooperative history, quantitative history, and intellectual and legal history.[2] Even though Rainbow and Froehlich admit that "chronological" is still an important approach for historical researchers to use, they identify psychohistory, quantitative social-scientific history, comparative history, and oral history as being significant newer techniques, although not as commonly used as the "traditional" or "chronological" approach.[3] (Oral history will be discussed later in this chapter because of its importance in music-education research.)

Barzun and Graff emphasize the importance of "narrative" history, but give some credence to the viability of approaches labeled "psychohistory" and "quanto" history.[4] However, they also view these approaches somewhat dimly and wonder whether the days of the "psycho" and "quanto" historian are finished. In a somewhat rhetorical tone, they write, "The desired extinction of narrative history at the hands of the newcomers [psycho- and quanto-historians] would seem . . . to entail their own ultimate suicide."[5] Brickman, a strong adherent of the narrative approach, reports that the historian's responsibility is to report accurately what has taken place, but only on rare occasions can he be in a position to report what he observes.[6] Leedy, in discussing historical research, makes reference to "psychological" or "conceptual" research. He states that this type of research is "concerned not only with events and personalities but with tracing the origin, development, and influence of ideas and concepts."[7] As if to clinch the issue, Barzun and Graff aver, *"History at its simplest is the story of past facts."*[8]

Since the main purpose of historical research reporting is to present a narrative or chronological account of events or persons and places, the main focus of this chapter will be devoted to those techniques. Other approaches will be discussed briefly before proceeding with the concepts of narrative history.

Psychohistory, according to Borg and Gall, involves the use of sampling techniques, defining and treating variables, and statistical analysis of the data obtained.[9] The psychohistorian, in addition to statistics, also uses content analysis, both of which are the hallmarks of the behavioral scientist. Rainbow and Froehlich write that the psychohistorian uses today's knowledge to understand what has happened in the past, with the assumption that the "social sciences may provide the researcher with a new understanding of past human behavior and with new tools to interpret such behavior."[10] Loewenberg lists three contributions psychohistory can make to history: (1) examine the unconscious in human behavior; (2) form an alliance between psychology and history; and (3) determine how the present is related to one's social status and the unconscious.[11] An example of a hypothetical psychohistorical study in music education would be how the string-class teaching methods of Albert G. Mitchell and his techniques impacted on the fledgling instrumental-music movement in the United States in the early twentieth century.

Comparative history, which made its appearance in the 1960s, according to Frederickson, systematically compares the same event in different societal settings.[12] Most of the studies to date have dealt with civil rights, slavery, and race relations. A comparison is made of how an event may be the same or different in different settings. Shafer gives as an example the treatment of slavery in English-, French-, Spanish-, and Portuguese-speaking America.[13]

Cooperative history, in the words of Shafer, refers to historical reference works.[14] In music education an example would be

Keene's seminal work, *A History of Music Education in the United States*.[15]

Quantitative history (or quanto-history) also is labeled as "cliometrics" by Barzun and Graff, because of its interdisciplinary emphasis on using statistics and computers to uncover new evidence from the past.[16] Kousser labels this approach, which first appeared about 1960, "quantitative social-scientific history." (The term also is used by Rainbow and Froehlich, you will recall.) According to Kousser, the quantitative social-scientific historian looks at old material, supplementing it with new procedures which are now possible because of data processing.[17] In a recent doctoral study, Frontèra combined a quantitative social-historical approach with aesthetic inquiry to examine the musical output of four nineteenth-century Puerto Rican composers. She reviewed the political, social, and economic conditions in Puerto Rico in the time period covered in her study to ascertain how these affected the musical output of four composers (Gutiérrez, Tavárez, Campos, and Quintón). She also traced the Indian, African, and Spanish cultural influences on these composers to determine if they developed a "nationalistic" style based on the *danza* indigenous to Puerto Rico.[18]

A hypothetical example in music education of the application of quantitative techniques would be to examine the funding of research by the U.S. Office of Education from the first music-education studies in the 1960s to the present. Such a study would review not only the specific grants awarded, but also the individual amounts of the grants, to whom they were awarded, and how social and/or political events influenced funding for those projects.[19]

Not much has been written about intellectual and legal history in education research textbooks, but an example listed by Shafer is Diggins's "Getting Hegel out of History: Max Eastman's Quarrel with Marxism."[20] Historical, legal, and policy studies are included under the rubric "analytical research" by McMillan and Schumacher. They write, "Analytical studies provide knowledge and understanding about past educational historical, legal, and policy events. Major ideas and concepts are clarified for meaning."[21]

Narrative or Chronological History

As already noted, collection of data pertaining to the past frequently is referred to as history. Vincent points out that this narrative is a statement of what persons do in various fields such as politics, law, music, or other arts.[22] Nevins presents a different viewpoint, stating that history is a bridge which connects the past and the present and leads to the future.[23]

Researchers in music education who employ the historical method are expected not only to obtain various kinds of data about the past related to their topic, but also to interpret them according to generally accepted techniques or historiography. Gray, in her study of the short-lived National Catholic Music Educators Association (NCMEA), discusses the importance of that organization to the field. It was significant because (1) the NCMEA had a tradition linking new and old; (2) the organization was most influential during the 1950s when Catholic student enrollment was at its height; and (3) the NCMEA encouraged its members to be aware of the needs and responsibilities of the professional music educator. When the role of the Catholic school music teacher diminished, the parish/church musician gained in importance and led to the formation of the National Association of Pastoral Musicians.[24]

Historical research, as is true with all methods or procedures for obtaining data, must employ the scientific method to solve problems in history. This could be the inclusion of approaches from other fields, as already indicated—quantitative, for example—or the generally accepted approaches of narrative history which are concerned with the external and internal criticism of data, to be discussed later. Defining an approach that is predicated on the scientific method, Fischer reports that history is involved with solving problems. The historian, continues Fischer, asks open-ended questions about events of the past, and the answers to these questions are based on facts which are arranged according to some type of paradigm to explain the phenomenon being studied.[25]

Historical research has not always been done by professional researchers and historians. Some of the more interesting and meaningful research has been by amateurs and "history buffs" whose main purpose has been to preserve artifacts and literary and other items that soon may be gone forever. Witness the spate of historical journals, pamphlets, and brochures prepared by local historians in cities and towns and even in rural areas during the bicentennial of the United States in 1976. Many of those persons were not trained as professional historians, but their accounts of local history, some using oral history techniques, have preserved much important information for posterity. Another example of the interest in history on the part of the general public as well as that of history buffs was the recent blocking of a proposed shopping mall on lands which were contiguous to the Manassas National Battlefield Park in Virginia. Manassas is one of the most famous of U.S. Civil War battlegrounds, where the First and Second Battles of Manassas (or Bull Run) were fought. The U.S. Congress, in December 1988, at the urging of citizens' groups and the National Park Service, bought six hundred acres of the threatened territory.[26]

The word "history" has several meanings and purposes. Shafer lists three meanings for the term: (1) to review past happenings, (2) to maintain a record of current events, and (3) to develop methods and evaluate evidence obtained to provide a meaningful documentation of events.[27]

Study of the past sometimes can serve as the basis for understanding the present or for predicting the future. Although this concept is not used as extensively in music education as it is in the social or political sciences, researchers may study stylistic periods in music, for example, with this objective in mind. The simpler and emotionally restrained classical period may be better understood when compared with the highly chromatic, introspective, and less formal Romantic era. Concepts of neoclassicism might become more evident when compared with classicism. Such studies could be labeled "comparative history," because of the comparisons in musical style.

Several applications of Shafer's second point to music education could result in learning more about the life and influence of significant music educators (contemporary or deceased), the development and contributions of a performing group, or the influence of a professional organization. This type of study might be identified as psychohistory. A historical study of the contributions to the development of music education by Charles H. Congdon (1856-1928) would be an example of this type of research.

Patrick Sarsfield Gilmore (1829-1892) was the subject of a recent psychohistorical study by Cipolla. In "Patrick S. Gilmore: The Boston Years," Cipolla reports on the influence the legendary P. T. (Phineas Taylor) Barnum (1810-1891) had on Gilmore, the best known bandmaster of the nineteenth century prior to John Philip Sousa (1854-1932). Gilmore's band played an important role in musical activities just before and during the Civil War. The band performed at the 1860 Democratic Convention in Charleston, South Carolina, when delegates adjourned because they could not agree on a proslavery platform, resulting in the departure of delegates from eight southern states. Gilmore's band also performed at the

Republican Convention in Chicago the same year, when Abraham
Lincoln (1809–1865) was elected to head the Republican ticket.
During the Civil War the band was on active duty for the Union at
New Bern, North Carolina, and in New Orleans, Louisiana.[28]

Another doctoral study with psychohistorical implications is
Ferguson's "The Bands of the Confederacy: An Examination of the
Musical and Military Contributions of the Bands and Musicians of
the Confederate States of America," which was discussed in the
first chapter.[29]

In a study on the life and influence of an important figure in
American music education, Howe, in her doctoral dissertation,
"Luther Whiting Mason: Contributions to Music Education in
Nineteenth Century America and Japan," reported on Mason's
authorship of the first graded music textbook series and the first
program to train classroom teachers to supervise elementary-school
music teaching. Mason also assisted in the establishment of music
education in Japan by editing the first graded series of music
textbooks for Japanese students.[30]

For a researcher at the master's level, an interesting study could
be a comparison of different versions of *The Star-Spangled Banner*.
For example, the senior author is a member of a community band
that regularly performs the 1855 version of *The Star-Spangled
Banner*. Obtained from the Smithsonian Institution in Washington,
D.C., this 1855 version is scored only for brass instruments. In
addition to several rhythmic deviations from the version normally
played by a full band or orchestra, it contains four short cadenzas
for solo trumpet.

The third meaning for history given by Shafer is only partially
applicable in music-education research. Music researchers normally do not develop methods, but they do evaluate historical
evidence and then present it in a meaningful context.

Undoubtedly the most significant reason for involvement in
history today is the same one given by Thucydides (c. 460–400
B.C.), sometimes referred to as the "father" of the modern historical
method, who remarked that his purpose was "not to write for
immediate applause but for posterity." This eminent Greek historian also explained very astutely that it was his duty to supplement
and compare, as accurately as possible, his own observations of the
Peloponnesian War (431–404 B.C.) with the reports of eyewitnesses.
It was the German historian Leopold von Ranke (1795–1886),
according to Barzun and Graff, who applied the rigorous approach of the scientific method to historiography.[31] The method

of von Ranke as applied to historical research is more nearly akin to that used by most scholars today in narrative historical studies.

Although historical research in music has often been guarded jealously by scholars in musicology, there really is little justification for this restrictiveness, as an examination of historical studies in music education over the past three dozen years will reveal. Garrett, in defining the function of the musicologist, insists that the researcher use scholarly procedures to locate and organize data relating to the evolution of all types of music.[32] These same conditions are incumbent upon the music educator engaged in historical research. There is no need for investigators who use the scientific method to be labeled according to some narrow, arbitrary distinction like "historian," "musician," or "educator." Rather, they should all be regarded as "research scholars." This is in harmony with the views of Hockett, who considers the usefulness of history as the "intellectual honesty which should be developed by the quest for truth in any field of knowledge, in defiance of all temptations to wander from the straight and narrow path which alone can lead to it."[33]

Historical Research Procedures

Historical research is based on certain steps or procedures that, Hockett states, consists of "the gathering of data, the criticism of data; and the presentation of facts, interpretations, and conclusions in readable form."[34] The first point is closely related to the sources and kinds of information needed for the study. External and internal criticism, to be discussed later in this chapter, are used respectively to determine the truthfulness and trustworthiness of the data. Hockett's final step, relating to exposition and interpretation of data, already has been referred to as historiography, but will continue to be discussed throughout this chapter.

Gottschalk's historical research focus involves (1) obtaining the facts; (2) placing the facts in appropriate order; (3) determining the adequacy of data collected; and (4) making certain the items follow seriatim.[35] Gottschalk's first two steps relate to what Hockett calls "gathering of data," but with positive or negative implications. Finally, Gottschalk's sequence of data placement is closely allied to Hockett's "interpretation and conclusions." Historical facts, according to Shafer, are "slippery." He suggests that we must be concerned with "different *forms* of evidence, and with the social and individual psychological factors that determine the *quality* and *credibility* of evidence."[36]

Barzun and Graff present a more succinct statement about research procedures applicable to historical research: the subject or topic "is defined by *that group of associated facts and ideas which, when clearly presented in a prescribed amount of space, leave no questions unanswered WITHIN the presentation, even though many questions could be asked OUTSIDE it.*"[37]

Historical researchers are sometimes criticized for being too subjective because historiographers are not always in a position to exercise the rigid controls that natural scientists regard as absolutely essential. Historiographers, unlike scientists, normally are concerned with more than an observation of the present. When involved in the preservation of today's chronology, which tomorrow will be history, historiographers must be just as accurate and precise as natural scientists in order to realize the ultimate objective of presenting and interpreting the truth. A music critic, attending the world premiere of a composition by either a renowned or unknown composer, is on the threshold of history, as it were. The critic's responsibility to the musical world in accurately reporting the performance of this new work is essentially no different from that of the reporter who writes the proceedings of a conference of the world's leaders for dissemination to the general public. Both have an obligation to provide information that is as objective, truthful, and unbiased as is humanly possible.

The classic "who, what, where, when, why," timeworn as it may seem, is another way to look at a procedure for collecting historical data. Researchers in history, however, should always be aware that they may never be able to acquire all the information needed and that additional sources may be discovered later that will refute what they believe to be true based on the evidence at that time.

Probability

The concept of "probability," in simplest terms, may be stated as, "What is the likelihood that the evidence I am considering is valid?" For the historical researcher it is as important to establish the truth of "probability" as it is to determine the veracity of other kinds of information. Rainbow and Froehlich point out that, like the historian, the philosopher can use inductive reasoning to establish probability.[38] Using more objective techniques, however, the historical researcher employs external criticism to verify probability. Discussing the importance of verification of statements, Shafer insists that a researcher "must judge as well as he or she can each statement that is important. The judgment is of varying degrees of *probability* of being near or far from truth. Since this cannot be measured, only care and judgment will serve."[39]

Bringing probability down to a personal level, in the senior author's duties as a docent at the North Carolina state capitol in Raleigh, he continually asks himself what is the "probability" that the legends he describes to tour groups are true. One example will suffice. Were the so-called "secret rooms" in the capitol actually used by Confederate spies during the Civil War? Since those rooms were unfinished, were inaccessible, and contained no flooring until recent renovations of the building, the probability of this legend's being true is very remote.

On a more positive note, a recent Associated Press dispatch from Israel indicates that archaeologists have uncovered a two-thousand-year-old flask from caves at Qumran that may have been used to anoint ancient Israelite kings. The reddish oil found in the small clay juglet has a honey-like consistency, and apparently came from a perfume known as persimmon oil extracted from a now-extinct bush. The probability of the genuineness of this oil is very strong, according to the chemists and other scholars who examined it.[40] Barzun and Graff sum up the notion of probability by concluding that *"truth rests not on possibility nor on plausibility but on probability."*[41]

Source Materials

Source materials used by the historiographer are normally of two kinds, *primary* and *secondary*. A primary source of data is "first-hand" information. It is a report by the observer on the spot, as it were. When data are not original to the one reporting they become "secondary" or "secondhand" sources. It is also possible to obtain information from a "tertiary" or other source even further removed from the original. Every effort should be made, though, to seek out original data because the basis of solid historical research is the primary or firsthand source. According to Mason and Bramble, historiographers recognize the necessity of directing their energies appropriately to get this kind of information.[42]

If you are preparing a biography of a living person you might use such primary source materials as correspondence by and to the subject; publications by the subject; legal and personal documents, such as contracts, wills, and diaries; newspaper items; photographs and photocopies; concert programs; oral and written reports by contemporaries; and tape recordings of personal interviews.

Secondary sources often have value but should be used only when primary sources are untrustworthy or difficult to procure. Brickman asserts, however, that reliable secondary sources are preferable to primary sources that are questionable or incomplete.[43] Secondary sources worthy of merit will be adequately documented since they should be based on primary materials. Accounts of a concert written by someone other than the person actually present to hear the concert are secondary, as are specially prepared summary accounts of the minutes of official meetings. History books and many encyclopedia articles are secondary even though their authors may have had recourse to primary materials. Likewise, publications by an individual may be primary sources, but when excerpts from them are quoted by another person they become secondary.

Biographical accounts of composers frequently include an analysis of some of their music to indicate how events in their lives may have influenced their contributions to the field of music. As an example, Madeja, in a doctoral dissertation entitled "The Life and Work of Herbert L. Clarke (1867-1945)," gathered information on the life and influence of this important trumpet soloist, conductor, and teacher. Clarke's style of playing, concert programming, and cornet method book have all left their mark on many of today's trumpet and cornet players.[44]

Selection of Topic

Although factors in the selection of a topic already have been discussed at considerable length earlier in this book, five that Brickman considers to be significant before an investigator decides on a historical-research topic are: (1) interest, (2) source materials available, (3) the time factor, (4) relevance to course, and (5) specialized knowledge.[45]

As already mentioned in this book, researchers in music education should direct their energies toward a topic in which they have an intense interest. A high-school choral director, for instance, might want to write a history of the high-school choral contest-festival movement in the United States. Preliminary investigation may reveal that source materials are so limited that it would be impractical to continue with the original idea without expanding its scope. Such expansion would obviously require additional time, a factor that might not be feasible in a situation where a deadline becomes an external factor imposed by the duration of the instructional period.

One aspect has not yet been mentioned: Brickman states emphatically that the topic of a research report should bear relevance to the objectives of the research class.[46] While there are exceptions, it is only logical that researchers in music education select a topic that they can develop in relation to music education. One of the principal objectives of a music-education research course ought to be to give students experience in making practical application of the precepts they learn there. Taking Brickman's enjoinder more seriously could result in fewer unsuitable music-education research studies.

In the realm of specialized knowledge, if you are proposing a history of music education in Germany, to cite a possibility, you obviously should possess both a knowledge of the history of music education in general and an adequate reading comprehension of German, the language in which most primary sources would likely appear. It would be very impractical to attempt logical translations with the use of a German-English lexicon exclusively, especially if you were unfamiliar with music-education terminology and philosophical principles, as well as with technical terms and idioms that might appear in the German language.

Oral History

Although Nevins is generally regarded as the first person to formally employ the techniques of oral history (in 1948), Hoover reports that the Forest History Society began reporting on the history of forest products in the United States and Canada in 1947.[47] One year later, Columbia University professor Allan Nevins conducted an oral-history interview with George McAney, a New York civic leader. The Columbia University Oral History Collection now includes the memoirs of over three thousand people and almost four hundred thousand pages of transcripts. Oral history is a procedure or method for obtaining and preserving historical information in spoken form based on the interview. Verbal evidence can be a primary source when written evidence is not available. Data gathered through oral-history interviews are largely intended for future use by historians rather than for the substantiation of hypotheses, as would be the case in experimental research or even psychohistory. Cutler states that "knowledge about the past passes by word of mouth from generation to generation, and not only must the scholar capture it but he must also try somehow to filter the significant from the inconsequential as well as the truth from the exaggerated."[48] The collection of data in oral-history research is based on a well-planned procedure rather than on spontaneous or random interviews, following these carefully planned steps:

1. researcher's invitation to individuals to participate;
2. preparation for the interview;
3. preinterview visit;
4. the interview session (tape-recorded);
5. preparation of verbatim transcript of the interview;
6. submission of transcript to interviewee for corrections and additions, along with legal draft agreement;
7. conclusion of the legal agreement and contract or statement of gift; and
8. preparation of final copy of interview.

Before sending an invitation to prospective interviewees you must identify the purposes of the research and the problem to be investigated. If the oral-history project involves working in a remote area, individuals able to provide the desired information must first be identified, and then necessary preparations arranged, such as housing for the researcher, equipment to be used (usually portable-operated cassette tape recorder or VCR and adequate supply of tapes), and mode of transportation to reach the interviewee. The researcher meets and establishes rapport with the interviewee, indicating the purpose of the interview and arranging a definite time and place for the next meeting. Researchers should use a portable tape recorder because they will not have time to write down everything of importance that the person being interviewed may say. In addition, portable recording systems are easier to transport. An added advantage is that a tape recording may be replayed as many times as necessary to get a literal transcript of the interview. A verbatim transcript allows the interviewee to make additions, corrections, or deletions and to protect both parties from any legal action that might result. There may be occasions when an interviewee will not permit the interview to be recorded. If this be the case, you must respect the wishes of the interviewee and not resort to some type of subterfuge. The result of this refusal would mean that you would need to write down as much as you can on the spot or, as is sometimes the case, write down what you can as soon as possible after the interview.

Legal documents should be worked out with your attorney. Once editorial and legal details have been clarified the final document is submitted for signature, and the contract or statement is made indicating the type of remuneration the interviewee is to receive. The oral-history process culminates in the preparation of the copy to be deposited in some archive or central repository for the benefit of other researchers or those who wish to read the account.

Oral-history studies in music education have been infrequent to date, but this could change as researchers become more interested in sociological and cultural studies that impinge on music, using qualitative techniques discussed earlier in this book. Hoover reports that one of the early oral-history studies in music was completed in the 1960s at Tulane University in New Orleans, Louisiana, and consisted of using tapes to supplement manuscripts on the history of jazz.[49] Recent national and regional meetings of the Music Educators National Conference have included sessions devoted exclusively to oral history. These should help to kindle interest and enthusiasm for oral-history research.

A recent oral-history study in music education was completed by Brobston.[50] In the first part of his study Brobston presented the antecedents of gospel music, music used by evangelists in the nineteenth and twentieth centuries, and the status of gospel music in the South at the time his study was completed, including singing conventions, publishers of gospel music, and performers. The second part of his study, "A Brief History of White Southern Gospel Music and a Study of Selected Amateur Family Gospel Music Singing Groups in Rural Georgia," contained the field research, or oral-history aspect. This was conducted in twenty-five counties of South Georgia selected at random, from which twenty-three family singing groups were interviewed and recorded in actual performance. Brobston concluded that there appears to be no significant diminution of gospel-singing activity in the geographical area included in his study.

The Oral History Association publishes two sources of information that should be helpful to music-education researchers: *Oral*

History Association Newsletter and the annual *Oral History Review*. Both contain articles, abstracts of recently completed studies, and a listing of recent publications dealing with oral history. One such citation is Cooper's "Popular Songs as Oral History: Teaching Black History Through Contemporary Audio Resources."[51] In addition, there are regional and state oral-history association which also publish reports.

Two important sources for the researcher interested in oral history are Baum's *Oral History for the Local History Society* and *Transcribing and Editing Oral History*. Both are published by the American Association for State and Local History. (See "Supplementary Sources" at the end of this chapter.)

Historical Research Data Gathering

Musicians involved in historical research will most likely find their data falling into one or more of the following categories: that of (1) heretofore-unknown information about an individual, group, object, or era; (2) uncovering heretofore-unknown creativity of someone; (3) discovering an authentic copy of a work or a more complete one; (4) locating creative efforts that were known to have been written but believed not to be extant; (5) collecting, codifying, or analyzing information of historical import from diverse sources; (6) verifying that documents, statements, or creative works of a reputed author are spurious; and (7) rectifying incorrect statements, dates, or information previously accepted as true.

In reference to the first point, one of the most gratifying by-products of historical research is the discovery of heretofore-unknown information. Although such data usually result from serendipity, opportunities for revelations of this kind are too infrequent in music and music education. The most likely sources of such information are newly discovered manuscripts, personal letters, or documents that previously were unavailable to the general public. Barzun and Graff give an interesting account of the former's discovery of a previously suppressed letter of Hector Berlioz (1803–1869) that appeared shortly after the first appearance of his "Rákóczy March" in 1846. The original was not only misdated but also distorted from a letter basically musical in content to one with "political" implications.[52]

Even more significant than Barzun's discovery is identifying heretofore-unknown creativity, the second category. Richard L.

Crocker, professor of music history at the University of California at Berkeley, announced that the deciphering of a song on clay tablets pushes the history of music back a thousand years to the second millennium B.C. Unearthed by French archaeologists in the 1950s in Ugarit, in what is now Syria, the cuneiform symbols were undecipherable until 1972. The song is based on the same heptatonic scale in use today in Western music. Crocker states that it sounds like a lullaby, hymn, or gentle folk song.[53]

Discoveries of heretofore-unknown creativity normally are of two kinds: items that have been identified positively as authentic and those about which some question remains regarding authenticity. Newspapers and periodicals like the *Journal of the American Musicological Society* and the *Music Quarterly* frequently contain accounts of the discovery of previously lost items. A case in point: a lost manuscript containing two movements of a Franz Joseph Haydn (1732-1809) Mass of 1786 was found in a cupboard in a northern Ireland farmhouse a few years ago. The renowned Haydn scholar H. C. Robbins Landon identified the work as being an important find. Among the clues used for identification, Robbins Landon reported that the ink had faded and the paper is from a mill on the Esterhazy Estate. The folder has a handwritten note by Vincent Novello, indicating that it was an unpublished work by Haydn which Novello bought in Vienna in 1829.[54]

The American concert pianist Byron Janis identified a hitherto-lost manuscript copy of Chopin's Waltz in G-Flat Major, Op. 70, No. 1. Found in the Château de Thoiry in Yvelines, France, the manuscript was unearthed in a box marked "old clothes" by the mansion's owner, Count Paul de La Panouse, who showed the work to Janis. The connection between Frédéric Chopin (1810-1849) and the Panouse family is that Chopin's friend, French writer Eugène Sue (1804-1857), was in love with the second wife of one of Count Paul's relatives. Janis, recognizing the importance of the manuscript, had it authenticated by Chopin expert François Lesure, of the Société Française Musicologie.[55] Discovered at the same time and in the same place was the E-Flat Waltz, Op. 18, "The Grand Valse Brillante."[56]

The discovery a few years ago of a Violin Concerto in C Major, reputedly by Beethoven, is an example of a composition the authenticity of which remains uncertain. Only further investigation will reveal whether this does belong in fact to Beethoven's catalog of works.

Another source of personal satisfaction to a researcher is to uncover a more complete or authentic copy of a musical composition or other creative work, the third category of data. While examining stacks of uncataloged instrumental music in the Moravian Archives in Old Salem (now part of Winston-Salem, North Carolina), the senior author located a complete set of the Three Trios, Op. 3, of John Antes (1740-1811) minus the last page of the violoncello part. John Bland of London published these undated trios, apparently about 1785, because Antes was known to have been in England then. Prior to Phelps's discovery the only known set in existence consisted of a second violin and a violoncello part owned by the Sibley Music Library of the Eastman School of Music in Rochester, New York. A comparison of the Eastman and Salem copies disclosed exact duplication. Thus, by using the Salem first- and second-violin parts and the Eastman violoncello part it was possible to present the first modern performance of Trio in D Minor, Op. 3, No. 2, the second of these charming Haydnesque trios, at the University of Iowa, Iowa City, on May 19, 1950, with violinists Stella Hopper and Joanne Dempsey and violoncellist Charles Becker as performing artists.

Antes, whose surname is the Greek equivalent of von Blume, was born at Fredrick-trop, Montgomery County, Pennsylvania, on March 24, 1740. In accord with the prevailing educational philosophy of the Moravians at that time Antes intensively pursued musical instruction in his youth, in addition to other studies. In 1769, after being ordained at Marienborn, Germany, he went to Egypt as a missionary. While recuperating from physical affliction Antes composed some quartets and other pieces before returning to Europe in 1782, where in Vienna, according to Grider, Antes met Haydn, who assisted other musicians in the performance of some of his compositions.[57] It was during his convalescence in Cairo that the trios were written, as indicated by the inscription of the title page, which states in part, "Composti a Grand Cairo dal Sigre Giovanni A-T-S. Dillettante Americano. Op. 3" [Composed at Grand Cairo by Mr. John A-T-S. American Dilettante. Op. 3]. Quite in keeping with the custom of the time, Antes perplexingly listed himself as A-T-S, a factor that resulted in his anonymity until 1940, when Carlton Sprague Smith, then chief of the Music Division of the New York Public Library, revealed the identity of this important Moravian composer.[58]

When any work is unearthed its importance ultimately may rest on its value when viewed in light of historical perspective. Under ordinary circumstances the discovery of works by someone such as Antes, who is relatively unknown to music educators, probably would go unheralded. In terms of historical perspective, however, the Antes Trios assume a new dimension. They represent, as far as the senior author has been able to discern, *the earliest extant chamber music written by a native-born American.*[59]

Another phase of historical research in music education relates to the fourth category, locating works previously believed not to be extant. At the Moravian Archives in Salem, in the same pile of uncataloged instrumental compositions that contained the Antes Trios, Phelps discovered the manuscript of "Parthia IX," by David Moritz Michael (1751–1825), generally regarded as the most important nineteenth-century Moravian instrumental composer. Rau and David, in their seminal catalog of American Moravian music, report that "Parthia IX" was not to be found in Bethlehem nor in Lititz in Pennsylvania.[60] Rau and David had indicated that the collections of Lititz and Bethlehem contained thirteen wind *partien.*[61] With the finding of "Parthia IX" it may safely be stated that Michael composed at least fourteen *partien*, all of which exist in manuscript in the Moravian Archives either in Bethlehem, Pennsylvania, which now contain the former Lititz holdings, or at Salem, North Carolina.[62] Since Bethlehem and Salem served as ecclesiastical headquarters for the northern and southern divisions of the Moravian church, respectively, the duplication in manuscript of some compositions in the archives of these two cities may be explained by the constant interchange of personnel. Michael, however, confined his activities to Bethlehem and Nazareth, Pennsylvania.

These *partien*, in accordance with the meaning of the word, were meant to be performed out-of-doors. Grider notes that they usually were performed from a balcony of the home of the Moravian Brethren on Wednesday evenings during the summer for the benefit of the citizens of the community.[63]

In four short, technically easy movements, "Parthia IX," except for the second movement, is scored for two clarinets in Bb, two French horns in Bb, and bassoon. The first (Allegro), third (Minuet), and fourth (Allegro) are in the key of Bb Major. The second (Andante), the key of F Major, is scored only for two Bb clarinets and bassoon.

A recent discovery of music, hidden for more than a century and thought to be lost, was four string quartets from Haydn's Op. 50. The disclosure was announced by Dr. Georg Feder, director of the

Joseph Haydn Institute in Cologne, Germany, in an interview in Sydney, Australia, in conjunction with the 250th anniversary celebrations for the birth of Franz Joseph Haydn (1732-1809). Feder stated that the works were authentic and were autographed by Haydn himself.[64]

The Polish-born violinist Henryk Szeryng, after a seven-year search, finally located a manuscript copy of Concerto No. 3 in E Major, by violin virtuoso Nicolò Paganini (1782-1840). It was known that Paganini had written five violin concertos, but prior to Szeryng's announcement, Concerto No. 3 was the only one that had not been found. Authenticity of the work was verified by French musicologists, according to Henahan.[65]

Collecting, codifying, or analyzing information of historical import from diverse sources, sometimes known as "documentary research," represents the fifth category of data for historical research in music education.

As an example of "documentary research," the Mendelssohn Quintet Club was the subject of an investigation the senior author made several years ago. This New England–based group, unless other evidence subsequently proves to the contrary, must be considered to be the *first professional group organized in the United States to devote itself exclusively to the performance of chamber music*. The ensemble remained in existence for forty-nine years, from 1849 to 1898, performing in many parts of the continental United States and in Hawaii, Australia, and New Zealand. The group also is reported to have been the first professional ensemble to organize a music conservatory.[66] Its focus on the performance of American music also is noteworthy.

Spearhead and driving force behind the Mendelssohn Quintet Club was Irish clarinetist, flutist, and violist Thomas Ryan (1827-1903), who emigrated from Ireland in 1844. Original members of the quintet were August Fries, first violin; Francis Riha, second violin; Thomas Ryan, viola and clarinet; Edward Lehmann, viola and flute; and Wulf Fries, violoncello. Ryan was the only member who remained with the group through its forty-nine-year existence.[67] Three New Englanders whose chamber works were featured by the quintet were Boston-born composers Charles Callahan Perkins (1823-1886) and James Cutler Dann Parker (1828-1916), and Vermont native Edward Jerome Hopkins (1836-1898).

In documentary research investigators assemble data from all available sources, codify them, and present their interpretations. The value of this type of study for both the musical layperson and the professional music educator is obvious. Someone who has neither the time nor the inclination to ferret out answers to questions usually welcomes the opportunity to acquire detailed and comprehensive information from one codified source. It is for this reason that dictionaries and encyclopedias of musical biography, terminology, and other kinds of information are so widely used by music educators who are seeking ready references.

The sixth category of data relates to documents, statements, compositions, or items that, although they may have been accepted at one time as authentic, subsequently have been proven to be spurious. An often-quoted example is the account of the fantastic and fanciful Cardiff Giant, unearthed in upstate Cardiff, New York, in the late nineteenth century. The Cardiff Giant had been buried by a scheming entrepreneur in that region of central New York State as a tourist attraction. The "giant" was a large, eight-foot gypsum image of a man. It even attracted the attention of the flamboyant P. T. Barnum (1810-1891), who wanted the "giant" for his circus. Unable to obtain it, he had another one made!

Good tells of a different type of chicanery involving a person who received a baccalaureate degree from a music school in 1950 and who, by 1963, through extensive forgery, was able to fabricate a transcript, complete with official registrar's seal, indicating this person had an Ed.D.[68] The senior author's evaluation of the authenticity of a string quartet allegedly by Benjamin Franklin (1706-1790), and a copy of a composition attributed to Sidney Lanier (1842-1881) will be discussed later in this chapter under "External Criticism or Authenticity."

Rectifying incorrect statements or information is the seventh category of data for historical research discussed in this book. Numerous examples exist in music as well as in general history for the rectification of statements, dates, or beliefs that previously have been accepted as correct. Brickman, Gottschalk, Hockett, and Nevins present several accounts to show that many anecdotes and statements attributed to George Washington (1732-1799), Thomas Jefferson (1743-1826), and Abraham Lincoln (1809-1865), among other distinguished Americans, have been proven to be illusory. Of local interest to Phelps has been the name of Bennett Place, near Durham, North Carolina, the site of the surrender on April 26, 1865, of the ninety-thousand-man Confederate Army of the Carolinas, Georgia, and Florida of General Joseph E. Johnston (1807-1891) to Union General William T. Sherman (1820-1891). This humble farmhouse of James and Nancy Bennett was the site of the largest troop surrender of the American Civil War. Historians of the North Carolina Division of Archives have found that the correct spelling of the surname should be *Bennitt*, rather than *Bennett*, although many historical accounts still spell the family name *Bennett*.

The correction of an improperly dated musical example well known to students of music history is cited. Hockett, in reporting on the English round *Sumer is icumen in*, says:

> A recent example of misdating due to unskilled use of evidence concerns an old musical piece known from its opening words as *Sumer is icumen*. Nineteenth-century historians thought it was written about 1240 because that was the date of another piece in the same manuscript. Not until the 1940s was the error discovered when a professor from an American university pointed out that the handwriting of the two pieces was not the same, and that the musical notation of the *Sumer* did not come into use until long after 1240, making the probable date of *Sumer* about 1310.[69]

This rectification of date was made by the late Manfred Bukofzer (1910–1955).

Another interesting example of misdating is the claim that Boston University, in 1876, was the first institution to grant the Bachelor of Music degree in the United States. Eells, however, relates that a report of the U.S. Commissioner of Education for 1873 confirms that the distinction properly belongs to Adrian College in Michigan. He notes that Trustees' Minutes of Adrian College, dated June 1873, list Mrs. Mattie B. Pease Lowrie as the first recipient of a Bachelor of Music degree in 1873.[70] Eells also reports that the first honorary degree in music was awarded by Georgetown University in Washington, D.C., to one Henry Dielman by Zachary Taylor (1784–1850), the twelfth president of the United States. Eells, quoting Shea, states that this apparently was the only time a president of the United States has been privileged to award honorary degrees.[71]

While reviewing archival records at New York University, you will recall, the senior author discovered the listing of an earned doctorate in music education in 1895, by New York University, of one John J. Dawson for his dissertation "The Education Value of Vocal Music." This dissertation was completed for the Doctor of Pedagogy degree, a common degree at that time for students in education. Since listings of doctoral degrees in music education have shown none earlier than 1912, Dawson must be recognized as the *first recipient of an earned doctorate in music education.*[72] Dawson's seventeen-page single-spaced document contains the following divisions: Vocal Music has been Overlooked, Vocal vs Instrumental Music, the Elements of Music, Reasons for Neglect of Music Culture, Character and Conduct in Education, in Physical Culture, in Intellectual Culture, in Emotional Culture, in Will Culture (Song as a means of Culture), Aesthetics, Conclusion. His closing statement is still appropriate today: "Song is a fundamental process in education—a true humanity subject—fitted to produce beneficial results in the evaluation and development of a more perfect manhood. The curriculum of elementary education is imperfect without it, while the curriculum of Higher Education cannot but be improved by it."[73]

Evaluating results of information has been discussed to some extent in conjunction with the seven categories of data mentioned earlier in this chapter. The historical method, however, is more explicitly concerned with external and internal criticism, or the "how" techniques.

External Criticism or Authenticity

Through the process of external (or lower) criticism the investigator learns whether or not the object of scrutiny is authentic. Many aspects constitute the overall meaning of external criticism, but the prime objective is to determine whether or not the item is genuine. Hockett, in defining external criticism, states, "It examines *documents*—a comprehensive term which . . . includes not only manuscripts but books, pamphlets, maps, and even ancient inscriptions and monuments."[74] Verification of authenticity also is part of the external-criticism procedure. Fischer, insisting that the successful outcome of factual verification may rest on the skill of the researcher, states that the historian must not only tell the truth, but show its truthfulness as well. The historian's veracity and skill at verification are important.[75]

Some of the questions that might be asked in the process of applying external criticism are: (1) Where was the item originally located? Where is it now? (2) Is the document an original version or a copy? If a copy, where is the original? (3) What is the estimated age of the item? Does it appear to be as old as it should be to be authentic? (4) Are there autographs or other identifications that will make the process of verification easier? (5) Is the handwriting (in the case of manuscripts) consistent with other items by the reputed writer? (6) Are there any indications (diaries, newspaper accounts, etc.) that such an item may have existed? and (7) Is there any reason to suspect that this item may be a hoax?

In the process of external criticism it often becomes necessary to probe auxiliary areas of knowledge. Some of the fields musicians most frequently consult seem to be photography, paleography, semantics, chronology, genealogy, and cartography. Sometimes you may even find yourself trying to determine the watermark of a document as well as the age and kind of paper used. You might locate a typewritten document with an indication that it was written before 1868. Such a statement would be inaccurate, because, according to Murphy, the typewriter was not patented until 1868 by Milwaukean Christopher Scholes.[76]

Applying the principles of external criticism to the questions posed above, consider an intriguing and beguiling flute-and-piano composition by Sidney Lanier (1842-1881) entitled "Danse des Moucherons." The senior author has in his possession a negative photostat of this short, rhapsodic, chromatic work which was obtained from Johns Hopkins University, in Baltimore, Maryland. In an attempt to locate the original manuscript he checked with the holdings of the Lanier Room at Johns Hopkins University, at Oglethorpe University in Georgia, and in other places, without success. In addition, personal correspondence with Lanier's children, each of whom courteously replied, failed to shed any light on manuscripts other than those at Johns Hopkins, where Lanier was known to have been but which, as just noted, does not possess the original to "Danse des Moucherons." Henry W. Lanier, who indicated that his manuscripts had been given to the Lanier collection at Johns Hopkins University, wrote the following regarding his father, a self-taught flutist and poet: "He once said to his wife what I believe to be literally true—that the difficulty with him was *not* to write down music. The moment he had time and strength, there were songs ready to be born."[77] Several brief sketches may be found in the Lanier Room at Johns Hopkins, including his projected "Quartette," "Tuno Religioso" (for two flutes or violas), "La Reve" (three flutes and bass flute), and "Trio for flute, pianoforte and violoncello."

Applying the tools of external criticism resulted in inconclusive answers to the first two questions. As to the third, Phelps was informed that his copy was reproduced directly from the original manuscript. The date 1873 appears after Lanier's name, yet the style of handwriting with regard to tempo and dynamics is inconsistent and suggests that it came from more than one hand. The tempo markings in particular appear to be in a more contemporary hand, especially on the last two pages of the six-page composition. In addition, the twelve-line manuscript paper on which the composition was written bears this inscription: "Carl Fischer, New York, Monarch Brand Warranted." It is true that Sidney Lanier spent some time in New York from 1870 to 1872, the year in which Carl Fischer arrived in the city. Fischer's first venture, however, was in musical instruments, according to city directories of that time. It was not until about 1880, moreover, that the publishing phase of the company began, so the colophon in question did not exist in 1873.

There are no autographs, holographs, or other identifications on Phelps's copy to suggest a positive answer to the fourth question. The composer's name is written in a combination of upper- and lower-case hand lettering. The tempo and dynamic terms, you recall, appear to be in different hands, making them difficult to compare with the written form of the composer's name and identification of the composition. Starke, in his biographical and critical account of Lanier's life, includes a photostatic copy of the flute part of the second and concluding pages of Lanier's "Gnat Symphony," which consists of only three-and-one-half lines.[78] The copy does contain Lanier's account, in a very neat and unhurried handwriting, of the composition, which the composer describes as a "translation of the sound," but this does not necessarily mean this description is in Lanier's handwriting. As already related, the senior author's copy contains six pages, including the piano part, but the last twelve measures of the flute part in the versions do not agree.

In response to the fifth question, a comparison was made of the item just cited and another one by Lanier, his unaccompanied flute solo "Wind Song," which Starke states was performed in October of 1874, but apparently was written earlier.[79] There is a strong similarity in handwriting; both appear in a style that shows a lighter, more delicate, and less hurried stroke than that in the Phelps copy of "Danse des Moucherons."

That such an item by this Georgia-born poet-musician may have existed, the object of the sixth question, has already been established in conjunction with the previous discussion, and the title is listed in Starke's bibliography under "Music by Lanier."[80] It also is listed in *Centennial Edition of the Works and Letters of Sidney Lanier*.[81]

In answer to the seventh question, it would appear that the authenticity of this copy of "Danse des Moucherons" just discussed must be open to serious question because of the discrepancies that exist, although the composition is listed by both Starke and Graham. Perhaps additional research will result in more convincing data to suggest otherwise. Hockett pinpoints the universal dilemma faced by historians who must pass judgment on a document, especially if there are some questions about its veracity, prudently noting that additional evidence eventually may appear to alter previously accepted ideas.[82]

To cite another example of the application of principles of external criticism, an item appeared in a now-defunct New York City newspaper a few years ago that intrigued Phelps. The article, a dispatch from Lynchburg, Virginia, stated in part that a previously unknown quartet for strings by Benjamin Franklin (1706-1790) was soon to have its initial performance in Philadelphia, Pennsylvania, largely through the efforts of a woman who was an associate professor of French at a local women's college. The professor's attention was called to this composition by the owner of a Parisian bookstore in which she was browsing. The article stated that the quartet was discovered by an eminent musicologist in a pile of forgotten works, although their location was not disclosed.[83]

Several factors should be noted relative to this quartet. The original manuscript, in tablature, was reputed by the transcriber to be housed in the Bibliothèque Nationale in Paris. In correspondence with the senior author, however, music librarian E. Lebeau indicated, "La Bibliothèque nationale, et la Bibliothèque du Conservatoire qui en fait partie, ne possèdent ni quatuor ni aucune oeuvre musicale de Banjamin (sic) Franklin."[84] [The national library and the library of the conservatory, which is a part of it, possess neither the quartet nor any other musical composition of Benjamin Franklin.]

The real motive behind the use of tablature would be interesting to learn. In the preface to his transcription, which was published in 1945, the transcriber reports that the original is in the handwriting of a professional copyist of the late eighteenth century, who otherwise remains unidentified. Benjamin Franklin served as U.S. Ambassador to France from 1776 to 1785, and it is known that he attended concerts in Paris, including performances of chamber music at the salon of Madame Helvetius d'Auteil. It does seem rather strange, though, that tablature would be used for a string quartet so late in the eighteenth century, since this type of writing, except for the guitar and other fretted instruments, had largely been replaced by the conventional system of notation currently in use. Also unexplained is the rationale for placing each of the four instruments (three violins and violoncello) in *scordatura*. The use of this system of mistuning by Heinrich Biber (1644-1704) is well known, but the simple, uninteresting, single melody line employed for each instrument in the alleged Franklin quartet suggests no need for *scordatura*, because instrumentalists can play each of the parts in the Franklin quartet entirely on open strings, another curious circumstance. Also, the instrumentation, three violins and violoncello, is rather unorthodox for a string quartet.

The quartet is in five short movements. The first bears no subtitle, but appears to be in march tempo. The second is a *menuetto*, the third a *capriccio*, the fourth also a *menuetto*, and last a *siciliano*. The *capriccio* and *siciliano* are basically triparte, while the others are in two parts structurally. Unusual, too, is the inclusion of five movements in a quartet of this period in musical history.

Information from the Franklin Institute of Philadelphia, where the first contemporary performance of the quartet was scheduled, was to the effect that the work had not yet been presented. Furthermore, all attempts to communicate with the discoverer and the transcriber of the work proved to be fruitless. These repeated efforts continued for approximately two years, until the death of the transcriber.

A review of a performance of the alleged Franklin quartet appeared in a New York City newspaper, but no additional information was provided to suggest that the work was genuine, except that the 1945 version had been further edited and corrected by yet another unidentified hand.[85]

Finally, no definite proof has been advanced to show that Franklin actually knew enough about the technique of musical composition to compose a quartet, or any other musical work for that matter. True, he often is credited with the invention of the armonica, or musical glasses, a distinction he disclaimed. Franklin, however, admittedly did make many improvements on the instrument, whose sweet and pleasant tinkling sounds were produced by moistened fingers massaging rotating tumblers of different frequencies. Even Mozart and Beethoven were so intrigued by the soothing sounds of the armonica that they composed several pieces for this instrument.

In view of the rather consistent pattern of negative evidence, and lack of positive evidence, it must be concluded that this work unquestionably is spurious. The Franklin quartet appears to be a musical joke, the product of an anonymous jester. It always is possible, though that more positive data may be forthcoming in the future that could result in a more exact evaluation.

Internal Criticism or Credibility

Had the evidence regarding the Lanier and Franklin compositions been more positive, investigation of other factors, known as internal (higher) criticism, could have proceeded. There are many occasions when this additional step is necessary. Even though external criticism may establish that a document, item, or statement is authentic, there may be inaccuracies or inconsistencies within. Nevins says that although it is sometimes time-consuming to establish authenticity of a historical source, to establish the integrity of a source is more difficult.[86] The purpose of internal criticism, according to Gottschalk, is to determine how credible the data collected may be.[87] Experienced researchers frequently engage in external and internal criticism simultaneously, in which they will use information from one to assist in the implementation of the other.

Some historiographers divide internal criticism into positive and negative phases. Making a distinction between them, Brickman states that through positive criticism a researcher tries to ascertain the true meaning of statements, whereas negative criticism concerns a researcher's rationale for discrediting them, as evidenced by the partiality or inefficiency displayed by the writer.[88]

The investigator who is dealing with internal criticism must answer questions such as these: (1) Is the document consistent stylistically with others by the writer? Are there major inconsistencies? (2) Are there any indications that the writer's reporting was inaccurate? (3) Does the writer actually mean what is said? (4) Could this work have been written by someone else in the style of the individual? and (5) Is there any evidence that the writer is biased or prejudiced?

It generally is conceded that artists do change their manner of expressing themselves stylistically due to the natural process of artistic growth and development. For example, students of music literature are often called upon to compare various characteristics of a composer's stylistic periods. Witness the three distinctive epochs in the creative life of Ludwig van Beethoven (1770-1827): the first ending about 1802, the second approximately in 1815, and the third in 1827.

Although composers may show stylistic changes during their lifetime, the musical idioms they favor usually persist throughout their creative life. Characteristic idioms serve as guides for you when you attempt to ascertain whether the composition in question is consistent with others by the same composer. Major inconsistencies may result from the composer's deliberately altering an accustomed style by using different idioms. On the other hand, the incongruent features also suggest that these works are indeed by two different people. In the instance of a composer like Arnold Schoenberg (1874–1951), a change in both stylistic characteristics and musical idioms is apparent in his transition from the post-Romantic style of the *Verklärte Nacht* to the dodecaphonic *Pierrot Lunaire*.

Occasionally inaccuracies will be suspected in a document. Barzun and Graff describe the incorrect dating of a letter by Hector Berlioz (1803–1869) to his publisher indicating that he was forwarding the table of contents to a book. Berlioz dated his communication "Thursday June 23"; Barzun and Graff point out that the year must have been 1852, in which case June 23 fell on Wednesday. They also remind their readers that it was not unusual for Berlioz to mistake the day of the week.[89]

A third question that might be raised in regard to internal criticism is whether or not the writer actually meant what he or she said. Although some confusion understandably could come from writers' assuming that their readers comprehend and agree with their definition and use of certain terminology, misunderstandings are often more than merely problems of semantics. Witness persons who use the word "cornett" when "cornet" is intended. Despite the difference of only a single *t* the instruments are vastly dissimilar in nature. You will recall that the former refers to an obsolete fifteenth- and sixteenth-century instrument, normally made of wood, containing six finger holes and played with a cup-shaped mouthpiece. The contemporary cornet, a three-valved instrument constructed of metal, is similar to the trumpet, but shorter. Furthermore, the cup-shaped mouthpiece of the cornett is larger and deeper than that of the cornet.

The next question, more applicable to music than to any other discipline, is concerned with compositions that may have been written by an imposter in the style of another person. Especially suspect are "newly discovered" works claimed to be by such well-known composers as Haydn and Mozart. Reasons for this type of deception vary, but one of the most common is to enable someone who is unheralded to capitalize financially on the name of an esteemed composer. On the other hand, there are numerous examples in which musicians, in good faith and with no attempt at deception, have completed works left unfinished by composers at the time of their death. A representative example is Mozart's *Requiem*, which was finished by his protégé and intimate friend Franx X. Sussmayer (1766-1803).

Despite the best of intentions, it is difficult to be completely unbiased or unprejudiced. Some writers, of course, deliberately present a unilateral point of view, as evidenced by some early textbooks on the history of music in the United States. The treatise by Frédéric L. Ritter, *Music in America*, for instance, is generally regarded as strongly prejudiced in the direction of German Romanticism. Or, consider the absence of references in many textbooks written more than forty years ago to the role the Moravians played in the early musical life of the United States.

In a general sense, the realm of aesthetic judgment is characterized by personal predilection and preference, just as is the choice of an automobile. It likely would be more difficult for a critic who prefers the piano music of Franz Liszt (1811-1886) to that of Frédéric Chopin (1810-1849) to present an unbiased account when reviewing the works of both composers than it would be for the one who has no preference. Likewise, two concert artists do not perform the same composition in precisely the same manner. Gottschalk believes differences of interpretation are not bad. Musicians, he says, really are historians who interpret past events in a particular manner.[90]

Historical research can provide many challenging opportunities for one to make significant contributions to human knowledge. However, it should be remembered that history is more than reporting facts. Winks succinctly avers that a balance must be maintained between historical facts based on research and history involving analysis, interpretation, and generalization.[91] By using principles of historiography the researcher in music can employ the scientific method to obtain and evaluate facts objectively.

Problems for Review and Discussion

1. For what reasons does a music-education researcher pursue historical research?

2. Differentiate between primary and secondary sources and give some specific examples of each. How do you determine whether primary or secondary sources should be used?
3. Into what categories might data for historical research in music education fall? Give specific examples.
4. Discuss the place of external criticism in historical research. What specific questions might a music-education researcher ask when involved in external criticism?
5. What function does internal criticism serve in historical research? Differentiate between the negative and positive phases of internal criticism. What specific questions might be asked by the music-education researcher engaged in applying the principles of internal criticism?
6. What is the purpose of oral history? What procedures should be followed to complete an oral-history research project?
7. Discuss alternative historical research approaches to traditional "narrative history."

Supplementary Sources

Almack, John C. *Research and Thesis Writing*. Boston: Houghton Mifflin, 1930. Chapter 7.

Altick, Richard D. *The Art of Literary Research*, 3rd ed.; rev. by John J. Fenstermaker. New York: W. W. Norton, 1981. Chapters 2-5.

Ary, Donald, Lucy C. Jacobs, and Asghar Razavieh. *Introduction to Research in Education*, 3rd ed.; New York: Holt, Rinehart and Winston, 1985. Chapter 11.

Barzun, Jacques, and Henry F. Graff. *The Modern Researcher*, 4th ed.; New York: Harcourt Brace Jovanovich, 1985. Chapters 3-10.

Baum, Willa. *Oral History for the Local History Society*, 3rd ed., rev.; Nashville, Tenn.: American Association for State and Local History, 1987.

_____. *Transcribing and Editing Oral History*. Nashville, Tenn.: American Association for State and Local History, 1977.

Best, John W., and James V. Kahn. *Research in Education*, 6th ed.; Englewood Cliffs, N.J.: Prentice-Hall, 1989. Chapter 3.

Borg, Walter R., and Meredith D. Gall. *Educational Research: An Introduction*, 5th ed.; New York: Longman, 1989. Chapter 19.

Brickman, William W. *Research in Educational History*. Norwood, Pa.: Folcroft Library Editions, 1975. Chapters 2, 4, 5.

Cohen, Morris R., and Ernest Nagel. *An Introduction to Logic and Scientific Method*. New York: Harcourt Brace, 1934. Chapter 17.

Cook, David R., and N. Kenneth LaFleur. *A Guide to Educational Research*, 2nd ed.; Boston: Allyn and Bacon, 1975. Chapter 3.

Dawson, John J. "The Education Value of Vocal Music," dissertation for the Ped.D., New York University, 1895. UMI 7233518.

Duckles, Vincent H., and Michael A. Keller. *Music Reference and Research Materials: An Annotated Bibliography*, 4th ed.; New York: Macmillan, 1988.

Fischer, David H. *Historian's Fallacies: Toward a Logic of Historical Thought*. New York: Harper and Row, 1970. Chapters 3, 5, 9-11.

Fox, David J. *The Research Process in Education*. New York: Holt, Rinehart and Winston, 1969. Chapter 14.

Frederickson, George M. "Comparative History," in Kammen, *The Past Before Us*, pp. 457-473.

Garrett, Allen M. *An Introduction to Research in Music*. Washington: The Catholic University of America Press, 1958. Chapters 9, 10.

Good, Carter V. *Essentials of Educational Research: Methodology and Design*, 2nd ed.; Englewood Cliffs, N.J.: Prentice-Hall, 1972. Chapter 4.

Gottschalk, Louis. *Understanding History*, 2nd ed.; New York: Alfred A. Knopf, 1969. Chapters 3, 5-7.

Grider, Rufus A. *Historical Notes on Music in Bethlehem, Pennsylvania*. Philadelphia: John L. Pile, 1873; foreword by Donald M. McCorkle, Winston-Salem, N.C.: Moravian Music Foundation, 1957.

Heller, George N. *Historical Research in Music Education: A Bibliography*. Lawrence, Kan.: University of Kansas Press, 1988.

Heller, George N., and Bruce Wilson. "Historical Research in Music Education: A Prolegomenon," *Bulletin of Council for Research in Music Education*, 1982, 69:1-20.

Hillway, Tyrus. *Introduction to Research*, 2nd ed.; Boston: Houghton Mifflin, 1964. Chapter 11.

Hockett, Homer C. *The Critical Method in Historical Research and Writing*. New York: Macmillan, 1955, pp. 13-70.

Hoover, Herbert T. "Oral History in the United States," in Kammen, *The Past Before Us*, pp. 391-407.

Hopkins, Charles D., and R. L. Antes. *Educational Research: A Structure for Inquiry*, 3rd ed.; Itasca, Ill.: F. E. Peacock, 1990. Chapter 9.

Humphreys, Jere T. "Bibliography of Theses and Dissertations Related to Music Education, 1895-1931," *The Bulletin of Historical Research in Music Education*, January 1989, 10,1:1-51.

Jones, Ralph H., ed. *Methods and Techniques of Educational Research*. Danville, Ill.: Interstate Printers and Publishers, 1973, pp. 151-180.

Kammen, Michael, ed. *The Past Before Us: Contemporary Historical Writing in the United States*. Ithaca, N.Y.: Cornell University Press, 1980, Part III, "Modes of Gathering and Assessing Historical Materials."

Keene, James A. *A History of Music Education in the United States*. Hanover, N.H.: University Press of New England, 1982.

Kousser, J. Morgan. "Quantitative Social-Scientific History," in Kammen, *The Past Before Us*, pp. 433-456.

Leedy, Paul D. *Practical Research Planning and Design*, 4th ed.; New York: Macmillan, 1989. Chapter 7.

Loewenberg, Peter. "Psychohistory," in Kammen, *The Past Before Us*, pp. 408-432.

Mason, Emanuel J., and William J. Bramble. *Understanding and Conducting Research: Applications in Education and the Behavioral Sciences*, 2nd ed.; New York: McGraw-Hill, 1989. Chapter 2.

McMillan, James H., and Sally Schumacher. *Research in Education: A Conceptual Introduction*, 2nd ed.; Glenview, Ill.: Scott, Foresman and Co., 1989. Chapter 12.

Mouly, George J. *The Science of Educational Research*, 2nd ed.; New York: Van Nostrand Reinhold, 1970. Chapter 8.

Nevins, Allan. *The Gateway to History*, rev. ed.; Garden City, N.Y.: Anchor Books, 1962.

_____. *The Gateway to History*. Boston: D. C. Heath, 1938; Robin Winks, ed. New York: Garland Press, 1984.

Phelps, Roger P. "The First Earned Doctorate in Music Education." *The Bulletin of Historical Research in Music Education*, January 1983, 4,1:1-6.

_____. "The Mendelssohn Quintet Club: A Milestone in American Music Education," *Journal of Research in Music Education*, Spring 1960, 8,1:39-44.

Rainbow, Edward L., and Hildegard C. Froehlich. *Research in Music Education: An Introduction to Systematic Inquiry.* New York: Schirmer Books, 1987. Chapter 6.

Shafer, Robert J., ed. *A Guide to Historical Method.* Homewood, Ill.: Dorsey Press, 1980. Chapters 2-7.

Smith, Henry L. *Educational Research, Principles and Practices.* Bloomington, Ind.: Educational Publications, 1944. Chapter 7.

Travers, Robert M. W. *An Introduction to Educational Research,* 4th ed.; New York: Macmillan, 1968. Chapter 14.

Van Dalen, Deobold B. *Understanding Educational Research: An Introduction,* 4th ed.; New York: McGraw-Hill, 1979. Chapter 11.

Vincent, John M. *Aids to Historical Research.* New York: Appleton-Century-Crofts, 1934. Chapters 2, 5, 12.

Whitney, Frederick L. *The Elements of Research,* 3rd ed.: Englewood Cliffs, N.J.: Prentice-Hall, 1950. Chapter 8.

Wiersma, William. *Research Methods in Education: An Introduction,* 3rd ed.; Itasca, Ill.: F. E. Peacock, 1980. Chapter 7.

Williamson, John B., David A. Karp, and John R. Dalphin. *The Research Craft: An Introduction to Social Science Methods.* Boston: Little, Brown, 1977. Chapter 10.

Wise, John E., Robert B. Nordberg, and Donald J. Reitz. *Methods of Research in Education.* Boston: D. C. Heath, 1967. Chapter 4.

PART FOUR

MUSIC EDUCATION RESEARCH—
A GLIMPSE INTO THE FUTURE

The authors present ten portents which suggest what the future of music-education research could be.

10. What Does the Future Hold for Music-Education Research?

No one can accurately predict the future in regard to research in music education. In some respects the future looks bright; in others it does not look so rosy. Yet, pushing the gloom aside, there are certain hopeful signs that give an indication of what may be expected in the near future. On a note of caution, progress in certain directions can be as unpredictable as the economy of the world. Fundamental, though, to any progress is the necessity to "dream" or "prognosticate." As pointed out throughout this book, some of the greatest advances in history have been the result of some "presage" or "prognostication." The writers are aware that statements made here in either a positive or negative direction may subject them to criticism, whether it is warranted or not. What if the portents which follow prove to be inaccurate? Nothing will be lost, because to reflectively consider what is possible is better for the health of the profession than to just be content to go along with the everyday status quo.

As long as they remain in the field of music education for any length of time, even the recipients of a graduate degree who do not plan to do more research themselves likely will be affected by some of the projected trends, should they become a reality. Although research courses usually require a thesis, dissertation, or research document as preparation for continued research activity, there are many more "doctors" who do not continue research activities than those who do. Among the valid reasons given for lack of further research are that funding is not available or that administrators will not give released time, with or without compensation, for research.

We present ten portents suggesting what the future for the music-education researcher *may be* or *could be*. These portents are not listed in any priority because to prioritize conjectures is extremely risky at best. These surmises are presented, however, as something to reflect upon, and eventually to act upon individually or as a profession.

(1). There is concern by many universities that graduate students should take less time to complete a doctorate. A dispatch from the New York Times News Service indicates that in the 1960s the median time to complete a doctorate was five-and-a-half years; the median time now is about seven years. Because of this concern, the Council of Graduate Schools is attempting to find an alternative to the traditional dissertation. According to Berger in the *New York Times* dispatch, there will be one-half million college teaching vacancies in the next decade.[1] This means that some colleges and universities may have to employ more teaching personnel who do not possess a doctorate, although many will be on the road to the terminal degree. Such a situation is unhealthy because additional pressure is placed on those who must not only teach but also work on the doctorate at the same time. Looking at specific fields, the median length of time it takes humanities students to complete doctoral degree requirements is almost eight-and-a-half years; in education it is about eight years. At the other end of the scale are engineering and the physical sciences, each with a median of almost six years for completion of the doctorate.[2] There are several reasons for the increase in length of time needed to complete doctoral degree requirements. One has already been mentioned: cutbacks in financial aid for graduate students, resulting in more students having to take part-time jobs, necessitating a reduced course load. A second reason is the explosion in knowledge that has taken place in the past five decades. It has conservatively been estimated that more knowledge has been generated in the past four or five decades than in all the previous centuries since the beginning of the Christian era. True, high-speed computers pour out reams of information in minutes, which formerly took weeks or even months to obtain by a hand-search. This means students must ferret out, synthesize, and organize data from many more sources than were available to them even in the 1940s. Third, as it now stands, many music students in performance programs must not only write a dissertation but also present several full-length recitals. These requirements ought to be reviewed to determine whether or not they can be lessened without diminishing the quality of the programs. Students in music educa-tion also are affected; many are required to take courses in other disciplines in order to meet the minimum requirements for a dis-sertation which is interdisciplinary in scope. Extra course require-

ments obviously lengthen the time necessary to complete all degree requirements, including writing the dissertation. A fourth reason for the increase in length of time to complete a doctorate is listed by Mason and Bramble, who report that research support is largely influenced by trends brought about by social and economic pressure groups. Following these trends results in less emphasis on the theoretical and scientific research preferred by many doctoral students.[3] Social and economic pressures must not be ignored; they need to be recognized if research is to solve some of today's pressing problems. Since one of the objectives of research is to solve problems affecting humanity, then social and economic research is needed. Because of the intricate methodology necessary to conduct effective social and economic research, these kinds of research normally take longer, meaning doctoral students must realize it will take them longer to complete their degree requirements. This is one of the reasons why the education doctorate, referred to earlier, takes almost as long to complete as one in the humanities.

(2). The number of students who will be entering colleges or universities in the next few years in the United States is steadily declining because there are fewer students graduating from high school due to the lower birth rates of the 1960s and 1970s. The percentage of students who continue on to graduate work from a baccalaureate has not risen markedly; therefore, fewer undergraduates eventually means fewer potential graduate students. As a result some colleges and universities have been freezing positions which become open due to declining class size or for budgetary or other reasons. Complicating the situation is the extension of the mandatory retirement age to seventy, contributing to the rising median age of college and university professors. The rising median age is even more pronounced in institutions which have no mandatory retirement-age requirement. This increasing median age of college and university professors poses a budgetary dilemma for administrators who must retain high-salaried, tenured professors who teach classes with declining enrollments. You recall reference was made earlier to the projected shortfall of persons to fill higher education vacancies in the near future. If a college or university music department is to function effectively the positions, which otherwise might be frozen, will need to be filled. Some institutions are offering attractive early retirement inducements to interested faculty. This, in turn, creates openings for new or recent doctoral recipients at lower

salaries, relieving the budgetary situation, somewhat. The senior author of this book used to remind students in his doctoral classes that they were undertaking graduate work at an excellent time, because the number of openings in the future should continue to increase substantially unless music departments are abolished or positions frozen. Budgets obviously determine whether or not a vacancy will be filled or frozen. In a survey conducted by a Florida institution a few years ago, the problem of funding/finance was reported by a majority of college and university music executives to be the single greatest problem facing their institutions.[4] Informally, there has been little change in this funding dilemma. Many new job-seekers will enter the field with fresh ideas and up-to-date skills and techniques, and eventually should make an even greater impact on the profession than have some of their predecessors who have resisted the fast-moving, inevitable changes taking place in the music-education profession.

(3). There are an increasing number of students coming to the United States from the Far East to work on graduate degrees. This influx is due to several reasons: English has largely become the language for universal scholarship; American universities are regarded with great respect in the Far East; and like their counterparts in the United States, these Far Eastern students are increasingly coming under pressure from administrators to earn a doctorate. The increase in students from the Far East is healthy and is likely to increase as Japan, Korea, and Taiwan continue to send more students to the United States. Also not to be overlooked are a small number of students from the People's Republic of China, the Philippines, Thailand, and Malaysia. The increase in foreign students is welcome news for universities, which are beginning to feel the financial crunch resulting from the decrease in number of students who enter higher education from the United States, as noted earlier. It is not surprising that many of these Far Eastern students opt to write dissertations which impinge on subjects from their native countries. As an example, a dissertation by Yeong-Kee Lee had just been completed while this book was being written. The title of Lee's dissertation is "An Analysis of the Relationship Between Korean Art Songs and Traditional Korean Vocal Music: A Unified Concept of Korean Music."[5]

(4). Reference has been made repeatedly to the overemphasis on behavioral studies in music education at the expense of other

approaches. You will recall from previous chapters that qualitative and other types of research are playing a greater role in graduate research studies. Mason and Bramble are among those who pinpoint the increase in completion of qualitative studies as well as those which are interdisciplinary.[6] The trend toward using other methodologies to obtain valid research data has not been bypassed by music-education researchers. More emphasis is being given to historical, philosophical, and qualitative problem-solving techniques. This is not to demean behavioral research, because it is the most effective way to get valid data for certain kinds of problems, but there are other problems which can be investigated better by other than behavioral-research techniques. In historical research, for instance, it may be expected that researchers will utilize the techniques of psychohistory or quantitative history when certain types of quantification are called for. Oral-history techniques and those incorporating phenomenology also will continue to receive greater emphasis. Regardless of the methodology used, research in the future must be relevant and utilitarian, report Mason and Bramble.[7]

(5). To say that the rapidly advancing technological world has been leaving many musicians in the dark is no understatement. The decade of the 1980s has been called the "computer age"; the 1990s is promising to be the decade of even higher-speed computers and fax machines. Fax machines make it possible for researchers to receive complete articles, prints, photographs, or other items that might not be accessible by computer alone. As graduate students become more and more sophisticated, their educational horizons and training will place them at higher levels of understanding. Technology can play a prominent role in enabling music-education students to achieve levels of competence never before possible. Microcomputers have become standard equipment in most elementary classrooms, and many colleges and universities are requiring students to possess a personal computer as a necessary part of course requirements, just as a slide rule or hand calculator was mandatory a few years ago. A doctoral student in music education can hardly afford to be without some type of computer or word processor. Proficiency in using personal computers is not beyond the realm of possibility for all music students. Most offices in music departments contain terminals which connect to mainframe computers, and the offices of professors contain modems that enable them to interface with many systems. On the other hand, a Fairlight,

Alpha-syntauri, or some other sophisticated instrument for music research and instruction is beyond the financial means of most persons individually, so they will need to make arrangements with a college or university which has one of these technological wonders if they want to use one for their research. Computers can be used for many tasks which now are done manually, such as inventory of instruments and music, purchase requisitions, staff and payroll forms, appointment forms for music faculty, course grade sheets, and student transcripts, to mention a few. Automating department offices should leave more time for staff to do the job they are supposed to do: namely, to serve students and faculty more efficiently. The use of computers to relieve departmental chairs and professors of dull administrative details likely will increase as computer prices come down and as researchers and professors become more intelligent in the application of computers for research and teaching.

(6). Music researchers are beginning to interface with researchers in health and other fields. The number of conferences and research projects in which musicians cooperate with health researchers is growing. Some of these projects involve musicians working jointly with experts in fields such as physiology, neurology, psychology, and biomechanics. A recent report which involved music researchers interfacing with health professionals is Lee's *Rehabilitation, Music and Human Well-Being*.[8] True, music-therapy researchers have worked cooperatively with researchers in various mental and health fields. As an example of some of the newer advances, persons affected with viral encephalitis, who often cannot speak or swallow, can communicate by passing a hand across a light-sensitive keyboard which ties into a synthesizer. Quadriplegics also can communicate by moving their eyes toward a screen which will then record images by a keyboard camera aimed at the face. It would have been impossible to use this advanced technology with seriously handicapped persons just a few years ago. Persons who formerly were bypassed educationally or placed on the "trash heap" of humanity now have an opportunity to learn. In another direction, a growing concern of health and other educators is the large number of older citizens in this country. The term "andragogy" is used when referring to an "aging" population. Andragogy relates to some of the problems associated with adult learning. Some music teachers are beginning to realize that there is a large untapped population of retired persons who still need music for recreational and other purposes. Many want to be active performers in choruses, bands, orchestras, or other musical groups rather than simply passive listeners. Technology can benefit these persons also. In some states community colleges offer courses free of charge to "senior citizens" who seek enrichment and stimulation by enrolling for courses they never had an opportunity to take before. The attention given to the ever-increasing aging population also has import for teacher-training institutions. They must realize that "another population" besides children and young people demands some attention and that personnel must be trained to deal with this challenge. Studies combining music and andragogy could provide nascent possibilities for researchers in music education who have an inclination to work in a field that badly needs more research.

(7). Many excellent basic interdisciplinary research techniques courses are being offered which are helpful to music researchers. The musician who understands basic concepts of research should be able to apply them to music research. There appears to be a growing need, however, for more specific courses which relate music to other disciplines, especially the arts, because it is difficult to complete arts research without using interdisciplinary methodologies. Specific courses to tie together the methodologies best suited for the arts could make a great contribution to the field. Such courses could be team-taught or taught by one person who has some expertise in research techniques suitable for music and the other arts. Would it not be best for music-education students to take a basic interdisciplinary course, then follow it with one or two specialized research courses in music? This, while desirable, likely would crowd a doctoral candidate's already complex academic program. The basic research course might replace another, already in the curriculum, of less value to the student, or total course requirements would need to be increased, a proposition that already is complicated by the longer time required to complete all degree requirements.

(8). The ever-spiraling cost of higher education has made it necessary for many graduate students to matriculate on a part-time basis or to seek scholarship aid or an assistantship so they can attend full-time. There has been considerable opposition from some accrediting agencies to part-time graduate instruction. One of the reasons given for opposing part-time instruction is that the students

do not achieve a sense of educational continuity and social unity because they are away from the campus so much of the time. Is not the motivation to achieve, partially based on the high costs of graduate education, more important to success than whether or not graduate students interact socially and complete their degree requirements with "their class"? The nonchalant, disinterested syndrome identified by some accrediting agencies as characteristic of part-time graduate instruction was not apparent to the senior author of this book when he was teaching doctoral students. In fact, many of his part-time students achieved better academically and developed closer friendships than did some of their full-time peers. Tuition costs undoubtedly will keep rising faster than the inflation rate in the next few years, a concern expressed by music executives in the study referred to earlier in this chapter.[9] Students who need to remain in their current positions for financial reasons will increasingly enroll in graduate work on a part-time basis, usually in late afternoons, in early evenings, or on Saturdays. This need not be unhealthy. It does present graduate education in a different perspective, but is this necessarily bad?

(9). Traditionally candidates for the Ph.D. have had to pass language examinations in French and German to satisfy "tool" requirements. Most of these examinations called for students to translate into English pages of material from the language in question. In other instances, spoken and written comprehension were evaluated individually by foreign-language faculty members. Exceptions were rarely made to the requirement of French and German as "tools." For years there was a "purist" school of thought which adamantly believed that one is not "educated" unless he or she has expertise in these languages. There still are some music professors and others who aver that a music student must know French and German since so much of the written literature is in these languages. If this be the case, why is Italian overlooked or disregarded? What about Spanish, Russian, Hebrew, or even Chinese? Now, it is true that many graduate students in the United States are monolingual, knowing only English, whereas in other countries students are required to learn English as a second language. It is encouraging to note that some of the newer degrees *require* no foreign language, substituting instead "research tools" which are related to the research being pursued. Foreign languages, however, still *may* be used to satisfy "tool" requirements. Even when foreign-language expertise is required or permitted, there is a trend toward relaxing the traditional requirement that only French and German can be used to satisfy the "tool." Statistics and computer science also can qualify as "traditional tools" in some institutions. "Nontraditional tools" used for many doctorates other than the Ph.D.—and in some instances even for the Ph.D.—can be almost anything relevant to the dissertation topic which has been approved by the candidate's dissertation committee. Advanced musical analysis, literary analysis, and oral history are some of the "nontraditional tools" which are permitted in doctoral programs. The question also has been raised why "tools" of any kind are needed at all. In view of the propensity to shorten the length of time for doctoral study, to dispense with "tools," foreign languages or otherwise, makes sense unless they are specifically needed for the dissertation. Why should a student whose dissertation deals with music in the elementary schools of the United States need to pass examinations in French, German, or any language, for that matter? The same argument holds true for dissertations relating to topics on Americana. If the researcher uses narrative historical approaches, why is it necessary to use statistics as a "tool"? On the other hand, in a psychohistorical study one would be expected to use statistics. Does it not make more sense to permit greater flexibility regarding "tool" requirements? As a result doctoral programs might become more utilitarian and meaningful to students. Better research documents could follow because less time and effort would be spent on meeting requirements that are meaningless in many instances. Teasing questions have been raised in this section—perhaps even heretical ones! The wisdom of continuing something which has been traditional for hundreds of years should be given serious consideration. If the tradition is valid, retain it; if not, change it!

(10). Postdoctoral research presumably should be an ongoing process after completion of a doctoral dissertation. Despite an ever-increasing number of completed doctorates, the amount of reported postdoctoral research has not been very significant. Why is so little under way? One reason is that federal and state funding have virtually disappeared for music. Some funds have been available from governmental agencies for research involving all the arts, as evidenced by the subsidy given to New York University by the National Endowment for the Arts and the U.S. Department of Education to establish the National Arts Education Research Center. You will recall this was discussed in the first chapter. Because of the cutbacks in governmental funding, researchers have had to

turn more and more to private funding, which also has been "drying up." On a positive note, some researchers still receive funding from various agencies. One of the junior authors of this book recently received a highly prized grant for research as a "Presidential Scholar" from the university where he teaches; the other junior author has received a Fulbright Award for study and research in the Malay archipelago. With belt-tightening and budget cuts at almost all levels, researchers have been forced to conduct research on their own, with little or no outside funding or released time. Moreover, professors also write textbooks without a sabbatical leave or released time. Fortunately, the quality of postdoctoral reports read by the authors of this book is excellent. It indicates that these doctoral recipients have learned their research lessons well! Emphasis on excellence in postdoctoral research is likely to continue, with or without external or internal funding. There now is a small corps of dedicated researchers anxious to "create" and implement research ideas in a manner similar to that which impels a composer or other creative person to function. The urge to find solutions to problems is overwhelming and too great to extinguish; this is encouraging for the profession. Unfortunately, without additional funding from various sources, some researchers will become frustrated, discouraged, and disillusioned, and their desire to develop and implement research projects will be extinguished.

Music-education researchers have made excellent progress since the first projects were funded by the U.S. Office of Education in the 1950s. The quality and quantity of research are better, problems are more clearly defined, and even though progress is slow, applications of completed research are being made by teachers in the classroom. Despite the gloomy financial picture, the future of research in music education does not look that bleak. Research funds still are available, so progress will not be stopped! Researchers must proceed to solve problems and obtain new knowledge. Research is like the blood that flows through your body; it can never be stanched except by the mind that refuses to think!

Problems for Review and Discussion

1. What are some of the optimistic signs on the horizon that bode well for the music-education graduate student?
2. Give some of the negative signs referred to in this chapter that could be discouraging to you.

Supplementary Sources

Berger, Joseph. "Scholars Urge Shorter Path to Ph.D." New York Times News Service, in Raleigh, N.C., *News and Observer*, May 4, 1989, 2A.

Brademas, John. *Signs of Trouble and Erosion: A Report on Graduate Education in America*. Report submitted by the National Commission of Student Financial Assistance. New York: New York University, 1983.

Bradford, Bruce C., and John K. Schorr. *Report on the Future of American Higher Education: A Survey of Deans of Arts and Sciences, Business, Law and Music at Phi Beta Kappa Institutions in the U.S., 1983*. Deland, Fla.: Social and Opinion Research Services, Inc., 1984.

Lee, Mathew H. M., ed. *Rehabilitation, Music and Human Well-Being*. St. Louis: MMB Music Inc., 1989.

Mason, Emanuel J., and William J. Bramble. *Understanding and Conducting Research: Applications in Education and the Behavioral Sciences*, 2nd ed.; New York: McGraw-Hill, 1989. Chapter 14.

Notes

Chapter 1

1. Deobold B. Van Dalen, *Understanding Educational Research: An Introduction*, 4th ed.; New York: McGraw-Hill, 1979, p. 1.
2. Donald Ary, Lucy C. Jacobs, and Asghar Razavieh, *Introduction to Research in Education*, 3rd ed.; New York: Holt, Rinehart and Winston, 1985, p. 39.
3. Lee S. Shulman, "Paradigms and Research Programs in the Study of Teaching: A Contemporary Perspective," in Merlin C. Wittrock, ed., *Handbook of Research on Teaching*, 3rd ed.; New York: Macmillan, 1986, p. 3.
4. Charles D. Hopkins and R. L. Antes, *Educational Research: A Structure for Inquiry*, 3rd ed.; Itasca, Ill.: F. E. Peacock, 1990, p. 21.
5. William Wiersma, *Research Methods in Education: An Introduction*, 3rd ed.; Itasca, Ill.: F. E. Peacock, 1980, p. 4.
6. James H. McMillan and Sally Schumacher, *Research in Education: A Conceptual Approach*, 2nd ed.; Glenview, Ill.: Scott, Foresman and Company, 1989, p. 8.
7. Edward J. Vockell, *Educational Research*, New York: Macmillan, 1983, p. 3.
8. Evelyn J. Sowell and Rita J. Casey, *Research Methods in Education*, Belmont, Calif.: Wadsworth Publishing Co., 1982, p. 6.
9. John W. Best and James V. Kahn, *Research in Education*, 6th ed.; Englewood Cliffs, N.J.: Prentice-Hall, 1989, p. 17.
10. Paul D. Leedy, *Practical Research Planning and Design*, 4th ed.; New York: Macmillan, 1989, p. 5.
11. Max D. Engelhart, *Methods of Educational Research*, Chicago: Rand McNally, 1972, p. 1.

12. Clifford K. Madsen and Charles H. Madsen, Jr., *Experimental Research in Music*, Raleigh, N.C.: Contemporary Publishing Co., 1970, p. 4.

13. Edward L. Rainbow and Hildegard C. Froehlich, *Research in Music Education: An Introduction to Systematic Inquiry,* New York: Schirmer Books, 1987, p. 56.

14. Arthur E. Clarke, "Jamaican Folk Psalms: Choral Settings of Selected Psalms Based on Jamaican Folk Melodies, Rhythms and Harmonies, Suitable for Jamaican Students in Secondary Schools, Churches, and Music Festivals," dissertation for the Ed.D., New York University, 1988. UMI 8812527.

15. Robert M. W. Travers, *An Introduction to Educational Research*, 4th ed.; New York: Macmillan, 1978, pp. 256-257.

16. Leedy, p. 173.

17. Richard M. Jaeger, ed., *Complementary Methods for Research in Education*, Washington: American Educational Research Association, 1988, Chapter 3.

18. Robert C. Bogdan and Sari K. Biklen, *Qualitative Research for Education: An Introduction to Theory and Methods*, Boston: Allyn and Bacon, 1982, p. 37.

19. David W. Ecker, ed., *Qualitative Evaluation in the Arts*, New York: New York University, 1981; and John V. Gilbert, ed., *Qualitative Evaluation in the Arts*, Vol. II, New York: New York University, 1984.

20. Nancy-Louise Howes, "Some Effects of Sequential Music Tasks on the Cognitive and Social Skills of Learning Disabled Adults," *Journal of the International Association of Music for the Handicapped*, Winter 1989, 4:3-14.

21. Beverly J. Jones and June K. McFee, "Research in Teaching Arts and Aesthetics," in Wittrock, p. 911.

22. Jones and McFee, p. 912.

23. John Brademas, *Signs of Trouble and Erosion: A Report on Graduate Education in America*, Report submitted by the National Commission on Student Financial Aid, New York: New York University, 1983, p. 7.

24. Paul L. Dressel, *College Teaching as a Profession: The Doctor of Arts Degree*. East Lansing, Mich.: Michigan State University Press, 1982, p. 1.

25. Hug writes that the Department of Music Education offered twenty courses in its first year of existence. Elsie A. Hug, *Seventy-Five Years in Education: The Role of the School of*

Education, New York University, 1890-1965, New York: New York University Press, 1965, p. 113.

26. John J. Dawson, "The Education Value of Vocal Music," dissertation for the Ped.D., New York University, 1895. UMI 7233518.

27. Paul E. Koefod, *The Writing Requirements for Graduate Degrees*, Englewood Cliffs, N.J.: Prentice-Hall, 1964, p. 11.

28. John Grossman, "Gorillacillins," *Health Magazine*, September 1983, 15,9:34.

29. Herbert Mitgang, "Catalog Reflects Jefferson's 'World View,' " *New York Times News Service*, June 2, 1989.

30. See Bruce Catton, *The American Heritage Picture History of the Civil War*, New York: American Heritage/Bonanza Books, 1982, pp. 293, 314-315; also, Jerry Korn, ed., *War on the Mississippi: Grant's Vicksburg Campaign*, Alexandria, Va.: Time-Life Books, 1985, p. 87.

31. Benny P. Ferguson, "The Bands of the Confederacy: An Examination of the Musical and Military Contributions of the Bands and Musicians of the Confederate States of America," dissertation for the Ph.D., North Texas State University, 1987. UMI 8723754.

32. Truman Lee Kelley, *Scientific Method*, New York: Macmillan, 1932, p. 1.

33. Gordon B. Davis and Clyde A. Parker, *Writing the Doctoral Dissertation: A Systematic Approach*, Woodbury, N.Y.: Barron's Educational Series, 1979, pp. 41-43.

34. Bruce W. Tuckman, *Conducting Educational Research*, 3rd ed.; New York: Harcourt Brace Jovanovich, 1988, p. 25.

35. M. M. Chambers, "Selection, Definition, and Delimitation of a Doctoral Research Problem," *Phi Delta Kappan*, November 1960, 42,2:73.

36. Koefod, p. 74.

37. Kelley, p. 3.

38. *Report: Year I. National Arts Education Research Center at the School of Education, Health, Nursing, and Arts Professions, New York University*, New York: New York University, 1989, p. 2.

39. Walter R. Borg and Meredith D. Gall, *Educational Research: An Introduction*, 5th ed.; New York: Longman, 1989, p. 4.

40. Jones and McFee, p. 911.

41. Cornelia Yarbrough, "A Content Analysis of the *Journal of Research in Music Education*," *Journal of Research in Music Education*, Winter 1984, 32,4:217.
42. Roger P. Phelps, "Critical Thinking: A Prerequisite for All Sound Research," *The New York State School Music News*, March 1978, 41,7:31-32.
43. Jacques Barzun and Henry F. Graff, *The Modern Researcher*, 4th ed.; New York: Harcourt Brace Jovanovich, 1985, p. 109.
44. Leedy, p. 3.
45. Emanuel J. Mason and William J. Bramble, *Understanding and Conducting Research: Applications in Education and the Behavioral Sciences*, 2nd ed.; New York: McGraw-Hill, 1989, p. 29.
46. McMillan and Schumacher, p. 8.
47. John C. Almack, *Research and Thesis Writing*, Boston: Houghton Mifflin, 1930, p. 57.
48. Joseph C. Brennan, *The Meaning of Philosophy*, 2nd ed.; New York: Harper and Row, 1967, p. 161.
49. Fred M. Kerlinger, *Foundations of Behavioral Research*, 2nd ed.; New York: Holt, Rinehart and Winston, 1973, p. 11.
50. Borg and Gall, pp. 16-17.
51. Vockell, p. 287.
52. Mason and Bramble, p. 7.
53. Morris R. Cohen and Ernest Nagel, *An Introduction to Logic and the Scientific Method*, New York: Harcourt Brace Jovanovich, 1934, p. 195.
54. Thomas Munro, *Scientific Method in Aesthetics*, New York: W. W. Norton, 1928, p. 23.
55. Best and Kahn, p. 17.
56. Van Dalen, p. 18.
57. Carter V. Good, *Essentials of Educational Research: Methodology and Design*, 2nd ed.; Englewood Cliffs, N.J.: Prentice-Hall, 1972, p. 25.
58. Phelps, "Critical Thinking," p. 31.
59. Herbert L. Searles, *Logic and Scientific Method*, 2nd ed.; New York: Ronald Press, 1956, pp. 4-5.
60. Samuel Gorovitz, Merrill Hintikka, Donald Provence, and Ron G. Williams, *Philosophical Analysis: An Introduction to Its Language and Techniques*, 3rd ed.; New York: Random House, 1979, p. 3.
61. Mason and Bramble, p. 77.
62. Best and Kahn, p. 4.

63. Ary, Jacobs, and Razavieh, p. 8.
64. Sowell and Casey, p. 6.
65. John Dewey, *How We Think*, Boston: D. C. Heath, 1933, p. 107.
66. Kelley, p. 24.
67. Tuckman, p. 37.
68. Roger P. Phelps, "The Doctoral Dissertation: Boon or Bane?" *College Music Symposium*, Fall 1978, 18,2:82-93.
69. Borg and Gall, p. 50.
70. Carter V. Good and Douglas E. Scates, *Methods of Research*, New York: Appleton-Century-Crofts, 1954, p. 51.
71. Wiersma, p. 30.
72. J. Francis Rummel, *An Introduction to Research Procedures in Education*, 2nd ed.; New York: Harper and Row, 1964, p. 29.
73. Almack, p. 48.
74. Leedy, p. 46.
75. Jacques Barzun, *New Letters of Berlioz 1830-1868*, New York: Columbia University Press, 1954.
76. Tyrus Hillway, *Introduction to Research*, 2nd ed.; Boston: Houghton Mifflin, 1964, p. 116.
77. George N. Heller, *Historical Research in Music Education: A Bibliography*. Lawrence, Kan.: University of Kansas Press, 1988.
78. Jere T. Humphreys, "Bibliography of Theses and Dissertations Related to Music Education, 1895-1931," *The Bulletin of Historical Research in Music Education*, January 1989, 10,1:1-51. (This source includes studies which were completed prior to the initial William S. Larson *Bibliography of Research Studies in Music Education 1932-1948.)*
79. Robert G. Petzold, "Directions for Research in Music Education," *Music Educators Journal*, January 1964, 50,5:40.
80. Koefod, p. 107.
81. *Subject Headings*, 10th ed., 2 vols., Washington, D.C.: Library of Congress, 1986. (Music books are listed in Volume 2, pp. 2142-2150.)
82. *Dewey Decimal Classification and Relative Index*, 20th rev. ed., 4 vols., Albany, N.Y.: Forest Press, 1989. (A somewhat revised classification exists in this new edition. The 780 classification for Music is included on pages 548-602, in Vol. 3. One example will suffice: 780.7 Education, research, performance, related topics, p. 552.)
83. *Books in Print*. New York: R. R. Bowker. The 1988-1989 Edition contains four kinds of entries: *Subject Guide* (4 vol-

umes), *Authors* (3 volumes), *Titles* (3 volumes), and *Publishers* (1 volume). (In the *Subject Guide*, Volume 3, Music is listed on pages 4581–4621. An example is Music—Data Processing, p. 4587.)

84. John E. Druesedow, Jr., *Library Research Guide to Music: Illustrated Search Strategy and Sources,* Ann Arbor, Mich.: Pierian Press, 1982.

85. Complete bibliographic information on these items is omitted here. Refer to your library card catalog for complete information. This is part of the research process.

86. Included no author indexing and no book reviews between 1961 and 1969.

87. The *Thirty-Fifth Yearbook*, Part II, 1936, and the *Fifty-Seventh Yearbook*, Part I, 1958, were devoted exclusively to music education. At the time of this writing an editorial committee was in the process of preparing another yearbook for music education.

88. In July 1988, Volume 49, No. 1, *DAI-A* and *DAI-B* began to include doctoral dissertations from fifty universities in Great Britain, identified by *BRD* or *BRDX*.

89. *Thesaurus of ERIC Descriptors*, 11th ed.; Phoenix, Ariz.: Oryx Press, 1987.

Chapter 2

1. John W. Best and James V. Kahn, *Research in Education*, 6th ed.; Englewood Cliffs, N.J.: Prentice-Hall, 1989, p. 36.

2. Donald T. Campbell and Julian C. Stanley, *Experimental and Quasi-Experimental Designs for Research*, Chicago: Rand McNally, 1966, pp. 47–48.

3. E. Paul Torrance, *Torrance Tests of Creative Thinking*, Columbus, Ohio: Personnel Press, Xerox Educational Center, 1966.

4. Roger P. Phelps, "The Doctoral Dissertation: Boon or Bane?" *College Music Symposium*, Fall 1978, 18,2:88.

Chapter 3

1. See Thomas Spencer Bayes, *An Essay on the New Analytical Logical Forms*, New York: Lenox Hill, 1971; Nino B. Cocchiarella, *Logical Studies in Early Analytical Philosophy*, Colum-

bus, Ohio: Ohio State University Press, 1987; Anthony Flew, *Logic and Language*, Garden City, New York: Anchor Books, 1965; Bas C. van Fraassen, *Formal Semantics and Logic*, New York: Macmillan, 1971; Max Hocutt, *The Elements of Logical Analysis and Inference*, Cambridge, Mass.: Winthrop Publishers, 1979; P. F. Strawson, *Philosophical Logic*, London: Oxford University Press, 1967; and Anna-Teresa Tymieniecka, *Contributions to Logic and Methodology in Honor of J. M. Bochenski*, Amsterdam: North-Holland Publishing Company, 1965.

2. For example, see Bennett Reimer, "Toward a More Scientific Approach to Music Education Research," pp. 1-22; George N. Heller, "Philosophical Research in Music Education: Two Cheers for Tolerance," pp. 22-26; Jack Heller and Warren Campbell, "View from the Fourth Estate," pp. 27-31; Peter Webster, "Reflections on Reimer," pp. 31-39; and Bennett Reimer, "A Reply by Reimer," pp. 40-42, all in *Bulletin of the Council for Research in Music Education*, Summer 1985, 83.

3. Reason in this usage includes observation, experimentation, data collection and treatment as well as inferring, deducing, and calculating.

4. See Bas C. van Fraassen, *The Scientific Image*, Oxford: Oxford University Press, 1980.

5. Walter R. Borg and Meredith D. Gall, *Educational Research, An Introduction*, 5th ed.; New York: Longman, 1989, pp. 15-22, 379-385.

6. Borg and Gall, pp. 22-25.

7. Martin Heidegger, "Plato's Doctrine of Truth," trans. by John Barlow, in William Barrett and Henry D. Aiken, eds., *Philosophy in the Twentieth Century*, vol. 3, *Contemporary European Thought*, New York: Harper and Row, 1962.

8. Martin Heidegger, *Early Greek Thinking*, trans. by David Farrell Krell and Frank A. Capuzzi, New York: Harper and Row, 1975.

9. René Descartes, "Meditations," 1641, in René Descartes, *Discourse on Method and Meditations*, trans. by Lawrence J. Lafleur, New York: The Bobbs-Merrill Company, 1966, pp. 118-143.

10. Karl R. Popper, "Of Clouds and Clocks," in Karl R. Popper, *Objective Knowledge*, Oxford: Clarendon Press, 1979, pp. 206-251.

11. An excellent source is A. J. Ayer, *Logical Positivism*, The Free Press, 1959. Also see Ernest Nagel, *The Structure of Science*, London: Routledge and Kegan Paul, 1961.

12. Max Weber, *The Protestant Ethic and the Spirit of Capitalism*, trans. by Talcott Parsons, New York: Charles Scribner's Sons, 1958, especially chapter 5.

13. Edward L. Rainbow and Hildegard C. Froehlich, *Research in Music Education, An Introduction to Systematic Inquiry*, New York: Schirmer Books, 1987, pp. 128-161.

14. Milton Babbitt, "Past and Present Concepts," in Benjamin Boretz and Edward Cone, eds., *Perspectives on Contemporary Music Theory*, New York: Norton, 1972, pp. 3-9.

15. Carl Hempel, *Aspects of Scientific Explanation and Other Essays in the Philosophy of Science*, New York: The Free Press, 1965.

16. Abraham Kaplan, *The Conduct of Inquiry*, San Francisco: Chandler Publishers, 1964.

17. Aristotle, *De Interpretatione*, trans. by E. M. Edghill, in R. McKeon, ed., *The Basic Works of Aristotle*, New York: Random House, 1941, pp. 5-7.

18. Ludwig Wittgenstein, *Tractatus Logico-Philosophicus*, trans. by G. E. M. Anscombe, Oxford: Basil Blackwell, 1963, 4. 01.

19. Bertrand Russell, "Introduction" to Wittgenstein, *Tractatus*, p. ix.

20. Ludwig Wittgenstein, *Philosophical Investigations*, London: Basil Blackwell, 1953.

21. This idea is developed in Lawrence Ferrara, "Research and Practice in Music Education: The Problem of Dislocation," *College Music Symposium*, Spring 1982, 22,1:65-72.

22. Immanuel Kant, *The Critique of Pure Reason*, trans. by J. M. D. Meikeljohn, New York: Everyman's Library, 1964.

23. David Hume, *Treatise of Human Nature*, New York: Everyman's Library, 1975.

24. Cf. Marjorie Greene, *The Knower and the Known*, Berkeley: The University of California Press, 1974, particularly the "Introduction"; and John Dewey and Arthur F. Bentley, *Knowing and the Known*, Boston: Beacon Press, 1949.

25. See D. Bohm, *Causality and Chance in Modern Physics*, London: Routledge and Kegan Paul, 1957; Rom Harre, *The Principles of Scientific Thinking*, London: Macmillan, 1970; Rom Harre, *Varieties of Realism, A Rationale for the Natural Sciences*, London: Basil Blackwell, 1986; Mary B. Hesse,

Models and Analogies in Science, London: Sheed and Ward, 1963; G. Maxwell, "The Ontological Status of Theoretical Entities," in H. Feigl and G. Maxwell, eds., *Minnesota Studies in the Philosophy of Science*, vol. 3, University of Minnesota Press; and J. J. C. Smart, *Between Science and Philosophy*, New York: Random House, 1968.

26. Harre, *Varieties of Realism*, pp. 177-190, 237-242.
27. Harre, *Varieties of Realism*, pp. 145-190.
28. Harre, *Varieties of Realism*, pp. 191-236.
29. Harre, *Varieties of Realism*, pp. 237-316.
30. Hesse, *Models and Analogies in Science*, pp. 162-165.
31. Harre, *Varieties of Realism*, p. 7.
32. Thomas S. Kuhn, *The Structure of Scientific Revolutions*, 2nd ed.; Chicago: University of Chicago Press, 1970.
33. Hilary Putnam, *Reason, Truth and History*, Cambridge: Cambridge University Press, 1981, p. 114.
34. Michael Polanyi, *Personal Knowledge, Towards a Post-Critical Philosophy*, Chicago: University of Chicago Press, 1962.
35. Polanyi, pp. 15-17.
36. Harre, *Varieties of Realism*, pp. 4-5.
37. See Harriet Martineau, *The Positive Philosophy of Auguste Comte*, vol. 1, London: John Chapman Publishers, 1953, pp. 61-62.
38. See Jacques Derrida, *Deconstruction and Philosophy*, John Sallis, ed., Chicago: University of Chicago Press, 1987.
39. Hans-Georg Gadamer, *Truth and Method*, New York: The Seabury Press, 1975, pp. 235-274.
40. Richard Rorty, *Philosophy and the Mirror of Nature*, Princeton, N.J.: Princeton University Press, 1979, pp. 315-316.
41. Rorty, pp. 361-362.
42. Rorty, p. 373.
43. Martin Heidegger, *Being and Time*, New York: Harper and Row, 1962, p. 122.
44. Hans-Georg Gadamer, *Philosophical Hermeneutics*, trans. and ed. by David E. Linge, Berkeley: The University of California Press, 1976, p. 9.
45. Gadamer, *Philosophical Hermeneutics*, pp. 18-44 and especially 21-26.
46. This is developed in Lawrence Ferrara, *Philosophy and Music Analysis: Bridges for Sound, Form and Reference*, Westport, Conn.: Greenwood Press, 1990. See the chapter, "Should the Method Define the Tasks?"

47. Martin Heidegger, "On the Essence of Truth," trans. by R. F. C. Hull and Alan Crick, in Martin Heidegger, *Existence and Being*, Werner Brock, ed., with an Introduction and Analysis by Werner Brock, Chicago: Henry Regnery Company, 1949, p. 303.
48. The analogy of experimental design to a metal pipe is loose at best. Its development in this section is a heuristic device to understand better, through such a contrast, philosophical inquiry. While the limited discussion of experimental design in this section accents observational activities, experimental and quasi-experimental practices in music-education research function at all three levels of scientific inquiry, as articulated by Harre. Therefore, this discussion of experimental design should not be interpreted as a presentation of the full scope of experimental studies in music-education research.

Chapter 4

1. For a succinct definition of "aesthetics" see the verso page of any issue of *The Journal of Aesthetics and Art Criticism*.
2. See Christopher Ballantine, *Music and Its Social Meanings*, New York: Gordon and Breach, 1984; Theodor W. Adorno, *Prisms*, trans. by Samuel and Sherry Weber, Cambridge, Mass.: M.I.T. Press, 1988, pp. 119-172; and Theodor W. Adorno, *Introduction to the Sociology of Music*, New York: Continuum Publishing Co., 1987.
3. For example, see Bruno Nettl, *The Study of Ethnomusicology*, Urbana: The University of Illinois Press, 1983; Mantle Hood, *The Ethnomusicologist*, Kent, Ohio: Kent State University Press, 1982; and Marcia Herndon and Norma McLeod, *Field Manual for Ethnomusicology*, Norwood, Pa.: Norwood Editions, 1983.
4. For a classic formalist approach to visual art, see Clive Bell, *Art*, London: Chetto and Windus, 1914.
5. Martin Heidegger, "On the Origin of the Work of Art," in Martin Heidegger, *Poetry, Language, Thought*, trans. by Albert Hofstadter, New York: Harper and Row, 1971, pp. 17-87.
6. Rom Harre, *Varieties of Realism, A Rationale for the Natural Sciences*, London: Basil Blackwell, 1986, pp. 145-190.
7. See Sigmund Freud, *Leonardo da Vinci: A Psychosexual Study of an Infantile Reminiscence*, New York: Moffet, Yard and Co.,

1916; and R. E. Frye, *The Artist and Psycho-Analysis*, London: L. and V. Woolf, 1924.

8. Rudolph Arnheim, *Toward a Psychology of Art*, Berkeley: University of California Press, 1966; Arnheim, *Visual Thinking*, Berkeley: University of California Press, 1969; Arnheim, *Art and Visual Perception*, Berkeley: University of California Press, 1974; Arnheim, *New Essays on the Psychology of Art*, Berkeley: University of California Press, 1986.

9. While highly trained musicians who utilize a psychological approach to music presumably could match Arnheim's collection of analyses, such a collection of works has not been registered by Ferrara. For example, John A. Sloboda, in *The Musical Mind: The Cognitive Psychology of Music*, Oxford: Clarendon Press, 1985, does not provide in-depth analyses of musical works. Chapter 4 does present a discussion of processes of composition and improvisation but no psychological framework is developed there, nor is there a systematic implementation of such a theoretical framework in music analysis.

10. Edmund Husserl, *Logical Investigations*, two vols., 1900-01, trans. by Dorion Cairns, The Hague: Martinus Nijhoff, 1969.

11. Edmund Husserl, *Ideas: General Introduction to Pure Phenomenology*, trans. by W. R. Boyce Gibson, Collier Books, 1931, p. 40.

12. Franz Brentano, *Psychology from an Empirical Standpoint*, trans. by Antos C. Rancurello, D. B. Terrell, and Linda McAlister, in Linda McAlister, ed., New York: Humanities Press, 1973, pp. 92-100.

13. George Dickie, *Art and Aesthetic, An Institutional Analysis*, New York: Cornell University Press, 1974.

14. Dickie, pp. 19-52.

15. George Dickie, "Is Psychology Relevant to Aesthetics?" *Philosophical Review*, July 1962: 285-302.

16. Dickie, *Art and the Aesthetic*, pp. 21-27. Also see Morris Weitz, "Family Resemblances and Generalizations Concerning the Arts," in *American Philosophical Quarterly*, July 1965: 219-228.

17. Dickie, *Art and the Aesthetic*, pp. 45-46.

18. Dickie, *Art and the Aesthetic*, pp. 37-38.

19. Dickie, *Art and the Aesthetic*, pp. 44-45.

20. Dickie, *Art and the Aesthetic*, pp. 45-46.

21. Recall the discussion in chapter 3 of this text concerning Martin Heidegger's essay "On the Essence of Truth," trans. by R. F.

C. Hull and Alan Crick, in Martin Heidegger, *Existence and Being*, Werner Brock, ed., with an Introduction and Analysis by Werner Brock, Chicago: Henry Regnery Company, 1949, pp. 292-324.

22. Leonard B. Meyer, *Emotion and Meaning in Music*, Chicago: The University of Chicago Press, 1956.

23. Bell, p. 6.

24. John Dewey, "The Theory of Emotion," *Psychological Review*, I. 1894: 553-569.

25. Meyer, pp. 35-39.

26. Susanne K. Langer, *Feeling and Form*, New York: Charles Scribner's Sons, 1953, especially chapters III and IV.

27. Susanne K. Langer, *Problems of Art*, New York: Charles Scribner's Sons, 1957, pp. 44-58.

28. Susanne K. Langer, *Philosophy in a New Key*, 3rd ed.; Cambridge, Mass.: Harvard University Press, 1957, pp. 246-248.

29. Langer, *Philosophy in a New Key*, p. 86.

30. Psychologism is a position in which all operations of thought and reason are reduced to psychological laws. In such a position, the mind is the ultimate center for knowledge.

31. Husserl, *Ideas*, pp. 91-100.

32. Husserl, *Ideas*, pp. 45-71, 181-184, 285-288.

33. Edmund Husserl, *Cartesian Meditations*, trans. by Dorion Cairns, The Hague: Martinus Nijhoff, 1960, pp. 108-117.

34. Edmund Husserl, *Phenomenology of Internal Time-Consciousness*, ed. by Martin Heidegger in 1928, trans. by James S. Churchill, Bloomington: Indiana University Press, 1964.

35. Martin Heidegger, *Being and Time*, 1927, trans. by John Macquarrie and Edward Robinson, New York: Harper and Row, 1962.

36. Heidegger, "On the Origin of the Work of Art," p. 42.

37. Heidegger, "On the Origin of the Work of Art," p. 42.

38. Heidegger, "On the Origin of the Work of Art," p. 46.

39. Heidegger, "On the Origin of the Work of Art," pp. 65-66.

40. For example, see Thomas Clifton, *Music as Heard, A Study in Applied Phenomenology*, Yale University Press, 1983.

41. There are many dissertations that provide excellent models for the phenomenological description of musical "sound-in-time." See Judith Lochhead, "The Temporal Structures of Recent Music: A Phenomenological Investigation," dissertation for the Ph.D., State University of New York at Stony Brook, 1982; Douglas Roy Bartholomew, "A Phenomenology

of Music: Themes Concerning the Musical Object and Implications for Teaching and Learning," dissertation for the Ph.D., Case Western Reserve University, 1985; Garry L. Brodhead, "Structural Time in Twentieth-Century Tonal Music," dissertation for the Ph.D., Indiana University, 1983.

42. Roman Ingarden, *The Literary Work of Art*, trans. by George G. Grabowicz, Evanston, Ill.: Northwestern University Press, 1973, pp. 34-62.

43. Roman Ingarden, *The Cognition of the Literary Work of Art*, trans. by Ruth Ann Crowly and Kenneth R. Olson, Evanston, Ill.: Northwestern University Press, 1973.

44. E. D. Hirsch, Jr., *The Aims of Interpretation*, Chicago: University of Chicago Press, 1976. Also see John Reichert, *Making Sense of Literature*, Chicago: University of Chicago Press, 1977.

45. This is often the case in Theodor W. Adorno's sociological accounts of music. For example, see the chapters on "Bach" and "Jazz" in his *Prisms*, pp. 119-146.

46. For two protracted examples of this ten-step eclectic method, see Chapters VIII and IX in Lawrence Ferrara, *Philosophy and Music Analysis Bridges to Sound, Form, and Reference*, Westport, Conn.: Greenwood Press, 1990.

47. Articles include Lawrence Ferrara, "Allowing Oneself to Be Moved, a Phenomenology of Musical Evaluation," David Ecker, ed., *Qualitative Evaluation in the Arts*, New York: New York University, 1981, pp. 125-151, and Ferrara, "Phenomenology as Tool for Musical Analysis," *The Musical Quarterly*, Summer 1984, 70,3:355-373.

48. See Donald Pirone, "The Solo Piano Music of Karol Rathaus," dissertation for the Ph.D., New York University, 1984; Ronald H. Sadoff, "The Solo Piano Music of Charles Ives: A Performance Guide," dissertation for the Ph.D., New York University, 1986; Hugo Goldenzweig, "The Chopin Etudes: A Schenkerian and Phenomenological Analysis," dissertation for the Ph.D., New York University, 1987; Paul Sung-Il Kim, "Olivier Messiaen's 'Catalogue D'oiseaux' for Solo Piano: A Phenomenological and Style Analysis," dissertation for the Ph.D., New York University, 1989; and David Reeves, "The Songs of Charles Griffes: An Eclectic Analysis," dissertation for the Ph.D., New York University, 1989.

Chapter 5

1. Egon G. Guba and Yvonna S. Lincoln, *Effective Evaluation*, San Francisco: Jossey-Bass, 1983, pp. 128-152. Guba and Lincoln's focus is qualitative *evaluation*. Distinctions between qualitative research and qualitative evaluation will be made later in the current chapter. However, the characteristics that Guba and Lincoln delineate bear upon both research and evaluation that utilize qualitative designs.

2. Guba and Lincoln, p. 130.

3. Guba and Lincoln, p. 131.

4. Guba and Lincoln, p. 132.

5. Michael Polanyi, *The Tacit Dimension*, Garden City, N.Y.: Doubleday and Co., 1967.

6. Guba and Lincoln, p. 136.

7. Guba and Lincoln, p. 137.

8. See L. A. Dexter, *Elite and Specialized Interviewing*, Evanston, Ill.: Northwestern University Press, 1970, p. 6.

9. John Lofland and Lyn H. Lofland, *Analyzing Social Settings, a Guide to Qualitative Observation and Analysis*, Belmont, Calif.: Wadsworth Publishing Co., 1984.

10. Oswald Werner and G. Mark Schoepfle, *Systematic Fieldwork*, vol. 1, Newbury Park, Calif.: Sage Publications Inc., 1987, pp. 198-199.

11. Werner and Schoepfle, p. 239.

12. Lofland and Lofland, chapter 4.

13. Werner and Schoepfle, pp. 273-274.

14. Marion Lundy Dobbart, *Ethnographic Research, Theory and Application for Modern Schools and Society*, New York: Praeger, 1982, pp. 259-266.

15. Lofland and Lofland, p. 54.

16. Judith Preissle Goetz and Margaret Diane LeCompte, *Ethnography and Qualitative Design in Educational Research*, New York: Academic Press, Inc., 1984, pp. 164-207.

17. James P. Spradley and David W. McCurdy, eds., *The Cultural Experience: Ethnography in Complex Society*, Chicago: Science Research Associates, 1972.

18. Rosalie H. Wax, *Doing Fieldwork, Warnings and Advice*, Chicago: University of Chicago Press, 1971.

19. Goetz and LeCompte, p. 110.

20. Goetz and LeCompte, p. 110.

21. Jack D. Douglas, *Investigative Social Research, Individualized and Team Field Research*, Beverly Hills, Calif.: Sage Publications Inc., 1976, pp. 167-171.
22. Douglas, pp. 172-174.
23. K. T. Erikson, "A Comment on Disguised Observation in Sociology," *Social Problems*, 1967, 14:368.
24. Raymond L. Gold, "Roles in Sociological Field Observation," *Social Forces*, 1958, 36:217-223.
25. Walter R. Borg and Meredith D. Gall, *Educational Research*, 5th ed.; New York: Longman, 1989, pp. 396-397.
26. James P. Spradley, *Participant Observation*, New York: Holt, Rinehart and Winston, 1980.
27. Goetz and LeCompte, pp. 112-113.
28. James P. Spradley, *The Ethnographic Interview*, New York: Holt, Rinehart and Winston, 1979.
29. Goetz and LeCompte, pp. 119-125.
30. Borg and Gall, p. 399.
31. Goetz and LeCompte, p. 123.
32. Goetz and LeCompte, p. 123.
33. Goetz and LeCompte, p. 124.
34. Werner and Schoepfle, pp. 291-292.
35. Werner and Schoepfle, p. 292.
36. B. Tymitz and R. L. Wolf, *An Introduction to Judicial Evaluation and Natural Inquiry*, Washington, D.C.: Nero and Associates, 1977.
37. Leonard Schatzman and Anselm L. Strauss, *Field Research: Strategies for a Natural Sociology*, Englewood Cliffs, N.J.: Prentice-Hall, 1973.
38. Guba and Lincoln, pp. 155-160.
39. Dexter quoted by Guba and Lincoln, p. 174.
40. Guba and Lincoln, p. 178.
41. Guba and Lincoln, p. 179.
42. Herbert J. Rubin, *Applied Social Research*, Columbus, Ohio: Charles E. Merrill Publishing Co., 1983, p. 363.
43. Guba and Lincoln, pp. 180-183.
44. Goetz and LeCompte, pp. 124-132.
45. Michael Quinn Patton, *Qualitative Evaluation Methods*, Beverly Hills, Calif.: Sage Publications Inc., 1980.
46. Pertti J. Pelto and Gretel H. Pelto, *Anthropological Research, the Structure of Inquiry*, 2nd ed.; Cambridge, England: Cambridge University Press, 1978.
47. Pelto and Pelto.

48. Pelto and Pelto, p. 50.
49. Patton, p. 46.
50. Schatzman and Strauss, *passim.*
51. Patton, p. 46.
52. Goetz and LeCompte, p. 128.
53. Goetz and LeCompte, p. 128.
54. Guba and Lincoln, p. 179.
55. Patton, p. 48.
56. Patton, p. 49.
57. Pelto and Pelto, p. 154.
58. Lofland and Lofland, p. 118.
59. Lofland and Lofland, p. 133.
60. Patton, p. 130.
61. Goetz and LeCompte, p. 129.
62. Goetz and LeCompte, p. 129.
63. Guba and Lincoln, p. 182.
64. Robert C. Bogdan and Sari Knopp Biklen, *Qualitative Research for Education*, Boston: Allyn and Bacon, Inc., 1982, pp. 145–170.
65. Goetz and LeCompte, p. 191.
66. Bogdan and Biklen, p. 156.
67. Bogdan and Biklen, pp. 157–162.
68. Goetz and LeCompte, p. 168.
69. Goetz and LeCompte, pp. 169–171.
70. Goetz and LeCompte, p. 170.
71. Guba and Lincoln, p. 186.
72. For example, see Elliott W. Eisner, *The Educational Imagination*, New York: Macmillan Publishing Co., 1979.
73. Goetz and LeCompte, pp. 205–206.
74. Bogdan and Biklen, pp. 195–207. Also see Robert Stake's seminal work in Robert Stake, ed., *Evaluating the Arts in Education, a Responsive Approach* (especially chapter 2), Columbus, Ohio: Charles E. Merrill Publishing Co., 1975.
75. Borg and Gall, pp. 743–744.
76. Borg and Gall, pp. 746–754.
77. Borg and Gall, pp. 755–758.
78. Bogdan and Biklen, pp. 198–201.
79. Guba and Lincoln, pp. 295–302.
80. See Todd D. Hick, "Mixing Qualitative and Quantitative Methods: Triangulation in Action," in John Van Maanen, ed., *Qualitative Methodology*, Beverly Hills, Calif.: Sage Publications Inc., pp. 135–148. Ongoing research conducted by Fadi Bejjani,

Lawrence Ferrara, Fred Rees, et al. in the "Human Performance Laboratory" at New York University has developed experimental designs that may converge with qualitative research designs for studies in performing arts medicine. For example, see Bejjani, Ferrara, et al., "Comparison of Three Piano Techniques as an Implementation of a Proposed Experimental Design," *Medical Problems of Performing Artists*, 4 (1989) pp. 109-113.

Chapter 6

1. Walter R. Borg and Meredith D. Gall, *Educational Research: An Introduction*, 5th ed.; New York: Longman, 1989, pp. 23-25.
2. Borg and Gall, pp. 23-24.
3. Borg and Gall, p. 24.
4. Paul D. Leedy, *Practical Research Planning and Design*, 4th ed.; New York: Macmillan, 1989, p. 152.
5. Borg and Gall, chapter 6.
6. Robert Rosenthal and Ralph L. Rosnow, *The Volunteer Subject*, New York: Wiley and Sons, 1975, pp. 195-196.
7. Borg and Gall, pp. 230-231.
8. Richard J. Colwell, *Music Achievement Tests*, Chicago: Follett Educational Corporation, 1967-1970 (four separate tests).
9. Borg and Gall, p. 264.
10. Richard W. Bowles, *The Belwin-Mills Singing Achievement Test*, Melville, N.Y.: Belwin-Mills, 1971.
11. James V. Mitchell, ed., *The Ninth Mental Measurements Yearbook*, Lincoln, Neb.: The University of Nebraska Press, 1985, p. xiv.
12. James V. Mitchell, ed., *Tests in Print III*, Lincoln, Neb.: The University of Nebraska Press, 1985.
13. Norman E. Gronlund, *Measurement and Evaluation in Teaching*, 4th ed.; New York: Macmillan, 1981, pp. 280-284.
14. Gronlund, pp. 280-281.
15. Gronlund, pp. 281-282.
16. Norman H. Hie, *SPSSX User's Guide*, New York: McGraw-Hill, 1983.
17. Fred N. Kerlinger, *Behavioral Research: A Conceptual Approach*, New York: Holt, Rinehart and Winston, 1979, pp. 71-74.

18. George L. Rogers, "Attitudes of High School Band Directors and Principals Toward Marching Band Contests," *Journal of Research in Music Education*, 1985, 33,4:259-267.
19. Richard E. Goodstein, "An Investigation into Leadership Behaviors in the United States," *Journal of Research in Music Education*, 1987, 35,1:13-25. Interestingly, the article preceding this Goodstein study also is by the same author: "An Introduction to Discriminant Analysis," *Journal of Research in Music Education*, 1987, 35,1:7-11.
20. William V. May, "Musical Style Preference and Aural Discrimination Skills of Primary Grade School Children," *Journal of Research in Music Education*, 1985, 33,1:7-22.
21. Kerlinger, pp. 71-74.
22. Kerlinger, pp. 71-75.

Chapter 7

1. Walter R. Borg and Meredith D. Gall, *Educational Research: An Introduction*, 5th ed.; New York: Longman, 1989, p. 12.
2. Borg and Gall, p. 446.
3. *SAS Users' Guide: Statistics for Personal Computers*, Cary, N.C.: SAS Institute, 1987; *SPSSX: Statistical Package for the Social Sciences*, New York: McGraw-Hill, 1983.
4. Annette H. Zalanowski, "The Effects of Listening, Instructions and Cognitive Style on Music Appreciation," *Journal of Research in Music Education*, 1986, 34,1:43-53.
5. Robert A. Cutietta, Joseph Millin, and David Royse, "Noise Induced Hearing Loss Among School Band Directors," *Bulletin of Council for Research in Music Education*, 1989, 101:41-49.
6. Fred N. Kerlinger, *Behavioral Research: A Conceptual Approach*, New York: Holt, Rinehart and Winston, 1979, p. 390.
7. Borg and Gall, p. 574.
8. Borg and Gall, p. 574.
9. Manny Brand, "Relationship Between Home Musical Environment and Selected Musical Attributes of Second-Grade Children," *Journal of Research in Music Education*, 1986, 34,1:111-120.
10. Robert A. Cutietta and Kelly J. Haggerty, "A Comparative Study of Color Association with Music at Various Age Levels," *Journal of Research in Music Education*, 1987, 35,2:78-91.

11. Borg and Gall, p. 423.
12. Borg and Gall, p. 429.
13. Borg and Gall, Chapter 11.
14. Carter V. Good, *Essentials of Educational Research: Methodology and Design*, 2nd ed.; New York: Appleton-Century-Crofts, 1972, p. 236.
15. Sharan B. Merriam and Edwin L. Simpson, *A Guide to Research for Educators and Trainers of Adults*, Malabar, Fla.: Robert E. Krieger, 1984, pp. 116-119.
16. Randall G. Pembrook, "Some Implications of Students' Attitudes Toward a Computer-based Melodic Dictation Program," *Journal of Research in Music Education*, 1986, 34,2:121-133.
17. Borg and Gall, pp. 444-446.
18. Borg and Gall, pp. 450-453.
19. Bruce W. Tuckman, *Conducting Educational Research*, 3rd ed.; New York: Harcourt Brace Jovanovich, 1988, p. 191.
20. Borg and Gall, p. 477.
21. Borg and Gall, p. 478.
22. Ned A. Flanders, *Interaction Analysis in the Classroom: A Manual for Observers*, Ann Arbor, Mich.: University of Michigan, 1966.
23. Anne C. Witt, "Use of Class Time and Student Attentiveness in Secondary Instrumental Music Rehearsals," *Journal of Research in Music Education*, 1986, 34,1:34-42.
24. Gilbert Sax, *Foundations of Educational Research*, 2nd ed.; Englewood Cliffs, N.J.: Prentice-Hall, 1979, pp. 77-78.
25. Merriam and Simpson, p. 96.
26. Patti J. Krueger, "Ethnographic Research Methodology in Music Education," *Journal of Research in Music Education*, 1987, 35,2:69-77.

Chapter 8

1. Fred N. Kerlinger, *Foundations of Behavioral Research*, 3rd ed.; New York: Holt, Rinehart and Winston, 1986, p. 17.
2. Donald T. Campbell and Julian C. Stanley, *Experimental and Quasi-Experimental Designs for Research*, Chicago: Rand McNally, 1963, pp. 1-71.
3. Thomas D. Cook and Donald T. Campbell, *Quasi-Experimentation: Design and Analysis Issues for Field Settings*, Boston: Houghton Mifflin, 1979, Chapters 1-5.

4. Cook and Campbell, pp. 51-55.
5. Cook and Campbell, p. 54.
6. Campbell and Stanley, pp. 5-6.
7. Philip J. Runkel and Joseph E. McGrath, *Research in Human Behavior*, New York: Holt, Rinehart and Winston, 1972, p. 104.
8. Campbell and Stanley, pp. 6-25.
9. Campbell and Stanley, p. 8.
10. Campbell and Stanley, pp. 34-36.
11. Richard E. Snow, "Representative and Quasi-Representative Designs for Research on Teaching," *Review of Educational Research*, 1974, 44:265-291.
12. Walter D. Borg and Meredith D. Gall, *Educational Research: An Introduction*, 5th ed.; New York: Longman, 1989, pp. 654-656.
13. Borg and Gall, p. 654, referring to Snow, pp. 265-291.
14. Snow, in Borg and Gall, p. 655.
15. Campbell and Stanley, pp. 40, 56.
16. Campbell and Stanley, p. 43.
17. Cook and Campbell, pp. 104-106.
18. J. Craig Peery and Irene W. Peery, "Effects of Exposure to Classical Music on the Musical Preferences of Preschool Children," *Journal of Research in Music Education*, 1986, 34,1:24-33.
19. Campbell and Stanley, p. 53.
20. Cook and Campbell, pp. 127-129.
21. J. H. Minton, "The Impact of Sesame Street on Reading Readiness of Kindergarten Children," doctoral dissertation, Fordham University, 1972, in Cook and Campbell, pp. 127-128.
22. Cook and Campbell, Chapter 5.
23. Campbell and Stanley, p. 51.
24. Thomas W. Goolsby, "The Parameters of Eye Movement in Vocal Music Reading," dissertation for the Ed.D., University of Illinois, 1987.
25. Stanley L. Schleuter and Lois J. Schleuter, "The Relationship of Grade Level and Sex Differences to Certain Rhythmic Responses of Primary Grade Children," *Journal of Research in Music Education*, 1985, 33,1:23-29.
26. Clifford K. Madsen and Carol A. Prickett, "Graduate Versus Undergraduate Scholarship: A Comparison of Essay Responses Concerning Professional Responsibilities of Music

Teachers," *Journal of Research in Music Education*, 1987, 35,3:191-197.

27. John W. Best and James V. Kahn, *Research in Education*, 6th ed.; Englewood Cliffs, N.J.: Prentice-Hall, 1989, pp. 288-290.

28. Bernadette Colley, "A Comparison of Syllabic Methods for Improving Rhythm Literacy," *Journal of Research in Music Education*, 1987, 35,4:221-235.

29. Charles P. Schmidt and Jean Sinor, "An Investigation of the Relationships Among Music Audiation, Musical Creativity, and Cognitive Style," *Journal of Research in Music Education*, 1986, 34,3:160-172.

30. Marilyn J. Kostka, "An Investigation of Reinforcements, Time Use, and Student Attentiveness in Piano Lessons," *Journal of Research in Music Education*, 1984, 32,3:113-122.

31. Albert LeBlanc and Carolyn Sherrill, "Effect of Vocal Vibrato and Performer's Sex on Children's Music Preference," *Journal of Research in Music Education*, 1986, 34,4:222-237.

32. Harry E. Price, "The Effect of a Music Appreciation Course on Students' Verbally Expressed Preferences for Composers," *Journal of Research in Music Education*, 1988, 36,1:35-46.

33. Roseanne Kelly Rosenthal, "The Relative Effects of Guided Model, Model Only, Guide Only, and Practice Only Treatments on the Accuracy of Advanced Instrumentalists' Musical Performance," *Journal of Research in Music Education*, 1986, 34,1:24-33.

Chapter 9

1. Paul D. Leedy, *Practical Research Planning and Design*, 4th ed.; New York: Macmillan, 1989, p. 125.

2. Robert J. Shafer, *A Guide to Historical Method*, 3rd ed.; Homewood, Ill.: Dorsey Press, 1980, p. 15.

3. Edward L. Rainbow and Hildegard C. Froehlich, *Research in Music Education: An Introduction to Systematic Inquiry*, New York: Schirmer Books, 1987, p. 108.

4. Jacques Barzun and Henry F. Graff, *The Modern Researcher*, 4th ed.; New York: Harcourt Brace Jovanovich, 1985, p. 260.

5. Barzun and Graff, p. 260.

6. William W. Brickman, *Research in Educational History*, Norwood, Pa.: Folcroft Library Editions, 1975, p. 91.

7. Leedy, p. 133.

8. Barzun and Graff, p. 46.
9. Walter R. Borg and Meredith D. Gall, *Educational Research: An Introduction*, 5th ed.; New York: Longman, 1989, p. 820.
10. Rainbow and Froehlich, pp. 115-116.
11. Peter Loewenberg, "Psychohistory," in Michael Kammen, ed., *The Past Before Us: Contemporary Historical Writing in the United States*, Ithaca, N.Y.: Cornell University Press, 1980, p. 409.
12. George M. Frederickson, "Comparative History," in Kammen, p. 458.
13. Shafer, p. 15.
14. Shafer, p. 15.
15. James A. Keene, *A History of Music Education in the United States*, Hanover, N.H.: University Press of New England, 1982.
16. Barzun and Graff, p. 239.
17. J. Morgan Kousser, "Quantitative Social-Scientific History," in Kammen, p. 444.
18. Nélida Muñoz de Frontèra, "A Study of Selected Nineteenth-Century Puerto Rican Composers and Their Musical Output," Volumes I-IV, dissertation for the Ph.D., New York University, 1988. UMI 8812518.
19. For additional insight into the quantitative method in history, see Shafer, 3rd ed., pp. 65-71; and Barzun and Graff, 4th ed., pp. 239-241, 265-266.
20. Shafer, p. 15, citing John P. Diggins, "Getting Hegel out of History: Max Eastman's Quarrel with Marxism," *American Historical Review*, February 1974, 38-70.
21. James H. McMillan and Sally Schumacher, *Research in Education: A Conceptual Introduction*, 2nd ed.; Glenview, Ill.: Scott, Foresman and Co., 1989, p. 435.
22. John M. Vincent, *Aids to Historical Research*, New York: Appleton-Century-Crofts, 1934, p. 139.
23. Allan Nevins, *The Gateway to History*, rev. ed.; Garden City, N.Y.: Anchor Books, 1962, p. 14.
24. Sharon Lee Gray, "A History of the National Catholic Music Educators Association, 1942-1976," dissertation for the D.M.E., University of Cincinnati, 1988. UMI 8822791.
25. David H. Fischer, *Historian's Fallacies: Toward a Logic of Historical Thought*, New York: Harper and Row, 1970, p. xv.
26. The Confederacy referred to the battleground as Manassas, whereas the Union, which lost both battles, preferred to use the term Bull Run, the name of the small stream which runs

through the battlefield. The Manassas National Battlefield is located about twenty-six miles southwest of Washington, D.C.

27. Shafer, p. 2.
28. Frank J. Cipolla, "Patrick S. Gilmore: The Boston Years," *American Music*, Fall 1988, 6,3:281-292.
29. Benny P. Ferguson, "The Bands of the Confederacy: An Examination of the Musical and Military Contributions of the Bands and Musicians of the Confederate States of America," dissertation for the Ph.D., North Texas State University, 1987. UMI 8723754.
30. Sandra Wieland Howe, "Luther Whiting Mason: Contributions to Music Education in Nineteenth Century America and Japan," dissertation for the Ph.D., University of Minnesota, 1988. UMI 8826463.
31. Barzun and Graff, p. 257.
32. Allen M. Garrett, *An Introduction to Research in Music*, Washington, D.C.: The Catholic University of America Press, 1958, pp. 2-3.
33. Homer C. Hockett, *The Critical Method in Historical Research and Writing*, New York: Macmillan, 1955, pp. 4-5.
34. Hockett, p. 9.
35. Louis Gottschalk, *Understanding History*, 2nd ed.; New York: Alfred A. Knopf, 1969, p. 207.
36. Shafer, p. 73.
37. Barzun and Graff, p. 19.
38. Rainbow and Froehlich, p. 168.
39. Shafer, p. 55.
40. Associated Press dispatch, February 15, 1989.
41. Barzun and Graff, p. 175.
42. Emanuel J. Mason and William J. Bramble, *Understanding and Conducting Research: Applications in Education and the Behavioral Sciences*, 2nd ed.; New York: McGraw-Hill, 1989, p. 34.
43. Brickman, p. 108.
44. James T. Madeja, "The Life and Work of Herbert L. Clarke (1867-1945)," dissertation for the Ed.D., University of Illinois at Urbana-Champaign, 1988. UMI 8823188.
45. Brickman, pp. 3-5.
46. Brickman, p. 14.
47. Herbert T. Hoover, "Oral History in the United States," in Kammen, p. 393.

48. William W. Cutler III, "Oral History—Its Nature and Uses for Educational History," *History of Education Quarterly*, Summer 1971, 11,2:184.

49. Hoover, p. 394.

50. Stanley H. Brobston, "A Brief History of White Southern Gospel Music and a Study of Selected Amateur Family Gospel Music Singing Groups in Rural Georgia," dissertation for the Ph.D., New York University, 1977. UMI 7808451.

51. Lee B. Cooper, "Popular Songs as Oral History: Teaching Black History Through Contemporary Audio Resources," *International Journal of Instructional Media*, 1977-78, 5,2:185-195.

52. Barzun and Graff, p. 126.

53. Lacey Fosburgh, "World's Oldest Song Reported Deciphered," *New York Times*, March 6, 1974, p. 1.

54. "A Hidden Haydn Found in Farmhouse," *Newsday*, February 20, 1984, p. 9.

55. Harold C. Schonberg, "Byron Janis Discovers Chopin MSS in a Chateau," *New York Times*, December 21, 1967, p. 1.

56. Muriel Brooks, "Chopin/Janis," *The American Music Teacher*, April-May 1979, 28,5:7-8. The waltzes were published in 1978 by Envolve Music Group, Ltd., New York, N.Y. 10019, under the title *Chopin/Janis: The Most Dramatic Musical Discovery in Ages.*

57. Rufus A. Grider, *Historical Notes on Music in Bethlehem, Pennsylvania*, Philadelphia: John L. Pile, 1873; foreword by Donald M. McCorkle, Winston-Salem, N.C.: Moravian Music Foundation, 1957, p. 57.

58. These trios have been reissued by Boosey and Hawkes and were recorded for the first time on New Records, *Music in America*, Karl Krueger, General Director, under the title "Instrumental Music in Colonial America: The Moravians," on Record NRLP 2016.

59. For additional information, see the microfiche version of the Phelps doctoral dissertation, *The History and Practice of Chamber Music in the United States from Earliest Times up to 1875*, Rochester, N.Y.: University of Rochester Press, 1980, pp. 241-257, 579-580, 654-726.

60. Albert G. Rau and Hans T. David, *A Catalogue of Music by American Moravians (1742-1842)*, Bethlehem, Pa.: Moravian College and Seminary for Women, 1938; New York: A.M.S. Press, 1970, p. 102.

61. Rau and David, p. 98.
62. Regarding the Michael *partien*, see the Phelps doctoral dissertation, pp. 277-381, 820-857.
63. Grider, p. 9.
64. "Four Haydn Scores Surface After More Than 100 Years," *San Juan Star*, June 20, 1982.
65. Donal Henahan, "Paganini's Concerto No. 3 Rediscovered," *New York Times*, January 14, 1971, p. 44.
66. Roger P. Phelps, "The Mendelssohn Quintet Club: A Milestone in American Music Education," *Journal of Research in Music Education*, Spring 1960, 8,1:39.
67. Phelps, "The Mendelssohn Quintet Club," p. 40.
68. Carter V. Good, *Essentials of Educational Research: Methodology and Design*, 2nd ed.; Englewood Cliffs, N.J.: Prentice-Hall, 1972, p. 174.
69. Hockett, p. 26.
70. Walter E. Eells, "First American Degrees in Music," *History of Education Quarterly*, March 1961, 1,1:36.
71. John G. Shea, *Memorial of the First Century of Georgetown College, D.C.*, New York: P. F. Collier, 1891, p. 164, as quoted by Eells, p. 39.
72. Roger P. Phelps, "The First Earned Doctorate in Music Education," *The Bulletin of Historical Research in Music Education*, January 1983, 4:2.
73. John J. Dawson, "The Education Value of Vocal Music," dissertation for the Ped.D., New York University, 1895, p. 16. UMI 7233518.
74. Hockett, p. 14.
75. Fischer, p. 40.
76. Richard W. Murphy, *The Nation Reunited*, Alexandria, Va.: Time-Life Books, 1987, p. 82.
77. Henry W. Lanier, New York, N.Y., personal letter to researcher, March 17, 1949.
78. Audrey H. Starke, *Sidney Lanier*, Chapel Hill, N.C.: University of North Carolina Press, 1933, opposite p. 174.
79. Starke, p. 184.
80. Starke, p. 462.
81. Philip Graham, ed., *Centennial Edition of the Works and Letters of Sidney Lanier*, Vol. VI, Baltimore: Johns Hopkins University Press, 1945, p. 389.
82. Hockett, p. 8.
83. *New York Tribune*, November 10, 1946.

84. E. Lebeau, Paris, personal letter to researcher, November 10, 1949.

85. Harold C. Schonberg, "Music: American Oddities," *New York Times*, September 24, 1968, p. 54.

86. Allan Nevins, *The Gateway to History*, Boston: D. C. Heath and Co., 1938; reprint ed., Robin Winks, ed., New York: Garland Publishers, Inc., 1984, p. 122.

87. Gottschalk, p. 138.

88. Brickman, p. 95.

89. Barzun and Graff, p. 126.

90. Gottschalk, pp. 219-220.

91. Winks, p. 276.

Chapter 10

1. Joseph Berger, "Scholars Urge Shorter Path to Ph.D.," New York Times News Service, in Raleigh, N.C., *News and Observer*, May 4, 1989, p. 2A.

2. Berger, p. 2A.

3. Emanuel J. Mason and William J. Bramble, *Understanding and Conducting Research: Applications in Education and the Behavioral Sciences*, 2nd ed.; New York: McGraw-Hill, 1989, p. 418.

4. Bruce C. Bradford and John K. Schorr, *Report on the Future of American Higher Education: A Survey of Deans of Arts and Sciences, Business, Law and Music at Phi Beta Kappa Institutions in the U.S., 1983*, Deland, Fla.: Social and Opinion Research Services, Inc., 1984, p. 33.

5. Yeong-Kee Lee, "An Analysis of the Relationship Between Korean Art Songs and Traditional Korean Vocal Music: A Unified Concept of Korean Music," dissertation for the Ph.D., New York University, 1989.

6. Mason and Bramble, p. 422.

7. Mason and Bramble, p. 416.

8. Mathew H. M. Lee, ed., *Rehabilitation, Music and Human Well-Being*, St. Louis: MMB Music, Inc., 1989.

9. Bradford and Schorr, pp. 32, 35.

Index

Adkins, Cecil, 53
Almack, John C., 37
American Education Research Association (AERA), 7, 241
Antes, John, 302, 303
Antes, R. L., 13
Arnheim, Rudolph, 119
Ary, Donald, 2, 32

Barzun, Jacques, 25, 39, 287, 288, 289, 292, 294, 295, 300, 313
Baum, Willa, 300
Bell, Clive, 125
Berger, Joseph, 322
Best, John, 3, 27, 32, 64
Bibliography of Research Studies in Music Education, 52
Biklen, Sari K., 8, 175, 176, 179, 181
Bogdan, Robert C., 8, 175, 176, 179, 181
Borg, Walter R., 8, 23, 26, 35, 161, 162, 165, 180, 181, 187, 192, 193, 225, 235, 238, 245, 248, 249, 269, 288
Brademas, John, 12
Bramble, William J., 25, 26, 30, 295, 323, 325
Brand, Manny, 229, 230
Brennan, Joseph C., 26
Brickman, William W., 288, 296, 297, 305, 312
Brobston, Stanley H., 299
Brook, Barry S., 55
Bulletin of Council for Research in Music Education, 23, 43, 52

Campbell, William G., 65, 259, 262, 263, 265, 268, 270, 272, 273, 274, 275
Casey, Rita J., 3, 32
Chambers, M. M., 20, 21, 23, 24
Clarke, Arthur E., 4
Cohen, Morris R., 26
Colley, Bernadette, 281

About the Authors

Roger P. Phelps (B.M., Eastman School of Music; M.M., Northwestern University; Ph.D., University of Iowa) is Professor Emeritus, New York University, where prior to his retirement to Cary, North Carolina, he was Chairman, Music and Music Professions Department. He has taught in the public schools of New York State and at Bob Jones University, the University of Southern Mississippi, and New York University. Dr. Phelps also has taught research courses at Duquesne University and at New York University's overseas centers in Israel and Puerto Rico. He has served as Chairman, Music Education Research Council and on the Editorial Committee of the *Journal of Research in Music Education*. Dr. Phelps has contributed to *Music Education in Action* and to *Mental Measurements Yearbooks*, in addition to several professional journals. He is serving on the International Advisory Board and on the Review Committee of the *International Journal of Arts Medicine*. He also is on the Advisory Committee of the *Bulletin of the Council for Research in Music Education*.

Lawrence Ferrara is Professor of Music at New York University where he is Director of Programs in Music Performance and Director of Doctoral Studies in the Department of Music and Music Professions. Dr. Ferrara is an active pianist and has appeared throughout the United States, Canada, and Europe. He has performed on ABC and CBS television, the Independent Cable Network, and on the BBC in England. In addition to numerous articles in journals concerning areas as diverse as music analysis, aesthetics, music education, performance practice, and performing arts medicine, Dr. Ferrara's published books include *Keyboard Harmony and Improvisation* (1986) and *Philosophy and the Analysis of Music*. Much of Dr. Ferrara's work is an attempt to synthesize quantitative and qualitative methods in music educational research and formal and phenomenological methods in music analysis and criticism.

Thomas W. Goolsby is on the music education faculty at the University of Washington in Seattle. Dr. Goolsby holds degrees in music education from Jacksonville State University, University of Georgia, and University of Illinois. He is active in the Music Educators National Conference and the Washington Music Educators Conference. He is a member of the Council for Research in Music Education since he was awarded "Outstanding Dissertation in Music for 1988" by that body. In 1989 he was selected as a Fulbright Scholar in Education Research Methodology. He has co-authored *The Teaching of Instrumental Music* with Richard J. Colwell and is published in *The Journal of Aesthetic Education, Music Educators Journal,* and *The Bulletin for the Council for Research in Music Education,* as well as journals abroad.